Artificial Intelligence for Educational Inclusion and Equity

Artificial Intelligence for Educational Inclusion and Equity

International Studies and Critiques

Edited by

Emmanuel Jean-Francois

Associate Professor, Educational Leadership, Division of Education and Counselling, Xavier University of Louisiana, USA

Micheal M. van Wyk

Professor in Economics Education, Department of Curriculum and Instructional Studies, University of South Africa

Edward Elgar PUBLISHING

Cheltenham, UK • Northampton, MA, USA

Published by

Edward Elgar Publishing Limited
The Lypiatts
15 Lansdown Road
Cheltenham
Glos GL50 2JA
UK

Edward Elgar Publishing, Inc.
William Pratt House
9 Dewey Court
Northampton
Massachusetts 01060
USA

Authorised representative in the EU for GPSR queries only: Easy Access System Europe – Mustamäe tee 50, 10621 Tallinn, Estonia, gpsr.requests@easproject.com

A catalogue record for this book is available from the British Library

Library of Congress Control Number: 2026934058

This book is available electronically in the Elgaronline Sociology, Social Policy and Education subject collection
https://doi.org/10.4337/9781035346431

MIX
Paper | Supporting responsible forestry
FSC® C013056

ISBN 978 1 0353 4642 4 (cased)
ISBN 978 1 0353 4643 1 (eBook)
ISBN 978 1 0353 9812 6 (ePub)

Printed and bound in Great Britain by
TJ Books, Padstow, Cornwall

Contents

List of contributors

Jimmy R. Caldwell is an Assistant Professor at Xavier University of Louisiana's Division of Education & Counseling. A proud graduate of Florida A&M University, he earned a PhD in Curriculum & Instruction with a specialization in Special Education and a cognate in Sociology of Education from the University of South Florida. Caldwell's research centers on investigating interconnected paradigms that impact the educational outcomes of Black students. His current research agenda focuses on the role of racism-white supremacy and the academic outcomes of Black boys. Other areas of inquiry include critical examinations of teacher preparation programs, discovering culturally transformative school disciplinary practices, and developing educational theories that best serve the academic outcomes for Black students.

Camila Carpio Frixone is a Special Project Assistant for the Psychological and Educational Sciences at the Universidad San Francisco de Quito.

Neil D. Grimes earned a PhD at Rutgers University's School of Communication and Information in the Department of Library and Information Science. He earned his B.A. in History from King's College in 2005 and his M.L.S. from Clarion University in 2006. Later, Grimes earned his second master's in Education with a Pennsylvania certification in Instructional Technology in 2012 from Wilkes University. He spent 13 years working in various roles in an urban school district in northeastern Pennsylvania as a certified K–12 school library media specialist, an elementary STEM teacher, and a middle school/high school social studies teacher. Grimes currently works as the Education & Curriculum Materials Librarian at William Paterson University in northern New Jersey. He works with faculty and students in the Department of Teacher Education Pre-K–12 and the Department of Educational Leadership. His research interests, publications, and conference presentations focus on libraries, equity issues in libraries and K–12, literacy, male mentorship, school-academic library partnerships, college and career readiness, microcredentials, professional development, information literacy, educational technologies in the Pre-K–12 environment, school librarianship, virtual professional development, how libraries address mental health and wellness, and how libraries address the digital divide through digital equity. He currently serves on ALA's EBSS Curriculum Materials Center Committee, as an Associate on ALA's Committee on Education, and recently served as co-chair of NJLA's Professional Development Committee in addition to serving on other national, state, and institutional committees. In addition to his scholarship and service, he has co-taught a section of the Honors Research Seminar since 2021 at William Paterson University centered on teaching freshmen research skills around issues of equity in the Pre-K–12 environment.

Sari Havu-Nuutinen holds a PhD in Education and is a Professor of Education, specializing in early years education. She works as a head of School of Applied Educational Science and Teacher Education, where she is actively involved in various educational initiatives. This includes contributions to minor studies in pre-primary education, an international master's degree program, and doctoral studies in education. With nearly 30 years of experience in teacher education in Finland, Havu-Nuutinen has played a significant role in curriculum development in teacher education as well as in basic education. Her international collaborative research focuses on the multidimensional teaching and learning of young children in science education. She has actively participated in science education research and teacher education developmental projects internationally. Currently, she works as a WP leader in a national project related to science capital and coordinates the international project about sustainability in teacher education. A decade ago, she served as a senior Fulbright scholar, conducting research at Ohio University, USA.

Emmanuel Jean-Francois is an Associate Professor of Educational Leadership at Xavier University of Louisiana. He earned his PhD in Curriculum and Instruction with a focus on Adult, Higher Education, and Human Resource Development, as well as a graduate certificate in College Teaching from the University of South Florida. He holds a master's degree in Organization Management and Leadership from Springfield College. He is a former secondary school teacher and headmaster (i.e., Principal). He served as President and Executive Director for various nonprofit organizations. He has been involved in scholarship and issues related to educational and organizational leadership since 1994. He has published: *Transnational Perspectives on Innovation in Teaching in Learning Technologies*, *Perspectives in Transnational Higher Education*, *Building Global Education with a Local Perspective: An Introduction to Global Higher Education*, *Financial Sustainability for Nonprofit Organizations*, and *Trans-cultural Blended Learning and Teaching in Post-secondary Education.* He has also published in several peer-reviewed journals.

Patrick Kersalé is an ethno-archaeo-musicologist and educator who has spent over 30 years exploring traditional music around the world. A prolific author, he has published books, films, scientific articles, and educational tools. As a lecturer, he passionately shares his research, combining meticulous documentation with accessible teaching to preserve and promote the world's musical heritage.

Sini Kontkanen works as a university lecturer at the University of Eastern Finland at the School of Applied Educational Science and Teacher Education. She is interested in how digitalization can enhance learning and teaching in different educational contexts and especially in-service and pre-service teachers' digital professional development from the point of view of Technological Pedagogical Content Knowledge (TPACK). She has published several articles on this topic, exploring how authentic learning experiences with digital tools and learning environments can enhance teachers' intentions and readiness to use ICT for teaching and learning. She is also currently involved as a researcher in the FINSCI project (Funded by Academy of Finland, STN), which examines parents' science capital and children's science literacy.

Cristina Adriana Kruger is a School Technical Supervisor of Region I – Ministry of Education of Chubut – Argentina. She has 21 years of teaching experience in the following educational levels: primary, secondary, and tertiary. She is a PhD candidate in Education – UNINI Mx. She earned a Master's in Education at UNINI Mx., a Master's in Education specialized in Organization and Management of Educational Centers – UNEATLÁNTICO, and a Bachelor's in Management of Educational Institutions – Blas Pascal – Córdoba. She has been a teacher of the 1st and 2nd cycle of E.G.B. – ME Chubut. She received a Higher Level Teaching Specialist in Primary Education and ICT (Information and Communication Technologies) and has a specialization in Management of Educational Institutions (FLACSO – Argentina).

María Dolores Lasso obtained her PhD from New Mexico State University. She holds a Master's degree in Education from Boston University and completed her undergraduate studies in Elementary Education from the Pontifical Catholic University of Ecuador. As the Dean of Undergraduate Studies and Academic Affairs at Universidad San Francisco de Quito (USFQ), Lasso is responsible for the academic operations of all undergraduate programs. Her role involves continuous improvement, institutional curriculum design strategies, and optimization of academic processes to ensure the best possible educational experiences for all USFQ students. With over two decades of teaching experience, Lasso currently teaches Education courses in the undergraduate and graduate programs.

Charles L. Lowery is an Associate Professor of Educational Leadership and Policy Studies at Virginia Tech. His interdisciplinary research explores bricolage, critical literacies, rural education, and place-based approaches in educational leadership, emphasizing leaders as moral democratic agents. His recent work addresses how educational leaders in under-resourced educational settings perceive and address educational challenges due to crisis, conflict, and controversy. Currently, he is co-editing a volume titled *Educational Leadership and Political Literacy: Empowering School Leaders for Informed Democratic Engagement.*

Sara Platt is an Assistant Dean, Director of Assessment and Accreditation, Assistant Professor of Special Education. Platt is Assistant Dean, Director of Assessment and Accreditation, and an Assistant Professor of Special Education at the University of Mississippi School of Education.

Claire Ramsey earned her doctorate in Educational Administration, with a cognate in Comparative International Educational Leadership. She cultivated a diverse background in education and community engagement. She taught in secondary classrooms both in the United States of America (USA) and abroad, coached swimming and triathlon athletes, and volunteered as a tutor for English literacy and English as a Second Language programs. Her professional journey spans teaching and research experiences across the USA, France, Bolivia, Kenya, Germany, and Finland, enriching her global perspective on education. Ramsey's research adopts an appreciative lens, focusing on themes such as place-based education, community and career-connected learning, sustainable education systems, and global educational leadership. Her work emphasizes fostering meaningful connections between educational institutions, communities, and careers while advocating for equitable practices in education worldwide.

Marie Rathmann is a Research Associate at Helmut Schmidt University at the Professorship for Continuing Education and Lifelong Learning. Her research interests center on learning and educational processes in informal settings in the context of digitalization. Here she especially researches how subjects acquire digital competencies. Ethnographic methodologies and praxis-theoretical heuristics comprise one of her primary areas of focus. In addition, Rathmann is a member of the interdisciplinary project *hpc.bw – Competence Platform for Software Efficiency and Supercomputing*, where she collaborates with the Professorship for High Performance Computing (HPC) to establish a competence platform for acquiring HPC competencies.

Therese Rosemann has been a Postdoc Researcher since 2021 in the *DigiTaKS** project at HSU where her main focus is on the identification of (digital) learning and communication networks of students. To this end, she is collaborating with the MINT project hpc.bw – Competence Platform for Software Efficiency and Supercomputing with the aim of implementing an individual feedback system on the digital learning and usage behavior of students. Her general research interest lies in learning activities in informal and non-formal learning contexts in professional and university contexts, with a special focus on the implementation of process-related survey procedures (esp. diary studies) in the workplace, which she also applied in her dissertation (2022) at Göttingen University (Germany).

Jan Schiller has been a Postdoc Researcher since 2016 at the professorship. His current research and teaching focus on questions of digitalization in adult and continuing education, European and national educational policy as well as continuing higher education. A special focus of his work is on time-related issues in the context of *Bildung* in connection with educational, sociological, and philosophical approaches, which he pursued in detail in his dissertation *Bildung for an Uncertain Future* (2022). In the *DigiTaKS** project, his focus lies on the concept of transformative digital competence as a connection between digital competences and critical educational theory.

Sabine Schmidt-Lauff holds the position of Professor of Continuing Education and Lifelong Learning within the Faculty of Humanities and Social Sciences since 2016. Prior to this, she served as a Professor of Adult Education and Continuing Education at Chemnitz University of Technology from 2008 to 2016. She is a member of the International and Continuing Education Hall of Fame (ICAE HoF) and serves as Co-Convenor of the Research Network STREAM (Spaces, Times, and the Rhythms of the Education of Adults and its Movements) within the European Society for Research on the Education of Adults (ESREA). Her academic research and scholarly work are primarily focused on international comparative studies in the field of lifelong learning, with particular attention to the concepts of time and temporality in adult education. Additionally, her research explores themes related to professionalization and professional identity in the context of digitalization and digital technologies.

Nomita Sharma is working as an Assistant Professor at the University of Delhi. She has earned her doctorate in Management of Innovation in SMEs from the Department of Business Economics, University of Delhi. She specializes in management of innovation in Small and Medium Enterprises. She has published articlesin international journals like the *International Journal of Innovation* and book chapters in the *Entrepreneurship in the Middle East and North Africa: Dynamics in Trends, Policy and Business Environment*, and *Globalization in Developing Economies*, to name a few. Some of her research papers include 'Influence of Innovation on Mechanisms of Institutional Change – A Global Perspective,' 'Management of Innovation in Developing Economies, India as a Paradise for Start-ups, Legend or Reality?,' 'Innovation for Survival: Entrepreneurial Response of Indian MSMEs to Demonetization,' 'Management of Innovation in Micro, Small and Medium Enterprises in the Middle East and North Africa (MENA),' and 'Innovative Behaviour of Indian Micro, Small and Medium Enterprises: An Empirical Study,' to name a few.

Jason Todd is an Associate Professor of English at Xavier University of Louisiana. He received his PhD from the Center for Writers at the University of Southern Mississippi in 2006. His fiction has appeared in journals such as *Southern California Review*, *Chicago Quarterly Review*, *Fiction Weekly*, and *971 Magazine*. He teaches courses on American literature, comics, and graphic novels, dystopian realities, and genre fiction. From 2010 to 2015, he served as Xavier's first QEP Director, managing the campus-wide Read Today, Lead Tomorrow initiative. From 2015 to 2021, he served as the first Associate Director for Programming for Xavier's Center for the Advancement of Teaching and Faculty Development. In 2021, he became the Director of Xavier's Digital Humanities program. He is a member of the Association for Interdisciplinary Studies, the South Atlantic Modern Language Association, and the Professional and Organizational Developers Network.

Micheal M. van Wyk is a Professor in Economics Education and an NRF-rated researcher at the College of Education, University of South Africa (UNISA). He is a qualified professional teacher, has published articles in highly impacted journals, supervised doctoral and master's degree students, read conference papers, published conference proceedings, edited academic books, and been awarded external grants. He is a flipped instructional designer researcher in ODeL research. In 2013, he was awarded for his novel educational contributions to Economics Education in teacher education, the Chancellor Award for Excellence in Research (UNISA). In 2018, he was awarded the Scholarship of Teaching and Learning for his groundbreaking research on the e-portfolio as an alternative assessment approach in teacher education at both the College of Education and the University of South Africa. One of his recent articles entitled 'Students' Perceptions of the Flipped Classroom Pedagogy in an Open Distance e-Learning University' (2020) was published in *Ubiquitous Learning: An International Journal* (SCOPUS) and voted as the best scholarly publication by the journal vetting panel, and was consequently awarded the International Award for Excellence for Research (2020), Common Ground Research Network, University of Chicago, USA. In 2023, he was an awardee of the Chancellor's Award for Excellence in Research (UNISA). He is serving on international journal editorial boards and vetting panels. He was recently awarded the Medal of Honor Education (2023) from the Education Association of South Africa. He is the Associate Editor for *Heliyon: Education*. His research interests are digital technologies, generative artificial intelligence, digital game-based learning, flipped pedagogy, e-portfolios, authentic assessment, and economics education.

1. Introduction

Emmanuel Jean-Francois and Micheal M. van Wyk

From access to schooling, quality education, academic achievement, and access and utilization of digital technologies for learning, educational disparities remain one of the critical issues that affect almost every country in the world. Obviously, the level and extent of educational disparities vary with the development level of a country. The differences also depend on whether a country is located in the Global North or the Global South. Furthermore, there are variations within countries when accounting for rural and urban areas, the socio-economic and socio-cultural backgrounds of students, as well as their immigration status. Educational disparities do not exist by chance. They result from overall realities of inequality, exclusion, and unfair policies in various societies, regardless of the region in the world. Although educational disparities have always existed, the global pandemic coronavirus (COVID-19) has exposed them in ways that were not so explicit for everyone to observe. In fact, the digital divide has generated disproportional teaching and learning opportunities that have given birth to learning loss in academic achievement for some categories of learners. This book argues that artificial intelligence (AI) provides the tools that can not only help reduce the digital divide but also address issues of educational disparities through inclusion and equity. The term equity refers to the need to provide every student the opportunities and resources based on their specific situation in order to achieve positive outcomes (Acai et al., 2019).

This scholarly publication serves as a vital resource for advancing education, inclusion, and equity in the age of AI. By offering both appreciative and critical perspectives, it equips scholars, educational leaders, educators, policymakers, and practitioners with insights needed to navigate the complex implications of AI integration. This publication underscores the importance of ensuring that AI technologies and detectors are implemented in a way that is fair, accessible, and responsive to the diverse needs of all students, particularly those from historically marginalized communities. As such, it contributes meaningfully to the ongoing critical conversations on how to harness AI to create more socially just and inclusive educational practices and systems.

Potential readers of this book will have an opportunity to:

1. Explore how educational leaders can combine AI with instructional leadership to provide support that helps address educational disparities and inequity;
2. Appreciate instructional strategies that enable using AI to foster educational inclusion and equity;
3. Discuss good practices to help students use AI ethically and to learn in ways that contribute to filling academic achievement gaps;
4. Analyze how AI can help foster equity and inclusion in adult and continuing education and lifelong learning programs;
5. Discuss community involvement policies and strategies for AI integration in education for social justice and equity;
6. Elaborate on leadership and policy approaches to ensure the integration of AI in education in an equitable and ethical manner.

OVERALL CONTEXT

Intelligence is one of the key factors that distinguish humans from other animals. What is human intelligence? Nowadays, this is a more complex question, given all the prominent scholars who have contributed to the literature, understanding, and perspective on intelligence. The intent here is not to review the literature on intelligence, but to simply introduce the concept, as it is part of the title and the overarching purpose of the book. Wechsler (1939), a pioneer of cognitive psychology, provided one of the classic definitions of intelligence, which is "the aggregate or global capacity of an individual to act purposefully, think rationally, and manage effectively with their environment" (p. 229). This definition encompasses both the aggregate and global capacity of a human being, the purposefulness of their action, rationality, effectiveness, and the surrounding environment. According to Sternberg (2012, p. 19), "Intelligence is the ability to learn from experience and to adapt to, shape, and select environments". Sternberg (2003) argued the triarchic theory, which is that intelligence can be analytical, creative, and practical. Sternberg (2012) also noted that race, as a social construct and not biological, is not a factor in intelligence. Obviously, given the cognitive psychology orientation of this definition, it is important to point to its limitations with respect to non-cognitive factors, such as social, cultural, and emotional intelligence.

As one can see from the list of definitions provided, intelligence is defined in a unitary fashion, even though there are some differences between the constructs from various scholars. In simple terms, human intelligence is the capacity of the human brain to learn from experience and use that knowledge to adapt to new situations and manipulate one's environment. Existing literature suggests several qualifiers of intelligence, such as social intelligence or the capacity to understand and manage social relationships effectively (Thorndike, 1920, p. 227); cultural intelligence, which involves the capability to relate and work effectively across cultures (Earley & Ang, 2003, p. 10); emotional intelligence, which refers to the ability to recognize, understand, and manage our own emotions and the emotions of others (Goleman, 1995, p. 6); and multiple intelligence (Gardner, 2006), encompassing linguistic, mathematical, spatial, musical, bodily, naturalist, interpersonal, and intrapersonal intelligence. Therefore, the use of the term artificial intelligence did not emerge from nothingness. What is artificial intelligence?

Although artificial intelligence (AI) has been used for several decades by professionals and the public at large, its recent development has caught many people by surprise. Obviously, there has been an acceleration in the amount and effectiveness of new AI tools and software that are being used in every walk of life, including in education. According to the American National Standards Institute/InterNational Committee for Information Technology Standards (ANSI INCITS, R2007), AI is:

(1) A branch of computer science devoted to developing data processing systems that perform functions normally associated with human intelligence, such as reasoning, learning, and self-improvement.
(2) The capability of a device to perform functions that are normally associated with human intelligence, such as reasoning, learning, and self-improvement. (para 2)

This definition articulates that some AI machines or computer applications can reproduce learning, perception, rationale, problem-solving, and decision-making outcomes that are similar to what a human being can do. In other words, AI is human-like intelligence in an artificial way (Mueller & Massaron, 2019). For example, in 1997, Gary Kasparov, a chess champion, got crushed in a chess game by a computer program called *IBM Deep Blue* (Mueller & Massaron, 2019, p. 16). That was AI in action, but not too many people paid attention to that. However, the alarm went off in 2023. Kelly (2023, January 26) reported that AI programs *ChatGPT* and AI chatbots passed the law and business schools' exams at the University of Minnesota and the University of Pennsylvania, respectively, at the level of a student who receives a C+ score. We had very passionate discussions about the danger of AI.

Creative writers who work in the media and movie industries see AI positioning itself to replace them almost immediately (Italie, 2023, August 13). Educators are playing tough on holding students accountable for plagiarism, even though students can use *ChatGPT* to write papers on their behalf. However, there is no actual consensus that using *ChatGPT* is considered to be plagiarism. While Science Po, a leading university in France (McGregor, 2023, February 3) banned the utilization of AI, the University of Helsinki (2024) encourages the use of AI and provides instructions on how to use it. As Peters (2023) argued, it might be a better idea to foster a culture of scholarly and academic integrity instead of trying to destroy AI. Artists see AI reproducing their songs and images almost accurately, so the panic button has been pressed. Politicians and regular citizens are crying foul and even making alarming predictions about the very existence of humankind being threatened by AI. Although the threat posed by AI is real, the end-of-the-world alarm sounded about AI is not new. Radio was supposed to die when TV emerged. Workers were supposed to lose all their jobs when robotization started. Not too long ago, the digitalization forced by the COVID-19 lockdown was supposed to eliminate the physical workplace. In all the aforementioned cases, there were some negative consequences, but the predictions were always wrong. Part of the reason is that the ingenuity that created the machines does not die after the machine becomes operational. There will always be a way to limit the damage caused by machines. And, until machines are completely eliminated, some people will always have access to them and hold an advantage over people who do not use them. As long as AI exists, some people will always use it to facilitate their educational experiences. The only losers will be people who refuse to find a way to limit the negative consequences of AI and ensure that it is used ethically and equitably as a complement to human productivity and efficiency. AI is already part of educational scholarship and practices. It will be almost impossible to reverse such a reality. The challenge is how AI can be used ethically and as a tool for enhancing inclusion and equity in education. The purpose of this book is to articulate how AI can be used as a tool to help bridge the gap in educational disparity and inequity. International studies and approaches will be offered to make that case.

CONTENT

This publication offers practical frameworks for creativity, critical thinking, and deep analysis while providing effective teaching and learning strategies. In addition, it addresses instructional leadership and presents policy recommendations to guide thoughtful integration of AI in education.

The book includes chapters covering the following topics:

- Human resource development and AI;
- Educational leaders in P-20 education: Instructional leadership using AI to address educational disparities and inequity;

- Faculty and teachers: Instructional strategies using AI to address educational disparities and inequity;
- Adult and continuing education and lifelong learning: Using AI to foster equity and inclusion;
- Equity and ethics: Using AI equitably and ethically.

The chapters are organized in three Parts that constitute the conceptual framework of the book. The Parts overlap around critiques and recommendations for diversity and equity in education.

Part I: AI and the Challenges of Diversity Inclusion, Equity, and Ethics

Chapter 2: Diversity inclusion, equity, and artificial intelligence by Emmanuel Jean-Francois

This chapter focuses on Diversity, Equity, and Inclusion (DEI) in organizational and social contexts. It identifies persistent disparities in representation and access across various demographic groups, highlighting systemic barriers and unconscious biases. Effective DEI initiatives correlate with improved workplace culture and performance. The findings underscore the necessity of sustained, multifaceted approaches to achieve meaningful equity and inclusion.

Chapter 3: Bridging the digital divide in education: Global and local perspectives by Neil D. Grimes and Sara Platt

Existing literature and data show that there is a digital divide globally between the countries of the Global North and those from the Global South. Such a digital divide is also manifest within countries of the Global North and Global South when considering the rural and urban areas. This chapter discusses the issues of a digital divide in education from a global and local perspective, its persistence, and its impact on educational outcomes and achievement, especially in the aftermath of COVID-19. The developmental AI systems carry the potential to reduce achievement gaps across learners from various backgrounds and promote educational inclusion and equity. The chapter discusses and illustrates approaches and strategies to bridge the gaps in the digital divide in education globally and locally.

Chapter 4: "A whole cartload of beautiful possibilities": Moral guidance and the paradigm shift of generative AI by Jason Todd

This chapter argues that the current focus on preventing misuse of Generative AI, while understandable, represents a missed opportunity for transformative educational reform. The proliferation of institutional policies that primarily address cheating concerns reflects what Nietzsche might have recognized as a preference for "a sure nothing" over "an uncertain something". Such approaches fail to engage with the more profound implications of these technologies for teaching, learning, and the mission of higher education. This disconnect is particularly problematic for institutions serving historically marginalized communities, where the failure to provide students with contemporary digital literacy skills may exacerbate existing inequities.

Chapter 5: Critical perspective on artificial intelligence in education by Patrick Kersalé

The primary objective of this chapter is to offer a critical perspective on the use of AI in education. We will examine the ethical, social, and pedagogical implications of these technologies, focusing on issues of accountability, equity, and privacy. Additionally, we will explore concrete case studies to illustrate the successes and failures of AI in various educational contexts. Finally, we will propose recommendations for the responsible integration of AI into educational systems. This chapter is organized into seven main sections. Following the introduction, it provides an overview of AI in education, defining key concepts and exploring common applications. The third section will present a critical perspective on the ethical and social challenges of AI, followed by detailed case studies in the fourth section. The fifth section discusses the challenges and limitations of AI in education, while the sixth section proposes recommendations for responsible integration. Finally, the conclusion summarizes the key points and offers future perspectives.

Part II: Human Resource Development and Educational Leadership for Inclusive and Equitable AI Integration

Chapter 6: Artificial intelligence and human resource development: Efficiency and equity by Nomita Sharma

This chapter involves a study that aims to understand how AI may increase the efficiency and equality of human resource development. It also explains how AI influences human resource development. AI refers to robots' ability to imitate some aspects of human intelligence, such as pattern recognition and decision-making. Companies from a wide range of industries employ AI for a variety of goals. These include employing individuals, risk assessment, financial counseling, and recommendations for criminal punishment. Although AI has the potential to exacerbate inherent prejudices, discrimination, and injustices, it is not an exception to the well-known fact that social connections and environments are mirrored and replicated in technology. The chapter employs the PRISMA technique. PRISMA (Preferred Reporting Items for Systematic Reviews and Meta-Analyses) is a widely used method for reporting systematic reviews and meta-analyses. It provides a short set of requirements that writers must include in their reports to ensure completeness and transparency. The findings of this study establish the framework for future research targeted at enhancing understanding of the connection of human development, labor, and technology, especially in light of AI's growing impact on the labor market. While AI can benefit poor groups, governments and corporations must collaborate to address equality in AI in order to mitigate its possible negative impacts.

Chapter 7: AI for educational inclusion and equity: Academic leadership and policy for ethical integration in the Global South by Micheal M. van Wyk

Studies reported that AI for "educational inclusion and equity" is an enabler for a transformative agenda for the future of the Global South higher education. This chapter selects a multiple case study design to examine institutional policies and guidelines to understand how leadership practices influence the ethical and inclusive implementation of AI in educational settings. The *Pedagogy of Freedom* and the theory of *Equity-Centred Design Thinking* underpin the study. The multiple case study research investigates current policies and practices, identifies barriers and opportunities, and proposes strategic recommendations for fostering inclusive AI-driven educational ecosystems aligned with the Global South's unique socioeconomic and infrastructural contexts. Moreover, the role of academic leadership and AI policy in ensuring equitable AI integration in higher education is explored. The chapter indicated implications for integrating AI for an educational inclusion and equity approach.

Chapter 8: AI as part of a process of change in Argentine educational management by Christina Adriana Kruger

Educational leadership involves the practices of leading educational organizations, including curriculum, instruction, and assessment in an educational institution through support and professional development provided to the teachers. The integration of AI into educational leadership is reshaping pedagogical practices and administrative strategies globally. In Argentina, a nation grappling with educational disparities, AI presents both opportunities and challenges in promoting equity and inclusion. This chapter examines how AI influences educational leadership in Argentina, focusing on its role in advancing equitable and inclusive education.

Chapter 9: AI and the ethical dimension of educational leadership by Charles L. Lowery

This chapter contemplates the convergence of AI and authentic ethical leadership in K–12 education. While AI tools can bolster school leaders' creativity, problem-solving, and scenario-based resourcefulness, this enhancement must be balanced with a preservation of *authentic* intelligence. By generating novel insights, AI can facilitate the generation of ideas and possible resolutions for complex dilemmas, crises, and conflicts, but educators must remain vigilant to potential biases, hidden agendas, and what is called *dilemma latency*. Through critically developed prompts and a continual ethical lens, leaders can engage and enhance their moral autonomy, enrich their ability to understand stakeholder perspectives, and maintain cultural sensitivity when leveraging the seemingly infinite number of AI-driven recommendations. Ultimately, the chapter considers the undeterred human aspect of leadership and decision-making—the irreducible role of empathy, democratic values, and the capacity for adaptive thinking that machines cannot replicate. The goal is to cultivate ethically prepared leaders who employ AI critically and competently, ensuring it complements—rather than constrains or diminishes—their moral agency and decision-making in contemporary educational environments.

Part III: AI for Inclusion and Equity in Curriculum and Instruction

Chapter 10: Trust in artificial intelligence: Challenges of educational equity and ethics in students' practices in German higher education by Therese Rosemann, Marie Rathmann, Jan Schiller, and Sabine Schmidt-Lauff

This chapter discusses the experience of adult students in the *DigiTaks* project, in Germany. The *DigiTaks* project aims to investigate the digital competence acquisition processes of adult learners in Germany. One of the sub-projects investigated how students use *ChatGPT* and other AI tools to conduct research equitably and ethically. The project uses a longitudinal research design approach, involving both quantitative and qualitative research methods. The chapter discusses the literature and conceptual framework of the study related to AI, the methodology, findings, analysis, and recommendations regarding the ethical utilization of AI in a manner that is inclusive and equitable.

Chapter 11: Digitalization and artificial intelligence for enhancing inclusive and equitable education in Finland by Sari Havu-Nuutinen and Sini Kontkanen

This chapter aims to provide an overview of policy and practices relevant to how digitalization and different forms of AI are recognized in Finnish education. The chapter reviews the use of digital learning to support learners' equity and inclusion in Finnish educational policy and practice. It provides examples of the implementation of AI in basic education and its potential benefits. In addition, the chapter reviews research outcomes related to how digitalization is applied in teacher education to foster equity and inclusion in Finnish education more broadly.

Chapter 12: Educational integration of artificial intelligence: Like it or not AI is changing the way we teach and learn by María Dolores Lasso and Camila Carpio Frixone

This chapter consists of a reflection about different ways to promote the integration of AI in different educational settings in Ecuador. The adoption of new technologies has always been a challenge for educational settings. In most cases, technologies are adopted due to outside pressure rather than the willingness of teachers to incorporate new trends into their teaching. During the past years, different institutions of the Ecuadorian government have published documents introducing the integration of AI as an expectation for different educational settings. Meanwhile, students of all educational levels are adopting different types of AI applications as part of their daily lives, including their academic work. Schools and universities are developing institutional policies about the use of AI for academic work and at the same time are finding ways to formally embrace AI in a pedagogical, ethical, and appropriate manner.

Chapter 13: Mitigating teacher burnout and facilitating career pathways by Claire Ramsey

As AI becomes increasingly embedded in educational practice, its potential to alleviate systemic challenges—such as high educator turnover and limited professional development opportunities—demands rigorous exploration. This chapter examines how AI, when implemented ethically and equitably, can mitigate unmanageable workloads, enable personalized career advancement, and promote long-term retention among K–12 educators. Framed by the Comprehensive AI Assessment Framework (CAIAF) and informed by the Artificial Intelligence Assessment Scale (AIAS), the analysis draws on recent empirical studies, policy reports, and case-based examples to assess how AI tools support teachers through automated grading, adaptive lesson planning, emotional wellness, and professional development. The chapter also considers how these interventions affect student academic success by enabling more stable and responsive learning environments. Central to this inquiry is the dual function of CAIAF, which evaluates the degree of AI integration while ensuring alignment with five core ethical pillars: transparency, equity, pedagogical alignment, accountability, and data protection. By highlighting both the promise and limitations of AI-enabled interventions, this chapter offers a structured, ethics-driven pathway for integrating AI into school systems to advance educator support, instructional quality, and educational equity.

Chapter 14: Reclaiming AI equity in special education: Justice in a post-federal era by Jimmy R. Caldwell

AI is rapidly transforming special education, offering both opportunities for inclusive innovation and risks of reinforcing structural inequities. This chapter critically analyzes how AI technologies shape access, assessment, and accountability for students with disabilities, especially those situated at the intersections of race, language, and socioeconomic status. Grounded in Universal Design for Learning (UDL) and Disability Critical Race Theory (DisCrit) frameworks, the chapter presents a justice-centered approach for evaluating AI implementation in educational settings. Through literature review and policy analysis, the chapter interrogates algorithmic bias, predictive labeling, ethical opacity, and the erosion of procedural safeguards. The chapter advances a multi-pronged agenda for reform, including policy redesign, equity-driven professional development, participatory co-design, and community-rooted research focused on algorithmic justice. Amid federal disinvestment in public education, the chapter concludes by proposing localized, coalition-based governance models to reclaim AI as a tool for equity rather than control.

FINAL CONSIDERATIONS

The chapters in this volume have addressed how AI can support educational equity and inclusion in a variety of international contexts. The diversity of the contexts and contributors constitutes a strength for this volume, as it aligns with the overall purpose of the volume and inherently sets the stage for multi-rationalist perspectives. Despite AI's promise, equity and inclusion in education are still difficult and contentious issues. The term "inclusion" describes the development of educational settings that serve all students, including those from marginalized socioeconomic backgrounds, minority ethnic groups, and people with disabilities. In contrast, equity places a strong emphasis on fairness in the allocation of resources, participation, and results. The way AI interacts with these ideas brings up issues related to algorithmic fairness, access, cultural sensitivity, and data ethics. Adaptive learning systems, automated grading, predictive analytics for student retention, and natural language processing tools are some of the newer uses of AI in education. There is potential for these tools to help students with learning disabilities, special education needs, and language barriers. Critiques also highlight the threat to data privacy, the perpetuation of preexisting biases, and the marginalization of voices in AI design processes. AI digital tools should be used comprehensively for diversity inclusion, equity, and ethical scrutiny and safeguards. Short of that, they run the risk of fostering algorithmic bias and digital divides even though they provide early intervention systems, individualized learning, and accessibility for students with disabilities. A multi-stakeholder strategy that prioritizes equity-minded and social justice leadership, comprehensive policies and guidelines, educator training, inclusive design, strong infrastructure, and regulation is needed to ensure inclusive and equitable AI. Overall, the ultimate aim of this volume is to advance conversations and discussion about the opportunities offered by

AI to address educational disparities by advancing educational inclusion and equity while being mindful of the various ethical challenges that must be continuously monitored and addressed adequately.

REFERENCES

Acai, A., Mercer-Mapstone L., & Guitman R. (2019). Mind the (gender) gap: Engaging students as partners to promote gender equity in higher education. *Teaching in Higher Education*, 27(1), 18–38. https://doi.org/10.1080/13562517.2019.1696296

Earley, P. C., & Ang, S. (2003). *Cultural intelligence: Individual interactions across cultures.* Stanford University Press.

Gardner, H. (2006). *Multiple intelligences: New horizons in theory and practice.* Basic Books.

Goleman, D. (1995). *Emotional intelligence: Why it can matter more than IQ.* Bantam Books.

Italie, H. (2023, August 13). *Fiction writers fear the rise of AI, but also see it as a story to tell.* Retrieved from: https://apnews.com/article/ai-novels-authors-f846ff75df37dacbdb87b4343a346c2a

Kelly, S. M. (2023, January 26). *ChatGPT passes exams from law and business schools. CNN Business.* Retrieved from: https://www.cnn.com/2023/01/26/tech/chatgpt-passes-exams/index.html

McGregor, K. (2023, February 3). *Sciences Po bans chatgpt amid HE quality, integrity fears.* University World News. Retrieved from: https://www.universityworldnews.com/post.php?story=20230203074335557

Mueller, J. P, & Massaron, L. (2019). *Deep learning for dummies* (2nd ed.). Wiley.

Peters, M. (2023). *Stop focusing on plagiarism, even though ChatGPT is here: Create a culture of academic integrity instead.* Retrieved from: https://hbsp.harvard.edu/inspiring-minds/stop-focusing-on-plagiarism-even-though-chatgpt-is-here

Sternberg, R. J. (2003). Intelligence. In D.K. Freedheim (Ed.). Handbook of psychology: History of psychology. (Vol. 1, pp. 135–156). Wiley & Sons.

Sternberg, R. J. (2012). Intelligence. *Dialogues in Clinical Neuroscience, 14(*1), 19–27.

Thorndike, E. L. (1920). Intelligence and its uses. *Harper's Magazine*, 140, 227–235.

University of Helsinki. (2024). *Using AI to support learning.* Retrieved from: https://studies.helsinki.fi/instructions/article/using-ai-support-learning

Wechsler, D. (1939). *The measurement of adult intelligence.* Williams & Wilkins.

PART I

AI and the challenges of diversity inclusion, equity, and ethics

2. Diversity inclusion, equity, and artificial intelligence

Emmanuel Jean-Francois

INTRODUCTION

The recent global COVID-19 pandemic and the murder of George Floyd by a police officer in the US have shed light on ethnic disparities across various sectors in American society. The death of George Floyd has generated global outrage and put on the forefront the issues of diversity, equity, and inclusion (DEI) as a critical area of inquiry, policy analysis, and policy making due to its profound impact on organizational effectiveness, social justice, and outcomes across multiple sectors (Tessema et al., 2022; Williams & Sahel, 2022). The DEI discourse spans multiple decades, but has mainly focused on representation, anti-discrimination efforts, and more importantly, tokenism. There was no clear consensus on issues of structural racism embedded in policies and practices, especially in American society. Consequently, DEI discourse was not primarily about systemic change, intersectionality, and belonging (Gichane et al., 2025; Tessema et al., 2022). The murder of George Floyd had created a shift. During the recent development of the DEI discourse in the US, I witnessed individuals from the majority groups acknowledging their awareness of their White privileges (regardless of gender, class, age, political leaning, or sexual orientation), their comfort to take advantage of it as much as possible, and their resort to denialism, meritocracy, or technicality when a given practice of discrimination or racism becomes too explicit. Most of the majority ethnic groups in the US have provided their support for systemic changes against structurally discriminatory and racist policies and practices. Obviously, the support is for the broad idea pending approval of the implementation and related implications. First, organizations and institutions have slowly adopted DEI initiatives and guidelines. Then, the election of Joseph Biden in 2020 led to the adoption of executive policy initiatives that lasted until the election of Donald Trump in 2024. It did not take too long for public and private organizations, including most educational institutions, to surrender and delete anything that sounds or smells DEI. It was not a surprise, for this is the reality of a capitalist society where money (not core values) is the primary driver of everything, including past DEI initiatives. It is fair to argue that the DEI discourse has both proponents and detractors, who are not entirely divided across ideological lines, because diversity-based discrimination and racist practices are legacies of both political parties in the US. It is evident that there is a lack of comprehensive understanding of DEI while the challenges of inequity, especially in education, persist. A complete eradication of initiatives and policies to address diversity inclusion and equity is not possible, given the need to manage diversity inclusion will remain and outlive any petty exclusionary policies. Therefore, any effort to promote exclusion and inequity, as is the case with the Trump administration, has an expiration date. The Trump administration may argue against that statement. However, it is factual. If the administration was not for exclusion and inequity, it would have reformed the obvious mistakes made in the implementation of some DEI policies and used a different approach. Having a radical approach against DEI reflects a profound ignorance at best of what DEI conceptually stands for. Diversity inclusion does not exclude competence and excellence. Equity is about fairness. How can someone be against fairness? When some farmers in the U.S. received subsidies from the Trump administration to alleviate their loss because of structual disadvantages caused by the trade war with China (U.S. Department of Agriculture, USDA, 2020), this was a practice of equity. When some businesses in the U.S. (e.g., bars, restaurants) received subsidies during the early period of COVID-19 to pay their employees while they were closed (U.S. Small Business Administration, 2020), this was a practice of equity. It was about providing them an opportunity to prevent their total collapse. Some businesses did not need such subsidies, because they were greedily profiting from the pandemic (Daniel, 2022). So, the subsidies were not distributed on the basis of equality, but on the basis of equity. And, it was the right thing to do, given COVID-19 affected some businesses disproportionately. It is the same thing in society and education. When some groups are affected disproportionately, those who are entrusted with the leadership of societies and organizations have a moral responsibility to use equity as a tool to negate the effect of disproportionate disadvanges. Now, it is up to the proponents of diversity inclusion and equity to be honest with themselves and reflect on what undermined the very purpose that they claim pursuing. It is important to note that equity that is based on self-profiteering, cronyism, superficial representation, and marginalization based on identity politics is exclusionary and unsustainable. Regardless of the nature of the political climate and divisiveness in society, artificial intelligence (AI) seems to offer a window of opportunities to find alternative ways to advance inclusion and equity in education. Globally, AI is revolutionizing educational systems by providing new avenues for efficiency, learner-centered methods, and customization, which carry the seeds to explore opportunities for taking initiatives and addressing educational inclusion and equity through digitalization. In that sense, AI digital technologies emerge as a promising tool for addressing systemic injustices in education because of their capacity to process vast amounts of data, identify patterns, and customize instruction for individual students (Luckin et al., 2016). In fact, due to its revolutionary potential to improve student engagement, personalize learning, and maximize administrative efficiency, research on the advantages of incorporating AI in educational settings has become a crucial field of study. Policymakers, educators, and researchers are paying more and more attention to the integration of AI as education institutions work to achieve the fourth Sustainable Development Goal (SDG) of the United Nations (UN), which is to ensure inclusive and equitable quality education for all. Having said that, so far, the digitalization of education has not comprehensively advanced inclusion and equity in education, given the reality of the digital divide that leaves some categories of educational stakeholders behind. Then, the question is: To what extent can such opportunities offered by AI comprehensively help address issues of diversity inclusion and equity in education?

DIVERSITY

What is diversity? Diversity is the global reality of a world made of many geographic regions, countries, cultures, religions, ideologies, individuals of different skin colors, genders, physical traits, ages, languages, sexual orientations, histories, lived-experiences, personalities, motivations, worldviews, political affiliations, thoughts, abilities, preferences, and socioeconomic status (Campbell et al., 2025). Therefore, the world is inherently diverse. Every country in the world includes a certain degree of diversity, even when a high level of homogeneity might exist in certain areas. In a nutshell, diversity is a fact of human life, but also of the overall ecosystem, which consists of recognizing the various distinctions of individuals, whether they are biological, geographic, cultural, economic, political, or ecological. As Campbell et al. (2025) assert, diversity is the acceptance, appreciation, and recognition of individuals or groups with unique identities and traits. Diversity has a significant impact on global workforce dynamics, social justice, and organizational effectiveness. Diversity as a concept has changed over time, moving from early ethical and legal concerns in the middle of the twentieth century to a strategic necessity in modern organizational settings (Brazzel, 2003). The importance of diversity has been further heightened by the growing globalization of markets and workforce demographics. Several scholars argue that companies that embrace diversity see increases in employee commitment and financial performance (Foster et al., 2021; Juhwan et al., 2023). Khan and Kalra (2022) explain that diversity exists at the surface-level differences (e.g., skin color, ethnicity, gender, age, physical abilities, language) and deep-level differences (e.g., attitudes, personalities, worldview, expertise, beliefs). When combined with inclusive environments and encouraging leadership, diversity improves financial performance, innovation, and creativity (Barak, 2016). The mediation of inclusion enables diverse perspectives to translate diversity into organizational benefits (Reinert & Buengeler, 2024). As I mentioned earlier, diversity is unavoidable in groups, organizations, institutions, communities, societies, and the world. The challenge to address is diversity inclusion.

DIVERSITY INCLUSION

Diversity inclusion refers to the intentional efforts to ensure individuals of all backgrounds or identities are not marginalized, but feel welcomed, respected, supported, and valued (Shore et al., 2011). Diversity exists and is observable. Diversity can be translated into representation. However, in contrast to mere representation, inclusion focuses on the active engagement and participation of diverse individuals within an institutional or organizational environment (Arsel et al., 2022). As Shultz et al. (2022) explain, diversity inclusion implies that individuals with different identities have full access to a system's opportunities and decision-making. In the context of education, diversity inclusion encompasses policies and practices that accommodate students of various racial, ethnic, gender, linguistic, ability, and other distinct backgrounds. It aims to eliminate barriers to learning and participation by recognizing and valuing the uniqueness of each learner. For example, inclusive education addresses the needs of students with disabilities through individualized support and curriculum adaptation (Florian & Black-Hawkins, 2011). Diversity inclusion helps ensure that stakeholders (e.g., students, parents, educators) from historically marginalized and disadvantaged communities have access to opportunities that the system would not allow them otherwise. Some strategies for diversity inclusion in education include, but are not limited to, universal design for learning (UDL), culturally responsive teaching, and anti-bias curriculum. Inclusive leadership combined with ongoing education and technology can help promote a sense of community and reduce prejudice. Diversity inclusion is meaningful and worthwhile. However, diversity inclusion must combine with equity to be effective and sustainable.

EQUITY

What is equity? Often, the terms equality and equity are used interchangeably. They overlap with one another. They do, however, have different conceptual meanings, particularly in the context of education. Theoretically, equality is frequently linked to the equitable allocation of opportunities or resources. In other words, equality means giving everyone the same opportunities or resources. That would be fair if some categories did not have long-standing structures, policies, and discriminatory policy implementation practices that give them an unfair advantage. Contrary to equality, equity is more complex and takes into account people's different needs and situations. It draws from conceptual frameworks like intersectionality, which study the relationship between overlapping social identities and oppressive and privileged systems, structures, and policies (Los Santos et al., 2020). Equity entails adjusting opportunities and resources to match the unique requirements of people or groups in order to produce just and fair results. Understanding how these ideas overlap and diverge in practice requires an awareness of this distinction.

According to Gorski (2017), equity is the fair treatment, advancement, opportunity, and access of all people while working to identify and remove obstacles that have kept some groups from fully participating in society. The idea of equity has become more important in discussions about social justice, healthcare, education, and policy. Equity is fairness that takes into consideration historical, social, and economic disadvantages that affect results. The World Health Organization (2021, para. 1) defines equity as "the absence of unfair, avoidable or remediable differences among groups of people, whether those groups are defined by social, economic, demographic, or geographic factors, or by other dimensions of inequality (e.g. sex, gender, ethnicity, disability, or sexual orientation)." Equity in education refers to the distribution of resources, instruction, and support based on each learner's needs in order to guarantee equal chances for academic success. Equity involves an acknowledgment that equal resources do not always translate into equal and fair outcomes if some students start with disproportional advantages related to facets of their identities. Consequently, it is important to develop customized learning pathways to guarantee that every student can gain academically, regardless of their identities. Even though diversity inclusion and equity are widely acknowledged to be important, there are still a lot of unanswered questions about how to implement them effectively and achieve quantifiable results. Institutions and organizations have encountered obstacles like lack of resources, inconsistent policies, and opposition from dominant groups when attempting to translate their commitments to diversity inclusion and equity into long-lasting structural changes (Bernstein & Salipante, 2023). The politization of the acronym DEI in the US is an illustration of that. Most people (e.g. Americans), even the detractors of DEI, would not want individuals to be excluded or not provided the resources they need to succeed based on their demographic, cultural, social, economic, political, or intersectional identities. Therefore, the problem is not necessarily in the acronym (i.e., DEI), but in its over-politicization for all kinds of noble and questionable purposes, to put it mildly. Diversity inclusion and equity in education are important not as a political slogan or an imaginary/invented issue. It is a reality manifested in almost all education outcomes and achievement metrics (Stanford Center for Education Policy Analysis, CEPA, 2025). It is also because initiatives and policies rooted in an equality framework contribute to increasing diversity, but help diversity inclusion on the margin; thus, expand and sustain inequality. In reality, implementing equality in education frequently leads to equal distribution of resources, which may result in inequal differences in results because of varying student needs. Infusing equity in education enables one to identify systemic disadvantages that exist historically and contemporarily, design fairness-oriented models, and successfully implement targeted interventions (e.g., resource allocation based on need and differentiated instruction) to reverse the course of educational exclusion and inequities. The hardest part is to acknowledge the challenges related to achieving educational equity and develop smart strategies to face them, and shape institutions and organizations that are fertile grounds for fairness to grow and prosper.

CHALLENGES AND RESISTANCE TO DIVERSITY INCLUSION AND EQUITY

Despite a growing body of knowledge about diversity, significant challenges remain in understanding and managing diversity inclusion effectively (Jones, 2025). Recent controversies in the US about the acronym DEI suggest the existence of an ambiguity and complexity surrounding the meaning and practical applications of diversity across different contexts. While diversity inclusion and equity are value-added and sustainable assets for a safe, peaceful, and stable society, it is not uncommon for some groups to see them as legal compliance to monitor and police. The conflict between diversity as a strategic asset and a compliance concern is one example of the significant gap in integrating diverse disciplinary perspectives and balancing conflicting approaches when advocating for or challenging against diversity inclusion and equity. There must be a balance between diversity inclusion and equity as a strategic asset and legal compliance. Diversity is a strength until it is weaponized through identity politics by one sector or another. And this is the reality some people are still too timid to admit in a supposedly democratic society where majority and minority groups exist. Diversity inclusion and equity should not have been an issue for debate, given that diversity is a fact and inequity has been structurally experienced by some categories or groups in society (Delgado & Stefancic, 2017). However, the implementation of policies can be challenged and corrected in ways that are dogmatic. Inadequate diversity inclusion and equity management strategies can worsen organizational inequality and fail to fully reap the benefits of workforce diversity. If diversity inclusion and equity are only handled as a matter of legal compliance rather than a resource that will benefit everyone within a system's opportunities, they may encounter opposition and become difficult to implement. Equity can be imposed by political power. However, in a relatively democratic society where power centers are cyclical, political power alone cannot sustain equity initiatives and policies. Political power must be combined with the power of consciousness raising, persuasion, and diverse coalition building to sustain equity. This is where a deconstructionist perspective (Derrida, 1997) is needed. Concepts, paradigms, and policies, even the most popular ones, cannot be immune to criticism at the risk of ostracism. This is to argue that while the positive effects of diversity inclusion and equity are irrefutable, the mismanagement or mishandling of their implementation can lead to unintended consequences that reach dogmatic territories and inappropriate resistance, as it has been the case from day one of the second Trump administration. On the other hand, even well-intended dogmatism on social, political, and economic issues is rooted in religious fanaticism, and risks opening a Pandora's box for over-policing, virtue signaling, identity politics, excesses, abuses, selective outrages, and other similar zealous behavior and/or decision-making that can become cyclical and detrimental to sustainable diversity inclusion, and equity. Dogmatism can infect both the proponents and the detractors of diversity inclusion and equity. Dogmatic, self-righteous, and overreaching discourses, policies, and practices by proponents of diversity inclusion and equity can have the unintended consequences of being as destructive as the actions of detractors. The anti-DEI federal and state legislations in the US that have already dismantled P-20 programs and support services illustrate how dogmatists from one camp can provide excuses to dogmatists from another camp to undermine diversity inclusion and equity. The minority groups that are most in need of diversity inclusion and equity policies become the only victims because some other groups or individuals that benefit from DEI initiatives and policies are part of dominant categories in society, thus are not as significantly affected by anti-DEI actions.

Particular diversity metrics and hiring practices have received more attention and priority than more significant cultural change and inclusion strategies (Toma et al., 2024). This is partly due to the fact that identity activism can be more aggressive and vocal in pushing the aspects of diversity inclusion and equity that are more beneficial to them. Due to differing legal frameworks and social norms, diversity inclusion and equity practices vary across national, regional, and cultural contexts. Given the spatial and temporal variability in diversity categories and priorities, it is crucial to localize the definitions and methods of diversity inclusion and equity (Chengere & Bekele, 2024). Challenges such as unconscious bias, intersectional discrimination, and digital divides remain inadequately addressed in many organizational and educational settings, especially in the US. As mentioned earlier, this partly results from the infusion of political partisanship and identity politics in diversity inclusion and equity initiatives and policies, which in turn fuels resistance to change in a society where conservative instincts predominantly drive a combined majority from both major US political parties. Oftentimes, the challenges of diversity inclusion and equity go beyond demographic differences (e.g., gender, skin color, sexual orientation, or immigration status), especially when it comes to the divide between rural versus urban areas, wealthy versus disadvantaged communities, affirmative action versus legacy recruitment, or center versus peripheral power privilege, and so on and so forth. The point is that advancing diversity inclusion and equity in education should not be discrete efforts by special interest groups and intersectoral rivalries. It should be approached as a systemic project that includes everyone while allowing opportunities for continuous improvement. Failure to do so will deepen disparities and exclusion.

DISPARITIES AND EXCLUSION IN EDUCATION

Educational disparities refer to unequal access, participation, and outcomes among student groups; exclusion is about the procedures that explicitly or implicitly hinder complete educational engagement (Hernández-Saca et al., 2023). This is even more complicated when considering the intersectionalities that exist in how individual identities are affected by disparities and exclusion. Skin color, ethnicity, gender, sexual orientation, and disability are just a few of the intersecting identities that have been included in scholarship in recent decades, as opposed to the previous focus on socioeconomic status. According to Crenshaw (1991), intersectionality theory offers a framework for examining how various identities interact to create distinct experiences of disadvantage. By demonstrating how systemic power structures create and maintain inequities, this framework connects disparities and exclusion. Creating inclusive educational practices and policies requires an understanding of these intersectional relationships.

Persistent gaps in economic opportunities, health outcomes, and educational attainment are intersecting issues that contribute to systemic inequities affecting marginalized populations (Kim et al., 2023) and worsen educational disparities. There are disagreements over how much systemic racism and discrimination contribute to educational disparities versus socioeconomic status (Kulkarni et al., 2022). This disagreement will continue to exist, given the subjective ontology that may inform them. However, disparities continue to remain an objectively observable fact, even when scrutinized through subjective interpretations. As such, the necessity for complex, intersectional approaches is further highlighted by ongoing discussions regarding the efficacy of current policies and interventions meant to close educational gaps (Scheurich & Mason, 2024). As recent political and economic crises showed, disparities affect not only the individuals who experience them, but also the stability of peaceful and safe societies. If gaps are not closed, there is a chance that cycles of disadvantage will continue, and threaten social cohesiveness and economic advancement (LaVeist et al., 2023).

As previously noted, the global COVID-19 pandemic exacerbated already existing inequities by drawing attention to differences in access to remote education (Ghosh, 2024). With marginalized groups continuously encountering obstacles to high-quality education, educational disparities in access and utilization of digital technologies, especially educational technologies, are important predictors of lifelong inequalities in employment, health, and social mobility (Farquharson et al., 2023). The need for a thorough understanding and intervention is highlighted by the gaps that persist despite policy efforts. The problem of educational exclusion manifests both explicitly and implicitly, affecting students through systemic barriers and social marginalization. Exclusion can be explicit exclusion through policy implementation that positively affects one group and negatively affects another group based on technicalities. It can also be implicit through systemic biases, cultural invisibility, or structural and institutional practices that marginalize certain groups without overt intent. Educational disparities are related to demographic, geographic, economic, policy, and intersectional factors.

Demographically, skin color, gender, ethnicity, language, caste, and migration status all influence educational participation and success, and intersectionally exacerbate disadvantages. In certain nations, where social identity has a significant impact on educational mobility and results, skin color and gender intersections are especially prominent. Differences in enrollment and achievement between males and females indicate that gender inequality in education is still a serious problem in some countries. Bruce and Venkatesh (2014) assert that disability, ethnicity, and migration status are also critical demographic factors that exacerbate exclusion, especially in marginalized communities.

Geographically, there are notable regional and urban-rural differences that impact educational outcomes and access, with a focus on marginalized areas and nations in the Global North and South. Geographic proximity and spatial dependence are important variables affecting academic achievement. Educational attainment disparities are noticeable between low- and middle-income nations (Bennet et al., 2024). Urban-rural locations are associated with educational disparities in both Global North and Global South countries. Rural and isolated sub-urban areas are more severely affected by these disparities.

Economically, numerous researchers note that educational attainment, resource availability, and access to high-quality education are strongly correlated with family socioeconomic status (Lian, 2024; Bennett et. al., 2024). In both rural and urban areas, educational disparities are made worse by parental education levels and infrastructure deficiencies, which frequently exacerbate economic disparities (Kumar et al., 2024; Lian, 2024). There are notable differences in educational attainment between kids from various socioeconomic backgrounds. These disparities are associated with wider economic inequality and are visible in both Global North and Global South nations (Blanden et al., 2022). Educational disparities are also apparent in the Science, Technology, Engineering, Arts, and Mathematics (STEAM) disciplines (Wang et al., 2023).

Policy-wise, political governments and economic systems have a significant influence on educational disparity. The effectiveness of equity-focused policies has been evaluated in a study by Sit (2024) who found that countries in the Global North generally demonstrate better funding stability and policy implementation than some Global South countries. Intersectional inequality is not adequately addressed by many policies that manage to relatively achieve goals and objectives set by donors at the expense of nuanced realities in communities, societies, and regions (André & Westerveen, 2024).

Intersectionally, the factors of inequities are overlapping with educational disparities based on demography, geography, economy, culture, and policy (Crenshaw, 1991). Minority and indigenous groups frequently experience systemic obstacles to education, which lower their educational attainment in comparison to majority groups. Systemic barriers restrict equitable access and success in education. Racial and ethnic minorities, women, low-income groups, and other minorities continue to experience educational disparities (Ghosh, 2024).

DIGITALIZATION OF EDUCATION, DIGITAL DIVIDE, AND THE EMERGENCE OF AI

The emergence of digital technology in society has positioned digitalization as an opportunity to achieve inclusion and equity in education. The digital transformation of education has been one of the most important trends of the twenty-first century. It has been further accelerated by worldwide disruptions like the COVID-19 pandemic (UNESCO, 2020). According to Selwyn (2016), the term *digitalization of education* refers to how digital tools and technologies are incorporated into administrative, instructional, and learning procedures. For example, virtual classrooms and Learning Management Systems (LMS) have revolutionized instructional delivery and expanded access to educational content. Online platforms, blended learning, and mobile education have all made education more accessible as a result of digitalization (OECD, 2021). Real-time feedback, lifelong learning, and increased student engagement are all made possible by the use of digital tools (Aydin, 2022). Zawacki-Richter et al. (2019) argue that infrastructure, teacher preparation, and policy alignment are crucial for successful digitalization. However, not everyone benefits equally or equitably from digitalization, thus the reality of the digital divide. Disadvantaged communities are still disproportionately impacted by the digital divide, which exacerbates educational disparities, especially in rural and low-income areas.

The Digital Divide

Originally defined as differences in access to information and communication technologies, the digital divide has expanded to include differences in digital literacy and meaningful use, which has an additional impact on social inclusion and educational equity (Liu, 2024). Similarly, Robinson et al. (2015) argue that the digital divide involves disparities in digital literacy, internet connectivity, and device access that disproportionately impact low-income and marginalized communities. The digital divide is observable in (a) unequal and inequitable access to educational technologies and online resources by learners from disadvantaged and minority ethnic backgrounds, rural areas, and low socioeconomic status; (b) lower digital literacy of marginalized students; and (c) lack of technology infrastructure necessary for the digitalization of education. The digital divide exists between countries of the Global North and the Global South, and within individual countries, regardless of their localization on either side of the global paradigm. The digital divide has become a crucial field of study and a matter of great concern because of its significant social, economic, and health ramifications, research on racial and ethnic diversity, gender inequality, and educational disparities.

While some learners are benefiting from the opportunity offered by digitalization to have successful academic experiences, others are still lagging behind and recording unsatisfactory academic outcomes. Due to socioeconomic, geographic, and infrastructure disparities, the digital divide exacerbates already existing educational inequalities. The digital divide continues to be a major obstacle to educational equity. According to van Dijk (2020), it appears on three levels: (a) through device/internet access; (b) through usage and skills; and (c) through results. Students from low-income, minority, or rural communities face additional difficulties in accessing and using digital resources. The OECD (2021) claims that COVID-19 made these differences worse all over the world. The rise of AI complicates and opens up this digital divide. The distribution of the digital divide still affects who gains from these developments in AI in education. UNESCO (2021) reported that while high-income areas welcome AI-enhanced education, low-resource environments frequently lack the necessary infrastructure. AI is integrating into education. What does that mean for individuals who are affected by educational disparities and inclusion?

The Emergence of AI in Education

AI is quickly becoming a disruptive force in the digitalization of education. According to Russell and Norvig (2021), AI is the creation of computer systems that are able to carry out tasks that normally require human intelligence, such as natural language processing (NLP), speech recognition, language translation, visual perception, video, sound, and image generation, and decision-making. From enabling autonomous vehicles to improving medical diagnostics through predictive analytics to automating repetitive tasks in manufacturing, AI is relevant in many domains.

AI applications, ranging from learning analytics and predictive modeling to automated grading systems and intelligent tutoring, have the potential to enhance institutional efficiency and personalize learning (Luckin et al., 2016; Holmes & Tuomi, 2022). Because AI provides tools for automated assessment, adaptive learning, and institutional analytics, it is being incorporated into educational ecosystems more and more (Luckin et al., 2016; Holmes & Tuomi, 2022). AI can improve individualized learning pathways and lessen administrative burdens. AI-powered solutions, for instance, have been used in personalized learning (i.e., adaptive platforms adjust content according to the behavior of each learner), intelligent tutoring systems (i.e., tutoring and feedback in real time), learning analytics (i.e., examining learning data to forecast dropout risks and recommend interventions), and automated assessment (i.e., formative feedback and automated essay grading are supported by machine learning and natural language processing).

AI-accelerated digitalization of education has opened up new avenues for efficiency, educational equity, and personalized learning. Nevertheless, these developments have also revealed and expanded pre-existing disparities through the digital divide (van Dijk, 2020). Careful, inclusive, and ethical application is required for AI to fully realize its potential. Future progress requires a well-rounded strategy that fosters equitable access, protects student data, and takes into account the human role in education. In the absence of intentional and inclusive policies, AI tools run the risk of making exclusion worse rather than better. For AI in education to be a tool of inclusion rather than division, it is imperative that human-centered AI design, strong teacher preparation, and data equity frameworks be in place.

ADVANCING EDUCATIONAL EQUITY AND INCLUSION THROUGH AI

As previously mentioned in this chapter, despite international pledges to promote inclusive and equitable education, educational inequalities continue to exist along racial, socioeconomic, linguistic, and ability-based lines

(UNESCO, 2020). Additionally, the preceding section made the case that AI can identify learning gaps, automate feedback, and personalize instruction—skills that could help achieve diversity inclusion and equity objectives. The use of AI in education has spurred an increasing amount of research on how it can promote equity, diversity, and inclusion. In addition to promoting inclusive teaching methods and fair access to educational resources, AI may aid in the reduction of educational inequalities and exclusion. With proper design and implementation, AI can be a potent tool for addressing educational disparities, preventing exclusion, and advancing diversity inclusion and equity in education.

AI and Instructional Leadership for Equity and Inclusion

Systemic injustices spanning socioeconomic, racial, linguistic, and geographic dimensions (Delgado & Stefancic, 2017) continue to impede equitable access to high-quality education, resulting in educational disparities. Thus, instructional leadership—defined as the strategic direction given by school administrators to enhance instruction and learning—is one of the most crucial instruments for closing achievement gaps (Hallinger, 2011). In the twenty-first century, the use of AI in education presents fresh opportunities to reevaluate instructional leadership with equity at its center.

Learning analytics, predictive modeling, and intelligent tutoring systems are examples of AI technologies that are being used more and more to optimize resource allocation, direct decision-making, and personalize learning. If there is leadership that is focused on equity, these tools could be used to address long-standing educational disparities that disproportionately impact students from marginalized backgrounds (Luckin et al., 2016). The two challenges facing educational leaders today are preventing bias from being replicated through opaque algorithms and using AI to enhance academic performance (Williamson & Piattoeva, 2022). An increasingly common tactic for improving teaching methods and lowering educational inequities is the use of AI in educational leadership. Here are some examples of key areas where AI can help with instructional leadership:

AI for student support and early intervention

AI-powered instructional leadership has the potential to significantly reduce educational disparities, but only if it is implemented with purpose, openness, and ethical supervision. One of the most promising applications of AI has been in early intervention. Numerous studies have shown that AI aids in the early detection of learning gaps and student risks (Bowers & Chen, 2019; Vieriu, & Petrea, 2025). Using predictive analytics and attendance-tracking algorithms, school administrators target interventions for students from underserved or marginalized communities. By using predictive analytics to identify students who are most likely to struggle academically or drop out, leaders can more fairly distribute resources (Bowers & Chen, 2019).

Support for individualized education and differentiated instruction

Instructional leaders can support differentiated instruction by utilizing AI-powered adaptive learning platforms, like intelligent tutoring platforms. These systems make inclusive education possible for English language learners, students with disabilities, and others who require specialized learning pathways. The diverse needs of students may be particularly well served by AI-powered personalized learning technologies. Differentiated instruction that previously required a lot of effort from teachers is made possible by instructional leaders through the use of adaptive platforms. However, success requires support from teachers, suitable training, as well as an explicit educational vision that is informed by equity principles.

Data-driven leadership in education

AI tools enable educators and leaders to make evidence-based decisions about instruction by giving them access to real-time data dashboards, according to studies (Zawacki-Richter et al., 2019). Improved performance in underprivileged schools and lower dropout rates have been associated with these practices. In addition to analyzing insights produced by AI, leaders need to challenge the presumptions underlying these technologies. In particular, biases that affect students of color, English language learners, and students with disabilities may be reinforced or amplified by algorithmic decision-making if it is not regulated (Holmes & Tuomi, 2022; Williamson & Piattoeva, 2022).

Ethics and bias in AI: equity risks

Implementing AI has risks despite its advantages. Numerous articles alert readers to the existence of biases in algorithms and the lack of ethical considerations (Holmes & Tuomi, 2022; Williamson & Eynon, 2020). Threats to equity arise from instructional leaders' frequent lack of training in evaluating algorithmic fairness. School administrators must strike a balance between ethical issues and AI's potential in order to advance social justice. Furthermore, in order to fully realize AI's transformative potential in reducing achievement gaps, professional development for educators and leaders is crucial. For instructional leadership practices to incorporate equity-driven AI solutions, policy frameworks, leadership development, and stakeholder collaboration are also required. Though encouraging, the road to AI-enabled equitable education necessitates thoughtful planning and leadership dedicated to inclusivity, justice, and ongoing evaluation.

Implementing ethics is still a major challenge. Leaders find it challenging to evaluate the methods used to arrive at conclusions because AI systems frequently operate as "black boxes." Particularly in diverse school communities, this opacity erodes trust and accountability. The adoption of AI must be accompanied by ethical frameworks, clear guidelines, and professional development to enable leaders to make decisions that are just and culturally sensitive.

AI and Instructional Strategies for Equity and Inclusion

The incorporation of AI into educational systems has drawn more attention in recent years due to its potential to address persistent problems with educational disparity and injustice. The potential for individualized, data-driven learning experiences that could lessen these disparities is presented by instructional strategies that integrate AI. However, deliberate design, implementation, and evaluation are necessary for these innovations to be effective and equitable.

Technologies including chatbots, automated feedback systems, adaptive learning platforms, and intelligent tutoring systems are examples of AI-driven teaching strategies. These tools can give underprivileged populations scalable solutions, real-time feedback, and support for individual learning needs (Luckin et al., 2016). Students who are frequently marginalized in traditional classroom settings can benefit from adaptive learning software, which can adjust the pace and content according to a learner's progress (Holstein et al., 2019). According to Zawacki-Richter et al. (2019), AI-powered language tools have also improved academic inclusion by helping students who have limited proficiency in the language of instruction.

Concerns about algorithmic bias, data privacy, fair access to AI technologies, and the possibility that AI systems could perpetuate systemic discrimination still exist despite these possible advantages (Eubanks, 2018). Furthermore, teachers must have a sophisticated awareness of both the technology and the sociocultural backgrounds of their students in order to successfully incorporate AI into their lessons. Educational institutions and leaders should provide appropriate training for teachers in AI literacy to ensure its efficient application as a tool to reverse existing disparities.

BEWARE OF ETHICAL CONCERNS ABOUT AI INTEGRATION IN EDUCATION

While AI can be used to advance diversity inclusion and equity in education, there is a growing awareness of the ethical and equity risks associated with such integration. A key concern is algorithmic bias, which disproportionately affects marginalized groups. AI is trained on data that reflect historical social inequalities. Therefore, AI is more likely to generate outputs that reproduce inequalities or even worsen them (Baker and Hawn 2021). For instance, students from historically underrepresented backgrounds may be wrongly penalized by AI-based predictive tools in admissions or disciplinary systems. There is a lack of data governance that raises concerns about student surveillance and third-party vendors that may misuse their data (Williamson & Eynon, 2020). Few educational institutions carry out thorough data audits or have explicit consent procedures in place. Policies at the national and institutional levels are still disjointed. As an illustration, Finland has introduced ethically focused inclusive AI curricula, whereas other countries have embraced more technologically oriented strategies that frequently ignore social justice issues (Luckin et al., 2022). Furthermore, excluding stakeholders continues to be a barrier. Families, teachers, and students frequently don't understand how AI systems affect the educational process. This prevents the development and nurturing of accountability and trust from growing. A democratization of AI governance is needed through the involvement of all stakeholders. Organizations around the world, including the European Commission (2025), the OECD (2021), and UNESCO (2021), have established ethical guidelines for AI, highlighting the necessity of human-centered, rights-based approaches. Despite these initiatives, there is still disparity in how high ethical standards are translated into legally binding educational policies. Because AI systems frequently function as "black boxes," it can be challenging to audit or justify their choices, which can reinforce preexisting biases or worsen disparities between students from various socioeconomic, racial, or linguistic backgrounds (Baker & Hawn, 2021). Universities and national ministries are starting to implement internal AI ethics policies, though these are frequently advisory rather than required. A coherent set of policies should include both legally binding standards and adaptable, context-sensitive procedures. Training educators, ensuring fair assessments for AI procurement, and promoting AI literacy for all stakeholders are critical.

CONCLUSION

As discussed throughout this chapter, educational disparities are a major worldwide problem that can take different forms, including variations in educational outcomes, quality, and access among various socioeconomic, geographic, and demographic groups. These differences are influenced by a wide range of factors, such as socioeconomic status, political and economic systems, and cultural settings. The evidence from existing literature emphasizes how intricate and multidimensional global educational inequality is. Access, persistence, and achievement are all impacted by educational disparities that continue to exist across racial, ethnic, gender, and socioeconomic divides. It is widely acknowledged that low-SES groups and racial/ethnic minorities experience ongoing disparities in educational access, persistence, and achievement, which are frequently exacerbated by systemic factors (Ghosh, 2024). Racial/ethnic minority, low-income, rural, and female students are disproportionately affected by the digital divide, which continues to be a major obstacle to diversity inclusion and equity in education.

It can never be said enough that the growing diversity of the populations served by healthcare and educational institutions, and the enduring inequalities in access and results highlight the social importance of diversity inclusion and equity (Gichane et al., 2025). According to Vela et al. (2022), despite new effort, structural inequity is still a devastating issue in health and education. Therefore, it is important to advance diversity inclusion and equity in order to promote fair participation and ensure everyone has not just the opportunities, but also, and more importantly, the resources to succeed in proportion to the structural and contemporary disadvantage gaps. Although the theoretical distinction between equality and equity is obvious, it can be difficult to put into practice. As demonstrated by political discussions surrounding racial equity initiatives, especially in the US, the implementation of equity policies can result in feelings of partiality or retaliation by the majority groups or categories. As I mentioned earlier, a deconstructionist perspective is needed to elucidate both the proponents and the detractors of equity. The reality is equity is needed because policies and practices based on racial supremacy have too often become the norms and gone unchallenged for long periods of time or managed to sustain the test of policy reform initiatives in societies where money is considered to be a voice, and corporations are legally considered as people. Furthermore, if equity initiatives are not based on a thorough comprehension of intersectionality and power dynamics, there is a chance that they will become superficial. Maintaining a balance between equity and equality necessitates constant critical evaluation and corrections to guarantee that interventions are just and successful (Espinoza, 2007).

It is crucial to take into account the larger context of these disparities even though the evidence points to notable educational gaps. Educational opportunities are greatly influenced by a number of factors, including, but not limited to, demography, geography, economy, policy, and intersectionality. Further complicating the issue of educational inequality is the interaction of socioeconomic status, geographic location, and cultural identity. Comprehensive policy interventions that take into account the particular circumstances of various regions and populations are necessary to address these disparities. Interventions like targeted scholarships, inclusive education, and support services have been shown to be successful in removing obstacles (Ghosh, 2024).

Because AI technologies can identify systemic biases, improve accessibility, and enable personalization, they present promising tools to support educational diversity inclusion and equity goals. AI can help education move toward a more equitable and just future when it is in line with diversity inclusion and equity values. If AI is carefully planned and applied, it can serve as a catalyst for diversity inclusion and equity in education. Access for underserved groups can be increased by assistive AI, while adaptive learning technologies could aid in customizing learning pathways.

These tools are not necessarily equitable, though. AI education raises a number of ethical and equity concerns, including algorithmic bias and fairness, privacy and surveillance, accessibility and technological ability bias, cultural and ideological balance, tokenism versus true inclusion, and resource allocation equity. The datasets used to develop many AI systems underrepresent learners with disabilities, students of color, and non-native English speakers. Furthermore, schools in low-income areas might not have the necessary infrastructure to implement AI, which would exacerbate the digital divide (Van Deursen, 2020). Insufficient training in ethical AI use may also put educators and administrators at risk of relying too much on opaque algorithms.

The effectiveness of the utilization of AI technologies to advance educational inclusion and equity depends on their deliberate creation, inclusive application, and continuous monitoring. It is critical that we move toward human-centered AI systems that are created in partnership with interdisciplinary researchers, educators, and diverse communities. Ensuring access to AI resources, addressing algorithmic bias, and incorporating diversity inclusion and equity principles into AI development are all crucial to building inclusive educational programs and institutions. When developing and implementing policies, it is important to make sure that AI in education advances equity efforts rather than impedes them. Initiatives like UNESCO's AI and Education: Guidance for Policy Makers (UNESCO, 2021) offer workable models for inclusive and moral AI governance. Overall, despite AI's potential to create more equitable learning environments, there are still issues, especially with algorithmic bias, data equity, and access to AI-enabled tools. For AI to reach its full potential in terms of diversity inclusion and equity, a more moral, inclusive, and human-centered approach is essential. Inclusive policy frameworks, cultural sensitivity, and equitable data inputs are necessary for these advantages.

REFERENCES

André, G., & Westerveen, L. (2024). Contrasting approaches to educational equality: An intersectional perspective on educational policies in Belgium. *Journal of Education Policy*, *40*(4), 587–605.

Aydin, C. H. (2022). The digital transformation of higher education: A framework for a sustainable digital ecosystem. *Education and Information Technologies*, *27*(1), 55–76.

Arsel, Z., Crockett, D., & Scott, M. L. (2022). Diversity, equity, and inclusion (DEI) in the Journal of Consumer Research: A curation and research agenda. *Journal of Consumer Research*, *48*(5), 920–933.
Baker, R. S., & Hawn, A. (2021). Algorithmic bias in education. *International Journal of Artificial Intelligence in Education*, *31*(3), 552–581.
Barak, M. E. M. (2016). *Managing diversity: Toward a globally inclusive workplace*. Sage.
Bennett, P., Foley, K., Green, D. A., & Salvanes, K. G. (2024). Education and inequality: An international perspective. *Fiscal Studies: The Journal of Applied Public Economics*, 429–454.
Bernstein, R. S., & Salipante, P. (2023). Embedding inclusive, equitable diversity practices in nonprofit organizations: Developing policy to account for system dynamics. *Nonprofit Policy Forum*, *15*(2), 97–120.
Blanden, J., Doepke, M., & Stuhler, J. (2022). Intergenerational mobility and inequality: The role of education. *National Bureau of Economic Research*. Working Paper Series, No. 29979.
Bowers, A. J., & Chen, J. (2019). Using machine learning to identify early warning indicators of dropout in K–12 education. *Educational Technology Research and Development*, *67*(4), 935–953.
Brazzel, M. (2003). Chapter 2. Historical and Theoretical Roots of Diversity Management. In D. L. Plummer (Ed.), *Handbook of Diversity Management*. University Press of America, 51–93.
Bruce, S. M., & Venkatesh, K. (2014). Special education disproportionality in the United States, Germany, Kenya, and India. *Disability & Society*, *29*(6), 908–921.
Campbell, C., Sands, S., McFerran, B. et al. (2025). Diversity representation in advertising. *Journal of the Academy of Marketing Science*, 53, 588–616.
Chengere, K. A., & Bekele, M. (2024). Cross-cultural leadership and diversity: A comprehensive literature review. *Science Innovation*, *12*(6), 109–112.
Crenshaw, K. (1991) Mapping the margins: Intersectionality, identity politics, and violence against women of color. *Stanford Law Review*, 43, 1241–1299.
Daniel, W. (2022). *U.S. companies post their biggest profit growth in decades by jacking up prices during the pandemic*. https://fortune.com/2022/03/31/us-companies-record-profits-2021-price-hikes-inflation/.
Delgado, R., & Stefancic, J. (2017). *Critical race theory: An introduction* (3rd ed.). NYU Press.
Derrida, J. (1997). *Politics of friendship* (G. Collins, Trans.). Verso.
Espinoza, O. (2007). Solving the equity-equality conceptual dilemma: A new model for analysis of the educational process. *Educational Research*, *49*(4), 343–363.
Eubanks, V. (2018). *Automating inequality: How high-tech tools profile, police, and punish the poor*. St. Martin's Press.
European Commission (2025). *European approach to artificial intelligence*.
Farquharson, C., McNally, S., & Tahir, I. (2023). Education inequalities. *Oxford Open Economics*, *3* (Supplement_1), i760–i820.
Florian, L., & Black-Hawkins, K. (2011). Exploring inclusive pedagogy. *British Educational Research Journal*, *37*(5), 813–828.
Foster, B. P., Manikas, A. S., Preece, D., & Kroes, J. R. (2021). Noteworthy diversity efforts and financial performance: Evidence from DiversityInc's top 50 for diversity. *Advances in Accounting*, *53*, 100528.

Ghosh, S. S. (2024). Navigating educational inequities in the USA: A statistical analysis of socio-economic and cultural barriers faced by young adults in formal education. *Studies in the Education of Adults, 56*(2), 158–176.
Gichane, M.W., Griesemer, I., Cubanski, L. et al. (2025). Increasing diversity, equity, and inclusion in the health and health services research workforce: A systematic scoping review. *Journal of General Internal Medicine, 40*, 1487–1497.
Gorski, P. C. (2017). *Reaching and teaching students in poverty: Strategies for erasing the opportunity gap*. Teachers College Press.
Hallinger, P. (2011). Leadership for learning: Lessons from 40 years of empirical research. *Journal of Educational Administration, 49*(2), 125–142.
Hernández-Saca, D. I., Voulgarides, C. K., & Etscheidt, S. L. (2023). A critical systematic literature review of global inclusive education using an affective, intersectional, discursive, emotive and material lens. *Education Sciences, 13*, 1212.
Holmes, W., & Tuomi, I. (2022). State of the art and practice in AI in education. *European Journal of Education, 57*, 542–570.
Holstein, K., Vaughan, J. W., Daume III, H., Dudik, M., & Wallach, H. (2019). Opportunities for machine learning research to support fairness in industry practice. Proceedings of the 2019 CHI Conference on Human Factors in Computing Systems, 1–16.
Jones, S. (2025). This fragile new world: Tales of futures without DEI in higher education. *Social Sciences, 14*(12), 695. https://doi.org/10.3390/socsci14120695
Juhwan, L., Yue, V., Jichul, J. (2023). Do employees' perceptions of diversity management enhance firms' financial performance: the moderating role of board members' diversity level. *International Journal of Contemporary Hospitality Management, 35*(11), 3990–4009.
Jurado de Los Santos, P., Moreno-Guerrero, A. J., Marín-Marín, J. A., & Soler Costa, R. (2020). The term equity in education: A literature review with scientific mapping in Web of Science. *International Journal of Environmental Research and Public Health, 17*(10), 3526.
Khan, U., & Kalra, A. (2022). It's good to be different: How diversity impacts judgments of moral behavior. *Journal of Consumer Research, 49*(2), 177–201.
Kim, S. J., Retnam, R. P., Sutton, A. L., Edmonds, M. C., Bandyopadhyay, D., & Sheppard, V. B. (2023). Racial disparities in opioid prescription and pain management among breast cancer survivors. *Cancer Medicine, 12*(9), 10851–10864.
Kulkarni, S. J., Lawrence, M., & Roberts, E. (2022). "We're constantly learning": Identifying and disrupting White supremacy within a victim services organization. *Journal of Interpersonal Violence, 38*(1–2), 1187–1203.
Kumar, A., Sharma, P., Patel, R., Gupta, A. S., & Singh, V. (2024). Educational inequality and its impact on social and economic opportunities in rural India. *International Journal of Humanities, Management and Social Science (IJ-HUMASS), 7*(2), 87–96.
LaVeist, T. A., Pérez-Stable, E. J., Richard, P., Anderson, A., Isaac, L. A., Santiago, R., Okoh, C., Breen, N., Farhat, T., Assenov, A., & Gaskin, D. J. (2023). The economic burden of racial, ethnic, and educational health inequities in the US. *JAMA, 329*(19), 1682–1692.
Lian, J. (2024). An analysis of inequality in educational resources in the United States. *Advances in Economics, Management and Political Sciences, 127*(1), 163–169.
Liu, T. (2024). Unveiling and addressing the causes of educational inequalities in China. *Journal of Education, Humanities and Social Sciences, 36*, 98–102.

Luckin, R., Holmes, W., Griffiths, M., & Forcier, L. B. (2016). *Intelligence unleashed: An argument for AI in education*. Pearson Education.

Luckin, R., George, K., & Cukurova, M. (2022). *AI for school teachers*. CRC Press.

OECD. (2021). *The state of school education: One year into the COVID pandemic*. OECD Publishing.

Reinert, C., Buengeler, C., Lehmann-Willenbrock, N., & Homan, A. C. (2024). Reviewing and revisiting the processes and emergent states underlying team diversity effects. *Small Group Research*, *56*(1), 114–163.

Robinson, L., Cotten, S. R., Ono, H., Quan-Haase, A., Mesch, G., Chen, W., ... & Stern, M. J. (2015). Digital inequalities and why they matter. *Information, Communication & Society*, *18*(5), 569–582.

Russell, S., & Norvig, P. (2021). *Artificial intelligence: A modern approach* (4th ed.). Pearson.

Scheurich, J. J., & Mason, M. (2024). An intersectionality-based research framework and methodology that emphasizes systemic inequities in public schooling, including racism, sexism, and classism. *Cultural Studies – Critical Methodologies*, *24*(5), 319–330.

Selwyn, N. (2016). *Education and technology: Key issues and debates* (2nd ed.). Bloomsbury Academic.

Shore, L. M., Randel, A. E., Chung, B. G., Dean, M. A., Holcombe Ehrhart, K., & Singh, G. (2011). Inclusion and diversity in work groups: A review and model for future research. *Journal of Management*, *37*(4), 1262–1289.

Shultz, C., Hoek, J., Lee, L., Leong, W. Y., Srinivasan, R., Viswanathan, M., & Wertenbroch, K. (2022). JPP&M's global perspective and impact: An agenda for research on marketing and public policy. *Journal of Public Policy & Marketing*, *41*(1), 34–50.

Sit, F., (2024). Global inequalities in access and success in higher education. *New Vistas*, *10*(1).

Stanford Center for Education Policy Analysis. (CEPA, 2025). *Racial and ethnic achievement gaps*. Retrieved from: https://cepa.stanford.edu/educational-opportunity-monitoring-project/achievement-gaps/race/.

Tessema, Z. T., Worku, M. G., Tesema, G. A., Alamneh, T. S., Teshale, A. B., Yeshaw, Y., Alem, A. Z., Ayalew, H. G., & Liyew, A. M. (2022). Determinants of accessing healthcare in Sub-Saharan Africa: A mixed-effect analysis of recent demographic and health surveys from 36 countries. *BMJ Open*, *12*(1), e054397.

Toma, C., Boroş, S. & Popa-Roch, M. (2024). Editorial: Paradoxes of diversity, equity and inclusion: From the lab to the social field. *Frontiers in Psychology*, *15*, 1511223.

UNESCO. (2020). *Global education monitoring report 2020: Inclusion and education: all means all*. Retrieved from: https://unesdoc.unesco.org/.

UNESCO. (2021). *AI and education: Guidance for policymakers*. Retrieved from: https://unesdoc.unesco.org/.

U.S. Department of Agriculture. (USDA, 2020). *Farmer first actions taken by the trump administration: The Trump Administration delivered $12 billion in farmer bridge aid*. https:\\www.usda.gov/farmers-first.

U.S. Small Business Administration. (2020). *Restaurant revitalization fund*. https://www.sba.gov/funding-programs/loans/covid-19-relief-options/restaurant-revitalization-fund.

Van Deursen, A. J. A. M. (2020). Digital inequality during a pandemic: quantitative study of differences in COVID-19-related internet use and outcomes among the general population. *Journal of Medical Internet Research*, *22*(8), e20073.
van Dijk, J. A. G. M. (2020). *The digital divide*. Polity Press.
Vela, M. B., Erondu, A. I., Smith, N. A., Peek, M. E., Woodruff, J. N., & Chin, M. H. (2022). Eliminating explicit and implicit biases in health care: Evidence and research needs. *Annual Review of Public Health*, 43, 477–501.
Wang, N., Tan, AL., Zhou, X. et al. (2023). Gender differences in high school students' interest in STEM careers: a multi-group comparison based on structural equation model. *International Journal of STEM Education*, 10, 59.
Williams, A.M., & Sahel, J.A. (2022). Addressing social determinants of vision health. *Ophthalmology and Therapy*, *11*(4), 1371–1382.
Williamson, B., & Eynon, R. (2020). Historical threads, missing links, and future directions in AI in education. *Learning, Media and Technology*, *45*(3), 223–235.
Williamson, B., & Piattoeva, N. (2022). Education governance and datafication: Technologies of control and resistance. *Education Policy Analysis Archives*, *30*(21).
World Health Organization (WHO, 2021). *Health equity*. Retrieved from: https://www.who.int/health-topics/health-equity#tab=tab_1
Zawacki-Richter, O., Marín, V. I., Bond, M., & Gouverneur, F. (2019). Systematic review of research on artificial intelligence applications in higher education – where are the educators? *International Journal of Educational Technology in Higher Education*, *16*(1), 39.

3. Bridging the digital divide in education

Global and local perspectives

Neil D. Grimes and Sara Platt

INTRODUCTION

The digital divide in education refers to the gap between those who have access to technology and digital resources and those who do not, leading to disparities in educational opportunities and outcomes in the K–20 educational environment and beyond. This divide is particularly pronounced on a global scale, with significant discrepancies between countries of the Global North, which tend to have better access to technology, and countries of the Global South, where access is often limited. The Global North comprises of more economically advanced countries, such as those in North America, Europe, Australia, Japan, and Russia (Cayli, 2014). In contrast, the Global South typically refers to regions with lower social and economic development, including developing countries in Asia, Africa, the Middle East, and Latin America (Cayli, 2014). Moreover, within countries themselves, disparities persist between urban and rural areas, further exacerbating inequities in education. With the onset of the COVID-19 pandemic, the importance of addressing the digital divide has been further underscored, as remote learning has become a necessity, highlighting the stark disparities in access to technology and its impact on educational continuity and equity.

This chapter, "Bridging the digital divide in education: Global and local perspectives," is part of the volume *Artificial Intelligence for Educational Inclusion and Equity: International Studies and Critiques*. The purpose of this chapter is to examine the global and local dimensions of digital inequity, with a particular focus on the role of artificial intelligence (AI) and educational technologies (EdTech) in addressing these disparities. It explores how access to AI-driven learning tools, government policies, and digital infrastructure shape educational opportunities across different regions. Through a comparative lens, this chapter highlights case studies from the Global North and the Global South, emphasizing the successes, challenges, and gaps in digital inclusion efforts worldwide.

By analyzing AI readiness, digital infrastructure, and policy interventions, this chapter aims to provide a structured understanding of the systemic inequalities that contribute to the digital divide. It also considers how AI can serve as both a tool for inclusion and a factor that may inadvertently reinforce existing inequities if access is not equitably distributed. The discussion underscores the importance of collaborative efforts among policymakers, educators, and technology developers to ensure that AI-driven educational tools promote equity rather than exacerbate disparities.

Ultimately, this chapter contributes to the broader themes of the volume by examining the intersection of AI and EdTech, education, and digital equity on a global scale. By doing so, it aligns with the overarching goal of exploring how AI and EdTech can be leveraged to create more inclusive educational systems, ensuring that no student—regardless of geography, socioeconomic status, or technological access—is left behind.

BACKGROUND: GLOBAL DIGITAL DIVIDES

The digital divide has both socioeconomic and educational implications as well as global impacts. Technological innovation is opening a new frontier in the development agenda for countries all over the world. It has been forecast that AI could contribute up to 15.7 trillion USD to the global economy by 2030 (PricewaterhouseCoopers, 2024). While all regions of the global economy stand to benefit from AI, it is evident that North America and China will see the largest GDP gains (Yu et al., 2023). Countries in the Global South will experience more moderate increases due to the much lower rates of adoption of AI technologies. In contrast, developed nations, with greater economic resources, can more easily fund research and implement advanced AI technologies. However, countries in the Global South are still committed to utilizing AI, as shown by initiatives like India's AIForAll strategy (Panday & Samdub, 2024; Yu et al., 2023).

An Oxford Insights Assessment (2024) of 181 countries around the world and their preparedness in using AI in public services highlights that the lowest-scoring regions include much of the Global South, such as countries in sub-Saharan Africa, some Central and South Asian countries, and some Latin American countries. The report emphasizes that governments require the appropriate operating environment to support AI development, which includes a robust technology sector, adequate data infrastructure, and strategic vision and attention to governance and ethics at the state (local) or government (national) level. Without an enabling operating environment, disparities in AI readiness will feed into global inequality (Yu et al., 2023) further increasing the existing global digital divide.

Pick & Nishida (2015) examine global digital divides through a comprehensive analysis of technological usage across different regions. They investigated disparities in internet access, mobile phone use, and other digital technologies using spatial and multivariate statistical techniques. Their analysis identified significant digital divides between developed and developing regions, with wealthier nations typically exhibiting higher levels of technological utilization. Key factors influencing these divides include economic development, education levels, infrastructure, government policies, and geographic conditions. Their study revealed regions such as North America and Europe, part of the Global North, lead in digital technology adoption, while sub-Saharan Africa, parts of Asia, and Latin America, part of the Global South, lag behind. Furthermore, Pick & Nishida (2015) emphasize the role of policy interventions in addressing these disparities, highlighting how infrastructure investments, education, and digital literacy programs can help bridge the gap. Their spatial analysis also shows that digital divides are not only global but also exist within countries, where rural areas often face greater challenges in accessing digital technologies compared to urban areas. They stress the need for continued efforts to reduce digital divides globally and locally, as technological access plays a critical role in social and economic development. Aissaoui (2022) explored how the COVID-19 pandemic exacerbated existing digital inequalities, particularly in access to technology, internet connectivity, and digital skills. He identified key dimensions of the digital divide, including socioeconomic status, education, and geographic location, and examined how these factors influence digital inclusion. Furthermore, Aissaoui (2022) highlighted the critical role of government policies, education systems, and technological infrastructure in addressing these disparities. Addressing these inequalities is vital for achieving more equitable outcomes throughout countries in the Global North and the Global South.

THEORETICAL FRAMEWORK

Applying the Digital Equity Framework to Bridging the Digital Divide in Education

The National Digital Inclusion Alliance (NDIA) defines digital equity as "a condition in which all individuals and communities have the information technology capacity needed for full participation in our society, democracy, and economy" (Tesfaye and Miller n.d., Definitions section). NDIA is a U.S.-based organization that believes digital equity is necessary for civic and cultural participation, employment, lifelong learning, and access to essential services.

Digital equity should be the goal that all organizations, including government leaders, work toward in the Global North and Global South as individual countries work toward achieving digital inclusion. Community libraries are central to bringing about digital equity and digital inclusion in fulfilling the new mission of libraries (Grimes & Porter, 2024). Additionally, schools and educational institutions of learning are also key to addressing digital equity through the work of P-20 educators.

The digital divide in education poses a significant challenge in ensuring equitable access to technology, digital resources, and learning opportunities across various regions and countries in the Global North and Global South. To provide a structured and comprehensive analysis, the authors selected the theoretical framework of Digital Promise's K–12 Digital Equity Framework (Jackson et al., 2024). This framework includes five components: (1) Leadership for Digital Transformation, (2) Coherent Systems, Resources, and Policies, (3) Consistent Access to Devices and Connectivity, (4) Digital Competency, and (5) Powerful Learning Propelled by Technology.

Component one emphasizes the intertwined leadership systems from schools, districts, and communities that guide technology integration. Component two addresses policies and resources that advance or restrict technology use and availability. Component three pertains to accessibility, infrastructure, and device maintenance. Component four focuses on basic digital literacy, mindsets, and technology training. Component five relates to pedagogy and the engagement and learning of both teachers and students through technology. These components assist in categorizing the critical dimensions of digital equity, assessing disparities in access and infrastructure, and analyzing policy interventions and technology adoption including AI and EdTech rates of adoption across various global contexts.

Digital Equity Framework: Categorizing the Dimensions of Digital Access and Inclusion

Digital Promise's K–12 Digital Equity Framework (Jackson et al., 2024) offers a structured approach to understanding how different factors contribute to digital inclusion or exclusion. This chapter explores several of the key dimensions related to Digital Promise's K–12 Digital Equity Framework:

1. *Infrastructure and Policy Support*: The development of digital infrastructure and supportive government policies plays a crucial role in closing the digital divide. This chapter discusses how infrastructural deficiencies, such as unreliable electricity and weak broadband networks, disproportionately affect students in the Global South. The Digital Literacy

Programme in Kenya (Ministry of Information, Communications and The Digital Economy, 2024) and India's AIForAll strategy (Panday & Samdub, 2024; Yu et al., 2023) are examples of government-led initiatives aimed at improving digital infrastructure, yet they face challenges related to scalability and sustainability. In contrast, Finland's policies ensure that even students in rural areas have equal access to technology.

2. *Affordability*: Economic constraints significantly affect students' ability to engage with digital learning resources. This chapter discusses how lower-income households in both developed and developing nations struggle with the cost of internet/broadband, digital devices, and software necessary for online education. In the U.S., for example, affordability remains a challenge for students in urban and rural underprivileged communities, despite the country's advanced technological infrastructure. Meanwhile, initiatives like India's Digital India campaign attempt to subsidize technology costs, yet implementation challenges persist.
3. *Access to Technology and the Internet*: Access remains one of the most fundamental barriers to digital equity, particularly in regions with inadequate infrastructure. This chapter highlights how students in low-income communities and rural areas, particularly in the Global South, struggle with limited access to internet connectivity, computers, and digital learning tools. The case studies on India and Kenya illustrate how disparities in broadband availability and digital device distribution impact students' ability to participate in digital learning. In contrast, nations like Finland, where strong governmental initiatives have ensured universal access, serve as a model for addressing these disparities.
4. *Digital Literacy and Skills Development*: While access to technology is essential, digital literacy—the ability to effectively use digital tools (e.g., AI, EdTech) for learning and problem-solving—is just as critical. This chapter emphasizes the need for digital literacy programs to equip students and teachers with the necessary skills to navigate digital environments. Studies cited in the manuscript illustrate how digital literacy remains a barrier, particularly in underserved regions, where many students lack foundational computer skills. Finland, in contrast, incorporates digital literacy into its national curriculum, demonstrating the effectiveness of integrating technology training into formal education.

By organizing the discussion around these dimensions of digital equity, this chapter can more systematically highlight how different factors interact to create disparities in learning experiences using digital learning tools including AI and EdTech. Moreover, it allows for a more targeted analysis of potential policy interventions to mitigate these challenges.

The Digital Equity Framework helps to break down the issue into its fundamental dimensions—access, leadership, digital literacy, infrastructure, and policy support—offering a structured way to examine how different factors interact to widen or bridge the digital gap. Applying these analytical lenses will not only enhance the depth of analysis but also offer clearer policy recommendations and a structured approach to addressing digital inequity across different contexts.

LITERATURE REVIEW

Factors Contributing to the Persistence of the Digital Divide in Education

Chen & Wellman (2004) examine the global digital divide, focusing on disparities in access to and use of digital technologies both within and between countries. They argue that the digital divide is influenced by a variety of factors, including income, education, infrastructure, government policies, along with social and cultural dynamics. Chen & Wellman (2004) further highlight that wealthier nations and individuals generally have better access to the internet and other digital resources, while lower-income countries and populations face significant barriers, such as poor infrastructure and limited governmental leadership and support. Additionally, they emphasize that even within countries, the digital divide persists due to differences in education levels, urban versus rural access, and social inequalities. A comprehensive analysis reveals that the persistence of the digital divide is influenced by a multitude of interconnected factors, including socioeconomic status, geographic location, educational attainment, infrastructure availability, and socio-cultural dynamics (Chen & Wellman, 2004).

Socio-Economic Status (SES)

Socio-economic status (SES) is a critical determinant of digital access and usage. Individuals from higher-income households are more likely to own digital devices and have reliable internet connections, facilitating greater engagement with educational technologies. Conversely, those from lower-income backgrounds often face financial barriers that limit their access to necessary digital tools, hindering their educational opportunities (Sun & Metros, 2011). Chen & Wellman (2004) indicate that students' academic performance is closely linked to their socio-economic status, which in turn affects their access to and use of technology.

Geographic Location

Geographic disparities, particularly between urban and rural areas, contribute significantly to the digital divide. Urban regions typically have better infrastructure, offering residents more reliable and faster internet services. In contrast, rural areas often lack such infrastructure, resulting in limited internet connectivity and access to digital resources. This urban-rural divide restricts educational opportunities for students in less-connected regions. A study found that Americans in rural areas are 12% less likely to have broadband internet access than those in urban areas, impacting their ability to utilize digital educational resources effectively (Whitacre et al., 2017).

Educational Attainment

There is a strong correlation between educational attainment and digital proficiency. Individuals with higher levels of education are more likely to possess the skills necessary to effectively use digital technologies. This proficiency enables them to leverage digital tools for educational advancement and professional development. Conversely, those with lower educational attainment may lack digital literacy, limiting their ability to engage with technology-based educational content. Hargittai (2010) highlighted that individuals with college degrees or higher are significantly more likely to have internet access and use digital skills at work compared to those with only a high school education.

Infrastructure Availability

The presence of robust technological infrastructure is essential for digital access. Regions with well-developed infrastructure provide residents with the necessary tools to engage in digital learning. In contrast, areas lacking such infrastructure face significant barriers, limiting residents' ability to participate in technology-enhanced education. For example, disparities in the ratio of students to computers within public schools have been observed, with schools having higher minority enrollments experiencing higher student-to-computer ratios, thus indicating less overall access to technology (Lake & Makori, 2020).

Sociocultural Dynamics

Cultural perceptions and societal norms can influence the adoption and use of digital technologies. In some communities, technology may be viewed with skepticism or deemed unnecessary, leading to lower adoption rates. These socio-cultural factors can impede the integration of technology into educational practices, thereby widening the digital divide. DiMaggio & Hargittai

(2001) noted that cultural differences, such as viewing computers as a luxury or concerns about technology isolating individuals from family activities, contribute to disparities in internet use among different social classes.

Impact of the Digital Divide on Educational Outcomes and Achievement

Pierce & Cleary (2024) explore the persistent educational digital divide and its role in exacerbating societal inequality. They highlight how disparities in access to digital technologies and internet connectivity, particularly among students from low-income, rural, and marginalized communities, continue to impact educational outcomes. Pierce & Cleary (2024) argue that while technological advancements have become increasingly integrated into education, unequal access to these resources limits opportunities for certain groups, reinforcing existing socio-economic divides. The article also examines how the digital divide affects students' academic achievement, long-term career prospects, and social mobility, emphasizing that digital literacy and access to digital tools are essential for success in the global modern economy. Furthermore, Pierce & Cleary (2024) call for targeted policies and interventions, such as infrastructure investments and inclusive digital education initiatives, to address these inequalities and promote a more equitable education system.

Sun & Metros (2011) explored issues related to the digital divide and its impact on academic performance. Their research indicated that proper use of technology by students is linked to increased academic performance outcomes. However, disparities in access to technology, influenced by socio-economic status, affect students' ability to utilize these resources effectively, thereby impacting their levels of academic achievement. The persistence of the digital divide in education is a multi-faceted issue rooted in socio-economic disparities, geographic location, educational attainment, infrastructure availability, and sociocultural dynamics. Addressing this complex challenge requires comprehensive strategies that encompass economic investment, educational reforms, infrastructure development, and cultural sensitivity to promote digital equity and enhance educational outcomes for all.

Understanding the Digital Divide in Education in the Global South and the Global North

A comprehensive understanding of the digital divide in education requires an examination of existing literature and data that highlight its various dimensions and implications. Factors contributing to the persistence of this divide are multi-faceted, including socio-economic status, geographic location, infrastructure development, and policy decisions. These disparities have profound effects on educational outcomes and achievement, perpetuating cycles of inequality. Case studies from around the world can provide concrete examples of how disparities in access to technology and resources translate into unequal educational opportunities for learners, further emphasizing the urgency of addressing this issue.

Cheshmehzangi et al. (2023) examined the widening digital divide in education during the COVID-19 pandemic, particularly among primary and secondary school children. They highlight how school closures and the sudden shift to online learning exacerbated existing inequalities, thus leading to increased social exclusion for students from disadvantaged backgrounds. They identify several factors contributing to this growing divide, including unequal access to technology, internet connectivity issues, and varying levels of digital literacy among students, teachers, and parents. Cheshmehzangi et al. (2023) emphasize the impacts of these disparities on students' learning outcomes, mental well-being, and social development, with marginalized groups being the most affected. This source also discusses the broader implications of these digital inequities for education equality, calling for more comprehensive policies to ensure equitable access to digital resources and support systems for students and families. Cheshmehzangi et al. (2023) further argue that addressing the digital divide requires more than providing technology; it necessitates targeted interventions that consider the socio-economic and cultural contexts of students.

CASE STUDIES: GLOBAL NORTH AND GLOBAL SOUTH

Case Study: United States (Global North)

Despite being one of the world's most technologically advanced countries, the United States continues to experience deep disparities in digital access, particularly along socioeconomic and geographic lines. A study by the Center for Reinventing Public Education (2022) found that approximately 30% of students from low-income households lacked consistent access to devices and reliable internet during the COVID-19 pandemic. These disparities are especially evident in low-income urban districts and in rural regions. For instance, students in urban Detroit and rural Mississippi struggled with inadequate internet infrastructure, limiting their participation in remote learning. In contrast, wealthier suburban districts had the financial resources to provide laptops, broadband subsidies, and digital learning tools, creating a stark divide in educational access and outcomes. The digital divide in the U.S. is not just about access—it also involves AI adoption and teacher training. According to Langreo (2024), a nationally representative EdWeek Research Center survey found that more than 7 in 10 teachers in the U.S. reported having received no professional development on using AI in the classroom. While the U.S. leads in technological innovation, it lags in AI adoption and digital literacy training among educators, limiting the potential of AI-driven education to enhance equity and inclusion.

Case Study: Finland (Global North)

Finland, widely regarded as having one of the world's best education systems, demonstrates how strong national policies and equitable digital access can bridge educational gaps. The Finnish government has prioritized digital equity, ensuring that all schools, regardless of location, have high-speed internet access and digital learning resources. The National Agency for Education has implemented policies aimed at providing equal access to digital tools. As a result, students in urban Helsinki and rural Lapland alike can benefit from AI-driven learning platforms, teacher training in digital pedagogy, and government-supported EdTech initiatives (OECD, 2023). During the COVID-19 pandemic, Finland's investment in digital literacy and comprehensive internet access enabled a smooth transition to remote learning, mitigating learning losses experienced by other countries. Unlike the United States, where digital disparities remain pronounced, Finland has demonstrated that a coordinated policy approach, combined with investments in teacher training and infrastructure, can significantly reduce digital inequities.

Case Study: India (Global South)

India, the world's most populous nation with 1.44 billion people (IMF, 2024), is home to a wide range of socio-economic disparities and provides a stark example of the digital divide in education. In rural areas, where more than 65% of its population resides, the lack of access to digital devices and reliable internet severely hampers educational opportunities. A study by UNICEF (2020) during the COVID-19 pandemic revealed that only 24% of Indian households had internet access, with rural areas having much lower penetration rates. Children in wealthier urban households could continue their education through online classes, while those in rural villages, particularly in states like Bihar and Jharkhand, were left behind. Government initiatives such as the "Digital India" campaign (Department of Electronics and Information Technology, Government of India, 2024a) aim to address these gaps. Specifically, this initiative aims to expand broadband infrastructure, distribute digital devices, and enhance digital literacy. However, despite its ambitious goals, the implementation of Digital India has been uneven, and socioeconomic disparities, gender inequities, and caste-based exclusions continue to limit equitable educational access. Girls and marginalized communities, in particular, face greater obstacles in obtaining digital literacy and technological resources, further reinforcing existing educational disparities.

Case Study: Kenya (Global South)

Kenya has made notable progress in integrating technology into education, primarily through initiatives such as the Digital Literacy Programme (DLP) (Ministry of Information, Communications and The Digital Economy, 2024). This government-led initiative was designed to provide laptops to primary school students and equip classrooms with digital learning resources. However, infrastructure challenges remain a major barrier, particularly in rural and low-income areas, where electricity shortages, high data costs, and lack of teacher training hinder the effective implementation of digital education. Furthermore, Kenya has expressed aspirations to integrate AI into education, but the lack of foundational digital infrastructure and AI literacy training has made this goal difficult to achieve. A global education survey conducted by UNESCO (2023) found that out of 51 countries studied, only 11 had developed and implemented AI curricula, with Kenya lagging in AI adoption due to resource limitations and insufficient teacher preparation. Without further investment in broadband access, teacher training, and localized digital literacy programs, Kenya's digital divide is likely to persist, limiting opportunities for students in underprivileged regions.

Similarities

- Urban-rural digital gaps: In the United States, India, Kenya, and Finland, rural regions have less access to broadband connectivity, access, and training in EdTech including AI than urban regions.
- Socioeconomic disparities: Low-income families in both high-income and developing countries face barriers to digital access, whether in Detroit (U.S.) or rural Bihar (India).
- Teacher training deficiencies: Across all four cases, teacher preparedness in digital literacy and AI adoption remains an issue. Even in technologically advanced nations like the U.S., a lack of professional development in AI-driven education hinders access and affects equity.

Differences

- Policy effectiveness: Finland's centralized policy approach ensures that all students receive equal digital access, while India and Kenya face inconsistent implementation due to economic constraints.
- AI and EdTech adoption: Finland and the U.S. have greater AI and EdTech adoption than Kenya and India, where AI infrastructure remains underdeveloped.

- Infrastructure investment: Government-led initiatives in Finland have successfully expanded digital access, while India and Kenya struggle with inadequate broadband infrastructure and affordability issues.

The digital divide is a global issue that transcends economic classifications, affecting students in both high-income and developing nations. While the Global North benefits from stronger infrastructure and policy investments, digital inequities persist within wealthier countries, especially among low-income and rural communities. Meanwhile, the Global South faces more fundamental challenges, such as unreliable broadband access, economic constraints, lack of professional development training on AI and EdTech, along with policy inefficiencies, which further widen the educational technology gap.

Addressing these disparities requires a multi-faceted approach, including government intervention, targeted infrastructure investments, AI integration, and teacher training programs. Without these coordinated efforts, the promise of digital equity in education will remain unfulfilled, leaving millions of students—regardless of geography—disconnected from the opportunities that AI, EdTech, and digital learning can offer.

FOCUS ON DIGITAL EQUITY AND INCLUSION IN EDUCATION

Comprehensive Analysis of Digital Equity and Inclusion in Education

Digital equity remains a pressing challenge in global education systems, with disparities in access to technology, digital literacy, and pedagogical inclusion shaping students' learning experiences. While access to devices and broadband connectivity remains a fundamental component of digital equity, it is only one part of a complex socio-economic and pedagogical challenge. A growing body of research emphasizes that digital equity efforts must move beyond simple access to infrastructure and instead address broader systemic inequities that affect students' engagement with technology. Viberg et al. (2024) highlight the role of AI-powered educational decision support systems (AI-EDSS) in promoting inclusive and equitable learning opportunities, while also cautioning against potential biases that may inadvertently reinforce existing disparities. Similarly, Pawar & Khose (2024) argue that AI can enhance educational inclusion by identifying at-risk students and providing personalized learning experiences, but they stress the need for deliberate policy interventions to ensure fair implementation. Furthermore, Almufareh et al. (2024) propose a conceptual model for leveraging AI to support students with disabilities, emphasizing the necessity of accessible digital tools to advance disability inclusion in education. Van Wyk (2024) explores the implications of generative AI, such as ChatGPT, in higher education, noting that while it offers new opportunities for learning, educators must adopt strategies to prevent academic misconduct and ensure responsible AI integration. These perspectives collectively reinforce the idea that achieving digital equity requires not just access to technology but a concerted effort to address pedagogical and systemic barriers to inclusion.

Digital Equity in OECD Countries: Infrastructure, Policy, and Teacher Training

Gottschalk & Weise (2023) provide a broad overview of digital equity efforts across the Organisation for Economic Co-operation and Development (OECD) countries, emphasizing the importance of national and regional policies that ensure equitable access to digital tools. Their analysis highlights that despite significant advancements in technology, socioeconomic disparities continue to affect students' access to digital resources, particularly in rural and economically disadvantaged regions. They emphasize the importance of digital skills development and inclusive pedagogical practices in ensuring that access to technology translates into meaningful learning opportunities.

One of the key findings from their study is that comprehensive policy frameworks are essential to addressing both technological and socio-economic barriers. Several OECD countries have implemented large-scale digital inclusion initiatives, such as subsidizing internet access for low-income families, investing in public digital infrastructure, and integrating digital literacy programs into national curricula. However, even within these countries, disparities persist between urban and rural areas, high-income and low-income families, along with technologically advanced and under-resourced schools. These findings underscore the need for policies that not only expand access but also support marginalized students in developing the digital competencies necessary to thrive in a technology-driven world.

A significant challenge that Gottschalk & Weise (2023) identify is the need for sustained teacher training in digital pedagogy. Teachers play a pivotal role in closing the digital divide, but many educators lack the necessary training to effectively integrate technology into instruction. Howard et al. (2022) expand on this issue by arguing that teacher preparation programs must incorporate digital equity frameworks to ensure that educators are not only technologically competent but also prepared to address the diverse needs of their students. Equipping teachers with the skills to leverage AI-powered tools, adaptive learning platforms, and data-driven instructional strategies can enhance inclusivity in digital learning environments.

Beyond Access: The Role of Social and Cultural Inequities in Digital Inclusion

While Gottschalk & Weise (2023) emphasize infrastructure and policy solutions, Collin & Brotcorne (2019) take a socio-critical approach to digital equity, arguing that digital inequalities cannot be solved merely by providing access to technology. They highlight the ways in which race, gender, and socioeconomic status shape students' interactions with digital tools, affecting their confidence, digital competencies, and ability to benefit from technology-enhanced education.

One of the critical insights from Collin & Brotcorne (2019) is that power dynamics within the education system influence how digital tools are used and who benefits from them. For example, marginalized students may have access to the same devices as their wealthier peers but lack the mentorship from educators, curriculum design, or digital literacy training needed to use these tools effectively. They critique the common assumption that simply increasing access to technology will automatically lead to more equitable educational outcomes. Instead, Collin & Brotcorne (2019) argue that educators and policymakers must develop strategies that account for structural inequalities and provide tailored interventions for students who face social and economic disadvantages.

Their research supports a shift toward a more inclusive and critical approach to digital equity, which includes not only increasing access to devices and the internet but also ensuring that educational technology is used in ways that empower students rather than reinforce systemic inequities. This aligns with Howard et al. (2022), who argue that teachers must be trained to recognize and address digital inequities in their classrooms, using technology in ways that are responsive to the diverse backgrounds and needs of students.

The Role of AI in Digital Equity and Inclusion

The rise of AI in education has introduced new opportunities and challenges in the quest for digital equity. AI-driven tools have the potential to personalize learning experiences, provide targeted interventions for struggling students, and automate administrative tasks to allow teachers to focus on instruction. However, as Holcombe & Wozniak (2024) point out, AI also introduces ethical and practical concerns that must be addressed to ensure that it contributes to inclusion rather than exacerbating inequities.

One of the key benefits of AI in education is its ability to create interactive and customized learning experiences. Holcombe & Wozniak (2024) explore how generative pre-trained transformers (GPTs) and other AI-powered tools can be used to generate personalized content, gamify lessons, and provide instant feedback to students. These tools can help bridge gaps in student engagement, motivation, and access to high-quality learning materials, particularly for students from under-resourced schools.

However, the responsible and ethical use of AI in education is a pressing concern. Holcombe & Wozniak (2024) warn that AI-generated content must be carefully monitored to ensure accuracy, relevance, and alignment with educational goals. Additionally, there is a risk that AI tools could reinforce existing biases if they are trained on historically biased datasets. For instance, if an AI-powered grading system favors students from certain demographic backgrounds due to biased training data, it could inadvertently contribute to widening educational disparities rather than closing them.

To mitigate these risks, Howard et al. (2022) and Gottschalk & Weise (2023) emphasize that teachers must be trained in AI literacy so they can critically evaluate AI tools, recognize biases, and use these technologies in ways that promote equity. Ensuring that AI-driven education remains student-centered, ethically designed, and accessible to all learners is crucial to its effectiveness in fostering digital inclusion.

A Holistic Approach to Digital Equity: Policy, Pedagogy, and AI Integration

The research reviewed in this section collectively underscores the multifaceted nature of digital equity. While access to technology and internet connectivity remains a fundamental concern, the real challenge lies in ensuring that all students regardless of their socioeconomic background, race, or geographic location can effectively engage with digital learning tools and benefit from technological advancements.

- Gottschalk & Weise (2023) highlight the importance of national policies and investments in digital infrastructure to provide equitable access.
- Howard et al. (2022) emphasize the role of teacher preparation and ongoing professional development in closing digital gaps.
- Collin & Brotcorne (2019) urge policymakers and educators to consider social and cultural inequities when designing digital equity initiatives, ensuring that technology is used to empower rather than exclude.
- Holcombe & Wozniak (2024) bring AI into the conversation, emphasizing its potential benefits and ethical challenges in promoting educational inclusion.

Together, these perspectives advocate for a holistic approach to digital equity, one that combines investments in infrastructure, teacher training, social inclusion efforts, and AI/EdTech integration to create learning environments that are truly inclusive, accessible, and empowering for all students. Without these coordinated efforts, digital technologies risk becoming another mechanism for reinforcing existing inequities rather than a tool for closing them. Therefore, ongoing research, cross-sector collaboration, and policy-driven interventions are necessary to ensure that digital equity in education becomes a reality rather than an aspiration.

How AI and EdTech Promote Digital Equity and Inclusion

AI and EdTech have emerged as powerful tools in advancing digital equity and inclusion, particularly for students who face systemic barriers to accessing quality education. Pedro et al. (2019) argue that AI has the potential to bridge educational gaps by personalizing learning experiences, supporting educators, and enhancing accessibility for marginalized groups. AI-driven tools can tailor instruction to individual learning needs, benefiting students with disabilities, language barriers, or those with limited access to traditional educational resources.

Moreover, AI-powered Educational Decision Support Systems (AIEDSS) have been recognized as critical in advancing equity and inclusion in education. Viberg et al. (2024) highlight that these systems utilize learning analytics and adaptive algorithms to enhance decision-making processes within educational institutions. AIEDSS can provide real-time insights into student progress, allowing teachers to make data-driven interventions that ensure equitable learning experiences. These tools can help identify at-risk students early, provide personalized support, and allocate educational resources more efficiently. However, Viberg et al. (2024) caution that bias in AI models must be addressed to prevent the reinforcement of existing inequities, calling for ethical AI governance frameworks that prioritize fairness, transparency, and inclusion in AI-driven education.

A key aspect of AI-enhanced educational inclusion is its ability to personalize learning environments, adjusting content to suit the pace, interests, and abilities of each student (Pedro et al., 2019). AI systems analyze student performance data to provide adaptive learning pathways, ensuring that learners receive the targeted support they need to succeed. This capability is especially valuable for addressing learning disparities caused by socioeconomic status, disabilities, or geographical location.

Beyond student learning, AI plays a crucial role in reducing educators' workload and improving pedagogical practices. Pawar & Khose (2024) explore how AI-powered tools help teachers by automating administrative tasks, such as grading assignments and tracking student engagement. These AI tools free up teachers' time, allowing them to focus on instruction, mentorship, and individualized support for students. Additionally, AI can assist in professional development by offering educators data-driven insights into classroom performance, helping them refine their teaching strategies.

However, unequal access to AI-powered tools remains a significant barrier to digital equity (Pedro et al., 2019). In many low-income and rural communities, AI-driven education remains inaccessible due to insufficient infrastructure, lack of digital literacy, and economic constraints. Without strategic policies and targeted investments, the benefits of AI-enhanced education will remain concentrated in wealthier countries and regions, exacerbating rather than mitigating digital divides.

Strategies for Promoting Digital Equity into Curriculum and Pedagogy

Promoting digital equity requires the integration of technology into curriculum and pedagogy, and the implementation of digital literacy programs to equip learners with essential skills for the digital age. Tailored interventions targeted at marginalized communities and underserved regions are necessary to address their unique needs and challenges. Monitoring and evaluation mechanisms play a critical role in assessing the effectiveness of interventions and guiding adjustments to strategies as needed. By adopting a holistic approach that combines technological innovation with targeted interventions, educational equity can be advanced for all learners.

Harris et al. (2009) present the TPACK (Technological Pedagogical Content Knowledge) framework as a way to conceptualize effective technology integration in education. They argue that teachers need to develop an understanding of how content, pedagogy, and technology intersect in order to use technology meaningfully in their teaching. Harris et al. (2009) emphasize that simply knowing how to use technology is insufficient; educators must also know how to integrate it in ways that enhance both subject matter understanding and instructional practices. Petko et al. (2025) revisit the TPACK framework, emphasizing the critical role of contextual factors in effective technology integration within education. They propose an enhanced model that integrates Contextual Knowledge (XK) alongside the original TPACK components—Technological Knowledge (TK), Pedagogical Knowledge (PK), and Content Knowledge (CK) to better address the complexities educators face in diverse teaching environments. This updated framework aims to provide a more comprehensive understanding of the dynamic interplay between technology, pedagogy, content, and context, thereby supporting educators in tailoring their instructional strategies, including those involving AI and EdTech, to meet the specific needs of their students and educational settings.

The TPACK framework (Harris et al., 2009; Petko et al., 2025) encourages teachers to align their technological choices with curriculum goals and pedagogical approaches, ensuring that technology supports, rather than detracts from, learning. Ultimately, the authors highlight the need for teacher education and professional development to focus on building TPACK, enabling teachers to incorporate technology in a way that is deeply connected to both pedagogy and curriculum.

Black et al. (2024) presents a structured approach for integrating AI education into teacher preparation programs. They argue that, as AI increasingly impacts various aspects of life and work, educators must be prepared to teach these concepts to students. The proposed framework focuses on building foundational AI literacy among educators, offering pedagogical strategies for teaching AI, and addressing ethical implications, such as AI bias and privacy concerns. Additionally, the framework emphasizes the interdisciplinary nature of AI, showing how it can be integrated across subjects like mathematics, science, and the humanities. Ultimately, they call for collaboration between educational institutions, policymakers, and the tech industry to successfully incorporate AI education into teacher training programs.

Black et al. (2024) also highlights the challenges of implementing AI in education, including limited resources, a lack of AI expertise among educators, and the need for continuous professional development. To address these challenges, the authors of this chapter suggest leveraging partnerships with technology companies, developing open-source AI teaching materials, and creating micro-credentials such as those offered to teachers in the U.S. through the National Education Association (NEA) (NEA, n.d.) focused on the broad areas of EdTech and AI literacy for educators. This can be done by working with organizations such as the NEA and the International Society for Technology in Education (ISTE), specifically through the Teach AI initiative, which involves ISTE but is led by the World Economic Forum (TeachAI, n.d.a), which offers an AI Guidance for Schools Toolkit (TeachAI, n.d.b).

Education preparation programs at higher education institutions must adequately prepare candidates to teach using pedagogy that utilizes the upper levels of Bloom's taxonomy, which include analyze, evaluate, and create (Oregon State University, 2024). AI has the potential to easily provide factual information, describe concepts, and apply information. But teachers need to develop student skill sets that can evaluate information that AI creates for accuracy, legitimacy, and bias. Teachers need AI literacy to learn how to use AI prompts to receive the information needed to complete tasks. But teachers also need to understand how to evaluate, analyze, and synthesize information to create new ideas and solve large-scale problems.

Universal Design for Learning 3.0 (CAST, 2024) provides a framework for reaching and teaching all learners through multiple means of engagement, representation, along wth action and expression. AI provides a medium for students to explore multiple means of action and expression. Students can use AI to use multiple tools for construction, composition, and creativity (UDL

Consideration 5.2). Furthermore, students with disabilities can use AI to assist in writing, reading, and math calculations to access curriculum that may have been inaccessible before. It is essential that pre-service teacher candidates have the training in technology to know how to use AI to increase accessibility for students with language learning needs and learning disabilities that could impact their academic performance. If students engage with AI tools that provide the basic level of information (factual knowledge, summaries), then students may be able to synthesize and create at the highest level of skills according to Bloom.

Challenges and Ethical Considerations in AI for Digital Equity

While AI presents numerous opportunities to bridge the digital divide, concerns remain regarding its ethical implications and potential risks. Van Wyk (2024) raises important questions about the potential threats posed by AI-driven large language models (LLMs), such as ChatGPT, in education. While these models offer new opportunities for personalized learning, they also present risks of misinformation, over-reliance on AI-generated content, and academic dishonesty. Educators must develop preventive strategies to ensure that AI is used responsibly, balancing its benefits with academic integrity.

Furthermore, bias in AI algorithms remains a persistent challenge. Viberg et al. (2024) caution that if AI models are trained on biased datasets, they may reinforce existing inequities in education. For example, AI-powered grading systems may favor students from certain backgrounds if not properly calibrated, leading to discriminatory outcomes. Therefore, transparent AI governance and ethical oversight are crucial in ensuring that AI-driven educational tools promote rather than hinder equity.

AI for Disability Inclusion and Multilingual Learning

AI can also play a transformative role in supporting students with disabilities by offering assistive technologies that enhance accessibility. Almufareh et al. (2024) propose a conceptual model for inclusive technology, which leverages AI to enhance disability inclusion in education. The model outlines AI-powered text-to-speech, speech-to-text, and real-time captioning technologies that enable students with visual, hearing, or learning disabilities to participate fully in digital learning environments. AI tools such as real-time transcription and AI-generated Braille materials can provide previously inaccessible educational content to students with disabilities, ensuring a more equitable and inclusive learning experience.

Additionally, AI bridges language barriers by offering instant translation and speech recognition tools, allowing non-native speakers to access educational materials in their preferred language (Pedro et al., 2019). This is particularly beneficial in multilingual classrooms and migrant education programs, where students may struggle with traditional language-based curricula. AI-powered chatbots and virtual assistants can provide real-time language support, making education more accessible to diverse linguistic communities.

AI as a Catalyst for Inclusive Education

AI and EdTech hold great promise for enhancing digital equity and inclusion in education. By offering personalized learning, assistive technologies, and data-driven interventions, AI can close learning gaps, improve accessibility, and empower marginalized students. However, unequal access, algorithmic bias, and ethical concerns must be addressed to ensure that AI serves as a tool for inclusion rather than exclusion. Policymakers, educators, and technology developers must work collaboratively to establish equitable AI governance frameworks, invest in digital infrastructure, and promote responsible AI use in classrooms. If implemented thoughtfully, AI has the potential to transform education into a more inclusive, accessible, and equitable experience for all learners, regardless of their geographic, economic, or social background.

AI has emerged as a transformative force in education, offering innovative solutions to promote equity and inclusion. By leveraging AI-driven interventions, educators can tailor learning experiences to meet the diverse needs of students, thereby narrowing achievement gaps and fostering a more inclusive educational environment.

Adaptive Learning Technologies

Developmental AI systems offer promising solutions to mitigate the impact of the digital divide in education. These systems, designed to adapt and evolve over time, have the potential to personalize learning experiences and address the diverse needs of learners from various backgrounds. By leveraging AI-driven interventions, such as adaptive learning platforms and intelligent tutoring systems, educators can better support students and narrow achievement gaps. Examples of successful AI-driven initiatives can demonstrate how technology can be harnessed to promote educational inclusion and equity, ultimately transforming the landscape of education.

The introduction to developmental AI systems in education highlights their potential to create adaptive, personalized learning environments that continuously evolve based on students' developmental stages and emotional responses. These systems use data analytics and machine learning algorithms to track student progress, predict learning needs, and adjust content in real time to optimize learning outcomes. Zhang & Aslan (2021) note challenges such as ethical concerns regarding data privacy, the current digital divide, and the need for teacher training to effectively implement AI tools. They call for further research to address these issues and explore how AI can be integrated responsibly into educational systems to enhance learning experiences for all students.

AI-powered adaptive learning systems personalize educational content by analyzing individual student performance and learning preferences. These systems adjust the difficulty and type of content in real-time, ensuring that each student receives instruction tailored to their unique needs. This personalization is particularly beneficial for underperforming or disadvantaged students, as it provides targeted support to help them catch up with their peers. For instance, research has shown that AI-driven adaptive learning platforms can significantly improve learning outcomes by customizing instruction to individual student needs (Viberg et al., 2024).

Intelligent Tutoring Systems

Intelligent Tutoring Systems (ITS) utilize AI to emulate the personalized guidance of human tutors. These systems provide real-time feedback and support, enabling students to work through problems at their own pace while receiving immediate assistance when needed. The adaptability of ITS allows for the accommodation of various learning styles and paces, making education more accessible to a broader range of students. Studies have demonstrated that ITS can enhance student learning outcomes, particularly in subjects like mathematics and science (McLaren et al., 2017). Chen et al. (2020) and Zhang & Aslan (2021) provide comprehensive reviews of the transformative role of AI in education, highlighting its potential to enhance teaching and learning through personalized learning systems, ITS, adaptive platforms, and automated assessment tools. Chen et al. (2020) emphasize how AI-driven systems can adapt to individual learning needs, offering real-time feedback that improves learning outcomes and educational equity, particularly for students from diverse backgrounds. Zhang & Aslan (2021) further explore how these technologies are being integrated across K–12 and higher education settings to offer tailored learning experiences, improve instructional efficiency, and address achievement gaps. Both studies discuss the benefits of AI for educators, including administrative automation and effective student progress monitoring, while acknowledging challenges such as data privacy, the need for teacher training, and the risk of over-reliance on automated systems. Together, these works underscore the importance of thoughtful AI integration to fully realize its potential to revolutionize education and support diverse learners effectively.

Monitoring and Predictive Analytics

AI-driven analytics tools can monitor student engagement and performance, providing educators with insights to identify at-risk students and intervene proactively. By analyzing patterns in student data, these tools can predict potential challenges and suggest timely support measures, thereby preventing students from falling behind. This proactive approach is crucial in addressing disparities in educational outcomes and ensuring that all students have the opportunity to succeed (OECD, 2023).

Owan et al. (2023) highlights the critical role that AI can play in monitoring and evaluating educational interventions. AI-driven tools offer powerful capabilities to assess the effectiveness of educational programs by collecting, analyzing, and interpreting vast amounts of data on student performance and engagement. These tools can provide real-time feedback, helping educators and policymakers to track progress and identify areas where interventions are succeeding or falling short. AI algorithms can also detect patterns and trends in educational data that may not be immediately apparent to human evaluators, offering deeper insights into the impact of different teaching strategies, technologies, and curricula on diverse student populations. Owan et al. (2023) further emphasize that AI tools can be used to dynamically adjust interventions based on the results of these evaluations. By continuously monitoring the outcomes of educational programs, AI systems enable decision-makers to make data-driven adjustments to teaching methods, resources, and strategies to enhance their effectiveness. Through the effective use of AI in monitoring and evaluation, educational systems can become more responsive, agile, and capable of meeting diverse student needs.

Language Accessibility

AI technologies, such as natural language processing and machine translation, can break down language barriers in education. For non-native speakers, AI-powered translation tools and speech recognition systems offer real-time assistance, enabling them to participate fully in educational settings. This capability is essential in multicultural classrooms and contributes to closing learning gaps for students facing language challenges (Nixon et al., 2024).

AI IN EDUCATION: CASE STUDIES

Case Study: AI in Special Education

A notable example of AI promoting educational inclusion is its application in special education. AI-driven tools have been developed to assist students with intellectual and developmental disabilities (IDD) by tailoring educational content to their specific needs. These tools can simplify complex information, provide interactive learning experiences, and adapt to the unique learning pace of each student. A study by the Special Olympics Global Center for Inclusion in Education highlighted that educators and parents are optimistic about AI's potential to foster inclusive learning for students with IDD (Special Olympics, 2024).

Case Study: Khan Academy's AI Integration

Khan (2024) illustrates how AI can revolutionize education by providing personalized, accessible, and scalable learning experiences. He introduces "Khanmigo," an AI-powered tutor developed by Khan Academy to provide personalized support across various subjects. It was designed to offer individualized support and emulate one-on-one tutoring for students worldwide. The tool also aids teachers in lesson planning and data analysis, allowing for more targeted instruction. Despite some challenges in implementation, such as students initially struggling to ask effective questions, the integration of AI tools like Khanmigo holds promise in revolutionizing education by providing personalized learning experiences. Khan (2024) further emphasizes that AI should augment, not replace, human educators, enabling them to focus more on fostering critical thinking and creativity while addressing ethical considerations and ensuring equitable access to technology.

Challenges and Considerations

While AI offers significant potential to enhance educational equity, challenges such as data privacy, algorithmic bias, and the digital divide must be addressed. Ensuring that AI systems are designed and implemented with ethical considerations is crucial to prevent the reinforcement of existing inequalities. Moreover, providing educators with adequate training to effectively integrate AI tools into their teaching practices is essential for maximizing the benefits of these technologies.

AI-driven interventions hold substantial promise in promoting educational inclusion and equity. Through adaptive learning technologies, intelligent tutoring systems, predictive analytics, and language accessibility tools, AI can cater to the diverse needs of learners and help close achievement gaps. However, careful consideration of ethical, practical, and infrastructural challenges is necessary to fully realize the potential of AI in creating a more equitable educational landscape.

Addressing the digital divide in marginalized communities and underserved regions requires tailored interventions that consider the unique challenges and cultural contexts of these populations. Aguilar (2020) emphasizes strategies focusing on both access to technology and the development of digital skills, advocating for affordable internet access, culturally relevant digital literacy training, and partnerships among schools, community organizations, and governments.

PEOPLE, PLACES, AND COMMUNITIES OF PRACTICE

Politicians and Education Leaders Drive Digital Equity in Schools

According to Resta & Laferrière (2008), politicians and education leaders also play a crucial role in addressing digital equity and inclusion by shaping policies and strategies that ensure all students, regardless of socio-economic background, have access to the latest technologies. Politicians, in particular, are responsible for creating legislative frameworks that allocate resources and funding for digital infrastructure in schools. This includes providing affordable internet access, devices, and necessary support systems for students from underserved communities. They also need to advocate for public-private partnerships to expand digital resources and ensure equitable access across countries in the Global North and the Global South.

Education leaders (e.g., Secretaries of Education, Superintendents, Chief Information Officers, Provosts, College of Education Deans, etc.) are tasked with implementing information and communication technologies policies at the institutional level. They must prioritize the integration of technology in the classroom, while also focusing on professional development for teachers to effectively use AI, EdTech, and other digital learning tools in instruction. Leaders in education must ensure that schools are equipped with the necessary hardware, software, and technical support, and address any gaps in digital literacy (including AI and information literacy) among students and educators. Collaboration between educators, government agencies, and community organizations is essential to address the diverse needs of students and support their participation in a digital world as digital citizens. Both politicians and education leaders must also work to address systemic inequalities that contribute to the digital divide. This includes addressing factors like poverty, infrastructure deficiencies, and regional disparities. They must promote inclusive educational practices that are sensitive to the diverse cultural and socio-economic contexts of students. In doing so, they can create long-term solutions that not only improve access to technology but also ensure that students are equipped with the skills and opportunities to succeed in a technologically driven world.

According to Passey et al. (2018), politicians and education leaders are essential in promoting digital equity and inclusion by creating policies that empower students through technology. Politicians are responsible for ensuring equitable resource distribution, such as access to digital devices and internet connectivity for all students, particularly those in marginalized communities. Their role includes crafting legislation that supports funding for educational technology and digital literacy programs, while also encouraging partnerships between the public and private sectors to bridge the digital divide. Education leaders, on the other hand, are responsible for implementing these policies within schools and fostering environments where AI and other digital tools can enhance learning for all students. They must focus on ensuring that teachers are trained in using technology effectively and that curriculum development on a local (state) or national level reflects the integration of digital skills. These leaders play a key role in supporting students' digital agency, helping them to use technology in ways that enhance their learning experiences and career readiness. By working together, politicians and education leaders can create systems that ensure all students, regardless of background, have the resources and skills needed to participate fully in a digital world that is driven by AI, EdTech, and advanced technologies that will come in the future.

Infrastructure Bridges for the Digital Divide

To bridge the digital divide in education in the K–20 environment, a multi-faceted approach is necessary, encompassing infrastructure development, policy initiatives, community engagement, and capacity building. Improving access to technology including AI, and internet connectivity is crucial, particularly in underserved areas. Policy interventions, such as writing curriculum that focuses on information literact including AI, along with funding incentives and regulatory measures, can stimulate investment in digital infrastructure and promote digital inclusion. Community engagement initiatives that involve collaboration with local stakeholders empower communities to address their specific needs and challenges. Capacity-building efforts, including training programs for educators, librarians, and learners, are essential to ensure that everyone can fully participate in the digital age. Through looking at future international, national or local (i.e. state, district, or school level) case studies that highlight successful initiatives, lessons can be drawn to help inform future strategies and actions.

Lynn et al. (2022) examine the critical role of infrastructure in supporting digital connectivity in rural areas, as part of broader efforts to foster digital transformation in rural societies and economies. The authors in Lynn et al. (2022) discuss various infrastructure solutions, including broadband expansion, wireless networks, and emerging technologies like 5G, emphasizing the need for government and private sector collaboration to bridge the urban–rural connectivity gap. They also highlight the importance of addressing both technical and social barriers to ensure equitable access to digital resources, which is key to promoting sustainable development in rural regions.

To further address the digital divide, learning needs to begin in pre-service teacher and librarian training to address these professionals' technological capacity and continue through professional practice in schools and libraries through the creation of Professional Learning Communities (PLCs) and Communities of Practice (CoPs).

Creating Communities of Practice (CoPs) around Educational Technologies Including AI and Immersive Technologies

The term "Communities of Practice" (CoP) was first used to describe a set of relations among persons, activity, and world, over time and in relation to other tangential and overlapping communities of practice (Lave, 1991; Wenger, 2000; Wenger, 2011). CoPs connect practitioners to share ideas and solve problems (Lave, 1991; Wenger, 2000). Williams (2013) identifies PLCs as a structured form of CoPs specifically designed to improve teaching practices and student outcomes within schools. Williams highlights several key aspects of PLCs in the context of education:

- *Collaborative Culture*: PLCs foster a collaborative culture where teachers work together to solve problems, share strategies, and support each other's professional growth. This collaboration is crucial in urban schools where challenges such as limited resources and diverse student needs are prevalent.
- *Focus on Student Achievement*: PLCs in urban education are particularly focused on improving student achievement. Teachers analyze student data, identify learning gaps, and develop targeted interventions to address these gaps.
- *Reflective Practice*: Williams emphasizes the importance of reflective practice within PLCs. Teachers regularly reflect on their teaching methods, student responses, and overall effectiveness to continually improve their practices.
- *Sustained Professional Development*: PLCs provide a platform for sustained professional development. Unlike traditional one-time workshops, PLCs involve ongoing learning and development, allowing teachers to continuously refine their skills.

The literature on CoPs and PLCs further emphasizes the importance of collaborative, social learning systems in educational improvement. Wenger (2000) provides a theoretical foundation for understanding the dynamics of CoPs, emphasizing the role of social interaction and shared practice in learning.

Williams (2013) extends this framework to the context of urban education, illustrating how PLCs can foster a collaborative culture, focus on student achievement, and provide sustained professional development for teachers and librarians. These practices can create opportunities for teachers and librarians to learn from each other when exploring and experimenting with using AI, immersive technologies such as augmented reality, virtual reality, the Metaverse, and new digital learning tools in their teaching and professional library work.

CONCLUSION

Addressing the digital divide in education is imperative for promoting equitable access to quality education for all. A collective effort is needed to bridge the gap and ensure that no learner is left behind. Emphasizing the importance of collaboration and partnerships, stakeholders must prioritize efforts to address the underlying causes of the digital divide and promote educational equity. By charting a course towards inclusive and accessible education, we can pave the way for a more equitable and prosperous future. Looking ahead, continued research and practice are essential to inform evidence-based interventions and drive meaningful change in the realm of digital inclusion and educational equity.

Our chapter highlights the persistent digital divide in education, where significant disparities exist in access to technology including AI, EdTech, and digital resources. These disparities are more pronounced between the Global North, who has more developed technological infrastructures, and the Global South, where access to technology including broadband connectivity and AI remains limited. Additionally, intra-country divides are evident, particularly between urban and rural areas. The COVID-19 pandemic magnified these inequities, revealing how remote learning was inaccessible for many students in underserved and underconnected regions. The digital divide impacts educational opportunities and outcomes, often reinforcing existing socio-economic inequalities and creating barriers to digital inclusion and literacy. Having access to AI and being skilled in AI will create a world of opportunities for job and career advancement for those with AI and other digital literacies, while those without access to AI and digital literacy training will be stuck in the "unskilled laborer" category in a technological and information-driven worldwide economy.

The authors of this chapter believe that ongoing research is needed to explore the long-term effects of digital inequities on educational outcomes and to identify the most effective strategies for intervention. Tailored interventions that address both technological access and culturally relevant digital and information literacy are essential for bridging the digital divide. By fostering partnerships among educational institutions, community organizations, and governments, and by empowering educators, librarians, and learners with the necessary skills and resources, these interventions can promote long-term sources of digital equity. Such comprehensive strategies are crucial for helping marginalized learners overcome barriers to participation in education and the workforce in an increasingly digital and AI-driven world. The use of emerging technologies, such as AI, in promoting digital equity should also be a focus of future studies, particularly in their potential to personalize learning and support underserved learners. Additionally, future research should examine the socio-cultural dimensions of digital inclusion, ensuring that interventions are country and context-specific and responsive to the needs of diverse nations and communities. Effective policy-making and implementation by education leaders and politicians must also be informed by evidence-based research that promotes sustainable, inclusive digital education practices for all students and communities in the Global North and Global South to effectively close the digital divide through digital equity.

REFERENCES

Aguilar, S. J. (2020). Guidelines and tools for promoting digital equity. *Information and Learning Sciences*, *121*(5/6), 285–299.

Aissaoui, N. (2022). The digital divide: a literature review and some directions for future research in light of COVID-19. *Global Knowledge, Memory and Communication*, *71*(8/9), 686–708.

Almufareh, M. F., Kausar, S., Humayun, M., & Tehsin, S. (2024). A conceptual model for inclusive technology: Advancing disability inclusion through artificial intelligence. *Journal of Disability Research*, *3*, 1–11.

Black, N. B., George, S., Eguchi, A., Dempsey, J. C., Langran, E., Fraga, L., ... & Howard, N. (2024, March). A Framework for approaching AI education in educator preparation programs. In *Proceedings of the AAAI Conference on Artificial Intelligence* (Vol. 38, No. 21, pp. 23069–23077).

CAST. (2024). Universal Design for Learning Guidelines version 3.0. https://udlguidelines.cast.org

Cayli, B. (2014). Global South/Global North. In L. H. Cousins (Ed.), *Encyclopedia of Human Services & Diversity* (1st ed.). Sage Publications. https://search.credoreference.com/articles/Qm9va0FydGljbGU6NDMyOTE2?aid=104946

Center on Reinventing Public Education. (2022). The state of the American student: Fall 2022. https://crpe.org/wp-content/uploads/CRPE-%E2%80%94-Profile-of-a-Student-Report.pdf

Chen, L., Chen, P., & Lin, Z. (2020). Artificial intelligence in education: A review. *IEEE Access*, *8*, 75264–75278.

Chen, W., & Wellman, B. (2004). The global digital divide–within and between countries. *IT & society*, *1*(7), 39–45.

Cheshmehzangi, A., Zou, T., Su, Z., & Tang, T. (2023). The growing digital divide in education among primary and secondary children during the COVID-19 pandemic:

An overview of social exclusion and education equality issues. *Journal of Human Behavior in the Social Environment, 33*(3), 434–449.

Collin, S., & Brotcorne, P. (2019). Capturing digital (in) equity in teaching and learning: A sociocritical approach. *The International Journal of Information and Learning Technology, 36*(2), 169–180.

Communities of practice (CoP). (2011). In H. Thota & Z. Munir (Eds.), *Palgrave key concepts: Key concepts in innovation* (1st ed.). Macmillan Publishers Ltd. https://search.credoreference.com/articles/Qm9va0FydGljbGU6MzkzMTQzNw==?aid=104946

Department of Electronics and Information Technology, Government of India. (2024a, October 14). Digital India. https://www.meity.gov.in/static/uploads/2024/03/Running-single-file.pdf

DiMaggio, P., & Hargittai, E. (2001). From the 'digital divide' to 'digital inequality': Studying Internet use as penetration increases. *Princeton: Center for Arts and Cultural Policy Studies, Woodrow Wilson School, Princeton University, 4*(1), 1–23.

Gottschalk, F., & Weise, C. (2023). Digital equity and inclusion in education: An overview of practice and policy in OECD countries.

Grimes, N. D., & Porter, W. (2024). Closing the digital divide through digital equity: The role of libraries and librarians. *Public Library Quarterly, 43*(3), 307–338. https://doi.org/10.1080/01616846.2023.2251348

Hargittai, E. (2010). Digital na(t)ives? Variation in internet skills and uses among members of the "net generation". *Sociological Inquiry, 80*(1), 92–113.

Harris, J., Mishra, P., & Koehler, M. (2009). Teachers' technological pedagogical content knowledge and learning activity types: Curriculum-based technology integration reframed. *Journal of Research on Technology in Education, 41*(4), 393–416.

Holcombe, A., & Wozniak, S. (2024). Using AI to fuel engagement and active learning. *Educational Leadership, 81*(9), 16–21.

Howard, N. R., Schaffer, R., & Thomas, S. (2022). *Closing the gap: Digital equity strategies for teacher prep programs.* International Society for Technology in Education.

IMF. (April 22, 2024). India: Estimated total population from 2019 to 2029 (in millions) [Graph]. In *Statista.* https://www.statista.com/statistics/263766/total-population-of-india/

Jackson, J., Starr, J., & Weaver, D. (2024, August). *A framework for digital equity. Digital Promise.* https://doi.org/10.51388/20.500.12265/223

Khan, S. (2024). *Brave new words: How AI will revolutionize education (and why that's a good thing).* Penguin.

Lake, R. & Makori, A. (2020). *The digital divide among students during COVID-19: Who has access & who doesn't?* Center on Reinventing Public Education. https://crpe.org/the-digital-divide-among-students-during-covid-19-who-has-access-who-doesnt/

Langreo, L. (2024, March 25). *Teachers desperately need AI training. How many are getting it?* Education Week. https://www.edweek.org/technology/teachers-desperately-need-ai-training-how-many-are-getting-it/2024/03

Lave, J. (1991). Situating learning in communities of practice.

Lynn, T., Rosati, P., Conway, E., Curran, D., Fox, G., & O'Gorman, C. (2022). Infrastructure for digital connectivity. In *Digital towns: Accelerating and*

Measuring the Digital Transformation of Rural Societies and Economies (pp. 109–132). Springer International Publishing.
McLaren, B. M., Adams, D. M., Mayer, R. E., & Forlizzi, J. (2017). A computer-based game that promotes mathematics learning more than a conventional approach. *International Journal of Game-Based Learning (IJGBL)*, *7*(1), 36–56.
Ministry of Information, Communications and The Digital Economy. (2024, January 31). *Digital literacy programme (DLP).* https://ict.go.ke/digital-literacy-programmedlp/.
National Education Association. (n.d.). *Micro-credentials.* NEA. https://www.nea.org/professional-excellence/professional-learning/micro-credentials
Nixon, J., Smith, A., & Johnson, M. (2024). Language accessibility in education: The role of AI technologies in breaking down language barriers. *Journal of Educational Technology*, 36(2), 102–115.
OECD. (2023). Finland. In *Country Digital Education Ecosystems and Governance: A Companion to Digital Education Outlook 2023.* OECD Publishing. Rhttps://doi.org/10.1787/468e6641-en
Oregon State University. (2024). Bloom's taxonomy revisited. https://ecampus.oregonstate.edu/faculty/artificial-intelligence-tools/blooms-taxonomy-revisited-v2-2024.pdf
Owan, V. J., Abang, K. B., Idika, D. O., Etta, E. O., & Bassey, B. A. (2023). Exploring the potential of artificial intelligence tools in educational measurement and assessment. *Eurasia Journal of Mathematics, Science and Technology Education*, *19*(8), em2307.
Oxford Insights. (2024, February 5). *Gov AI Readiness Index.* Oxford Insights. https://oxfordinsights.com/ai-readiness/ai-readiness-index/
Panday, J., & Samdub, M. T. (2024, March 12). *4. Promises and pitfalls of India's AI industrial policy.* AI Now Institute. https://ainowinstitute.org/publication/analyzing-indias-ai-industrial-policy#:~:text=India's%20national%20AI%20strategy%2C%20%23AIForAll,smart%20cities%2C%20and%20smart%20mobility
Passey, D., Shonfeld, M., Appleby, L., Judge, M., Saito, T., & Smits, A. (2018). Digital agency: Empowering equity in and through education. *Technology, Knowledge and Learning*, *23*, 425–439.
Pawar, G., & Khose, J. (2024). Exploring the role of artificial intelligence in enhancing equity and inclusion in education. *International Journal of Innovative Science and Research Technology (IJISRT)*, *9*(4), 2180–2185.
Pedro, F., Subosa, M., Rivas, A., & Valverde, P. (2019). *Artificial intelligence in education: Challenges and opportunities for sustainable development.* UNESCO. Working Papers on Educational Policy.
Petko, D., Mishra, P., & Koehler, M. J. (2025). TPACK in context: an updated model. *Computers and Education Open*, 100244.
Pick, J. B., & Nishida, T. (2015). Digital divides in the world and its regions: A spatial and multivariate analysis of technological utilization. *Technological Forecasting and Social Change*, *91*, 1–17.
Pierce, G. L., & Cleary, P. F. (2024). The persistent educational digital divide and its impact on societal inequality. *PLOS ONE*, *19*(4), e0286795.
PricewaterhouseCoopers. (2024). *PwC's global artificial intelligence study: Sizing the prize.* https://www.pwc.com/gx/en/issues/data-and-analytics/publications/artificial-intelligence-study.html#:~:text=AI%20could%20contribute%20up%20to,come%20from%20consumption%2Dside%20effects

Resta, P., & Laferrière, T. (2008). Issues and challenges related to digital equity. In J. Voogt & G. Knezer (Eds.), *International handbook of information technology in primary and secondary education* (pp. 765–778, 1st ed.). New York: Springer.

Special Olympics Global Center for Inclusion in Education. (2024). Attitudes towards education and AI. Special Olympics International.

Sun, J. C. Y., & Metros, S. E. (2011). The digital divide and its impact on academic performance. *Online Submission.*

TeachAI. (n.d.a). Home. https://www.teachai.org/

TeachAI. (n.d.b). AI Guidance for Schools Toolkit. https://www.teachai.org/toolkit

Tesfaye, T., and M. Miller (n.d.). Definitions – the words behind our work: The source for definitions of digital inclusion terms. *National Digital Inclusion Alliance.* https://www.digitalinclusion.org/definitions/

UNESCO. (2023). *Global Education Monitoring Report – Technology in Education: A Tool on Whose Terms?* UNESCO. https://unesdoc.unesco.org/ark:/48223/pf0000385723/PDF/385723eng.pdf.multi

UNICEF. (2020). How Many Children and Young People Have Internet Access at Home? https://data.unicef.org/wp-content/uploads/2020/11/How-many-children-and-young-people-have-internet-access-at-home-2020_v2.pdf

Van Wyk, M. M. (2024). Is ChatGPT an opportunity or a threat? Preventive strategies employed by academics related to a GenAI-based LLM at a faculty of education. *Journal of Applied Learning and Teaching*, *7*(1), 35–45.

Viberg, O., Kizilcec, R. F., Wise, A. F., Jivet, I., & Nixon, N. (2024). Advancing equity and inclusion in educational practices with AI-powered educational decision support systems (AI- EDSS). *British Journal of Educational Technology*, *55*(5), 1974–1981.

Wenger, E. (2000). Communities of Practice and Social Learning Systems. *Organization*, *7*(2), 225–246.

Wenger, E. (2011). Communities of practice: A brief introduction. https://scholarsbank.uoregon.edu/server/api/core/bitstreams/d1fddebc-8756-4647-9aef-80046f02df59/content

Whitacre, B. E., Wheeler, D., & Landgraf, C. (2017). What can the national broadband map tell us about the health care connectivity gap? *The Journal of Rural Health*, *33*(3), 284–289.

Williams, D. J. (2013). Urban education and professional learning communities. *Delta Kappa Gamma Bulletin*, *79*(2), 31.

Yu, D., Rosenfeld, H., & Gupta, A. (2023, January). The "AI divide" between the Global North and Global South. In *World Economic Forum* (Vol. 16).

Zhang, K., & Aslan, A. B. (2021). AI technologies for education: Recent research & future directions. *Computers and Education: Artificial Intelligence*, 2, 100025.

4. "A whole cartload of beautiful possibilities"

Moral guidance and the paradigm shift of generative AI

Jason Todd

> The eagerness and subtlety, I should even say craftiness, with which the problem of "the real and the apparent world" is dealt with at present throughout Europe, furnishes food for thought and attention; and he who hears only a "Will to Truth" in the background, and nothing else, cannot certainly boast of the sharpest ears. In rare and isolated cases, it may really have happened that such a Will to Truth—a certain extravagant and adventurous pluck, a metaphysician's ambition of the forlorn hope—has participated therein: that which in the end always prefers a handful of "certainty" to a whole cartload of beautiful possibilities; there may even be puritanical fanatics of conscience, who prefer to put their last trust in a sure nothing, rather than in an uncertain something.
>
> (Friedrich Nietzsche, *Beyond Good and Evil*)

A BRIEF HISTORY

I used to have a department chair who disliked most any change imposed at our school by what she, like many of the faculty, termed "The Administration." She used to say, whenever some new policy or some new system was implemented, "They didn't need all these policies when Oxford was founded." I always found it a strange attitude, especially given that we were on the faculty of a historically Black and Catholic university. Weren't we the change makers? Weren't we teaching at a school that was founded to fight against the exclusionary history of higher education? Despite such questions, I also understood the impulse. Change can be good, but change can be difficult. As humans, as creatures with both self-awareness and long-term memory, we distrust change, especially when it comes suddenly. And, as academics, we have a deeply rooted belief that we and we alone know what is best for our classes, our research, and our work–life balance.

The concept of higher education in the Global North has been evolving over the past 1,000 years, since the founding of the University of Bologna in the eleventh century, which was influenced, in part, by the University of al-Qarawiyyin, founded in Morocco in the ninth century (Guoddar & Ennam, 2025). This longstanding tradition has often been a point of pride for those of us living and working within the world of academia, as well as something of a hindrance. Tradition is critical. We teach what we were taught. Many of us teach as we were taught.[1] Any suggestion of change can be interpreted as a criticism, both of our predecessors and of ourselves.

Compare this history, then, to the history of computing. Although in some ways we can say that the concept of computing—of thinking machines—predates the concept of the university,[2] we must accept that the primary history of computing spans less than a century. Since the creation of IBM's "Accounting Apparatus" and NCR's "Calculating Machine" in 1940, computers have evolved with an ever-increasing rapidity. In 1946, Mauchly and Eckert introduced ENIAC, the first Turing-complete machine; in 1964, Cray unveiled the CDC 6600, the first supercomputer; in 1976, Texas Instruments released the TI-99, the first computer to run on a 16-bit microprocessor; in 1983, Apple released the Lisa, the first publicly available desktop computer. Then, in 1989, Tim Berners-Lee proposed the World Wide Web, the first globally linked information system (Berners-Lee, 1990), and changed everything all over again.

In 1965, as our understanding of how computers could and would work was still developing, Gordon Moore, who would go on to co-found Intel Corporation, published an article called "Cramming More Components onto Integrated Circuits," noting that the industry's ability to fit components onto an integrated circuit (what we today call a microchip) was doubling every year and predicting that the trend would likely continue for the next decade. Ten years later, Moore modified his prediction, which has since been dubbed "Moore's Law," to suggest that the doubling would occur every two years, which it did for the next 50 years. In 2022, the year ChatGPT was unveiled to the public, the CEO of NVIDIA, the company that produces the GPUs that have been the primary enabler of the development of Generative AI, pronounced that "the ability for Moore's Law to deliver twice the performance at the same cost, or at the same performance, half the cost, every year and a half, is over" (Witkowski, 2022).[3]

I find the intersection of these two mindsets fascinating, and while many faculty for many years could, for the most part, choose to ignore any new technology that came along, even as others of us were always looking for new ways to incorporate those new technologies into our classes, the second decade of the twenty-first century has intertwined and confounded both these traditions. Generative AI, through its overwhelming need for processing power, has highlighted the inevitable end of Moore's Law, just as through its ease of use and conversational style, it has forced all faculty to pay attention and consider its impact on their teaching.

The public unveiling of ChatGPT in November 2022 caught many people by surprise; even so, ChatGPT quickly became the most rapidly adopted internet application, gathering over 100 million users during its first two months (Milmo, 2023). That, of course, was the public response to ChatGPT. The academic response, as we will see, was, to say the least, more reserved. We were, after all, only three years out from the beginning of the COVID-19 pandemic, a paradigm shift both in daily life and in academic life from which many of us may never recover. Just as the Spring 2020 term saw a chaotic scramble to figure out how to deliver meaningful learning experiences remotely, the Spring 2023 term saw a flurry of discussions about how faculty should "deal with" ChatGPT. There was little consensus. As with most any paradigm shift, when our understanding of the world changes so radically that we don't recognize it anymore, we attempt, in vain, to hold on to the ethical frameworks that have served us in the past. I would like to suggest that this is the third tech-related paradigm shift academics and academic institutions have been challenged by during the first two decades of the twenty-first century. The first was caused by the creation of Wikipedia.

Wikipedia began much more quietly in the early 2000s, but by 2007, as the free online encyclopedia was announcing its 2 millionth article, it was being banned by faculty, who had concerns both about the reliability of the user-generated content and a clear lack of effort by students ("History of Wikipedia," 2025; Jaschik, 2007). However, even as some faculty were issuing such outright bans, students were learning to use Wikipedia effectively. A study conducted in 2009 found that over half of the students surveyed considered themselves "frequent" users of Wikipedia — sometimes, even, despite faculty telling them not to. More interesting, though, were the findings about how these students were using Wikipedia. 82% reported using Wikipedia "to obtain background information or a summary about a topic," and 76% reported using it to help them start the research project (Head & Eisenberg, 2010). The same year that report was published, Wikipedia began a program to help faculty incorporate the editing of Wikipedia articles into their classes ("About Us," 2015). Within a decade, Wikipedia went from being the end of education to being an effective educational tool.

Other writers and theorists have noted the commonalities in the academic reactions to Wikipedia and to Generative AI. Fister and Head (2023) note that not only did the fear of Wikipedia corrupting the educational process subside, but many academics and scientists now serve as editors, significantly elevating the quality of many of the almost 7 million (English-language) articles currently available on Wikipedia.

Of course, there is a significant difference between a student using a Wikipedia article to write an essay and a student using ChatGPT to write an essay. The concerns over Wikipedia were a combination of trusting unreliable sources and the threat of plagiarism, but this was plagiarism easily identified. The concerns over ChatGPT, while also including concerns of inaccurate information, are more focused on students using Generative AI to write their essays for them, creating a work that is not copied from other sources, but instead creating a work replicated from so many sources that it reads like something entirely new. Although numerous systems have been introduced claiming to detect when a piece of writing has been generated by one of these systems, the validity of those results is questionable at best.[4] It is fairly easy for a faculty member to look at something a student has written, compare it to another piece of writing (identified by a plagiarism detector), and determine if the student writing is plagiarizing the other writing. It is not so easy to look at a report generated by an algorithm that says something a student has written was generated by AI and say with any certainty that it was generated by AI. According to Weber-Wulff et al. (2023), the publicly available AI detection systems "are neither accurate nor reliable" (p. 28). More recent research has found that such detectors are more likely to incorrectly identify the work of non-native English speakers and of Black students as being generative by Generative AI (Liang et al., 2023; Madden et al., 2024).

Let's be honest: Generative AI does pose a unique threat to academic integrity, a threat significantly more existential than the threat Wikipedia posed. It is all too easy for students to ask the many available chatbots to do their work for them—to produce a research paper or to solve a complex mathematical problem or to assemble a presentation or to create a drawing—and for those chatbots to produce something that cannot be unquestionably identified as AI-generated. Academic dishonesty has been a threat for an exceptionally long time,[5] and it will likely be with us for a long time to come. The rapid evolution of technology will continue to produce tools that can be used to save us time and effort, and there will always be some people who choose to misuse those technologies.

Recognizing those challenges, this chapter considers how institutions of higher learning can best respond to the rapidly changing reality of Generative AI. As many colleges and universities have struggled over the past two years with the questions raised by the public introduction of Generative AI, the students, faculty, and staff of those institutions have generally been left to develop their own responses without clearly defined frameworks. Such an ethical vacuum engenders chaos. Students need to know what is and what is not acceptable when using Generative AI to complete their coursework and studies.

Faculty need to know what is and what is not acceptable when deciding their classroom policies, while also needing to know what is and what is not acceptable in using these systems in their own work, be it creating course content, grading, researching, or writing. Likewise, the staff and administrators at the institution need to know what is and what is not acceptable in their own professional use of Generative AI.

THIS IS THE END

Within a week of the public unveiling of ChatGPT in late 2022, *Inside Higher Ed* ran an article discussing faculty concerns that the system would be "the end of writing assignments" (Warner, 2022). Within another week, *The Chronicle of Higher Education* ran an article (under its "Dystopian Times" column, no less) that began by asking, "Is the college essay dead?" (McMurtrie, 2022). These articles and others like them followed the clickbait model that has, unfortunately, become the standard for journalism in the twenty-first century: offer the most extreme take at the beginning, distill it into a headline, and then offer a nuanced analysis that explains why that extreme take is not realistic in the body of the article that most people probably won't read. In Warner's (2022) "Freaking Out about ChatGPT—Part I," he quickly explains that "ChatGPT may be a threat to some of the things students are asked to do in school contexts, but it is not a threat to anything truly important when it comes to student learning."

There was, of course, significant concern about how ChatGPT would disrupt the work of education early on, and over the months, as ChatGPT improved and as similar Generative AI engines were released to the public, much of that concern expanded. As we've discussed, there was a similar concern throughout academia about the introduction of Wikipedia. Perhaps there should be little surprise that the introduction of Generative AI would encourage a similar response.

In June 2023, *The Chronicle of Higher Education* ran a story called "Caught Off Guard by ChatGPT" (McMurtrie & Supiano, 2023). While the article relies more on anecdotal accounts rather than survey data, it captures exceptionally well the confusion of the Spring 2023 term. While that semester was perhaps not as traumatically disruptive as the COVID-19 lockdown three years earlier, the combination of chaos and anxiety was reminiscent, perhaps too reminiscent. Faculty (and administrators) were not prepared and, as a result, did not know how to respond to this new technology. According to the article, misuse by students was the greatest concern for classroom faculty: Is the use of Generative AI a form of cheating? Faculty were scrambling to define what was and what was not appropriate within their classes. However, the larger issue that comes to the surface in the article is lack of guidance: students didn't know how to deal with Generative AI because their faculty didn't know how to deal with Generative AI because their administrations didn't know how to deal with Generative AI. One faculty member's comment quoted in the article sums up the problem: "The silence about AI on campus is shocking" (McMurtrie & Supiano, 2023).

Almost a year later, during the Spring 2024 term, Ithaka S+R produced a survey of faculty in the United States designed to offer a more precise reflection of the attitudes of academics toward Generative AI. At the time, while 66% of respondents said they had at least some familiarity with Generative AI, and 72% said they had used Generative AI at least once for educational purposes, only 35% said they saw the potential for Generative AI to "have a positive effect" on the educational methods of their disciplines, and 42% reported that they had completely banned the students in their classes from using Generative AI. As the authors of the report explain, "familiarity with generative AI is not necessarily associated with enthusiasm for it" (Ruediger et al., 2024). The results of the survey were perhaps only surprising in the way it codified the uncertainty of faculty regarding the academic uses of Generative AI.[6]

Not long afterwards, in November 2024, three writing professors published an online manifesto called "Refusing Generative AI in Writing Studies" (Fernandes et al., 2024). Narrowly focused on the discipline of Writing Studies, the statement and supporting documents offer greater insight into faculty attitudes about Generative AI. Refusal here does not mean outright rejection, but rather "the range of ways that individuals and/or groups consciously and intentionally choose to refuse GenAI use, when and where we are able to do so" (Fernandes et al., 2024). The use of Generative AI in the classroom and by the students is a matter of academic freedom according to the manifesto. Unless required by the program in which the instructor is teaching, the instructor should have the right to determine how and when Generative AI is used for their classes. While this may sound like a more formal version of the reactions already discussed by faculty, the manifesto helps to codify the wide-ranging concerns of faculty.

In the two years since the public release of ChatGPT, we have seen a variety of reactions, still ranging between full-scale adoption—the creation of new classes, even new academic programs, focused on Generative AI—and full-scale resistance. Although the headlines have tended to focus more on those two extremes, I would suggest that most faculty fall somewhere in between those two poles. At my school, we have faculty developing classes within our core curriculum that challenge students to struggle with the complex question of the benefits and dangers of Generative AI; we have faculty finding new and creative ways to use Generative AI in and out of the classroom; and we have faculty who have chosen to focus on the more traditional aspects of education.

Many schools, I gather, are seeing similar responses. Much as with Wikipedia and with COVID-19, faculty are finding their own ways to deal with the latest technological disruption. But to what end?

EVERYTHING OLD IS NEW AGAIN

Long before Generative AI was a reality, university faculty were being challenged (or were challenging themselves) to integrate new technologies into their curricula. Some brief personal anecdotes: In 1996, while spending a semester of my senior year in London, I completed an independent study with one of my professors in St. Louis via the still new technology of email. Every week, I had to submit a response paper about the book I'd read (it was a class on post-modern thought, no less), so I would write the papers by hand and then walk a mile to Cyberia, billed as the world's first internet café, that had six computers that could be rented for half an hour at a time (Pfanner, 2004), to type and send my papers. Was this a good short-term solution? Yes, since the fax machine at the London school wouldn't let me make international calls. Was this a feasible model for large-scale distance education? No. Only five years later, when I enrolled in graduate school, students were being issued university email addresses and faculty were requiring them to use online databases to conduct research and to create PowerPoint slides to present that research. Yet another five years later, as I was beginning my teaching career, every school had a Learning Management System and some faculty were having their students create social media accounts so they could share their research with the general public.

While the incorporation of new media into the classroom might seem to some like a desperate attempt to stay relevant in a rapidly evolving world, there can be great value in embedding technological skill development within a curriculum. Despite the label of "Digital Natives" applied to anyone born after 1980, humans are not born with an innate ability to use technology. Within the Global North, Millennials, Gen Z, and Generation Alpha may not know a world without easy access to technology, but they do not necessarily know how to effectively (or ethically) use that technology without training and practice. Whether faculty are integrating technology instruction into their classes to increase student engagement (Lumpkin et al., 2015), to encourage and enhance collaboration and discussion (Dabbagh, 2019), to better prepare students for the twenty-first-century workforce (Crittenden et al., 2019; Tanjung, 2019), the research has shown that the best approach is to integrate and align that technology use and instruction with existing learning outcomes (Huffman & Huffman, 2012).

Since its founding, academia has prepared students to become productive members of one workforce or another. According to Axtell (2016b), in his sweeping history of the history of the modern university, throughout the first few hundred years of the medieval universities, there evolved three sets of students: members of the clergy, the sons of the noble class, and even sons of the working class. Regardless of their background, all were sent, whether by their Church superiors or by their parents, for professional training: "The universities' primary goal, the reason for their creation, was not to produce edified Christians or zealous clergymen, but to prepare professionals to maintain and lead the established social order, secular as well as religious" (pp. 14–15). This pattern remained for the first few hundred years of the history of the university. Even as the models established in England were transferred abroad, including to the North American colonies, the universities were producing graduates with the skills to improve their career options and contribute to the mechanism of society (Axtell, 2016a).

Today, if we are honest, it is difficult to predict what the world will look like in another year, let alone another three hundred years. Despite that ambiguity, the college students of today need to graduate ready to work (and live) in a world in which Generative AI is a significant factor. Whether those students join large corporations or start their own small businesses, whether they go on to law school or medical school, whether they pursue graduate degrees and return to teach the next generation of college students, their careers (and personal lives) will involve engagement with Generative AI. Pandya, Ruhi, and Patterson (2023) argue that colleges and universities "play a significant role in influencing the awareness, readiness, and confidence of their students to work in the new world of work in 2030." Even if their classes are not teaching them the specific skills necessary for working with Generative AI, they can help the students improve their preparation for that work. The attitudes of recent college graduates and of employers reflect this concern. According to the "2024 Graduate Employability Report" (2024) produced by Cengage, 70% of polled recent graduates think colleges should integrate the use of Generative AI into their curricula, while 62% of polled employers said that new applicants should have some proficiency in working with Generative AI.

The timing of this paradigm shift, in the opinion of many, could be particularly beneficial to Historically Black Colleges and Universities (HBCUs) and other Minority Serving Institutions (MSIs). For many decades, there has been a digital divide between Americans who have easy access to computers and the internet and those who do not. A report produced by Deutsche Bank Securities two years before the public introduction of ChatGPT suggested that members of Black and Hispanic communities in the United States were "10 years behind Whites in levels of broadband access" (Walia & Ravindran, 2020, p. 3). Moreover, according to a report from the McKinsey Institute for Economic Mobility, if something does not change, the Black community is expected to lose $350 billion in tech-based income by 2030 (Brown et al., 2023).

Since the introduction of ChatGPT, though, there has been an increasing call for HBCUs, in particular, to embrace this new technology as a means of bridging both the access and the income divides. A joint report published by the Online Learning Consortium, Wiche Cooperative for Educational Technologies, and Complete College America argues that HBCUs, given their history of serving underrepresented communities, promoting academic excellence, and cultural competence, are in a unique position to shape the future of AI, thereby significantly contributing to the improvement of these demonstrably flawed systems while also shrinking the technology wage gap. In addition, given HBCUs' long-standing commitment to serving their local communities, they can also help shrink the technology access gap by teaching AI literacy to their neighbors (Long et al., 2024, pp. 31–33).

Not long after the public introduction of ChatGPT, which was quickly followed by the public introductions of other large language model systems, such as Perplexity AI (December 2022), Google Bard and Microsoft Copilot (February 2023), and Anthropic's Claude (March 2023), academic institutions began discussing the need for "AI policies." Since that time, many colleges and universities have published some kind of statement online in response to this need. There has been little consistency in these statements, be it in terms of what they say or in terms of who has published them. Recently, the website Campus AI Exchange unveiled a global map documenting the "higher education institutions shaping AI through policies, guidelines, and governance frameworks" (Sabado, 2025). The visualization demonstrates the inconsistency we have seen so far with this still nascent process. Focusing currently on mostly institutions in the United States and the United Kingdom, the map shows a random scattering of the schools that have attempted to put forth some formal stance on how Generative AI tools might fit into their institutions.

A variety of studies between 2022 and 2025 have looked at the documents published by universities in response to the development of Generative AI. The purpose of this chapter is not to rehash the analyses that have already taken place and which are, likely, already out of date at the time of writing. However, it is worth considering the patterns and themes that emerge in some of those studies. Looking at the public websites of the 100 institutions included in the 2024 U.S. News Best National Rankings list, Wang et al. (2024) found that most had enacted a modestly non-restrictive approach to the use of Generative AI by students. Many of these schools were also providing resources to help their faculty craft appropriate policies for their individual classes and often stressing the need to consider the ethical implications of Generative AI use. The greatest concern, based on the focus of the reviewed policies, was the misuse (either intentional or unintentional) of Generative AI in student academic writing. In a similar study, McDonald et al. (2024) coded and analyzed the publicly available documents from 131 institutions classified as R1 by the

Carnegie system. Here the researchers found slightly more diverse institutional attitudes toward Generative AI, but still a generally hesitant acceptance of its use. Again, a prominent focus was on how Generative AI further complicates the issue of plagiarism. Interestingly, while McDonald's team also found a significant focus on concerns of plagiarism with Generative AI, they also found a number of schools embracing the introduction of Generative AI as an opportunity to reconsider the standard models of teaching and learning. Meanwhile, Luo (2024) takes a different approach. In a review of the published Generative AI policies of the 20 universities at the top of the 2024 QS World University Rankings, Luo's consideration of what problems those policies are attempting to mitigate finds that, perhaps not surprisingly, the top concern was the use of Generative AI to cheat on academic work.

Through this very cursory review, two trends seem obvious: first, that institutions of higher learning—the academy—recognize some substantial potential for this new technology; and second, that the individuals within those institutions—academics—are still highly focused on how this new technology will be misused. As Fister and Head (2023) have rightly suggested, this is, perhaps, an intensified repeat of the response to the new technology of Wikipedia we saw 15 or so years ago. I don't mean to suggest here that academics (and the academy as a whole) should not be concerned about cheating by students; rather, I want to suggest that that concern over cheating should not be the guiding factor in our response to Generative AI (or any future technology, for that matter). When a faculty member sits down to create an assignment, the first and most prominent thought should not be about how students might cheat on that test; it should be, instead, on what the students will learn by completing that assignment. In their foundational work, *Understanding by Design*, Wiggins and McTighe (2005) explain the importance of starting any academic planning process with the end result in mind. As with the creation of an assignment or of a new course or a new academic program, when developing policies that will affect students, we need to start that process by focusing not on the problems but on the benefits to the students.

A POLICY FOR THE FUTURE

In 1886, having given up his career as a university lecturer, Friedrich Nietzsche published his ninth book, *Beyond Good and Evil*, a book he subtitled, "Prelude to a Philosophy of the Future." In it, he laments the modern philosophers "who prefer to put their last trust in a sure nothing, rather than in an uncertain something" (2013). It's from this work that I have taken the title for this chapter because I see a certain parallel in the concerns Nietzsche expresses and the challenge those of us in the academy face today. Many of us have become rather nihilistic about the future of higher education. In the past twenty years, we have struggled through challenges none of us could have predicted, and as a result, many of us have become the "fanatics of conscience" Nietzsche criticizes. I myself initially responded to the advent of Generative AI in this way: I didn't want to deal with it. I didn't want to adapt my teaching yet again in response to some unprecedented change. Eventually, though, I took some time and learned not just how to interact with these new systems but how they worked—a little, at least—and over the past year, I've begun to integrate the use of these tools into my classes. It has been a struggle. For one, things keep changing. But the greatest challenge is that I haven't had a clear explanation of what is appropriate. Much like the philosophers in Nietzsche's time who struggled to understand Truth in a world without a clear moral framework, I struggled to understand how I could use this new technology. My students have struggled as well, as have my colleagues.

As we've discussed, for the schools that have published some kind of document about Generative AI, the focus has been on the students. Most of those, in one form or another, explain that what is appropriate and inappropriate use of Generative AI is determined by their individual instructors. While this, in theory, is good guidance, as it supports the idea of academic freedom that has, as we've seen, been a part of the university experience since its founding, it can also lead to frustration for the students. Faculty must give their students clear and precise explanations of how Generative AI can and cannot be used for their classes. In order to do so, faculty need an understanding of what Generative AI is, how it works, and how it is being integrated. In Spring 2023, it was fairly easy for me to tell my students in the syllabus that they could not use ChatGPT for any of the assignments for my classes. Today, such a statement has little meaning. They need more clarity. I have for many years now been a proponent of the Transparency in Learning and Teaching (TILT) model developed by Mary-Ann Winkelmes (2023), whose research has found that by providing detailed explanations of the purpose of an assignment, the steps necessary to complete the assignment, and the expectations that will be used to evaluate the assignment, faculty can help students avoid making mistakes that will impact their grade, even if their work demonstrates successful learning. More specifically, Winkelmes says,

> The TILT Framework is more than an outline for how teachers can explain academic work to students. It is also a guide for students' metacognitive awareness of their learning and a process for inviting students to share their expertise about their own learning experiences with their instructors. (p. 4)

This is the kind of reciprocity we need when we discuss Generative AI in academia.

Perkins et al. (2024) have proposed an effective method for helping students understand when and how Generative AI can and cannot be used in a given class. Their Artificial Intelligence Assessment Scale (AIAS) separates AI usage into five scales, ranging from "No AI" (for an activity in which Generative AI may not be used in any form) to "Full AI" (for an activity in which students are instructed to use Generative AI as a "co-pilot"). This allows a faculty member to label any activity the students will do with a clear indication of acceptable AI use. This also demonstrates to the students, I think, the fluidity of technology. We are far past the world of binary thinking. Students need to practice not only using Generative AI, but also making decisions about how and when to use it.

Of the institutions that have posted statements about Generative AI, as we've seen, most make clear that the individual faculty can decide what is appropriate within their classes. This guidance needs to be clear for all, from senior faculty to adjunct faculty. It needs to be filtered down from the top and through the multiple layers of academic bureaucracy: from Chief Academic Officers and Deans, from Department Chairs and Program Directors. Ideally, all these academic leaders should be considering how Generative AI might need to be integrated into their various curricula. Here too the faculty need guidance. Program Directors need to know what their Department Chairs consider appropriate; Chairs need to know what their Deans consider appropriate; Deans need to know what their Chief Academic Officers consider appropriate.

As faculty, though, we have more responsibilities than just our classes, and thus, we need more guidance about Generative AI use. Universities need to make clear how and when faculty can use Generative AI in their own research and writing. Will tenure committees recognize scholarship that was assisted by Generative AI? Can they publish articles about their experiments with Generative AI in the classroom? Again, these considerations need to be filtered through the levels of academia.

Finally, universities need to consider and make clear how the many members of the non-faculty staff can use Generative AI. Once again, there needs to be a top-down, tiered set of guidelines. The director of the institutional research office can only provide guidance once they have been given guidance by their supervisor, who likely will need guidance from their supervisor.

As we are making all these decisions about when the use of Generative AI is appropriate, we need to make sure that we are fully aware of the risks of using Generative AI. I often explain to my students, that no matter how clever these chatbots may seem, all they are actually good at doing is recognizing patterns. One of the tempting uses of them is to give them a set of data or a set of documents and ask them to identify trends and themes. But we—students, faculty, staff—need to be mindful of what data we give these systems, as it is not always clear how that data will be used. Policies that explain when Generative

AI can be used will do no good if they fail to consider and explain *how* they can be used. The University of Illinois Urbana-Champaign offers a detailed policy to its entire community that clearly describes the risks and benefits of giving data over to Generative AI (*Privacy Considerations for Generative AI*, 2025).

Three years before the public introduction of ChatGPT, Floridi and Cowls (2019) proposed a set of principles for an ethical and socially beneficial AI. Adapting standards long held within the bioethics community, they present a framework that can easily be followed by any institution developing its own set of guidelines for the use of what we now call Generative AI. The five principles they propose are as follows:

- *Beneficence*: How does the policy contribute to public well-being and the common good?
- *Non-Maleficence*: How well does the policy respect privacy and maintain data security?
- *Autonomy*: To what extent does the policy allow individuals to choose when and how they engage with this technology?
- *Justice*: In what ways does the policy promote unity and equity within the community?
- *Explicability*: How does the policy ensure transparency and accountability when this technology is used?

An academic AI policy built around these standards would empower the entire university community to not only embrace Generative AI, but to become skillful at using it responsibly and ethically. HBCUs and other MSIs, I think, are well-positioned to implement AI policies along these lines, given their longstanding commitment to social justice. Generative AI can be a tool that moves these schools forward, but only if they embrace it with these goals in mind. Long et al. (2024) make a strong argument for HBCUs to stay true to their course while embracing this revolutionary technology. It offers, in the words of Nietzsche (2013), "a whole cartload of beautiful possibilities" for those who are willing to embrace it with the proper moral foundation.

CONCLUSION

The journey from the medieval universities to today's institutions grappling with Generative AI reveals a fundamental tension that has always existed in higher education: the struggle between preserving tradition and embracing necessary change. As this chapter has demonstrated, the academic response to Generative AI mirrors historical patterns we have seen before—initial resistance, gradual experimentation, and eventual integration—but with stakes that may be uniquely consequential for educational equity and institutional relevance.

This chapter has argued that the current focus on preventing misuse of Generative AI, while understandable, represents a missed opportunity for transformative educational reform. The proliferation of institutional policies that primarily address cheating concerns reflects what Nietzsche might have recognized as a preference for "a sure nothing" over "an uncertain something." Such approaches fail to engage with the more profound implications of these technologies for teaching, learning, and the mission of higher education. This disconnect is particularly problematic for institutions serving historically marginalized communities, where the failure to provide students with contemporary digital literacy skills may exacerbate existing inequities.

For HBCUs and other MSIs, the emergence of Generative AI represents both a challenge and an unprecedented opportunity. As this chapter has demonstrated, the digital divide that has historically disadvantaged Black and Hispanic communities in technology access and employment could be addressed through strategic institutional responses to AI integration. However, this requires moving beyond defensive policies focused on preventing misuse toward proactive frameworks that position these institutions as leaders in ethical AI implementation.

The recommendations presented throughout this chapter focus on the need for comprehensive institutional policies that extend beyond student use to encompass faculty research, staff operations, and administrative functions. Rather than the current fragmented approach that leaves individual faculty to navigate these challenges alone, institutions require systematic frameworks that move beyond prohibition toward thoughtful integration. The ethical principles of beneficence, non-maleficence, autonomy, justice, and explicability provide a foundation for policy development, while practical assessment tools can translate broad institutional values into specific classroom guidance.

Most importantly, this chapter has argued that the current moment represents a unique opportunity for educational institutions to reassert their relevance and leadership in preparing students for an AI-integrated future. The rapid pace of technological change means that institutions that fail to engage meaningfully with these developments risk becoming increasingly disconnected from the realities their graduates will face. For institutions serving historically marginalized communities, this risk is particularly acute, as it could perpetuate or even amplify existing educational and economic inequities.

The "cartload of beautiful possibilities" that Nietzsche envisioned requires courage: the courage to move beyond the comfortable certainties of prohibition and control toward the uncertain terrain of genuine integration and innovation. For higher education, this means recognizing that Generative AI is not simply another technological tool to be managed and contained, but rather a transformative force that requires us to reconsider fundamental assumptions about teaching, learning, and the production of knowledge.

The institutions that will thrive in this new landscape will be those that embrace both the opportunities and the responsibilities that come with AI integration. They will develop policies that are both protective and permissive, that safeguard academic integrity while enabling innovation, and that prepare students not just to use these tools, but to use them wisely, ethically, and effectively. Most crucially, they will recognize that the goal is not simply to adapt to technological change, but to shape that change in ways that advance the fundamental mission of higher education: to foster critical thinking, promote social justice, and prepare engaged citizens for democratic participation in an increasingly complex world.

The choice before us is clear: we can continue to respond to Generative AI with the same defensive mechanisms that have characterized academic responses to technological change throughout history, focusing primarily on prevention and control, or we can seize this moment as an opportunity to reimagine higher education in ways that better serve our students, our communities, and our democratic ideals. The latter path is more challenging, but offers the possibility of transformation rather than mere adaptation. In choosing to embrace uncertainty over the false security of prohibition, we choose possibility over paralysis, and in doing so, we honor both our historical mission and our future potential.

NOTES

1. In fact, it has only been about 40 years since universities began to realize that faculty might need some training to help them become more effective teachers.
2. Just as universities like Oxford and Cambridge were being established, the Majorcan scholar Ramon Llull was investigating the possibility of what he called "logical machines." Llull was heavily influenced by Arabic thought. As is likely clear by now, this chapter is written from a Global North perspective. The impact upon academics by Generative AI is likely much more substantial in the Global South. This is a topic outside my area of expertise, but worthy of further study.
3. I should note that not long after Jensen Huang made his pronouncement, the current CEO of Intel, Pat Gelsinger, publicly refuted the idea (Machkovech, 2022).
4. As I was completing the final revisions for this manuscript, I ran it through one of these AI detection systems, which told me that 82% of the manuscript was likely AI-generated.
5. The Roman poet Martial, writing in the first century CE, offers one of the first uses of the Latin word *plagiarius*, which literally means *kidnapper*, to accuse someone of literary theft (Seo, 2009).

6. The survey, too, is perhaps skewed through self-selection of the participants: it's unlikely that faculty who chose to largely ignore Generative AI in that first year would feel compelled to respond to a survey about their attitudes toward Generative AI.

REFERENCES

2024 Graduate Employability Report: Preparing students for the GenAI-driven workplace. (2024). https://cengage.widen.net/s/bmjxxjx9mm/cg-2024-employability-survey-report

About Us. (2015, May 26). Wiki Education. https://wikiedu.org/about-us/

Axtell, J. (2016a). A land of colleges. In Wisdom's Workshop: The Rise of the Modern University (pp. 147–220). Princeton University Press. https://doi.org/10.2307/j.ctv7h0s90.9

Axtell, J. (2016b). Foundings. In Wisdom's Workshop: The Rise of the Modern University (pp. 1–42). Princeton University Press. https://doi.org/10.2307/j.ctv7h0s90.6

Berners-Lee, T. (1990, May). Information Management: A Proposal. World Wide Web Consortium. https://www.w3.org/History/1989/proposal.html

Brown, J. S., Finney, M., McMillan, M., & Perkins, M. (2023, February 3). How to close the Black tech talent gap. McKinsey Institute for Economic Mobility. https://www.mckinsey.com/institute-for-economic-mobility/our-insights/how-to-close-the-black-tech-talent-gap

Crittenden, W. F., Biel, I. K., & Lovely, W. A. (2019). Embracing digitalization: Student learning and new technologies. *Journal of Marketing Education*, 41(1), 5–14. https://doi.org/10.1177/0273475318820895

Dabbagh, N. (2019). Student Perspectives of the Value and Effectiveness of Technology Use for Learning in Higher Education. Proceedings of the 2019 AERA Annual Meeting. 2019 AERA Annual Meeting. https://doi.org/10.3102/1426202

Fernandes, M., McIntyre, M., & Sano-Franchini, J. (2024, November). Refusing Generative AI in Writing Studies [Blog]. Refusing Generative AI in Writing Studies. https://refusinggenai.wordpress.com/

Fister, B., & Head, A. J. (2023, May 4). Getting a Grip on ChatGPT. Inside Higher Ed. https://www.insidehighered.com/opinion/views/2023/05/04/getting-grip-chatgpt

Floridi, L., & Cowls, J. (2019). A Unified Framework of Five Principles for AI in Society. Harvard Data Science Review. https://doi.org/10.1162/99608f92.8cd550d1

Guoddar, H., & Ennam, A. (2025). The role of early female Muslim scholars in the development of world knowledge. Journal of Education in Muslim Societies, 6(2), 109122. https://dx.doi.org/10.2979/jems.00032

Head, A. J., & Eisenberg, M. B. (2010). How today's college students use Wikipedia for course-related research. First Monday, 15(3). https://doi.org/10.5210/fm.v15i3.2830

History of Wikipedia. (2025). In Wikipedia. https://en.wikipedia.org/w/index.php?title=History_of_Wikipedia&oldid=1273905393

Huffman, W. H., & Huffman, A. H. (2012). Beyond basic study skills: The use of technology for success in college. Computers in Human Behavior, 28(2), 583–590. https://doi.org/10.1016/j.chb.2011.11.004

Jaschik, S. (2007, January 25). A Stand Against Wikipedia. Inside Higher Ed. https://www.insidehighered.com/news/2007/01/26/stand-against-wikipedia

Liang, W., Yuksekgonul, M., Mao, Y., Wu, E., & Zou, J. (2023). GPT detectors are biased against non-native English writers. Patterns, 4(7). https://doi.org/10.1016/j.patter.2023.100779

Long, K. C., Gunder, A., Robinson, B., Davis, V. L., & Barth, D. (2024). Leading the AI Revolution: The Crucial Role of HBCUs in Steering AI Leadership. https://onlinelearningconsortium.org/research/leading-the-ai-revolution-the-crucial-role-of-hbcus-in-steering-ai-leadership/

Lumpkin, A., Achen, R., & Dodd, R. (2015). Using technology-nested instructional strategies to enhance student learning—InSight Journal. InSight: A Journal of Scholarly Teaching, 10, 114–125. https://doi.org/10.46504/10201509lu

Luo, J. (2024). A critical review of GenAI policies in higher education assessment: A call to reconsider the "originality" of students' work. Assessment & Evaluation in Higher Education, 49(5), 651–664. Crossref. https://doi.org/10.1080/02602938.2024.2309963

Machkovech, S. (2022, September 27). Intel: "Moore's law is not dead" as Arc A770 GPU is priced at $329. Ars Technica. https://arstechnica.com/gadgets/2022/09/the-intel-arc-a770-gpu-launches-october-12-for-329/

Madden, M., Calvin, A., Hasse, A., & Lenhart, A. (2024). The dawn of the AI Era: teens, parents, and the adoption of generative AI at home and school. Common Sense. https://www.commonsensemedia.org/sites/default/files/research/report/2024-the-dawn-of-the-ai-era_final-release-for-web.pdf

McDonald, N., Johri, A., Ali, A., & Hingle, A. (2024). Generative artificial intelligence in higher education: Evidence from an analysis of institutional policies and guidelines. arXiv.Org. https://doi.org/10.48550/ARXIV.2402.01659

McMurtrie, B. (2022, December 13). Teaching Experts Are Worried About ChatGPT, but Not for the Reasons You Think. The Chronicle of Higher Education. https://www.chronicle.com/article/ai-and-the-future-of-undergraduate-writing

McMurtrie, B., & Supiano, B. (2023, June 14). Caught Off Guard by AI. The Chronicle of Higher Education. https://www.chronicle.com/article/caught-off-guard-by-ai

Milmo, D. (2023, February 2). ChatGPT reaches 100 million users two months after launch. The Guardian. https://www.theguardian.com/technology/2023/feb/02/chatgpt-100-million-users-open-ai-fastest-growing-app

Nietzsche, F. (2013). Beyond Good and Evil (H. Zimmern, Trans.). Project Gutenberg. https://www.gutenberg.org/files/4363/4363-h/4363-h.htm

Pandya, B., Ruhi, U., & Patterson, L. (2023). Preparing the future workforce for 2030: The role of higher education institutions. Frontiers in Education, 8. https://doi.org/10.3389/feduc.2023.1295249

Perkins, M., Furze, L., Roe, J., & MacVaugh, J. (2024). The Artificial Intelligence Assessment Scale (AIAS): A framework for ethical integration of generative AI in educational assessment. Journal of University Teaching and Learning Practice, 21(06). https://doi.org/10.53761/q3azde36

Pfanner, E. (2004, September 2). "The world's first," Café Cyberia in London, takes a bow: A decade of Internet cafés. The New York Times. https://www.nytimes.com/2004/09/02/business/worldbusiness/the-worlds-first-caf-cyberia-in-london-takes-a-bow-a.html

Privacy Considerations for Generative AI. (2025). Univiersity of Illinois Urbana-Champaign, Privacy & Cybersecurity. https://www.cybersecurity.illinois.edu/policies-governance/privacy-considerations-for-generative-ai/

Ruediger, D., Blankstein, M., & Love, S. (2024). Generative AI and Postsecondary Instructional Practices: Findings from a National Survey of Instructors. Ithaka S+R. https://doi.org/10.18665/sr.320892

Sabado, J. (2025). AI in Academia: Policies, Guidelines, and Governance. Campus AI Exchange. https://campusaiexchange.com/ai-policies-guidelines-map

Seo, J. M. (2009). Plagiarism and poetic identity in martial. The American Journal of Philology, 130(4), 567–593. https://www.jstor.org/stable/20616209

Tanjung, R. F. (2019). Answering the challenge of industrial revolution 4.0 through improved skills use of technology college. International Journal for Educational and Vocational Studies, 1(1), Article 1. https://doi.org/10.29103/ijevs.v1i1.1374

Walia, A., & Ravindran, S. (2020). America's Racial Gap & Big Tech's Closing Window. Deutsche Bank Securities. https://www.dbresearch.com/PROD/RPS_EN-PROD/America%27s_Racial_Gap_%26_Big_Tech%27s_Closing_Window/RPS_EN_DOC_VIEW.calias?rwnode=PROD0000000000464258&ProdCollection=PROD0000000000511664

Wang, H., Dang, A., Wu, Z., & Mac, S. (2024). Generative AI in higher education: Seeing ChatGPT through universities' policies, resources, and guidelines. Computers and Education: Artificial Intelligence, 7, 100326. Crossref. https://doi.org/10.1016/j.caeai.2024.100326

Warner, J. (2022, December 5). Freaking Out About ChatGPT—Part I. https://www.insidehighered.com/blogs/just-visiting/freaking-out-about-chatgpt%E2%80%94part-i

Weber-Wulff, D., Anohina-Naumeca, A., Bjelobaba, S., Foltýnek, T., Guerrero-Dib, J., Popoola, O., Šigut, P., & Waddington, L. (2023). Testing of detection tools for AI-generated text. International Journal for Educational Integrity, 19(1), 26. https://doi.org/10.1007/s40979-023-00146-z

Wiggins, G., & McTighe, J. (2005). Understanding by Design (Expanded 2nd ed). ASCD; eBook Academic Collection (EBSCOhost). https://research.ebsco.com/linkprocessor/plink?id=57c586d5-d50e-33ae-98ac-319106f043a7

Winkelmes, M.-A. (2023). Introduction to transparency in learning and teaching. Perspectives in Learning, 20(1), 4–12.

Witkowski, W. (2022, September 22). "Moore's Law's dead," Nvidia CEO Jensen Huang says in justifying gaming-card price hike. MarketWatch. https://www.marketwatch.com/story/moores-laws-dead-nvidia-ceo-jensen-says-in-justifying-gaming-card-price-hike-11663798618

5. Critical perspective on artificial intelligence in education

Patrick Kersalé

INTRODUCTION

Context of Artificial Intelligence in Education

Artificial intelligence (AI) is revolutionizing numerous sectors, and education is no exception. Since the early experiments with intelligent tutoring systems in the 1970s, AI has evolved into a powerful tool in modern classrooms. Today, technologies such as machine learning, natural language processing, and recommendation systems are being used to personalize learning, automate administrative tasks, and provide real-time feedback to students. According to HolonIQ (2022), the global market for artificial intelligence applications in education is projected to reach approximately 6 billion USD by 2025, indicating sustained growth in investment and technological adoption within the sector. However, the integration of AI in education is not without challenges. Ethical concerns, algorithmic biases, and issues surrounding student privacy are among the problems that must be addressed to ensure the responsible use of these technologies. This chapter aims to critically explore these challenges, providing an in-depth analysis of the benefits and drawbacks of AI in education.

The primary objective of this chapter is to offer a critical perspective on the use of AI in education. We will examine the ethical, social, and pedagogical implications of these technologies, focusing on issues of accountability, equity, and privacy. Additionally, we will explore concrete case studies to illustrate the successes and failures of AI in various educational contexts. Finally, we will propose recommendations for the responsible integration of AI into educational systems.

This chapter is organized into seven main sections. Following this introduction, we will provide an overview of AI in education, defining key concepts and exploring common applications. The third section will present a critical perspective on the ethical and social challenges of AI, followed by detailed case studies in the fourth section. The fifth section will discuss the challenges and limitations of AI in education, while the sixth section will propose recommendations for responsible integration. Finally, the conclusion will summarize the key points and offer future perspectives.

ARTIFICIAL INTELLIGENCE IN EDUCATION: AN OVERVIEW

Definition and Key Concepts

AI in education refers to the use of algorithms and computer systems to facilitate and enhance teaching and learning processes. Key concepts include:

- *Machine Learning (ML)*: A branch of AI that enables systems to learn from data and improve their performance without being explicitly programmed (Russell & Norvig, 2021). For example, adaptive learning systems use machine learning algorithms to personalize educational content based on the individual needs of students.
- *Natural Language Processing (NLP)*: A technology that allows machines to understand and generate human language (Jurafsky & Martin, 2023). Educational chatbots, such as those used by universities to answer student questions, rely on NLP.
- *Expert Systems*: Expert systems are computer-based systems that emulate human decision-making by applying rules and domain-specific knowledge Computer systems that mimic human decision-making using rules and domain-specific knowledge (Jackson, 2019). For example, automated grading systems utilize predefined rules to evaluate student work.

Common Applications of AI in Education

The integration of AI in education has led to transformative applications that enhance learning experiences, streamline administrative tasks, and provide personalized support. Below are key applications with expanded explanations and supporting references:

Adaptive learning platforms

Adaptive learning systems use AI algorithms to analyze student performance and dynamically adjust content to meet individual needs. These platforms provide customized learning paths, ensuring students receive appropriate challenges and support.

- Khan Academy employs machine learning to recommend exercises and instructional videos based on student progress. Its AI-driven dashboard helps teachers identify struggling students (Khan Academy, 2023). Pane et al. (2017) found that adaptive learning technologies improve math outcomes by 22% compared to traditional instruction.
- Duolingo uses AI to personalize language lessons, adjusting difficulty based on user mistakes. A study by Vesselinov & Grego (2016) demonstrated that 34 hours of Duolingo usage equates to a university semester of language study (Duolingo, 2023).

Automated grading systems

AI-powered grading tools reduce instructor workload while providing consistent and immediate feedback. These systems evaluate written responses, code, and even complex problem-solving tasks.

- Turnitin's Gradescope enables instructors to grade assignments faster using AI-assisted rubric scoring. A case study at the University of California, Berkeley, showed a 50% reduction in grading time (Gradescope, 2023).
- E-rater by ETS assesses GRE essays with 92% agreement with human graders, demonstrating reliability (Attali & Burstein, 2006).

Educational chatbots

AI chatbots provide 24/7 student support, answering queries, explaining concepts, and guiding coursework.

- Georgia Tech's Jill Watson, an AI teaching assistant, handled over 10,000 student questions with 97% accuracy in an online course (Goel & Polepeddi, 2016).
- IBM Watson Tutor offers personalized explanations in STEM subjects, improving comprehension by 30% (IBM, 2023).

Intelligent tutoring systems (ITS)

ITS simulate one-on-one tutoring by adapting to student responses in real time.

- Carnegie Learning's MATHia uses AI to provide step-by-step guidance, increasing test scores by 15% (Koedinger et al., 2015; Carnegie Learning, 2023).

Predictive analytics for student success

AI analyzes student data (e.g., engagement, grades) to identify at-risk learners and recommend interventions.

- Civitas Learning uses predictive models to boost retention rates by 10–15% (Civitas Learning, 2023).

POTENTIAL BENEFITS OF AI IN EDUCATION

AI is transforming education by offering innovative solutions that enhance learning experiences, optimize administrative processes, and support both students and educators. Below is an expanded analysis of key benefits, supported by scholarly research and empirical evidence.

Personalized Learning

AI-driven adaptive learning systems tailor educational content to individual student needs, improving engagement and academic performance. Pane et al. (2017) argue that "adaptive learning technologies can personalize instruction at scale, addressing diverse learner needs more effectively than one-size-fits-all approaches" (p. 72).

- *Customized Learning Paths*: AI analyzes student data (e.g., response times, error patterns) to adjust lesson difficulty and pacing. For example, DreamBox Learning, an AI-powered math platform, improved student achievement by 60% in schools with high usage (Pane et al., 2017).
- *Reduced Performance Gaps*: A meta-analysis by Kulik & Fletcher (2016) found that AI tutors narrowed achievement gaps by 20–30% for struggling students compared to traditional instruction.
- *Learning Style Adaptation*: Platforms like Squirrel AI use machine learning to identify optimal teaching methods (e.g., visual vs. auditory) for each student, boosting retention rates by 35% (Luckin et al., 2022).

Improved Administrative Efficiency

AI automates time-consuming tasks, freeing educators to focus on pedagogy and student interaction. According to Luckin et al. (2016, p. 23), "AI automation in administrative tasks can reclaim 10–15 hours weekly for teachers, enabling deeper student engagement."

- *Automated Grading*: Tools like Gradescope reduce grading time by 50–70% while maintaining accuracy (Barrie et al., 2019). A Stanford study found AI grading of essays correlated with human graders at $r = 0.85$ (Shermis & Hamner, 2013).
- *Streamlined Enrollment*: AI chatbots have been shown to handle a large share of routine student inquiries, reducing administrative workload and

enabling institutions to reallocate staff resources to higher-value tasks (Labadze, Grigolia & Machaidze, 2023).

- *Resource Allocation*: Predictive analytics help institutions identify course demand trends, optimizing staffing and budgets (Baker & Inventado, 2014).

Instant Feedback

AI provides real-time, actionable feedback to students, fostering self-regulated learning. VanLehn (2011, p. 218) asserts that "immediate feedback loops powered by AI correlate with significant gains in metacognitive skills and academic persistence."

- *Writing Assistance*: Grammarly's AI detects grammar errors and suggests improvements, increasing writing quality by 40% (Crossley et al., 2019).
- *STEM Problem-Solving*: Platforms like ASSISTments offer step-by-step hints in math, reducing frustration and improving completion rates (Koedinger et al., 2015).
- *Language Learning*: Duolingo's AI corrections improve language proficiency two times faster than classroom-only instruction (Vesselinov & Grego, 2016).

CRITICAL PERSPECTIVES ON AI IN EDUCATION

Ethics and Accountability

Ethics and accountability are foundational pillars of education systems. For students, this includes the right to fair treatment, transparent evaluations, and data privacy (Biesta, 2015). Educators bear professional responsibility for fair grading, unbiased instruction, and safeguarding student welfare (Noddings, 2013). Administrators must ensure institutional policies align with equity, due process, and societal values (Strike, 2007).

Traditional education operates on clear accountability frameworks:

- Teachers answer for grading accuracy.
- Schools oversee curriculum fairness.
- Regulatory bodies enforce standards.

However, AI undermines ethical practices and accountability in several ways, encompassing:

- *Diffused responsibility*: When an AI grading system makes errors (e.g., mis-scoring essays), accountability blurs between developers, teachers, and institutions (Selwyn, 2019). For example, in 2020 the United Kingdom's controversial A-level grading algorithm disproportionately downgraded the results of many students and sparked widespread criticism over fairness and bias, ultimately leading authorities to abandon the automated method in favour of teacher-assessed grades (BBC News, 2020).
- *Opacity of "black box" systems*: Many AI algorithms (e.g., recommendation engines) lack explainability, violating transparency principles (Floridi et al., 2018). Consequently, teachers cannot verify if a student's AI-generated learning path is truly unbiased (UNESCO, 2021).
- *Erosion of student autonomy*: AI-driven personalized learning may override student agency, reducing education to algorithmic control (Zuboff, 2019). For example, proctoring software like Proctorio has been criticized for making punitive decisions (e.g., flagging "suspicious" eye movements) without human review (Harwell, 2021).
- *Bias amplification*: Facial analysis AI often misidentifies emotions of non-white students, affecting feedback validity (Buolamwini & Gebru, 2018).

AI introduces structural irresponsibility when (a) developers defer to "technical limitations"; (b) institutions claim reliance on "objective" systems; and (c) teachers lack training to challenge outputs. As Selwyn (2019) argues, "When ethics become embedded in code, they cease to be negotiable."

Algorithmic Biases and Inequalities in Educational AI

Algorithmic bias occurs when AI systems produce systematically prejudiced outcomes due to flawed assumptions in their development or biased training data (Mehrabi et al., 2021). In education, this manifests when technologies favor certain groups while disadvantaging others, often replicating existing societal inequalities (Noble, 2018). Key characteristics of algorithmic bias include:

- *Data bias*: Training datasets often overrepresent dominant groups (e.g., native English speakers) while underrepresenting minorities, leading to skewed outcomes and fairness issues in algorithmic systems (Obermeyer et al., 2019).
- *Design bias*: Developers' unconscious prejudices embedded in system architecture (Benjamin, 2019).
- *Feedback loops*: Biased outputs reinforce and amplify initial prejudices over time (Eubanks, 2018).

Algorithmic biases in educational AI manifest through language and cultural bias, gender stereotyping, and socioeconomic discrimination. With respect to *language and cultural bias*, automated essay scoring tools penalize non-native English speakers for "non-standard" phrasing (Baker & Inventado, 2014). Similarly, speech recognition software struggles with accented English, disadvantaging ESL students (Koenecke et al., 2020). Regarding gender stereotyping, career recommendation systems steer girls away from STEM fields based on historical enrollment patterns (UNESCO, 2019, p. 47). Also, avatar-based tutors use gender-coded visuals (e.g., female tutors for "soft" subjects) (UNESCO, 2019, p. 52). Finally, socioeconomic discrimination becomes a significant issue. For example, predictive analytics flag low-income students as "at-risk" based on neighborhood data rather than individual potential (O'Neil, 2016). Adaptive learning systems recommend cheaper, less rigorous pathways to disadvantaged students (Eubanks, 2018). Harwell (2021) conducted a study on Proctorio's racial bias and found that proctoring software flagged Black students' head movements as "suspicious" 2.3 times more often than White students and misinterpreted natural hair textures as *potential cheating devices*.

The UNESCO (2019) report on the challenges and opportunities that AI in education poses for sustainable development. The report provides some critical insights that require attention. Some key problems identified include the following:

- 73% of analyzed educational AI systems showed gender bias in career recommendations (p. 48).
- 68% of language processing tools performed significantly worse for minority dialects (p. 51).
- Algorithmic tracking systems disproportionately targeted students with disabilities for behavioral interventions (p. 55).

The report proposes policy solutions, such as:

- *Mandatory bias audits*: Third-party testing of all educational AI systems (p. 62).
- *Diverse development teams*: Minimum 40% representation of women and minorities in AI design teams (p. 65).
- *Student data rights*: Opt-out provisions for algorithmic decision-making (p. 70).

Impact on Teachers and Educational Roles

The introduction of AI in classrooms is changing the traditional roles of teachers. Some fear that AI will replace teachers, while others argue that it can complement them by automating tedious administrative tasks and allowing teachers to focus on more creative and relational aspects of teaching. According to Anderson (2020), AI can enhance teachers' capabilities by providing precise data on student progress and suggesting personalized interventions. For example, an AI system can identify students struggling with a particular concept and recommend additional resources or tailored teaching strategies. This enables teachers to provide more targeted and effective support. However, the use of AI in education requires adequate training for teachers. According to a study by Luckin et al. (2016), many teachers are not prepared to use AI technologies effectively. This can lead to resistance to adopt these technologies and limit their positive impact. Finally, AI raises questions about the added value of human input in the educational process. If AI systems can provide personalized instruction and instant feedback, what is the role of teachers in a modern classroom? According to Selwyn (2019), teachers play a crucial role in providing emotional support and fostering an inclusive and collaborative learning environment. These aspects cannot be replicated by machines.

Privacy and Data Security

The collection and analysis of large amounts of student data raise major concerns about privacy and security. Online learning platforms often collect sensitive data, such as academic performance, learning behaviors, and even student emotions through biometric sensors.

According to a UNESCO report (2019), this data can be vulnerable to privacy breaches and cyberattacks. For example, in 2018, a data leak in a popular educational platform exposed the personal information of millions of students, including their names, email addresses, and academic results. This highlights the need for robust security measures to protect student data.

Furthermore, the use of student data by AI systems raises ethical questions. For instance, data collected by adaptive learning platforms can be used to influence student behavior, such as encouraging them to spend more time on the platform or purchase additional services. This raises concerns about manipulation and exploitation of students.

Finally, it is essential to ensure that student data is used ethically and transparently. According to Anderson (2020), educational institutions must establish clear policies regarding the collection, storage, and use of student data. This includes obtaining informed consent from students and their parents, as well as ensuring that data is not used for commercial purposes without their authorization.

CASE STUDIES AND CONCRETE EXAMPLES

Adaptive Learning Platforms

Adaptive learning platforms use AI to personalize educational content based on individual student performance. Below are two well-documented examples with references:

Khan Academy is an online educational platform offering free courses in a wide range of subjects, from mathematics to history. The platform leverages AI-driven algorithms to monitor student progress and recommend exercises and instructional videos tailored to individual learning needs. For instance, when a student struggles with a particular concept, the system can provide additional resources to reinforce understanding. Empirical evaluations indicate that students who engage consistently with Khan Academy demonstrate measurable improvements in mathematics and science performance compared to peers with lower engagement (Khan Academy Efficacy Study, 2025). These findings highlight the potential of AI-enabled platforms to support personalized learning and improve academic outcomes.

Duolingo is a language-learning application that uses AI algorithms to adapt lessons based on users' progress and preferences. For example, if a user finds a specific type of exercise challenging, the app can adjust the difficulty or provide additional explanations. Vesselinov and Grego (2016) found that 34 hours of using Duolingo is equivalent to a semester of university-level language courses, demonstrating the effectiveness of this approach.

Automated Grading Systems

AI-powered grading tools reduce instructor workload while maintaining accuracy.

Turnitin is a widely used plagiarism detection and automated grading tool in higher education institutions. The system employs natural language processing algorithms to analyze students' work and detect similarities with other texts. In addition to plagiarism detection, Turnitin offers an automated grading system called Gradescope, which enables educators to grade assignments quickly and accurately. According to Barrie et al. (2019), the use of Gradescope reduced grading time by 50% while improving the consistency of evaluations.

E-rater (ETS) is an automated grading system developed by Educational Testing Service (ETS) to evaluate essays in the GRE (Graduate Record Examination). The system uses AI algorithms to assess the structure, grammar, and content of essays. Attali and Burstein (2006) demonstrated that scores assigned by E-rater are strongly correlated with those assigned by human graders, showcasing the reliability of this system.

Educational Chatbots are AI systems designed to interact with students and provide instant support. Below are two examples:

Jill Watson is a chatbot developed by the Georgia Institute of Technology to answer student questions in an online course on AI. The chatbot uses natural language processing algorithms to understand students' questions and provide accurate responses. Goel and Polepeddi (2016) assert that Jill Watson answered over 10,000 questions with a 97% accuracy rate, demonstrating the effectiveness of this technology.

IBM Watson Tutor is an educational chatbot designed to offer personalized support to students. The system uses AI algorithms to analyze students' queries and provide detailed explanations and additional resources. For example, if a student asks about a complex mathematical concept, the chatbot can offer a step-by-step explanation and suggest practice exercises. According to Chen et al. (2020), the use of Watson Tutor improved students' academic performance in several fields, including mathematics and science.

CHALLENGES AND LIMITATIONS OF AI IN EDUCATION

Technological Limitations

Despite significant advances in AI, current technologies still have notable limitations. For example, AI systems often struggle to understand context and nuances in human interactions. This can pose problems in areas such as essay evaluation, where understanding cultural and emotional context is crucial. According to a study by Warschauer and Matuchniak (2010), automated grading systems may misinterpret idiomatic expressions or cultural references, leading to inaccurate assessments. Additionally, AI systems are often limited by the quality and quantity of data available for training. For instance, if the training data for an adaptive learning system is biased or incomplete, the system risks replicating those biases in its recommendations. A study by O'Neil (2016) found that biases in training data can result in discriminatory outcomes, disproportionately affecting marginalized groups. Finally, AI systems often lack flexibility and adaptability. For example, an educational chatbot may be highly effective at answering frequently asked questions but may struggle with complex or unexpected queries. According to a study by Luckin et al. (2016), AI systems need to be continuously updated and improved to remain relevant and effective.

Cultural and Institutional Resistance

The adoption of AI in education can be hindered by cultural and institutional resistance. For instance, many teachers and administrators may be skeptical about the effectiveness and impact of these technologies. According to a study by Selwyn (2019), this resistance may stem from a lack of understanding of AI technologies, concerns about job displacement, or distrust in decisions made by machines. Moreover, educational institutions may face challenges in integrating AI technologies into their existing systems. For example, AI systems often require sophisticated technological infrastructures, such as cloud servers and databases, which may not be available in resource-limited institutions. A study by Zawacki-Richter et al. (2019) noted that integrating AI technologies into existing educational systems may require significant investments of time and resources. Lastly, concerns about the impact of AI on traditional educational values persist. For example, some educators fear that AI could reduce education to a mechanical and dehumanized process, neglecting important aspects such as creativity, critical thinking, and social interactions. According to a study by Biesta (2015), it is essential to ensure that AI technologies are used to complement and enrich education rather than replace it.

Costs and Accessibility

Integrating AI into education can be costly, raising questions about accessibility and equity. For example, AI systems often require substantial investments in hardware, software, and training. According to a study by HolonIQ (2022), the average cost of implementing an AI system in a school can range from $50,000 to $200,000, depending on the project's complexity and scale.

In addition, the costs of maintaining and updating AI systems can be high. For instance, AI algorithms must be continually updated to remain relevant and effective, which requires ongoing investments of time and resources. A study by Zawacki-Richter et al. (2019) highlighted that many educational institutions may lack the resources needed to sustain these costs over the long term. Finally, there are concerns about the accessibility of AI technologies for students and institutions with limited resources. For instance, students from disadvantaged socioeconomic backgrounds may lack access to the necessary technologies to benefit from AI systems, such as computers and high-speed internet connections. According to a study by van Deursen and van Dijk (2019), this digital divide can exacerbate existing inequalities in education, limiting access to the benefits of AI for marginalized groups.

RECOMMENDATIONS FOR RESPONSIBLE AI INTEGRATION

Ethical and Regulatory Frameworks

To ensure the responsible use of AI in education, robust ethical and regulatory frameworks must be established. These frameworks should address key issues such as *transparency*, *accountability*, *fairness*, and *privacy protection*.

- *Transparency*: AI systems must be transparent in their decision-making processes. For instance, algorithms used for automated grading or course recommendations should be explained in a way that is understandable to teachers and students. According to a study by Selbst et al. (2019), transparency is crucial for building trust in AI technologies.
- *Accountability*: Clear accountability must be defined in cases of errors or harm caused by AI systems. For example, if an automated grading system assigns an incorrect grade, mechanisms should be in place to correct the error and determine responsibility. A study by Floridi et al. (2018) emphasizes that accountability should be shared among developers, educational institutions, and end users.
- *Fairness*: AI systems must be designed to avoid biases and promote fairness. For example, the data used to train algorithms should be representative of the diversity of students. According to a study by O'Neil (2016), regular audits of AI systems can help identify and mitigate biases.
- *Privacy protection*: Student data must be safeguarded and used ethically. For example, educational institutions should obtain informed consent from students and their parents before collecting and using their data. A UNESCO (2019) study highlights the need for strict data protection policies to ensure the confidentiality and security of information.

Teacher Training and Awareness

To maximize the benefits of AI in education, it is essential to train and raise awareness among teachers about these technologies.

- *Technical training*: Teachers need to be trained in using AI technologies, including adaptive learning platforms, automated grading systems, and educational chatbots. For instance, workshops and online courses can be organized to teach teachers how to use these tools effectively. According to a study by Luckin et al. (2016), technical training can help teachers integrate AI into their teaching practices.

- *Awareness of ethical issues*: Teachers should also be made aware of the ethical challenges associated with AI, such as algorithmic biases and privacy concerns. For example, seminars and discussions can be organized to explore these issues and share best practices. A study by Selwyn (2019) found that ethical awareness helps teachers use AI responsibly.
- *Continuous support*: Teachers need access to ongoing support to help them troubleshoot issues and improve their skills. For instance, online communities of practice can be created for teachers to share experiences and collaborate on projects. According to a study by Chen et al. (2020), continuous support is critical for maintaining teacher engagement and motivation.

Stakeholder Involvement

Involving stakeholders—including *students, parents,* and *teachers and administrators*—is crucial to ensuring that AI technologies meet real needs and are accepted by the educational community.

- *Students*: Students should be consulted on the design and implementation of AI technologies. For example, surveys and focus groups can be conducted to gather student opinions and suggestions. A study by Williamson (2017) found that student involvement helps create AI systems better tailored to their needs.
- *Parents*: Parents should also be involved in the process to ensure that AI technologies are used ethically and benefit their children. For instance, informational meetings and workshops can be held to explain the benefits and risks of AI. According to a study by Selwyn (2019), collaboration with parents can build trust and promote acceptance of AI technologies.
- *Teachers and administrators*: Teachers and educational administrators should be engaged in the planning and implementation of AI technologies. For example, advisory committees can be formed to involve administrators in key decisions. A study by Zawacki-Richter et al. (2019) highlights that administrator engagement is essential to align AI technologies with educational goals and institutional values.

CONCLUSION

Future Perspectives

In the future, AI will likely continue to play an increasingly significant role in education. However, to maximize its potential, it will be crucial to continue exploring and assessing its impact on educational systems. Here are some future perspectives to consider:

- *Development of more advanced technologies*: Future AI technologies may include systems capable of understanding and responding to students' emotions, offering even more personalized and empathetic support. For instance, ongoing research is focused on developing AI systems that can detect stress or frustration in students and adjust learning content accordingly.
- *Expanding access*: Ensuring that the benefits of AI in education are accessible to all students, including those from disadvantaged backgrounds, will be essential. This could involve initiatives to lower the costs of AI technologies and improve technological infrastructure in resource-limited regions.
- *International collaboration*: Collaboration among countries and educational institutions will be vital to sharing best practices and developing common standards for the use of AI in education. For example, international organizations like UNESCO could play a key role in promoting equity and inclusion in digital education.
- *Ongoing research*: Continuous research is necessary to evaluate the impact of AI on learning outcomes, teaching practices, and educational inequalities. Such research can help identify best practices and guide educational policies.

In conclusion, AI offers exciting opportunities to transform education, but its integration must be approached with caution and responsibility. By establishing ethical frameworks, training teachers, and involving stakeholders, we can ensure that AI technologies are used to promote equity, inclusion, and excellence in education.

REFERENCES

Anderson, J. (2020). *Artificial intelligence in education: Promises and implications.* Springer.

Attali, Y., & Burstein, J. (2006). Automated essay scoring with e-rater® v.2. *Journal of Technology, Learning, and Assessment*, *4*(3). https://ejournals.bc.edu/index.php/jtla/article/view/1650

Baker, R. S., & Inventado, P. S. (2014). Educational data mining and learning analytics. In J. A. Larusson & B. White (Eds.), *Learning analytics* (pp. 61–75). Springer.

Barrie, J., McCredie, M., & Wild, S. (2019). Automated grading and feedback systems in higher education. *Journal of Educational Technology & Society*, *22*(1), 45–60.

BBC News. (2020, August 20). Coronavirus: A-level and GCSE results in England to be based on teacher assessments after algorithm row.

Benjamin, R. (2019). *Race after technology.* Polity Press.

Biesta, G. (2015). *Good education in an age of measurement: Ethics, politics, democracy.* Routledge.

Buolamwini, J., & Gebru, T. (2018). Gender shades: Intersectional accuracy disparities in commercial gender classification. *Proceedings of Machine Learning Research, 81*, 1–15.
Carnegie Learning. (2023). *MATHia software.* https://www.carnegielearning.com
Chen, X., Xie, H., & Hwang, G. J. (2020). A multi-perspective study on artificial intelligence in education: Opportunities, challenges, and future directions. *Journal of Educational Technology & Society, 23*(2), 1–14.
Civitas Learning. (2023). *Student success analytics.* https://www.civitaslearning.com
Crossley, S. A., Bradfield, F., & Bustamante, A. (2019). Using human judgments to examine the validity of automated grammar, syntax, and mechanical errors in writing. *Journal of Writing Research, 11*(2), 251–270.
Duolingo. (2023). *How Duolingo's AI works.* https://blog.duolingo.com/
Eubanks, V. (2018). *Automating inequality: How high-tech tools profile, police, and punish the poor.* St. Martin's Press.
Floridi, L., Cowls, J., Beltrametti, M., Chatila, R., Chazerand, P., Dignum, V., Luetge, C., Madelin, R., Pagallo, U., Rossi, F., Schafer, B., Valcke, P., & Vayena, E. (2018). AI4People – An ethical framework for a good AI society: Opportunities, risks, principles, and recommendations. *Minds and Machines, 28*(4), 689–707. https://doi.org/10.1007/s11023-018-9482-5
Goel, A. K., & Polepeddi, L. (2016). *Jill Watson: A virtual teaching assistant for online education* [Technical report]. Georgia Institute of Technology.
Gradescope. (2023). *AI-assisted grading.* https://www.gradescope.com
Harwell, D. (2021, April 2). Cheating-detection companies made millions during the pandemic. Now students are fighting back. *The Washington Post.* https://www.washingtonpost.com
HolonIQ. (2022). *The global education technology market.* https://www.holoniq.com
IBM. (2023). *Watson Tutor.* https://www.ibm.com/watson
Jackson, P. (2019). *Introduction to Expert Systems* (4th ed.). CRC Press.
Jurafsky, D., & Martin, J. H. (2023). Speech and Language Processing (3rd ed., draft). Stanford University. https://web.stanford.edu/~jurafsky/slp3/
Khan Academy. (2023). *Our mission.* https://www.khanacademy.org
Khan Academy Efficacy Study. (2025). Khan Academy efficacy results: Learning gains associated with platform use. Khan Academy.
Koedinger, K. R., McLaughlin, E. A., & Heffernan, N. T. (2015). Learning factors transfer analysis: Using learning curve analysis to automatically generate domain models. *Proceedings of the Second (2015) ACM Conference on Learning @ Scale*, 269–278. https://doi.org/10.1145/2724660.2724668
Kulik, C. A., & Fletcher, J. D. (2016). Effectiveness of intelligent tutoring systems: A meta-analytic review. *Review of Educational Research, 86*(1), 42–78. https://doi.org/10.3102/0034654315581420
Luckin, R., Holmes, W., Griffiths, M., & Forcier, L. B. (2016). *Intelligence unleashed: An argument for AI in education.* Pearson Education.
Luckin, R., Holmes, W., Griffiths, M., & Forcier, L. B. (2022). AI in Education: Promise and Implications for Teaching and Learning. UCL Knowledge Lab/Centre for Teacher AI.
Mehrabi, N., Morstatter, F., Saxena, N., Lerman, K., & Galstyan, A. (2021). A survey on bias and fairness in machine learning. *ACM Computing Surveys, 54*(6), 1–35. https://doi.org/10.1145/3457607
Noble, S. U. (2018). *Algorithms of oppression: How search engines reinforce racism.* NYU Press.

Noddings, N. (2013). *Caring: A relational approach to ethics and moral education* (2nd ed.). University of California Press.

Obermeyer, Z., Powers, B., Vogeli, C., & Mullainathan, S. (2019). Dissecting racial bias in an algorithm used to manage the health of populations. *Science, 366*(6464), 447–453. https://doi.org/10.1126/science.aax2342

O'Neil, C. (2016). *Weapons of math destruction: How big data increases inequality and threatens democracy.* Crown.

Pane, J. F., Griffin, B. A., McCaffrey, D. F., & Karam, R. (2017). Effectiveness of cognitive tutor algebra I at scale. *Educational Evaluation and Policy Analysis, 39*(1), 59–81.

Russell, S., & Norvig, P. (2020). *Artificial intelligence: A modern approach* (4th ed.). Pearson.

Selbst, A. D., Boyd, D., Friedler, S. A., Venkatasubramanian, S., & Vertesi, J. (2019). Fairness and abstraction in sociotechnical systems. *Proceedings of the Conference on Fairness, Accountability, and Transparency*, 59–68. https://doi.org/10.1145/3287560.3287598

Selwyn, N. (2019). *Should robots replace teachers? AI and the future of education.* Polity Press.

Shermis, M. D., & Hamner, B. (2013). Contrasting state-of-the-art automated scoring of essays. In M. D. Shermis & J. Burstein (Eds.), *Handbook of Automated Essay Evaluation: Current Applications and New Directions.* Routledge.

Strike, K. A., & Soltis, J. F. (2007). *The ethics of teaching* (5th ed.). Teachers College Press.

UNESCO. (2019). *Beijing consensus on artificial intelligence and education.* https://unesdoc.unesco.org

UNESCO. (2021). *Recommendation on the ethics of artificial intelligence.* Adopted by the 41st UNESCO General Conference, 23 November 2021.

van Deursen, A. J. A. M., & van Dijk, J. A. G. M. (2019). The first-level digital divide shifts from inequalities in physical access to inequalities in material access. *New Media & Society, 21*(2), 354–375. https://doi.org/10.1177/1461444818797082

VanLehn, K. (2011). The relative effectiveness of human tutoring, intelligent tutoring systems, and other tutoring systems. *Educational Psychologist, 46*(4), 197–221. https://doi.org/10.1080/00461520.2011.611369

Vesselinov, R., & Grego, J. (2016). *Duolingo effectiveness study.* City University of New York.

Warschauer, M., & Matuchniak, T. (2010). New technology and digital worlds: Analyzing evidence of equity in access, use, and outcomes. *Review of Research in Education, 34*(1), 179–225. https://doi.org/10.3102/0091732X09349791

Williamson, B. (2017). *Big data in education: The digital future of learning, policy and practice.* SAGE.

Zawacki-Richter, O., Marín, V. I., Bond, M., & Gouverneur, F. (2019). Systematic review of research on artificial intelligence applications in higher education. *International Journal of Educational Technology in Higher Education, 16*(1), 1–27. https://doi.org/10.1186/s41239-019-0171-0

Zuboff, S. (2019). *The age of surveillance capitalism: The fight for a human future at the new frontier of power.* PublicAffairs.

PART II

Human resource development and educational leadership for inclusive and equitable AI integration

6. Artificial intelligence and human resource development

Efficiency and equity

Nomita Sharma

INTRODUCTION

The human resources (HR) department of a corporation is in charge of managing day-to-day operations and improving the organization's overall culture. In addition to boosting employee morale, strengthening an HR department may improve its efficacy. However, this process may change from one business to the next, necessitating a range of techniques. This chapter examines human resource development, explains its significance, and offers suggestions on how to improve development processes.

The term "human resource development" at the organizational level refers to the full set of strategies, tools, procedures, processes, and structures utilized by a specific organization to improve the workforce's ability to accomplish its goals Desimone, Werner, and Harris (2002) define human resource development as "a set of systemic and planned activities designed by an organization to provide its members with the opportunities to learn necessary skills to meet current and future job demands" (p. 5). In exchange, this technique improves an organization's overall effectiveness.

Hiring and selection, training and development, performance reviews, and remuneration are among the strategies used by human resource professionals to manage employees. Furthermore, the nature of these techniques has evolved as company settings and workforces become more diverse. As a result, in order to better manage a diverse workforce, human resource professionals must consider diversity while executing any method or plan. The human resources department deals with concerns of inequality in hiring, training, performance appraisals, and incentives (Goodman et al., 2003; Kabongo et al., 2013). Managers have progressively improved the status of equitable job opportunities and fostered creativity in multicultural workforces by utilizing human resource management toolkits.

Workplaces are changing dramatically; communities are growing more diverse and global; and digitization is changing behavior and knowledge. In the era of expanding global capitalism and lucrative developments in the economic environment, talent management has become one of the main goals for all commercial entities. The quality of a company's human capital determines how well it does, and methods for enhancing those resources can increase staff capabilities. By examining several theoretical and empirical studies, this chapter aims to provide an examination of the relationship between HRD efficiency and equity using artificial intelligence. Therefore, the study focuses on the following research topics:

1. How does artificial intelligence fit into the core HRD tasks of today?
2. What effects does AI have on equity and efficiency in HRD?
3. How does the integration of artificial intelligence into HRD impact HRD theory and practice? What are some of the main outcomes of this integration?

TECHNOLOGY AND HRD EFFICIENCY AND EQUITY

Given how technology affects various industries and improves performance, instructional technologies could support the training and development duties of HRD (Barlett, 2008). Swanson and Holton (2009) conceptualized three levels of technology for HRD: IT and HRD, which emphasizes the decentralization of HRD activities in the workforce; application-oriented technology that provides HRD activities (workforce technology); and process-oriented technology that explains job-specific tasks and skills to enhance performance output. Internet technologies (IT) have a broad, complex, and pervasive influence on our society. Amazon has altered how we purchase goods, Facebook has altered how we communicate with others, and learning technology has fundamentally altered how we learn. Digital devices have also infiltrated the workplace and transformed the way work is done. Technology has long been a driving force behind organizational changes, including those pertaining to HRD. Cloud-based work systems, virtual teams, and telecommuting are examples of innovative work practices that have resulted from IT breakthroughs that have kept up with the times. These strategies have allowed businesses to hire skilled and bright individuals from all around the world. The management, evaluation, and development of an increasingly diverse and dispersed workforce present significant challenges for HRD.

Technological innovation has unquestionably been credited with creating opportunities for performance improvement by achieving more efficacy and efficiency for both individuals and businesses. According to a Pew Research study (Purcell & Rainie, 2014), the majority of American workers (n = 1,066) who took part in the survey stated that although IT has given them more freedom, it has also caused them to work longer hours. According to Purcell and Rainie (2014), a significant majority of them believed that technology has increased their productivity. The ability of both individuals and organizations to embrace and adjust to new workplace technology has improved. HRD professionals are responsible for adopting and leading this IT-focused organizational change.

Automation and artificial intelligence (AI) are bringing forth a new era of opportunities and challenges that is changing many industries, including human resource development (Wilson & Daugherty, 2018; Bennett, 2022). HRD has undergone a paradigm shift as a result of the introduction of AI and automation technologies. It has forced an examination of long-standing procedures and methods. Because of its revolutionary potential, the use of these state-of-the-art technologies in HRD is generally praised (Bhatt & Muduli, 2023; Stone et al., 2015). By encouraging fairness and inclusivity in the workplace, technology is revolutionizing human resource development. Fair compensation, equal access to learning and development, and a reduction in hiring prejudice are all made possible by HR technologies, such as artificial intelligence (AI) and data analytics. Organizations can establish a more inclusive and equitable workplace by utilizing these resources. Bias in recruiting and promotion has decreased due to technology. Applications and resumes can be analyzed by AI-powered technologies, which can detect and lessen unconscious bias during the first screening step. Instead of depending only on traditional qualifications, candidates might be evaluated based on their talents through the use of skills-based exams and interview procedures. Promotions can be tracked by automated methods, which also guarantee that opportunities are allocated equitably to all employee groups.

METHODOLOGY

In order to examine the literature on automation and AI in HRD, this systematic review followed guidelines for Preferred Reporting Items for Systematic Reviews and Meta-Analyses (PRISMA) (Liberati et al., 2009; Moher et al., 2010). For conducting systematic reviews, the PRISMA framework provides an organized technique that guarantees thorough coverage and scientific rigor. It provides a clear and reproducible proposition to analyze the previous research by directing the methodical gathering, analysis, and synthesis of the literature (Moher et al., 2010). This paradigm is especially useful for compiling and assessing research that deals with the complex issues of technology in HRD. On the other hand, because it offers an organized method of analyzing the relationship between HRD and technology results in many contexts of organizations. This method also aids in determining the ways in which technology influences HRD procedures and results. Additionally, it aids in identifying potential barriers and facilitators in diverse organizational settings (Denyer et al., 2008). Variables such as eligibility requirements, identification of information sources, selecting pertinent research, data extraction, evaluating research quality, synthesizing data, and evaluating and interpreting the results are all parts of the review process.

Eligibility Standard

Research documents that specifically looked at how automation and artificial intelligence affect strategic HRD functions were considered in this evaluation. They also looked at the opportunities and problems that come with automating and using AI to change HRD procedures. These studies provide insight into how HRD professionals' roles are changing in the modern world. Empirical studies that are both qualitative and quantitative as well as non-empirical like book chapters and reviews were included in the studies. These studies explicitly looked at the impact of automation and artificial intelligence on HRD including how they affect HRD procedures such as skill development, employee happiness, and organizational effectiveness. Research that failed to address these subjects or publications that are not available in English were not included.

Literature Search Strategies

To find pertinent research on automation and artificial intelligence in human resource development, a thorough search strategy was created. The use of important phrases associated with human resource development, artificial intelligence, and automation through Boolean operators "AND" and "OR" were searched in databases like Web of Science, Scopus, Google Scholar, and Semantic Scholar. The terms "artificial intelligence," "machine learning," "automation," "human resource development," "equity," "efficiency," "talent management," "workforce upskilling," "employee development," "workforce development," "knowledge management," "workforce planning," and "learning and development" were included in the search. The keywords, theoretical concepts, and publications published in the year range of 1997 to 2023 were the main focus in the search. To find other research that satisfied the inclusion requirements, the reference lists of pertinent publications were also examined. This iterative search approach ensured that as many relevant papers were taken into consideration and increased the review's comprehensiveness.

Selecting Studies, Extracting Data, and Evaluating Quality

Studies were chosen after a rigorous full-text evaluation based on predetermined qualifying criteria, which included a study of the titles and abstracts. A carefully crafted data extraction form was used to gather the data that was taken out of the studies. The authors, the year of publication, the study design, and the main themes covered were all included in this form. The data extraction procedure was carried out methodically and thoroughly, guaranteeing precision and consistency in the information that was extracted. This made it possible to conduct a thorough examination of the ways in which automation and artificial intelligence are applied in HRD, including the elements that impact their uptake, the processes that propel them, and the results they produce.

Summary of the Included Research

After refining the search terms, the number of items from the initial search—1,074—dropped to 1,000. This was further reduced to 74, of which 35 were eliminated following abstract and title screening and 39 satisfied the inclusion requirements. The critical appraisal skills program (CASP) checklist was used to evaluate the included papers' quality, yielding a final 39 number of the papers sample for the review. The final research documents came from 25 peer-reviewed journals, one conference paper, nine books, and four online sources. The research papers are from journals such as *Human Resource Development Review*, *Safety Science*, *Journal of Enterprise Information Management*, etc. (see Table 6.1)

SYNTHESIS AND ANALYSIS OF DATA

This chapter synthesizes the results from the included studies using a method of narrative synthesis (Popay et al., 2017). The ability of a narrative synthesis approach to logically combine many methodological findings and provide a comprehensive understanding of the intricate phenomena being studied was the primary factor in its selection. Finding voids, themes, and patterns within the research documents is made easier using this method, which makes it possible to combine data from many research documents, including both quantitative and qualitative research (Lisy & Porritt, 2016; Popay et al., 2017).

Table 6.1 Summary of research documents

S.No.	Author	Year of publication	Type of publication (e.g., peer-reviewed journal, conference paper, book, online document)	Study design (where applicable)	Main themes
1.	C. Ravanera & S. Kaplan	2021	Online document	N.A.	Artificial intelligence and equity
2.	A. Schosser	2024	Online document	N.A.	AI and HRM
3.	O. Itsese	2003	Journal	Case study	Study and survival of Nigerian economy
4.	J.S. Goodman et al.	2003	Journal	Exploratory	Organization, woman status
5.	J.D. Kabongo et al.	2013	Journal	Empirical study	
6.	J. Barlett	2008	Journal	Solomon four group design	Technology in HRM
7.	E.F. Holton & R.A. Swanson	2011	Online document	N.A.	Foundations of HRD
8.	K. Purcell & L. Rainie	2014	Online document	N.A.	Impact of technology on workers.
9.	E.E. Bennett	2022	Book	N.A.	Leveraging HRD
10.	H.J. Wilson & P.R. Daugherty	2018	Journal	Descriptive	Human and AI
11.	P. Bhatt & A. Muduli	2023	Journal	Descriptive	AI for learning

S.No.	Author	Year of publication	Type of publication (e.g., peer-reviewed journal, conference paper, book, online document)	Study design (where applicable)	Main themes
12.	D.L. Stone et al.	2015	Journal	Review	Technology and HRM
13.	R.A. Noe	2020	Book	N.A.	Employee training
14.	J.G. Ruiz et al.	2006	Journal	Review	Impact of E-learning
15.	E. Salas et al.	2012	Journal	Review	T&D in organizations
16.	J.H. Marler & S.L. Fisher	2013	Journal	Investigative	e-HRM and strategic HRM
17.	T.H. Davenport & J. Kirby	2016	Book	N.A.	Smart machines
18.	T. Davenport et al.	2020	Journal	Explorative	AI & Marketing
19.	A. Agarwal	2022	Journal	Descriptive	AI & HRM
20.	S. Agarwal et al.	2023	Book	N.A.	AI & HRM
21.	D. Denyer et al.	2008	Journal	Explorative	Design propositions
22.	A. Liberati et al.	2009	Journal	Review	PRISMA statement
23.	D. Moher et al.	2010	Journal	Review	PRISMA statement
24.	J. Popay et al.	2017	Book	N.A.	Narrative synthesis
25.	K. Lisy & K. Porritt	2016	Journal	Explorative	Narrative synthesis
26.	B. Sivathanu & R. Pillai	2020	Journal	Investigative	Technology and talent analytics
27.	E.T. Albert	2019	Journal	Review	AI applications in HR

S.No.	Author	Year of publication	Type of publication (e.g., peer-reviewed journal, conference paper, book, online document)	Study design (where applicable)	Main themes
28.	S. Jose	2019	Journal	Descriptive	Innovation in HRM
29.	A. Hemalatha et al.	2021	Book	Descriptive	Impact of AI
30.	T. Karaboˇga	2023	Book	Review based	Industry 4.0 and talent management
31.	J. Huang et al.	2021	Journal	Review based	AI in education
32.	E. Brynjolfsson et al.	2021	Journal	Descriptive	IT and digitisation
33.	S. Kim	2022	Journal	Descriptive	HRD & robot interaction
34.	J.C. Meister & K. Wiiyerd	2021	Book	N.A.	Innovation at workplace
35.	T.L. Mamela et al.	2020	Conference	N.A.	AI, big data, computing
36.	S. Bhattacharya	2021	Book	N.A.	AI in talent management
36.	Y. Qamar et al.	2021	Journal	-	Technology & people
37.	W. Tarken	2019		N.A.	Measurement of HR performance
38.	Wang et al.	2020	Article	N.A.	AI in health safety
39.	E.W.T. Ngai et al.	2020	Journal	Thematic analysis	AI applications

Note: HRM is the process of recruiting, selecting, training and compensating the employees of an organization.

Findings

The synthesis of the findings offers a number of important new perspectives on how automation and AI fit into HRD. The findings imply that automation and artificial intelligence (AI) have the potential to greatly enhance HRD procedures and results. This might revolutionize the way businesses handle their human capital. The search process is presented in Figure 6.1. Figure 6.2 shows different sources of research covered in the chapter. Figure 6.3 presents the different journals referred to in the study. Most of the papers were considered from Human Resource Development Review. Figure 6.4 describes the year of publication considered in the study. Most of the research papers are from 2021.

Artificial Intelligence and HRD Efficiency and Equity

This section looks at how automation and AI have been integrated into knowledge management, best practices, trends, and patterns that guide future development, as well as learning, performance management, talent development, and workforce planning. Examining how these technologies are used in these vital HRD tasks will reveal how AI and automation are used. The integration of technology in HRD is a growing field with origins in earlier technological developments.

Computer-based training systems initially took the role of conventional, instructor-led education techniques in the 1960s and 1970s (Noe, 2020). The introduction of the internet in the 1990s allowed employees to participate in learning and development in a more flexible and useful way (Ruiz et al., 2006). The emergence of Web 2.0 technologies in the early 2000s sparked yet another shift, paving the way for social learning platforms, collaborative learning environments, and online communities of practice (Salas et al., 2012). This democratization of education allowed for richer, more engaging experiences, expanding the scope of HRD (Marler & Fisher, 2013). Examples of recent advancements that aid in the creation of a highly personalized and engaging enriched environment include immersion technology and mobile learning tools like augmented and virtual reality (Wilson & Daugherty, 2018).

Smooth transitioning of automation and AI into HRD ushers in a new era in the development of the discipline. These technologies are employed in a range of HRD activities, such as learning and development, talent development and management, and workforce planning, claim Agarwal et al. (2023). For example, in learning and development, automation and AI are transforming the identification and meeting of learning needs through analysis of data pattern recognition.

AI algorithms also use machine learning and natural language processing to evaluate employee input in order to find pertinent information regarding skill gaps among employees and particular learning needs (Agarwal et al., 2023). In order to ensure that every employee receives training that they understand, the application of AI in the human resources domain allows for a customized

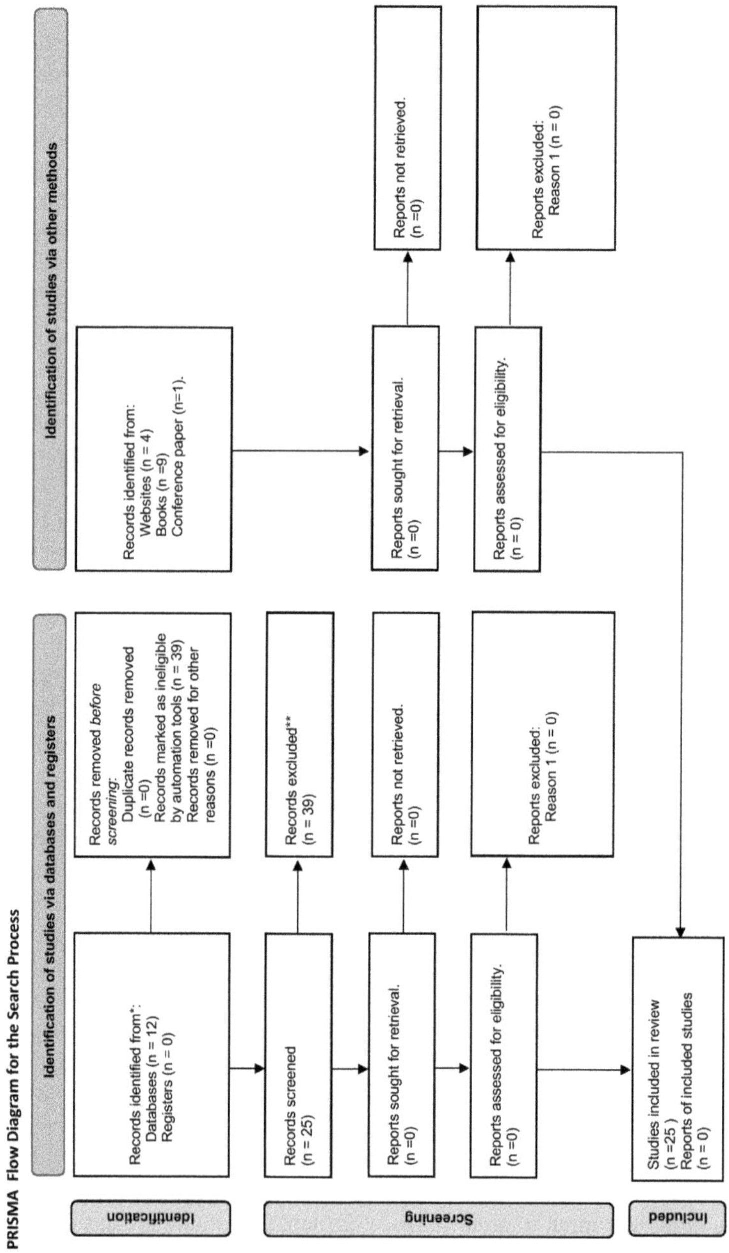

Figure 6.1 *Search process*

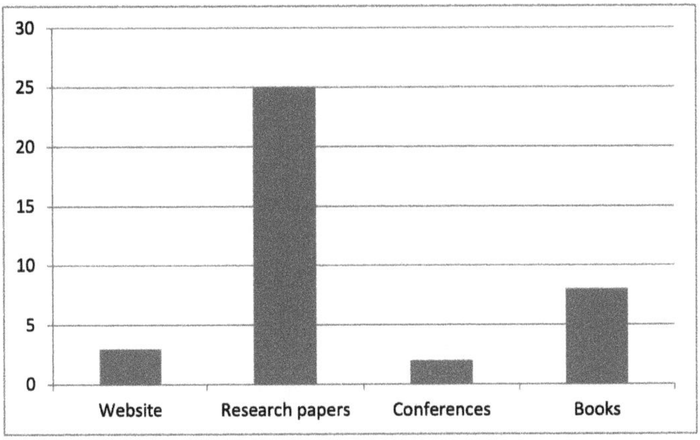

Figure 6.2 *Sources of research covered*

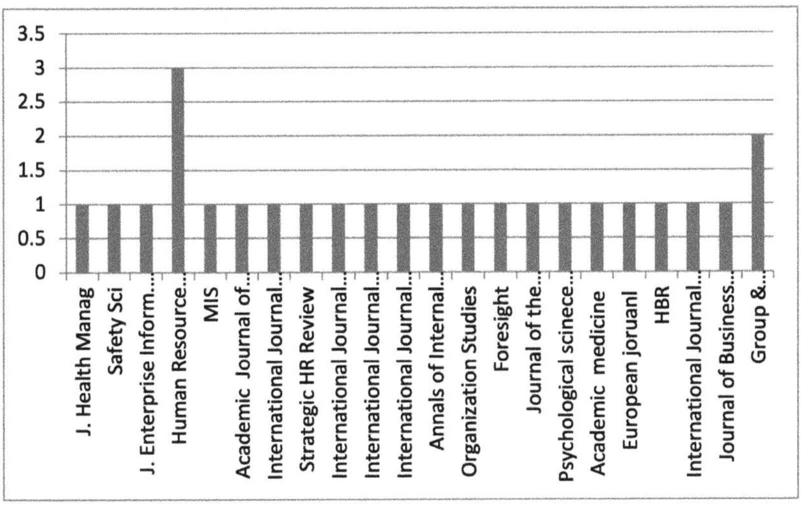

Figure 6.3 *Journals referred to in the study*

learning experience and assists in identifying skill gaps through analytics. In people management and development, AI serves two purposes: it gathers and assesses performance indicators and forecasts trends, enabling preemptive actions (Davenport & Kirby, 2016; Davenport et al., 2020). AI-powered predictive analytics not only assists human resource managers with talent

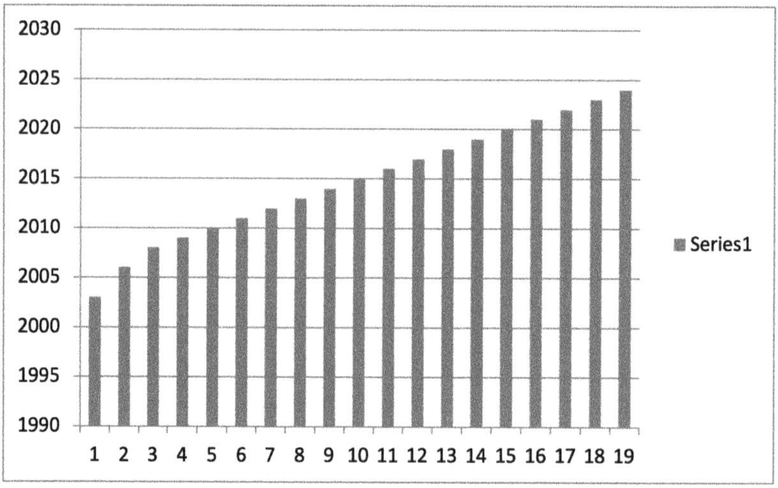

Figure 6.4 *Years of publication considered in the study*

management, but it also helps with workforce planning. In an agile organization, HR still manages hiring, development, performance management, and other HR responsibilities, but using agile methodologies. HR agility consists of three components: (1) the ability to quickly and efficiently identify issues that need attention, (2) the ability to reduce the time needed to develop and implement a response, and (3) the integration of design and analysis thinking to predict, plan, and target programs with the highest chance of success (Tarken, 2019; Qamar et al., 2021).

AI in Training and Learning

Predictive analytics and personalized learning systems are two AI-driven technologies that help find the best talent and provide more insightful data (Karaboğa, 2023). Features of AI, including machine vision, natural language processing, automation, and augmentation, have a big influence on personnel management procedures and can result in higher productivity as well as time and cost savings, Hemalatha et al. (2021) claim. Tasks like training and evaluation can also be streamlined with AI and automation (Albert, 2019; Jose, 2019). Together, the documents show how automation and AI are revolutionizing education by offering individualized, data-based learning opportunities. To provide employees with individualized and enriching experiences, these technologies make use of adaptive learning platforms and intelligent tutoring systems (Huang et al., 2021). By identifying individual learning preferences and styles, closely tracking progress, and offering personalized information and recommendations, utilizing automation and AI has the ability to improve the experience of learning. This increases employee engagement and improves information retention in addition to producing better learning results (Sivathanu & Pillai, 2020).

AI for customization and flexibility

Because AI-driven tools are personalized and adaptable, HRD professionals can tailor solutions to each individual employee's needs (Huang et al., 2021). This is seen in learning and development, where employees can use adaptive learning systems that provide customized learning experiences to reach their maximum potential. Brynjolfsson et al.'s (2021) major argument is that automation and artificial intelligence (AI) can improve HRD by utilizing the vital mechanisms of flexibility and personalization. More effective and engaging learning experiences brought about by personalization can result in better skill development and improved employee satisfaction (Kim, 2022).

AI for better decision-making

Businesses can make informed, fact-based decisions because of AI and automation for HRD processes (Meister & Willyerd, 2021). Executives can gain a deeper understanding into workforce trends, expertise advancement, employee performance, and engagement through the use of predictive modeling and analytics powered by AI. They are able to make strategic decisions with confidence and effectiveness by utilizing real-time data (Mamela et al., 2020).

Workplace safety and health improvements

The detection and avoidance of workplace dangers can be aided by the application of AI in HR. AI-powered systems analyze data from various sources, such as sensors, cameras, and other devices, to detect potential workplace risks. With the use of this information, workers may operate in a safer environment (Wang, 2020). AI can also be used to help detect health risks. For example, AI-powered solutions can monitor employee health data and identify any patterns that might indicate health issues. With the use of this information, employees can obtain personalized health recommendations and prevent future health problems (Ngai et al., 2020).

Influence of AI on HRD Efficiency and Equity

According to the review, better organizational performance and an application of artificial intelligence in HRD are positively correlated (Brynjolfsson et al., 2021). AI-powered human resource procedures can assist businesses in streamlining a number of HRD tasks, which will boost output and improve hiring and training of personnel (Bhattacharya, 2021). AI-driven HRD processes have advantages beyond decision-making, productivity, and hiring and developing personnel. By offering individualized learning and development opportunities, implementing AI tools can increase engagement and retention of employees (Alqahtani et al., 2022). By removing bias from hiring and performance management procedures, AI can assist firms in advancing diversity, equity, and inclusion (Coombs et al., 2020). Huang et al.'s (2021) study demonstrates the encouraging possibilities of AI-powered solutions. Employee dedication, motivation, and general job satisfaction can all be improved by these changes (Shao & Shi, 2020). It is critical to take into account the possible negative effects of AI-driven performance management, such as increased levels of stress and crucial issues (Chamorro-Premuzic et al., 2019). This crucial discussion centers on the potential for AI-powered HRD tools to raise employee satisfaction while acknowledging the potential risks associated with these technologies. In addition to enhancing the workforce in general, AI and automation are altering the skill set needed by HRD professionals. Recent research indicates that because of the combination of these technologies, HRD practitioners today must possess exceptional change management skills, develop a solid understanding of data analysis, and understand the applications of artificial intelligence. To effectively lead digital transformation in firms, certain abilities are required (Kim, 2022).

IMPLICATIONS OF THE STUDY

For lawmakers and HRD professionals wishing to employ automation and artificial intelligence (AI) to improve HRD procedures, this systematic review offers a number of useful ramifications. It provides logical insights into how automation and artificial intelligence are being adopted and how they affect the HRD landscape. In particular, the research emphasizes how important it is for businesses to do thorough evaluations of their preparedness for implementing automation and artificial intelligence. These assessments need to examine a wide range of elements, such as organizational culture, worker competencies, and current technology infrastructures. A diversified approach is necessary to minimize potential obstacles and maximize beneficial results. Fostering an atmosphere that is favorable to AI and automation is not only a technical improvement but rather a whole organizational transformation (Harrison et al., 2020; Meister & Willyerd, 2021).

LIMITATIONS OF THE STUDY

The analysis revealed a number of gaps in the study of AI and HRD that need more research because they haven't been adequately covered in this review or the body of current literature. For instance, the body of research examining the long-term effects of automation and artificial intelligence on HRD procedures and results is currently severely lacking in longitudinal studies. While current research provides some insight into the short-term effects of these technologies on HRD, more thorough and time-based study is desperately needed to properly grasp the long-term effects of AI and automation on HRD practices and the labor market as a whole. This would provide a more thorough comprehension of the evolution and sustainability of AI-driven HRD initiatives.

CONCLUSION

This chapter shows that the application of artificial intelligence improves the potential of human resources and also elevates productivity levels. It emphasizes how AI can enhance HRD effectiveness, flexibility, and decision-making based on data while highlighting the significance of organizational culture, moral principles, and competencies. With the help of the PRISMA methodology, the paper examines the many uses of AI in HRD, pointing out possible advantages like improved output and worker happiness while also recognizing hazards like job loss and moral dilemmas. Given the increasing impact of AI in human resources, the findings provide a basis for further research aimed at expanding understanding of the relationship between technology, labor, and human growth. Organizations can sustainably leverage the advantages of technology in HRD processes by having expertise, which is essential for effectively navigating the ever-changing work and technological world.

REFERENCES

Albert, E. T. (2019). AI in talent acquisition: A review of AI-applications used in recruitment and selection. *Strategic HR Review, 18*(5), 215–221.

Alqahtani M., Alqahtani K., Aksoy M. S. (2022). The role of artificial intelligence and information technology in promoting knowledge management in business firms: a review. SSRN. 2022. http://dx.doi.org/10.2139/ssrn.4109705.

Agarwal, A. (2022). AI adoption by human resource management: a study of its antecedents and impact on HR system effectiveness. *Foresight, 25*(1), 67–81.

Agarwal, S., Gupta, A., & Roshani, P. (2023). Redefining HRM with artificial intelligence and machine learning. In *The adoption and effect of artificial intelligence on human resources managemen*t (Part A, p. 113). Emerald Publishing Limited.

Barlett, J. (2008). Instructional technologies in human resource development: Impact, models, and changes. *International Journal of Instructional Technology & Distance Learning*, *5*, 51–65.

Bennett, E. E. (2022). Leveraging technology to design and deliver human resource development. In *The Emerald handbook of work, workplaces and disruptive issues in HRM* (pp. 261–276). Emerald Publishing Limited.

Bhatt, P., & Muduli, A. (2023). Artificial intelligence in learning and development: A systematic literature review. *European Journal of Training and Development*, *47*(7/8), 677–694.

Bhattacharya, S. (2021). AI in talent management for business excellence. In *Industry 4.0 technologies for business excellence* (pp. 255–266). CRC Press. Retrieved from: https://www.taylorfrancis.com/chapters/edit/10.1201/9781003140474-15/ai-talent-management-business-excellence-subhajit-bhattacharya

Brynjolfsson, E., Wang, C., & Zhang, X. (2021). The economics of IT and digitization: Eight questions for research. *MIS Quarterly*, *45*(1), 473–477.

Chamorro-Premuzic, T., Polli, F., & Dattner, B. (2019). Building ethical AI for talent management. *Harvard Business Review*, *21*(November), 1–15.

Coombs, C., Hislop, D., Taneva, S. K., & Barnard, S. (2020). The strategic impacts of intelligent automation for knowledge and service work: An interdisciplinary review. *Journal of Strategic Information Systems*, *29*(4), Article 101600.

Davenport, T. H., & Kirby, J. (2016). *Only humans need apply: Winners and losers in the age of smart machines*, 1–281. Harper Business.

Davenport, T., Guha, A., Grewal, D., & Bressgott, T. (2020). How artificial intelligence will change the future of marketing. *Journal of the Academy of Marketing Science*, *48*, 24–42.

Denyer, D., Tranfield, D., & van Aken, J. E. (2008). Developing design propositions through research synthesis. *Organization Studies*, *29*(3), 393–413. Retrieved from: https://doi.org/10.1177/0170840607088020

Desimone, R. L. Werner, J. M., & Harris, D. M. (2002). *Human resource development. (3rd ed.)* Harcourt College Publishers.

Goodman, J. S., Fields, D. L., & Blum, T. C. (2003). Cracks in the glass ceiling: In what kinds of organizations do women make it to the top? *Group & Organization Management*, *28*(4), 475–501.

Harrison, P., Nichol, L., & Gold, J. (2020). Redefining HRD roles and practice in the machine learning revolution. In *The future of HRD, volume I: Innovation and technology* (pp. 143-166). Cham: Springer International Publishing.

Hemalatha, A., Kumari, P. B., Nawaz, N., & Gajenderan, V. (2021, July 10). Impact of artificial intelligence on recruitment and selection of information technology companies. In *2021 International Conference on Artificial Intelligence and Smart Systems (ICAIS)* (pp. 60–66). IEEE. Retrieved from: https://doi.org/10.1109/ICAIS50930.2021.9396036

Holton III, E. F., & Swanson, R. A. (2011, December 1). *Foundations of human resource development.* Retrieved from: https://lsms.ac/wp-content/uploads/2023/02/18.pdf

Huang, J., Saleh, S., & Liu, Y. (2021). A review on artificial intelligence in education. *Academic Journal of Interdisciplinary Studies*, *10*(3), 206–206.

Jose, S. (2019). Innovation in recruitment and talent acquisition: A study on technologies and strategies adopted for talent management in IT sector. *International Journal of Marketing & Human Resource Management*, *10*(3), 1–8.

Kabongo, J. D., Chang, K., & Li, Y. (2013). The impact of operational diversity on corporate philanthropy: An empirical study of US companies. *Journal of Business Ethics*, *116*, 49–65.

Karaboğa, T. (2023). The impact of industry 4.0 on talent management practices: A systematic review. In *Leadership perspectives on effective intergenerational communication and management*, 53–71. IGI Global. Retrieved from: https://doi.org/10.4018/978-1-6684-6140-2.ch004

Kim, S. (2022). Working with robots: Human resource development considerations in human robot interaction. *Human Resource Development Review*, *21*(1), 48–74.

Liberati, A., Altman, D. G., Tetzlaff, J., Mulrow, C., Gøtzsche, P. C., Ioannidis, J. P., Clarke, M., Devereaux, P. J., Kleijnen, J., & Moher, D. (2009). The PRISMA statement for reporting systematic reviews and meta-analyses of studies that evaluate health care interventions: Explanation and elaboration. *Annals of Internal Medicine*, *151*(4), 65.

Lisy, K., & Porritt, K. (2016). Narrative synthesis: Considerations and challenges. *International Journal of Evidence-Based Healthcare*, *14*(4), 201.

Mamela, T. L., Sukdeo, N., & Mukwakungu, S. C. (2020, August 6–7). The integration of AI on workforce performance for a South African Banking Institution. In *2020 International Conference on Artificial Intelligence, Big Data, Computing and Data Communication Systems.*

Marler, J. H., & Fisher, S. L. (2013). An evidence-based review of e-HRM and strategic human resource management. *Human Resource Management Review*, *23*(1), 18–36.

Meister, J. C., & Willyerd, K. (2021). *The 2020 workplace: How innovative companies attract, develop, and keep tomorrow's employees today.* HarperCollins Publishers Inc.

Moher, D., Liberati, A., Tetzlaff, J., & Altman, D. G., PRISMA Group. (2010). Preferred reporting items for systematic reviews and meta-analyses: The PRISMA statement. *International Journal of Surgery*, *8*(5), 336–341.

Ngai E. W. T., Chan T. K. H., & Moon K. K. L. (2020). Artificial intelligence applications in healthcare: A thematic analysis. *Journal of Health Management*, *22*(2), 220–234.

Noe, R. A. (2020). *Employee training and development.* McGraw-Hill.

Popay, J., Roberts, H., Sowden, A., Petticrew, M., Arai, L., Rodgers, M., Britten, N., Roen, K., & Duffy, S. (2017). *Guidance on the conduct of narrative synthesis in systematic reviews: A product from the ESRC methods programme.* Institute for Health Research.

Purcell, K., & Rainie, L. (2014, December 1). *Technology's impact on workers.* Retrieved from: https://www.pewresearch.org/internet/2014/12/30/technologys-impact-on-workers/

Qamar Y., Agrawal R. K., Samad T. A., & Jabbour C. J. C. (2021). When technology meets people: The interplay of artificial intelligence and human resource management. *Journal of Enterprise Information Management, 34* (5), 1339–1370.

Ravanera, C. & Kaplan,S. (2021, July 10). *An equity lens on artificial intelligence.* Retrieved from: https://www.gendereconomy.org/artificial-intelligence/

Salas, E., Tannenbaum, S. I., Kraiger, K., & Smith-Jentsch, K. A. (2012). The science of training and development in organizations: What matters in practice. *Psychological Science in the Public Interest*, *13*(2), 74–101.

Shao, Y., & Shi, W. (2020). Artificial intelligence (AI) and human resource development. In *4th International Conference on Education, Management and Social Science (EMSS 2020) Proceedings* (pp. 126–133). Clausius Scientific Press.

Ruiz, J. G., Mintzer, M. J., & Leipzig, R. M. (2006). The impact of e-learning in medical education. *Academic Medicine, 81*(3), 207–212.

Sivathanu, B., & Pillai, R. (2020). Technology and talent analytics for talent Management – a game changer for organizational performance. *International Journal of Organizational Analysis, 28*(2), 457–473.

Stone, D. L., Deadrick, D. L., Lukaszewski, K. M., & Johnson, R. (2015). The influence of technology on the future of human resource management. *Human Resource Management Review, 25*(2), 216–231.

Swanson, R.A. & Holton, E.F. (2009). *Foundations of human resource development (2nd. Ed.).* Berrett-Koehler, San Francisco.

Tarken W. (2019, February 4). *How to measure your agile HR operating performance?* Retrieved from: https://www.linkedin.com/pulse/how-measure-your-agile-hr-operating-performance-tarken-sphr-csm/.

Wang L., Li Y., Du J., & Huang X. (2020). An Artificial Intelligence-enabled health and safety management system for industry 4.0. *Safety Science, 124*, Article 104618.

Wilson, H. J., & Daugherty, P. R. (2018). Collaborative intelligence: Humans and AI are joining forces. *Harvard Business Review, 96*(4), 114–123.

7. AI for educational inclusion and equity

Academic leadership and policy for ethical integration in the Global South

Michael M. van Wyk

INTRODUCTION

Studies reported that artificial intelligence (AI) for "educational inclusion and equity" is an enabler for a transformative agenda for the future of the Global South higher education—one where AI is harnessed to bridge gaps rather than widen them (Domínguez et al., 2025; Guerrero, 2024). It is argued that since the "hype" of generative AI, and possible the potential of AI to create more inclusive and equitable learning environments could change perceptions for inclusion and equity. With reference to South African students who have historically been marginalised due to socioeconomic status, disability, language barriers, or geographic isolation, for which inclusion is an option for a transformative agenda (Chopra et al., 2024; Dewa, 2024). Semantically, inclusion in higher education means ensuring that every student has access to meaningful learning opportunities regardless of their background or abilities. Moreover, AI can support this by offering personalised learning experiences tailored to individual needs. For example, adaptive learning platforms can adjust the content difficulty in real-time, while speech-to-text tools can assist students with hearing impairments or learning disabilities (Chopra et al., 2024; Kharbat et al., 2021; Salawa et al., 2024).

Equity, on the other hand, goes beyond equal access—it involves providing the specific resources and support each student needs to succeed. AI can help identify learning gaps early through data analytics, enabling timely interventions. It can also democratise access to high-quality educational content, especially in under-resourced schools or remote areas.

However, the argument invites critical reflection on these constructs for AI to be inclusive and equitable in Global South higher education institutions, which seems to be a concern. Therefore, academic leadership show "leadership tenacity" and reliance on creating opportunities to address inclusiveness and equity. For AI to truly serve inclusion and equity, it must be designed and implemented with fairness, transparency, and cultural sensitivity. Bias in algorithms, lack of access to digital infrastructure, and data privacy concerns are real challenges that must be addressed. Ultimately, "AI for Educational Inclusion and Equity" is not just a technological proposition—it is a call to action for university management, academics, policymakers, and technologists to collaborate in shaping an educational future where every learner has the opportunity to thrive.

Despite the growing potential of AI to transform education, its integration in the Global South remains uneven, often exacerbating existing inequalities rather than alleviating them. While AI tools can support personalised learning, improve access, and enhance educational outcomes, their deployment frequently lacks ethical oversight, contextual relevance, and inclusive design. Academic institutions and policymakers in the Global South face significant challenges, including limited digital infrastructure, insufficient regulatory frameworks, and a lack of capacity to guide AI adoption in ways that prioritise equity and inclusion. Moreover, there is a critical gap in academic leadership and policy direction to ensure AI technologies are implemented ethically and effectively within diverse educational contexts. For example, a newspaper article by Rebecca Davis (2025, p. 5) reported:

> Now, they face an insidious new challenge: across the country, students use ChatGPT and other ever-more-sophisticated large language models (LLMs) to generate essays, solve assignments, and cheat their way through their degrees. The institutions are scrambling for ways either to stop them or to turn their use of AI into a positive academic tool.

This newspaper article stressed that South African university students used AI technologies to write assignments, research papers, and online tasks. Without deliberate and informed leadership, the promise of AI risks reinforcing systemic disparities rather than addressing them. This research seeks to address this gap by examining how academic leadership and policy can shape the ethical integration of AI to promote educational inclusion and equity across the Global South.

Based on this view, specific initiatives emerged in AI in the Global South higher education, particularly within the South African context. The digital divide and historical inequalities in South African higher education remain a significant challenge for the Department of Higher Education and Training (DHET). To address this challenge of inclusion and equity, the DHET aligns with national priorities such as the G20 Task Team on Digitalisation

Transformation to address the digital divide and data privacy, the National Development Plan 2030, the White Paper on Post-School Education and Training, and global frameworks like UNESCO's AI and Education guidelines. In the context of the South African higher education space, this prompted a critical examination of the role of academic leadership and policy frameworks in guiding the ethical integration of AI for educational inclusion and equity in the Global South.

This chapter selects a multiple case study approach to examine institutional policies and guidelines to understand how leadership practices influence the ethical and inclusive implementation of AI in educational settings. The case study research investigates current policies and practices, identifies barriers and opportunities, and proposes strategic recommendations for fostering inclusive AI-driven educational ecosystems aligned with the Global South's unique socioeconomic and infrastructural contexts.

LITERATURE REVIEW

Global Perspectives on AI and Educational Equity

AI has emerged as a transformative force in education, offering tools for personalised learning, predictive analytics, and administrative efficiency. Globally, AI is being leveraged to address disparities in access and learning outcomes, particularly in underserved communities. UNESCO emphasises the importance of ethical AI integration to support Sustainable Development Goal 4 (SDG 4), which advocates for inclusive and equitable quality education (Dewa, 2024; Stirling & McGloin, 2015). Studies from the Global North highlight the potential of AI to support differentiated instruction, assist learners with disabilities, and reduce teacher workload. However, concerns persist regarding algorithmic bias, data privacy, and the reinforcement of existing inequalities when AI systems are trained on non-representative datasets.

South African Context: Challenges and Opportunities

In South Africa, the integration of AI in education is still in its nascent stages, with most initiatives concentrated in higher education institutions. A systematic review by Khoalenyane and Ajani (2024) found that while AI tools are being adopted for personalised learning and administrative support, their implementation is uneven and often hindered by infrastructural and digital literacy gaps. Dewa (2024) conducted a bibliometric analysis of AI in the South African school system, revealing that research and implementation primarily focus on urban and well-resourced schools, leaving rural and township schools behind. The report highlights that the digital divide exacerbates existing educational inequalities rooted in Apartheid-era spatial and economic legacies.

Leadership and Policy Gaps

Leadership plays a critical role in shaping AI's ethical and equitable deployment in education. However, Khoalenyane and Ajani (2024) indicated that South African policy frameworks, such as the National Digital and Future Skills Strategy and the White Paper on Science, Technology and Innovation, lack specific guidelines on AI ethics, data governance, and inclusion in the education sector. Moreover, Dewa and Tshidi (2025) emphasise the need for transformative leadership prioritising inclusive innovation and community engagement in AI adoption. It is argued that AI risks becoming a tool that benefits only the digitally privileged without deliberate academic leadership policy interventions.

Theoretical Insights

The literature suggests that the framework for this study, underpinned by Paulo Freire's *Pedagogy of Freedom* (1998) and the theory of *Equity-Centred Design Thinking* (Gamboa & Fernando, 2022; Khalil & Kier, 2021), offers valuable lenses for evaluating AI in higher education. These frameworks advocate for participatory approaches that centre the voices of marginalised students and academics in designing and deploying AI systems. Freire's *Pedagogy of Freedom* emphasises education as a practice of liberation rooted in ethics, respect, and critical thinking. From a Freirean view, teaching should not be about transferring knowledge but about fostering autonomy and dialogue between teachers and students. Freire believes educators must be committed to justice, love, and hope, empowering learners to shape their world actively. Freire stresses that proper education involves competence and a deep sense of responsibility. Ultimately, it is based on Freire's critical pedagogy, which calls for a humanising approach to education that nurtures freedom, dignity, and the potential for transformative social change (van Wyk, 2025).

On the other hand, the *Equity-Centred Design Thinking* perspective integrates social justice into the design process, ensuring that solutions are inclusive and address systemic inequities. It challenges traditional design thinking by centring the voices and experiences of marginalised communities. This theory emphasises co-creation, empathy, and reflection, encouraging designers to examine their biases and power dynamics. Equity-centred design seeks to solve problems and transform systems by prioritising equity, dignity, and justice. It involves continuous learning, accountability, and a commitment to creating fair and empowering outcomes for all, especially those historically excluded from decision-making processes.

In sum, this dualistic framework focuses on the academic leadership of ethical AI use in higher education, which is based on the need for inclusive leadership to guide AI integration.

METHODOLOGY

This chapter uses a qualitative research approach (Bogdan & Biklen, 1997), which was employed to explore academic leadership in the context of ethical and equitable AI use in higher education. The choice of a qualitative methodology was deliberate, aiming to capture the nuanced perspectives, institutional values, and policy-driven practices that shape ethical AI integration. The research sought to understand how different universities interpret and implement ethical AI principles within their academic frameworks. The data collection process relied heavily on document analysis, a content analysis method well-suited for qualitative inquiry (Grant, 2018). This involved examining institutional documents that directly or indirectly influence AI use in academic settings. The documents analysed included the Assessment Policy, AI Policy, Academic Integrity Policy, AI Guidelines, and the Academic Integrity Course. These texts were selected for their relevance to ethical considerations in AI deployment, particularly in teaching, learning, and assessment contexts. The Assessment Policy provided insights into how universities adapt traditional evaluation methods to accommodate AI tools while maintaining fairness and academic standards. It revealed the extent to which institutions are rethinking assessment design to prevent misuse of AI and ensure that student learning outcomes remain authentic and measurable. The AI Policy was a central document outlining the institution's stance on AI use. It typically included definitions, acceptable use cases, and boundaries for AI integration in academic work. This policy was instrumental in understanding how leadership envisions the role of AI in education and the ethical frameworks they employ to guide its use. The Academic Integrity Policy was another critical document, offering a lens into how institutions respond to AI's challenges to originality, authorship, and honesty in academic work. This policy often intersects with AI guidelines, highlighting the need for clear definitions of misconduct in the age of generative AI.

The AI Guidelines provided practical instructions for academic staff and students on responsibly engaging with AI tools. These guidelines often included examples of acceptable and unacceptable uses, emphasising transparency, citation practices, and the importance of human oversight in AI-assisted work. The Academic Integrity Course, typically a mandatory course for students, was analysed to understand how institutions educate their communities about ethical AI use. This course often included interactive content, case studies, and assessments designed to raise awareness about the implications of AI in academic contexts. Throughout the research process, ethical considerations were rigorously observed (Arifin, 2018; Cacciattolo, 2015). The study adhered to institutional research ethics protocols, ensuring that the analysis of policy documents was conducted with integrity and respect for institutional confidentiality. Although the study did not involve human participants, the ethical use of institutional data and the responsible interpretation of policy content were prioritised. The qualitative nature of this study allowed for a rich, contextualised understanding of how academic leadership is navigating the complex terrain of AI ethics. Rather than seeking generalisable results, the research aimed to uncover patterns, tensions, and innovations within and across institutions. The use of multiple case studies enabled comparative analysis, revealing both common strategies and unique approaches to ethical AI governance. This approach also highlighted the role of academic leadership in shaping institutional culture around AI. Leaders were found to play a pivotal role in initiating policy development, fostering dialogue among stakeholders, and ensuring that ethical considerations are embedded in institutional practices. Their influence was evident in the tone, scope, and enforcement mechanisms outlined in the policies.

In conclusion, this qualitative study, grounded in document analysis and multiple case studies, provided valuable insights into how higher education institutions respond to AI's ethical challenges. By examining key policy documents, the research illuminated the principles, priorities, and practices that define ethical AI use in academia. It also underscored the importance of proactive, inclusive, and transparent leadership in guiding institutions through this evolving landscape.

FINDINGS

In each of the case studies, the specific role of institutional and governmental leadership was examined. Two specific case studies of successful leadership in AI-driven education were used to examine institutional policies and guidelines to understand how leadership practices influence AI's ethical and inclusive implementation in educational settings.

Academic Leadership for AI Integration

Case A

The University of South Africa (UNISA) was established on 26 June 1873 as the oldest higher education institution in South Africa. Since 2013, UNISA has been established as an open distance e-learning university (ODeL) and the largest in the Global South with a registered student population of approximately 389,700 students. In 2019, the university's leadership successfully introduced several proctoring measures, such as "AI guardrails," to invigilate all online courses, assessments, and final-year examinations. A year later, the Council approved the strategic objective of ten catalytic niche areas, namely, one of the catalytic niche areas, the Fourth Industrial Revolution and Digitalisation, was chosen to drive AI for sustainable development, equity and the African Agenda 2063. Since the hype of AI, several initiatives of awareness on the ethical use of AI for professional development were initiated through seminars, panel discussions, online workshops, and the writing of an AI policy and specific AI literacy guidelines as part of the academic leadership. The Senate approved and introduced several successful AI-driven initiatives to empower and protect the university's academic project and integrity. First, the Senate and Council approved the 2022 Revised Assessment Policy and Academic Integrity Policy to streamline all academic assessment practices and procedures to combat academic dishonesty. Second, at the last November 2023 meeting, the University Senate and Senior Management of the university reported that an increase in academic dishonesty cases, such as plagiarism, cheating, and copyright infringements, had compelled the institution to act to protect the image and credibility of all programmes. The University Senate introduced a compulsory *Academic Integrity Course* (University of South Africa, 2025) to all students registered for undergraduate and postgraduate qualifications. This course empowers students with ethical principles, such as accountability, honesty, trust, fairness, courage, respect, and responsibility. Ultimately, this course aims to foster a culture of trust, honesty, ethical AI use, and the importance of ethical decision-making in teaching, learning, and research. In March 2025, an academic leadership collaborative project between UNISA and the Department of Basic Education (DBE) launched the *FutureMinds Bootcamp*. This initiative focuses on developing school learners' mathematics, agriculture, accounting, physics, natural sciences, and economics competencies. This project focuses on developing the competencies of teachers and learners (Grades 8–12) in robust AI skills development.

Case B

The University of Pretoria (UP) was gazetted on 4 March 1908 and since been established as a research-intensive institution within the South African Higher Education sector. The senior management and the University Senate introduced a new strategic direction. Currently, 56,708 undergraduate and postgraduate students are registered in different programmes. Since 2020, UP has implemented several successful leadership roles in AI-driven strategies to address inclusiveness and equity. In October 2023, the Department of Library Services, in collaboration with the Department of Education Innovation and the Department of Research Innovation, hosted a workshop on academic integrity targeted at postgraduate students, academics, and researchers at the University of Pretoria. Several academic integrity series are created to raise awareness of AI use and ethical practices to empower academic staff and students. Second, the senior leadership of the university and University Senate approved the University Integrated Academic Framework (2023–2026), as a leading research-intensive university, internationally recognised for our quality education, relevance and impact and for developing people and creating knowledge, and for making a difference locally and globally. As part of academic leadership, several AI-driven initiatives were presented by the University Transformation Hub, which implemented a community-based project, *Bridging The Digital Divide: Youth Empowerment Through AI Training*, at the UP Mamelodi Campus. This initiative hosted high school learners from Mamelodi, a "township" which was developed as a segregated area during Apartheid for only Africans. In this area, the learners are from different socioeconomic statuses, and the university leadership reaches out to empower learners with AI technologies. Similar projects have been conducted since the hype about AI, particularly for students with learning disabilities and visual impairments.

POLICY FRAMEWORKS FOR ETHICAL AND EQUITABLE AI

Policy frameworks for ethical and equitable AI ensure the responsible development and deployment of AI technologies. These frameworks emphasise transparency, accountability, fairness, and inclusivity. They guide higher education institutions to prevent bias, protect privacy, and promote human rights. Incorporating diverse stakeholder input, they help align AI systems with societal values and legal standards. Equitable AI policies also address access disparities, ensuring benefits are shared across communities. As AI evolves, adaptive governance and continuous oversight are essential to upholding ethical principles and fostering public trust. Ultimately, these frameworks are a foundation for building AI that supports justice and social good. Currently, analysis of existing South African policies, for example, the National Digital and Future Skills Strategy and the White Paper on Science, Technology and Innovation provided directions for higher education institutions (HEIs) to develop contextualised AI policies and guidelines for implementation. In 2024, South Africa's National AI Policy Framework, published by the Department of Communications and Digital Technologies (DCDT), outlines the country's strategic approach to AI. The National AI Policy Framework (Department of Communications and Digital Technologies, 2025, p. 11) aims to:

- Position South Africa as a leader in responsible AI innovation.
- Promote ethical, inclusive, and human-centred AI development.
- Support socioeconomic transformation through AI in education, health, agriculture, and public services.
- Ensure regulatory alignment with global standards while addressing local challenges.
- Foster partnerships between government, academia, industry, and civil society.

Based on this AI Policy Framework, South African higher education institutions must implement policy objectives. Furthermore, this AI Policy Framework provides an outline and

> alignment with global AI governance standards and addressing socioeconomic disparities. South Africa can leverage AI to drive economic transformation, foster social equity, and enhance its global competitiveness in AI innovation.

As the drivers for AI directives, UNISA and UP have either developed or revised the existing Assessment Policy, Academic Integrity and Copyright Policies to streamline all academic assessment practices, procedures, and ethical use of AI. For example, the UNISA Senate introduced a compulsory *Academic Integrity Course* (University of South Africa, 2025). UP introduced an *Innovation for Transformation Hub* (University of Pretoria, 2024) to empower students registered for undergraduate and postgraduate qualifications with AI literacy skills. These two cases updated or revised current policy gaps in frameworks regarding AI ethics, data privacy, and algorithmic bias, which are clearly articulated in the revised policies. Furthermore, both cases stand for inclusive policy developments, inculcating a participatory approach to policymaking, aligning with South African constitutional values and integrating indigenous knowledge systems.

INCLUSIVITY AND EQUITY IN HUMANISING THE USE OF AI

As AI becomes an integral part of our lives, making it more human-like is not just a preference but a necessity. One of the biggest challenges with AI is that it often feels cold and unrelatable. Humanising AI bridges this gap by making technology more intuitive and emotionally aware. This is especially crucial in learning, where empathy plays a key role. Bridging the gap between technology and people means creating systems, tools, and experiences that are innovative but also accessible, inclusive, and human-centred (van Wyk, 2025). As technology rapidly evolves, it is essential to ensure that all individuals—regardless of background, ability, or socioeconomic status—can benefit from its advancements. This involves designing with empathy, prioritising user needs, and fostering digital literacy. It also requires ethical leadership and policies that protect rights and promote equity (Khoalenyane & Ajani, 2024; Freire, 1998; Tolman, 2019). By involving diverse voices in the design and implementation of technology (Yaneske & Oates, 2010; Young et al., 2019), we can build solutions that reflect real-world challenges and aspirations. Ultimately, bridging this gap is more than access—empowerment, trust, and ensuring that technology serves humanity, not vice versa (Chopra et al., 2024; Dewa, 2024). When people feel seen, heard, and supported by the tools they use, technology becomes a powerful force for connection, creativity, and positive change.

DISCUSSION

This chapter's findings from a multiple case study document analysis revealed that institutional policies, guidelines and procedures were revised to adapt to the National AI Policy Framework. These cases have shown that specific academic leadership practices influence AI's ethical and inclusive implementation in higher educational settings. The case study research has informed current policies and practices, identified barriers and opportunities, and proposed strategic recommendations for fostering inclusive AI-driven educational ecosystems aligned with the Global South's unique socioeconomic and infrastructural contexts. The driving force behind AI policy and guidelines revisions was influenced by the National AI Policy Framework, which compelled universities to implement ethical and equitable AI systems and ensure the responsible development and deployment of AI technologies.

It emerged that decisive academic leadership impacted building trust in AI systems. People are more likely to trust AI systems that feel relatable and ethical. Transparent and human-centred AI creates confidence, making users feel secure about their interactions with technology. Rudolph et al. (2023) asked whether AI is a "personal digital assistant or job killer" and responded as follows:

> The developments in the generative AI space are progressing at a dizzying speed. Teachers can benefit from using generative AI . . . if they know how to use generative AI critically, substantial productivity gains are possible. (p. 9)

Academics have praised the benefits of ChatGPT and similar AI conversational tools but also expressed concerns about ethical considerations, plagiarism, data privacy, and the protection of personal information. This prompted the management of UNISA and UP to take advantage of the benefits of

AI-powered tools and implement awareness sessions on the ethical use of AI-powered tools. Studies reported that universities had planned continuous professional development (CPD) training sessions, organised webinars, online discussion sessions, and off-campus training to increase awareness of AI literacy and to train academics in AI-generated tools for teaching and learning (Limongi & Marcolin, 2024; Valenzuela, 2025). Based on these initiatives, some academics employed what they had learned during the CPD sessions, but others remain reluctant to integrate AI technologies into teaching spaces. Improving accessibility is essential for creating inclusive environments where everyone, regardless of ability, can participate fully. One effective strategy is adopting universal design principles, ensuring that products, services, and spaces are usable by the broadest range of people without needing adaptation (Story, 1998). This includes designing websites compatible with screen readers, using high-contrast colours, and providing alternative text for images. According to Burgstahler and Cory (2010), policy development also plays a crucial role—universities should implement clear accessibility policies and regularly review them to align with evolving standards. Moreover, Kandlhofer et al. (2023) posit that training and awareness are equally important; staff and educators must have the knowledge and tools to support diverse needs. Damodaran (1996) highlighted that user involvement is another key strategy—engaging people with disabilities in the design and evaluation process ensures that solutions are grounded in real experiences.

Additionally, Jensen and Pedersen (2009) offer multiple modes of communication and content delivery, such as captions, transcripts, and sign language interpretation, which helps accommodate different learning and communication styles. Finally, Gascon et al. (2022) supported continuous evaluation and feedback loops to allow for ongoing improvement, ensuring that accessibility is not a one-time effort but a sustained commitment. Together, these strategies foster environments that are compliant, genuinely inclusive, and empowering for all individuals. The hype around generative AI technologies has changed higher education operations in the Global South through digitalisation to enhance staff and student experience. AI that understands emotions can dramatically improve user experiences. For example, a human-like AI virtual assistant can adjust its tone and response style depending on whether a user is happy, confused, or annoyed. Integrating AI technologies has become increasingly pervasive in the rapidly evolving HEIs, transforming how students learn and engage with course materials. As academic institutions strive to adapt to the demands of the 21st century, concerns surrounding the digital divide, data privacy, and the ethical implications of using AI in digitalised curricula have emerged as critical issues that warrant in-depth examination (Anderson & Rivera-Vargas, 2020). The digital divide highlights the disparities in access to technologies and the internet, which can significantly impact education equity

(Gorski, 2005; Memon & Memon, 2025; Tolman, 2019). Efforts to bridge this divide aim to ensure all students have equal access to digital resources like laptops and data for a digitalised curriculum (Afzal et al., 2023; Damarin, 2000). The increasing digitalisation of higher education institutions (HEIs) while offering expanded access to learning resources through digital learning spaces (Bygstad et al., 2022; Hamadi & El-Den, 2024).

Promoting Ethical and Inclusive AI

With concerns about AI bias and fairness, Humanise AI focuses on ethical development. This ensures that systems do not discriminate and are inclusive of all users, regardless of their backgrounds or abilities.

Promoting ethical and inclusive AI is essential to ensuring that technological advancements benefit all members of society fairly and responsibly. Ethical AI prioritises transparency, accountability, and fairness in algorithms' design, training, and deployment (Akinrinola, Okoye, Ofodile & Ugochukwu, 2024). This includes addressing biases in data, ensuring privacy and security, and making decision-making processes explainable and auditable. Inclusivity in AI means involving diverse voices—across race, gender, ability, and socio-economic status—in the development and governance of AI systems (Emma, 2024). It also means designing AI tools that are accessible and beneficial to marginalised communities rather than reinforcing existing inequalities. To achieve this, higher education institutions must adopt clear ethical guidelines and frameworks, such as those aligned with human rights and social justice principles. Education and training are also critical—developers, policymakers, and users need to understand the ethical implications of AI and how to mitigate harm. Young et al. (2019) employed a Diverse Voices method in quality multiple case studies to create a space for diverse voices in the design and implementation of AI technology to build solutions that reflect real-world challenges and aspirations by policymakers, administrative staff and frontline staff (Yaneske & Oates, 2010). Collaboration across sectors—government, academia, industry, and civil society—is key to creating robust, inclusive AI ecosystems. Additionally, continuous monitoring and evaluation of AI systems help ensure they remain aligned with ethical standards. Ultimately, promoting ethical and inclusive AI is not just a technical challenge but a societal commitment to equity, dignity, and shared progress in the digital age.

The two cases established in the context of this chapter present specific challenges and opportunities in integrating AI for educational inclusion and equity. Currently, based on the business model of the two case studies, which are facing challenges of budgetary constraints. For example, the government brought several cost-cutting measures and guidelines to be followed by universities. These measures had major consequences on the budgets of universities, which had effected the implementation of academic projects. This significantly impacted infrastructure disparities when investing in AI-smart architecture and infrastructure, which can be costly. Universities must also take note of the type of learning management system to include and not exclude students with learning disabilities and barriers. Some academic staff lack knowledge of AI literacy, and insufficient training and digital literacy remain a challenge. Academic leadership must be aware of the risk of AI, which could cause algorithmic bias and data sovereignty to become a concern. However, both cases and Global South universities had ample opportunities like personalised learning, assistive technologies for learners with disabilities, and AI for multilingual education, particularly for mother-tongue speaking students.

Implications for the Integration of AI for Educational Inclusion and Equity Approach

To achieve the National AI Policy Framework objectives, universities must revise or establish clear AI policy and AI guidelines to achieve strategic objectives stipulated in the framework. Higher education institutions must adopt clear AI ethical guidelines and frameworks, such as those aligned with human rights and social justice principles. Higher education must have continuous professional development targets, strategies, and in-service training that are critical for curriculum developers, policymakers, and users for an inclusive approach to understanding the ethical implications of AI and how to mitigate harm. The AI policy must be developed with inclusive, transparent, and adaptive AI policies. Socially, AI can either bridge or exacerbate existing educational inequalities, the digital divide, and stereotyping, depending on how it is implemented. It is feasible that AI can enhance operational efficiency and personalise learning, but it requires significant investment in infrastructure, training, and integration. Practically, participants agreed that the training, webinars, and online discussion forums had empowered them with AI literacy skills. Academic leaders must foster ethical leadership and digital transformation, which includes all stakeholders for transparency.

CONCLUSION

This chapter's findings from a multiple case study document analysis revealed that institutional policies, guidelines and procedures were revised to adapt to the National AI Policy Framework. These cases have shown that specific academic leadership practices influence AI's ethical and inclusive implementation in higher educational settings. Furthermore, ethical leadership and inclusive policy for AI in higher education are crucial for inclusion and equity. This chapter made a call to action for South African stakeholders based on the ethical use of AI technologies, not to exclude the marginalised but to be inclusive and create equitable opportunities for all within the higher education space. This chapter employed a case study focusing only on two universities; a larger study will yield different findings. Future research should explore how ethical AI policies are implemented and experienced by stakeholders in higher education. While this study focused on document analysis, further studies could include interviews with academic leaders, faculty, and students to understand policy impact. Comparative research across institutions and regions could reveal diverse approaches to AI governance. Longitudinal studies may track policy evolution and effectiveness over time. Additionally, examining how AI ethics are integrated into curricula and addressing equity in AI access and use are critical. These directions will deepen understanding of ethical AI practices and support the development of inclusive, adaptive policy frameworks.

REFERENCES

Afzal, A., Khan, S., Daud, S., Ahmad, Z., & Butt, A. (2023). Addressing the digital divide: Access and use of technology in education. *Journal of Social Sciences Review*, *3*(2), 883–895.

Akinrinola, O., Okoye, C. C., Ofodile, O. C., & Ugochukwu, C. E. (2024). Navigating and reviewing ethical dilemmas in AI development: Strategies for transparency, fairness, and accountability. *GSC Advanced Research and Reviews*, *18*(3), 50–58.

Anderson, T., & Rivera-Vargas, P. (2020). A critical look at educational technology from a distance education perspective. *Digital Education Review*, *37*, 208–229. https://doi.org/10.1344/der.2020.37.208-229

Arifin, S. R. M. (2018). Ethical considerations in qualitative study. *International Journal of Care Scholars*, *1*(2), 30–33. https://doi.org/10.31436/ijcs.v1i2.82

Bogdan, R., & Biklen, S. K. (1997). *Qualitative research for education* (Vol. 368). Boston, MA: Allyn & Bacon.

Burgstahler, S. E., & Cory, R. C. (Eds.). (2010). *Universal design in higher education: From principles to practice*. Harvard Education Press.

Bygstad, B., Øvrelid, E., Ludvigsen, S., & Dæhlen, M. (2022). From dual digitalization to digital learning space: Exploring the digital transformation of higher education. *Computers & Education*, *182*, 104463. https://doi.org/10.1016/j.compedu.2022.104463

Cacciattolo, M. (2015). Ethical considerations in research. In *The praxis of English language teaching and learning (PELT) Beyond the binaries: Researching critically in EFL classrooms* (pp. 61–79). Rotterdam: SensePublishers.

Chopra, A., Patel, H., Rajput, D. S., & Bansal, N. (2024). Empowering inclusive education: Leveraging AI-ML and innovative tech stacks to support students with learning disabilities in higher education. In *Applied assistive technologies and informatics for students with disabilities* (pp. 255–275). Singapore: Springer Nature. https://doi.org/10.1007/978-981-97-0914-4_15

Damaris, S. K. (2000). The 'Digital Divide' versus digital differences: Principles for equitable use of technology in education. *Educational Technology*, *40*(4), 17–22. https://www.jstor.org/stable/44428620

Damodaran, L. (1996). User involvement in the systems design process is a practical guide for users. *Behaviour & Information Technology, 15*(6), 363–377. https://doi.org/10.1080/014492996120049

Davis, R (2025). CheatGPT crisis – SA universities face a burgeoning degree of AI-written academic assignments. Daily Maverick. Johannesburg. https://www.dailymaverick.co.za/article/2025-04-05-cheatgpt-crisis-sa-universities-faced-with-a-burgeoning-degree-of-ai-written-academic-assignments/

Department of Communication and Digital Technologies (2025). National AI Policy Framework. Pretoria. https://www.dcdt.gov.za/sa-national-ai-policy-framework/file/338-sa-national-ai-policy-framework.html

Dewa, A. (2024). Artificial intelligence for educational sustainability in the South African school system: A bibliometric analysis and literature review. *International Journal of Education and Development Using Information and Communication Technology, 20*(3), 60–78.

Dewa, A., & Tshidi, M. (2025). Harnessing the existing digital technologies to enhance student engagement for knowledge creation and inclusion in diverse classes: a systematic review. *Inted2025 Proceedings*, 5308–5315.

Domínguez, J. C. E., Munar, L. S., Beltrán, P. A. C., Ayala, C. A. P., Solano, A., & Galindez, J. A. O. (2025). Inclusive interactive multimedia experiences in school contexts with learning analytics integration. *IEEE Revista iberoamericana de tecnologias del aprendizaje.*

Emma, L. (2024). The ethical implications of artificial intelligence: A deep dive into bias, fairness, and transparency.

Freire, P. (1998). Pedagogy of freedom. (P. Clarke, Trans.). Lanham, MD: Rowman & Littlefield.

Gamboa, P. A., & Fernando, T. (2022). Community-engaged education in health promotion: Exploring equity and ethical dimensions to problem-solving in community. In *International handbook of teaching and learning in health promotion: Practices and reflections from around the world* (pp. 667–685). Cham: Springer International Publishing. https://doi.org/10.1007/978-3-030-96005-6_41

Gascon, G. M., Chen, H. T., Morosanu, L., Chen, V. H., Cass, P., & Falcone, R. (2022). Evaluation of the processes and outcomes of a physician leadership program: the continuous feedback loop design. *Journal of Continuing Education in the Health Professions, 42*(4), 284–290.

Grant, A. (2018). *Doing excellent social research with documents: Practical examples and guidance for qualitative researchers.* Routledge.

Gorski, P. (2005). Education equity and the digital divide. *AACE Review (Formerly AACE Journal), 13*(1), 3–45. https://www.learntechlib.org/primary/p/6570/

Guerrero, M. B. (2024). Pedagogical transformation in the age of AI: Advancing toward a more inclusive and sustainable education. *Neuropedagogy Research Journal, 1*(1).

Hamadi, M., & El-Den, J. (2024). A conceptual research framework for sustainable digital learning in higher education. *Research and Practice in Technology Enhanced Learning, 19*, 1–25.

Jensen, P. A., & Pedersen, E. F. (2009). User involvement and the role of briefing. *Architectural Management: International Research and Practice*, 172–185.

Kandlhofer, M., Weixelbraun, P., Menzinger, M., Steinbauer-Wagner, G., & Kemenesi, Á. (2023, October). Education and awareness for artificial intelligence. In *International Conference on Informatics in Schools: Situation, Evolution, and Perspectives* (pp. 3–12). Cham: Springer Nature Switzerland.

Khalil, D., & Kier, M. (2021). Equity-centered design thinking in STEM instructional leadership. *Journal of Cases in Educational Leadership, 24*(1), 69–85. https://doi.org/10.1177/1555458920975452

Kharbat, F. F., Alshawabkeh, A., & Woolsey, M. L. (2021). Identifying gaps in using artificial intelligence to support students with intellectual disabilities from education and health perspectives. *Aslib Journal of Information Management, 73*(1), 101–128. https://doi.org/10.1108/AJIM-02-2020-0054

Khoalenyane, N. B., & Ajani, O. A. (2024). A systematic review of artificial intelligence in higher education-South Africa. *Social Sciences and Education Research Review, 11*(1), 17–26.

Limongi, R., & Marcolin, C. B. (2024). AI literacy research: frontier for high-impact research and ethics. *BAR-Brazilian Administration Review, 21*(3), e240162.

Memon, F. N., & Memon, S. N. (2025). Digital divide and equity in education: Bridging gaps to ensure inclusive learning. In *Impact of digitalization on education and social sustainability* (pp. 107–130). IGI Global.

Rudolph, J., Tan, S., & Aspland, T. (2023). Editorial 6(2): Personal digital assistant or job killer? Generative AI and the teaching profession in higher education. *Journal of Applied Learning and Teaching*, 6(2), 7–16.

Salawa, J. S., Sebastian, P., Nyatega, C. O., Ally, J. S., Karawa, C. J., Koola, E. O., & Mwanjalila, R. (2024). Development of artificial intelligence (AI)-driven aid to enhance visual and hearing-impaired students. *African Journal of Education, Science and Technology (AJEST), 8*(1), 129–140.

Stirling, J., & McGloin, C. (2015). *Critical pedagogy and social inclusion policy in Australian higher education: Identifying the disjunctions.*

Story, M. F. (1998). Maximizing usability: The principles of universal design. *Assistive Technology, 10*(1), 4–12.

Tolman, S. (2019). Considerations for using critical pedagogy to promote social justice in higher education. In *Strategies for fostering inclusive classrooms in higher education: International perspectives on equity and inclusion* (pp. 197–212). Emerald Publishing Limited.

University of Pretoria. (2024). Innovation and transformation hub. Innovation Africa. Pretoria. https://tipconsortium.net/tiah/

University of South Africa. (2025). Academic integrity course. Pretoria. https://mooc.unisa/mod/page/news.php?id=306

Valenzuela, J. M. (2025). Developing teachers' AI literacy through professional development. In *Innovative approaches to staff development in transnational higher education* (pp. 215–244). IGI Global Scientific Publishing.

van Wyk, M. M. (2025). Integrating GenAI tools by academics to humanise pedagogical spaces: An AI humanising pedagogical perspective. *Journal of Applied Learning and Teaching*, 8(1), 58–66. https://doi.org/10.37074/jalt.2025.8.1.24

Yaneske, E., & Oates, B. (2010). Using voice boards: pedagogical design, technological implementation, evaluation and reflections. *Australasian Journal of Educational Technology*, *26*(8). https://doi.org/10.14742/ajet.1022

Yin, R. K. (2003). Design and methods. *Case study research*, *3*(9.2), 84.

Young, M., Magassa, L., & Friedman, B. (2019). Toward inclusive tech policy design: a method for underrepresented voices to strengthen tech policy documents. *Ethics and Information Technology*, *21*, 89–103.

8. AI as part of a process of change in Argentine educational management

Cristina Adriana Kruger

The integration of Artificial Intelligence (AI) into educational leadership is reshaping pedagogical practices and administrative strategies globally. In Argentina, a nation grappling with educational disparities, AI presents both opportunities and challenges in promoting equity and inclusion. This chapter examines how AI influences educational leadership in Argentina, focusing on its role in advancing equitable and inclusive education. The following research questions guided the inquiry and analytical process: (1) How is AI being integrated into educational management practices in Argentina? (2) What are the challenges that Artificial Intelligence propuse for educational management in Argentina? (3) How can AI be used as part of a process of change in Argentine educational management in pursuit of equity and inclusion? This chapter used an integrative literature review approach (Snyder, 2019) to address the research questions. A comprehensive search was conducted across databases including Google Scholar, Web of Science, Scopus, ScienceDirect, and Elsevier, using key search terms such as "Artificial Intelligence in Argentine education," "AI and educational management in Argentina," "AI for equity and inclusion in education," and other similar keywords. This process yielded relevant articles, which were analyzed to extract themes and insights pertinent to the research questions.

OVERVIEW OF THE ARGENTINE EDUCATION SYSTEM

The federal structure of the Argentine educational system is typified by the sharing of governance between national and provincial authorities. There have been periods of authoritarianism and democracy throughout the history of the Argentine educational system. The Federal Education Law of 1993, which gave the provinces more authority over education, was the main tool used to advance efforts to decentralize the educational system following the return to democracy in 1983 (Tiramonti, 2001). A major shift in Argentina's educational history was brought about by the Federal Education Law No. 24.195, which created a new organizational and regulatory framework for the educational system.

The National Education Law No. 26,206, which was passed in December 2006 as a result of discussion and analysis of the Argentine educational system, is a crucial step in the process of reclaiming education for the creation of a more equitable and just society. Currently in effect, Law No. 26,206 declares that education is a national priority and a state policy, ensuring that everyone has the right to an education and working to ensure equal opportunities for all people, regardless of their backgrounds.

Since the National Education Law No. 26,206 was passed, the state has formally recognized knowledge and education as a social and personal right as well as a public good. Additionally, it plays a crucial role in guaranteeing a consistent level of education along with fair opportunities and prospects, thereby preventing social or regional disparities. Within the educational system, the aforementioned law creates initial, primary, secondary, and higher education levels. Special education, rural education, intercultural bilingual education, technical professional education, artistic education, permanent education for adults and children, education in contexts of deprivation of liberty, and hospital and home education are among the eight modalities that are outlined as organizational and curriculum options. Despite Argentina's long history of providing free, mandatory public education, this specific law makes it mandatory from the age of four until the conclusion of secondary school.

Since the National Education Law went into effect, one of the challenges of the educational system has been ensuring that compulsory education is fulfilled in ways that are suitable for the needs and characteristics of the rural population. This is known as rural education. Similar emphasis was placed on the significance of rural schools achieving quality standards on par with urban schools. As a result of this recognition, the National Ministry of Education developed and implemented a number of policies in coordination with the jurisdictions to ensure quality, equality, and institutional strengthening, as stated in CFE Resolution No. 128/10.

Additionally, as one of the eight modalities acknowledged by the State to ensure respect for the ethnic, cultural, and linguistic identity of indigenous peoples, Intercultural Bilingual Education (EIB) is being incorporated into the national education system on an institutional basis. It is coordinated by the National Directorate of Educational Management of the National Ministry of Education (Resolution Number 119/10 CFE). This directorate supports a variety of initiatives, such as the development of pertinent proposals that incorporate indigenous knowledge, values, customs, and languages; research; and the involvement of indigenous peoples through their organizations and representatives. In order to achieve this, it collaborates with the Autonomous Educational

Council of Indigenous Peoples (CEAPI), the group that represents the indigenous peoples of the nation.

Nonetheless, there are still significant social disparities in Argentina's educational system that show up in a number of ways, including academic performance, teaching quality, and access to the system. The socioeconomic status of families, the location of schools, and the accessibility of resources and technology are all strongly correlated with these disparities.

The funding of public education and teacher salaries have been greatly impacted by economic instability, especially during the financial crisis of 2001 and more recent inflationary periods. Budgetary restrictions frequently lead to inadequate resources and infrastructure in public schools, particularly in the most impoverished provinces (Galiani et. al., 2008). However, education continues to play a crucial role in the public conversation about social mobility and economic development. It should be mentioned that a variety of historical, social, economic, and political factors have an impact on education in Argentina. As a result, the system is always changing, overcoming obstacles, and aiming for constant improvement to guarantee inclusive and high-quality education for all of its citizens.

The need to improve children's and youth's literacy through the development of literacy plans and programs, initial and ongoing teacher training, access to high-quality resources, monitoring and evaluation of instruction and learning, curriculum reform, teachers' labor rights, and the relative importance of national versus provincial control over education policy have been the main topics of recent policy discussions.

Disparities still exist despite large investments in education, particularly in underserved and rural areas. Issues include regional differences in educational outcomes, insufficient infrastructure, and unequal access to high-quality education. These structural issues highlight the necessity of cutting-edge strategies, like Artificial Intelligence, to advance inclusion and equity. Therefore, school leaders will most likely be able to define the vision and strategies for educational transformation through AI with the help of educational leadership and management.

Argentina is not an exception to how quickly AI is changing many industries around the world. Thus, in order to guide the use of AI, the Argentine Republic has established guidelines. The primary goal of these guidelines is to prioritize respect for the fundamental rights of individuals, confidentiality, privacy, and integrity of information, as well as adherence to computer security regulations and practices. These guidelines aim to prevent human rights violations by emphasizing prevention and demonstrated responsibility (Office of the Chief of Staff, Provision Number 02/23, Argentina).

In 2019, Argentina's Ministry of Science, Technology, and Productive Innovation (MINCYT) created El Plan Nacional de Inteligencia Artificial

(PNIA), which brings together the government, business, academia, and international partners to promote innovation and guarantee that AI technologies maximize benefits and minimize harm. This plan's strategic priorities include concentrating on ethical AI, enhancing AI infrastructure, and creating a regulatory framework (Robiolo & Martello, 2024).

Argentina is the fourth-highest adopter of the technology in South America, behind Chile, Brazil, and Uruguay, according to the Latin American Artificial Intelligence Index (CENIA, Latin Artificial Intelligence Index, 2024). Argentina's research, development, adoption, and governance are all well-balanced. Under the direction of the National Artificial Intelligence Center of Chile (CENIA, 2024), institutions and governments from all over the region collaborated to create this index. This rigorous study groups more than 70 sub-indicators that formed the basis for its construction, covering the circumstances of 19 Latin American countries. It organizes the factors and variables that influence the development of AI ecosystems around three dimensions: Enabling Factors (40% relative weight), Research, Development, and Adoption (35%), and Governance (25%).

An examination of Latin America's AI regulations shows that the region is still adjusting to the difficulties presented by this technology. International frameworks like the OECD Principles on AI and the UNESCO Recommendation have had a significant impact on this adaptation process, helping to lay the groundwork for the regulations that these nations implement (Ulloa, 2024).

SCHOOL LEADERSHIP IN EDUCATIONAL TRANSFORMATION

Leadership is an interactive process that enables a leader to exert influence on other people, so that they can take the proposed lines as a premise for their action. This influence, not based on formal power or authority, can be exercised in different dimensions, especially at the organizational level, when a leader strives to reach consensus and mobilize the organization around common goals (Leithwood et al., 2006). Similarly, educational leadership refers to a leading interactional process between an educational leader and their subordinates to achieve shared academic goals (Northouse, 2021). Educational leadership is consequential to the academic success of schools. Vega et al. (2023) assert that an effective educational leader can motivate and lead a school toward achieving increased or even optimal performance and achieving optimal outcomes for all stakeholders. More specifically, an educational leader can use instructional leadership strategies to mentor and support teachers, consequently improve their performance. Improved teacher performance can in turn positively affect the academic performance of students (Tambingon, et al., 2024).

Educational leadership theories provide a lens through which leaders can integrate change into organizations, including educational institutions (Fadhilah et al., 2024). For example, transformational leadership emphasizes inspiring and motivating stakeholders to achieve collective goals, aligning well with the adoption of innovative technologies like AI (Northouse, 2021). Distributed leadership focuses on shared responsibilities, facilitating collaborative decision-making in implementing AI tools (Bolden et al., 2009). Instructional leadership centers on improving teaching and learning, highlighting the potential of AI to enhance educational practices (Song & Rizal, 2023, cited by Bajarlía, 2023).

According to Bajarlía (2023, p. 110),

> a true leader must be a person with an open mind to new ideas, willing to take risks without fear of losing while having a clear objective. He must also be able to guide a whole team of people or an organization towards the achievement of goals.

This work is aimed at improving student learning, we speak of pedagogical or educational leadership. Therefore, educational leadership can be understood as that which gives a common sense to the school organization and influences the behavior of its members, having as its north the improvement of quality, which is tangibly expressed in student learning, as pointed out by Robinson et al. (2009). Studies have shown that school leadership has the second largest impact on student learning outcomes, only behind classroom teaching (UNESCO, 2023; VVOB, 2018). According to UNESCO (2023) educational leadership is that which potentiates academic achievement.

Among the successful leadership practices that research has highlighted is "professionally developing its staff," as the ability to enhance those capabilities of the members of the organization, which is necessary for the achievement of the goals of the establishment (Bolivar, 2014). A director shares leadership in view of adequately influencing his collaborators and leading them to achieve the institutional goal (Acevedo-Muriel, 2020, p. 26). As Timperley (2008 cited by Bolívar, 2014) points out principals have the responsibility to promote learning and professional development opportunities for teachers.

In addition, nowadays, given the complexity of globalized processes in the digital era, Fullán (2020) indicates that leadership must be updated depending on the current challenges so that all students have the same opportunities. Therefore, it is necessary to respond to the challenges of AI in education, as stated by UNESCO (2021). In this way, educational leadership involves an improvement in the excellence and confidence of the institution (Martínez-García & Gil-Flores, 2018).

Based on the above, it can be affirmed that instructional leadership is a key tool to optimize teacher performance and a privileged way of change for school improvement.

For this reason, the principal must manage the conditions for the improvement of learning and guide the pedagogical processes, assuming an active role that collaborates with the promotion of innovation and change for educational improvement, promoting the curricular integration of AI according to the needs and specific educational projects, and adopting a critical and responsible vision in order to provide a quality education in line with the current times. Recognizing the challenges, scope, limitations, and risks involved in the use of AI in schools, and prioritizing the continuous training of the teaching staff in the development of pedagogical, technological, and ethical skills. It is also important to design educational experiences that help students understand, reflect on, and discuss these social and cultural tensions.

APPLICATIONS AND USES OF AI IN MANAGEMENT

AI is the ability of machines to use algorithms, learn from data, and use what they learn in decision-making just as a human would (Rouhiainen, 2018, p. 17).

AI can also be defined as the simulation of human cognitive functions through artificial systems or intelligent agents. The cognitive functions that are tried to be reproduced are pattern identification, vision, analytics, data, decision making, and language, among others (UNESCO, 2023). The rapid advancement of AI has important implications in various fields, including education.

However, the definition of AI must be modified with technological change and educational objectives, as expressed in the document "Recommendation on the Ethics of Artificial Intelligence" (UNESCO, 2023). In addition, it is emphasized that AI is a tool for processing information by technology through the integration of different algorithms and models, which must respect certain ethical guidelines (UNESCO, 2022).

To understand the application of AI in educational management, it is necessary to properly understand what we mean by educational management. According to UNESCO, educational management is based on complex institutional systems and administrative arrangements that mobilize resources such as teachers, educational infrastructure, materials, and equipment, in order to provide the population with quality educational services.

The approach made in the "Beijing Consensus on Artificial Intelligence and Education," which mentions the importance of the systematic integration of AI and education in order to innovate education, teaching, and learning, and for AI to contribute to the acceleration of achieving open and flexible education systems that enable equitable, relevant, and quality lifelong learning opportunities for all, will contribute to the achievement of the SDGs and the shared future of humanity (UNESCO, 2019a).

Consequently, AI provides the necessary potential to address some of the major challenges in education today, innovate teaching-learning practices, and accelerate progress towards the achievement of Sustainable Development Goal 4 (SDG 4). SDG 4 and its corresponding targets aim to "ensure inclusive, equitable and quality education and promote lifelong learning opportunities for all" (UNESCO, 2015, p. 11).

The equity framework understands that all people are different, so they require an educational and social response adjusted to their needs that minimizes the situation of inequality (Sánchez & Ainscow, 2018, p. 16). Considering the vision of the Organization for Economic Cooperation and Development (Organization for Economic Cooperation and Development, 2012), equity in education implies that personal or social circumstances cannot be obstacles to developing educational potential (justice) under a constant process of improvement where all people reach a basic level of skills-inclusion (Sánchez & Ainscow, 2018, p. 16). And that the potentiality of educational inclusion lies in its understanding as a process of endless search for the best way to respond to diversity (Acevedo-Muriel, 2020, cited by Sánchez & Ainscow, 2018, p. 16).

In the Argentine Republic, the National Education Law No. 26,206 in its Title I General Provision, Chapter I, Article 2 states that education and knowledge are a public good and a personal and social right, guaranteed by the State. Chapter I, Article 2 establishes that education and knowledge are a public good and a personal and social right, guaranteed by the State, and Article 4 states that the National State, the Provinces and the Autonomous City of Buenos Aires are responsible for the education of their citizens.

> The National State, the Provinces and the Autonomous City of Buenos Aires have the primary and non-delegable responsibility to provide a comprehensive, permanent and quality education for all the inhabitants of the Nation, guaranteeing equality, gratuity and equity in the exercise of this right, with the participation of social organizations and families.

The objectives of the national education policy are to ensure quality education with equal opportunities and possibilities, without regional imbalances or social inequities, and to guarantee educational inclusion through universal policies and pedagogical and resource allocation strategies that give priority to the most disadvantaged sectors of society.

Therefore, the application of AI in education has the potential to revolutionize the way teaching and learning takes place, as well as to make educational management more efficient. Indeed, AI can adapt the teaching-learning process to the individual needs and preferences of each student, offering learning resources and activities tailored to their level of knowledge, learning style, and rate of progress (Vera, 2023, p. 20). Bearing in mind that the role of the principal is to generate the conditions for teaching and learning to take place, he/she manages different dimensions: technical-administrative, pedagogical-didactic, and socio-community as expressed by Gvirtz et al. (2011) in order to build an inclusive and quality school.

The technical-administrative dimension includes administrative, bureaucratic, and organizational tasks, such as attending to suppliers, filling out forms with information, and organizing the use of common areas. This dimension is part of the functioning of the school as an organization, hence its importance. However, it is common for the management team to be absorbed by these tasks, which takes time away from the other dimensions.

The pedagogical-educational dimension is the *raison d'être* of the management team. It involves knowing and coordinating what and how to teach. The management team must lead the curricular process of the organization; it must propose and guide reflection on teaching strategies and student learning processes; it must guide teachers in the face of problems or difficulties that arise; it must accompany them in the planning, design of sequences, and selection of resources, etc. All actions of the management team should aim at improving the school's educational practices.

And the socio-community dimension implies creating and maintaining links with the school. As Lucero-Tello et al. (2024, p. 125) points out, understanding school management and its multiple facets within an institution is fundamental to generate the desired change in education and in all its actors. In this sense, school management is positioned as a dynamic and changing element that not only adapts to the needs of society, but also guides the positive development of education and ensures a more inclusive and successful future for all.

One of the main problems in educational management is managing large amounts of data and making informed decisions based on it (Vera et al., 2023). Educational institutions must deal with a large amount of information, from enrollment management and academic progress tracking to resource management and curriculum planning. This data overload can make it difficult to identify meaningful patterns and make effective decisions (Litardo et al., 2024, p. 203).

Consequently, the incorporation of AI in school management is presented as a technology that allows improving administrative effectiveness and efficiency, and freeing up time to enhance pedagogical leadership. In other words, AI is presented as a potential solution to mitigate the administrative burden of principals and allow them to devote more time to activities related to the improvement of the educational process (UNESCO, 2021).

The integration of AI in education allows streamlining the development of administrative tasks such as registration, attendance, and monitoring of students; loading staff licenses; generating reports; making technical circulars; planning activities; and organizing the agenda, among others, which contributes to decision-making and time optimization, allowing for more efficient work.

As well, AI allows teachers to perform administrative and routine tasks, thus helping them to free up time and resources, and to focus on more creative and value-added pedagogical activities. For example, automatic test marking and data management can streamline the assessment and feedback process, allowing teachers to spend more time interacting with students, providing meaningful feedback and offering additional support to those who need it (Vera, 2023, p. 20).

As institutions adopt these technologies, it will be essential to ensure that they are used responsibly and equitably, maximizing their benefits for all students.

It is also recommended that educational institutions consider safeguarding information, privacy, and data security. Taking into account that AI is based on the analysis and processing of large amounts of data, concerns are raised about the protection of privacy and information security (Vera, 2023, p. 19). According to Loayza Flores et al. (2022) the quality of education is closely linked to the use and appropriation of technology. Therefore, it is crucial that educational institutions innovate and adopt AI as a key tool to improve educational quality and training. Litardo et al. (2024) point out that the integration of AI can be a transformative catalyst because when educational management is supported by this tool, it can solve fundamental problems and make a difference in areas such as personalization of learning, optimization of institutional administration, and adaptability to the changing demands of the school environment.

In this way, AI becomes a valuable tool to support school management and contribute to the integral development of students.

ARTIFICIAL INTELLIGENCE POSES CHALLENGES FOR ARGENTINE EDUCATION

In the current context, the main challenges of AI integration in Argentine education are the digital divide, digital literacy, and overcoming inequal access to technology.

Although the concept of the digital divide has evolved over time, at first it basically referred to connectivity problems. Subsequently, concern began to be introduced for the development of the capabilities and skills required to use Information and Communication Technologies (ICTs) (training and education), and recently it has also referred to the use of resources integrated into technology (Camacho, 2005, p. 3). The author proposes three types of digital divide: access, based on the difference between people who can access ICTs and those who cannot; use, based on people who know how to use them and those who do not; and quality of use, based on the differences between the same users (Camacho, 2005, p. 3).

In Argentina, the digital divide in terms of access to new technologies and the Internet continues to be a problem that affects different sectors of the population for different social, economic, and/or geographic reasons. Although progress has been made in terms of infrastructure and policies to improve connectivity, there are still significant differences in the quality of Internet service between the different regions of the country, with better quality in urban areas and large cities. Rural areas and the most economically disadvantaged sectors are at a disadvantage.

Socioeconomic inequalities create significant barriers to equitable access to technological devices, such as personal computers, tablets, and smartphones, as well as accessibility to internet service. This disparity in access to technology increases social inequalities and limits educational opportunities for a sector of the population in terms of access to online resources, educational platforms, and digital tools.

Another challenge to overcome is the digital divide related to the skills of understanding and use of technologies by the population that has access to them.

Digital literacy is considered to promote the development of skills necessary to be a user of digital information (García-Ávila, 2017, p. 70). In general, digital literacy includes knowledge of different sources of digital information, ethical criteria for using information, and using and owning devices, among other elements (García-Ávila, 2017, p. 73).

Although AI has the potential to democratize access to education, as it can provide online learning opportunities to a large number of students, there is a risk that only those with access to technology and sufficient resources can fully benefit from it (Vera, 2023, p. 20).

Therefore, in Argentina, it is essential to implement public policies and programs for access to technological devices for low-income families. At the same time, it is necessary to review and update curricula, since there is a lack of teaching digital literacy and Artificial Intelligence literacy. The latter is an issue of growing concern in the educational context, given the rapid evolution of technology and the need to prepare students and teachers for the challenges and opportunities of this century.

It is essential to address this problem in depth and from educational policies to propose possible solutions to ensure that the education system can accompany and train students to face the challenges of the future. As Vera (2023) states, the growing dependence on ICT in daily life forces us to reflect on how we can narrow the so-called digital divide in our students and thus leverage the digital era (Vera, 2023, p. 18).

As expressed by Litardo et al. (2024) it is important that both teachers and students are familiarized and trained in the use of AI and its potential in the entire educational field. In this way, they will be able to develop more effective pedagogical strategies. In this sense, training in technology and digital skills is therefore essential for a successful implementation of AI in education.

OPPORTUNITIES AND LIMITATIONS

The emergence of new digital technologies is a great opportunity to help marginalized students, those with disabilities, and those belonging to linguistic and cultural minorities. These technologies can help to personalize learning and create more flexible educational systems, and can also serve to overcome geographical and temporal barriers to generate immersive learning (UNESCO, 2015, p. 3).

AI has the potential to be a valuable tool in the inclusive education of persons with disabilities. It can help to eliminate barriers and create inclusive environments, adapt and personalize resources, and provide support and materials that align with the rights set forth in Article 24 of the Convention on the Rights of Persons with Disabilities. This article recognizes the rights of persons with disabilities to inclusive, quality, and free education under equal conditions and opportunities. It is essential to guarantee that reasonable accommodations are made in accordance with individual requirements, that the necessary support is provided to facilitate effective training, and that personalized and effective measures are implemented in environments that encourage maximum academic and social development.

Consequently, AI presents novel prospects for learning and education. It should thus be regarded as a supplementary instrument in the teaching-learning process, rather than as an end in itself. Some of the applications of Artificial Intelligence in education include the automatic evaluation of tasks, the development of personalized curricula, academic and professional writing, and others. Additionally, there are numerous free or low-cost Artificial Intelligence tools available for teaching practice, which can facilitate more efficient management both inside and outside the classroom (Bajarlía, 2023).

Among the limitations that we have both nationally and regionally to ensure a positive and beneficial development of AI in education is the lack of teacher training in the use and application of AI.

Therefore, it is crucial for teachers to constantly adapt and update themselves to face the challenges of the digital era and to form critical and skilled citizens for today's complex world. Collaboration between government, educational institutions, and technology providers is essential to overcome digital divides and maximize the benefits of AI in education (Apolo Buenaño et al., 2023). Some Argentine provinces are working on the incorporation of new curricular spaces crossed by digital tools in teacher training careers in order to ensure the training of future professionals who generate learning strategies mediated by digital technologies.

The integration of AI in higher education poses both challenges and opportunities for institutions, faculty and students. One of the key challenges of AI integration in higher education is the access and equity gap. It is critical to ensure that the integration of AI in higher education is inclusive and equitable, ensuring that all our students have the opportunity to access and reap the benefits of the technology (Vera, 2023, p. 19).

And finally, another important challenge is ethics and privacy in the integration of AI in higher education. Massive data collection and the use of AI algorithms for analysis and decision making raise concerns about the privacy and security of student information (Vera, 2023 p. 20).

For such reason, it is imperative to address and develop consensual policy frameworks to regulate and raise awareness of the ethical use of AI in education. This must go through the design and implementation of a Digital and AI Literacy Plan, considering that the main obstacle to the widespread adoption of AI technologies is the lack of solid evidence on their effectiveness and impact on students' academic achievement (Flores Vivar & García Peñalvo, 2023, p. 244).

USE OF ARTIFICIAL INTELLIGENCE IN EDUCATION IN AN ETHICAL AND EQUITABLE WAY

It is essential to keep in mind the multidisciplinary nature of artificial intelligence and its impacts, as well as to align the use of AI in education with public policies, particularly education policy, in order to adopt whole-of-government, cross-sectoral, and multi-stakeholder approaches to the planning and governance of AI in education; and to establish strategic priorities based on local challenges related to the achievement of SDG 4 and its targets, as well as the other SDGs (UNESCO, 2019a).

At the national level with the aim of addressing the advancement and application of Artificial Intelligence, the Undersecretariat of Information Technologies under the Secretariat of Public Innovation approved and published in the official gazette by Provision 2/2023 Article 1 the "Recommendations for a Reliable Artificial Intelligence" in order to generate ethical regulatory frameworks, and which seeks to ensure the responsible and beneficial development of AI, taking as a reference the Recommendation Guide on Ethics of Artificial Intelligence (UNESCO, 2023).

In June 2023, UNESCO warned that AI was being deployed too rapidly in schools and that there was a worrying lack of control, standards, and regulations (UNESCO, 2023, p. 8). Therefore, living in digitizing societies demands new educational practices, ethical reflection, critical thinking, responsible design practices, and new competencies, given the implications for the labor market, employability, and civic participation (UNESCO, 2023, p. 11). UNESCO reacted immediately and invited its Member States to adopt protections and to monitor that AI is developed according to ethical principles. It considers ethics as a dynamic basis for the evaluation and normative guidance of AI technologies, taking as a reference human dignity, welfare, and prevention of harm and relying on the ethics of science and technology (UNESCO, 2023, p. 10).

In August 2024, our country, in conjunction with 17 other Latin American countries, ratified its position on the implementation of AI. This was done by signing the Declaration of Cartagena de Indias, in which they ratified their commitment to implement the UNESCO Recommendation on the Ethics of Artificial Intelligence.

Consequently, the Argentine state endeavors to facilitate the development of transparent, equitable, and reliable AI, ensuring that the resulting technology is developed in a people-centered manner with a gender and human rights perspective.

From the perspective of student-centered education, one of the main benefits of AI application is the personalization of learning. AI makes it possible to tailor educational content and learning strategies to the individual needs of our students, which can improve the effectiveness of the formative process and increase the motivation and engagement of our students (Vera, 2023, p. 19).

Therefore, Artificial Intelligence can provide help and support to educational institutions to improve their learning outcomes, which contributes to the achievement of inclusive and fair education. In addition, it is possible to provide support to teachers and students to overcome different barriers in the teaching-learning process and thereby realize the goals of education with the needs of the twent-first century (Plitnichenko, 2020; University of San Diego Online Degrees, Schroer, 2023 cited by Bajarlía, 2023).

FINAL REFLECTION

From the perspective of strategic educational management, the role of the principal is of paramount importance to provide pedagogical leadership, encourage teamwork, foster an open attitude towards learning and innovation, and facilitate the achievement of institutional objectives. This is achieved by creating safe, inclusive, and equitable learning environments, establishing conditions that support learning, and providing guidance and support to teachers, with the ultimate goal of enhancing pedagogical processes and educational quality.

That is, the principal has the opportunity to manage change and create an opportune environment to forge a shared project. The way in which leadership is exercised influences everything that happens in the institution, having high expectations of students, involving its community, growing the teaching teams and achieving a joint project (Porres, 2018).

According to Bolivar, (2010) educational leadership makes sense in the school organization and influences the behavior of its members, whose objective is the improvement of quality, concretely expressed in student learning.

Educational management today faces a series of complex challenges, ranging from the optimization of administrative processes to the personalization of learning for each student (Cárdenas et al., 2022). These challenges can hinder the performance and effectiveness of educational institutions, affecting both students and educators. However, AI emerges as a promising tool to address these problems in innovative and efficient ways (Litardo et al., 2024).

The future of AI in educational management is promising despite the challenges and risks it presents. It offers significant potential for improving administrative tasks, teaching and learning, communication, and decision-making. With the advancement of this technology, further integration of AI into classrooms is expected, leading to more effective teaching and more efficient management. It is therefore essential to address the ethical and equity challenges that arise with its implementation.

Nevertheless, in Argentina, there are still constraints in terms of access to technology and teacher training in the use of digital tools, which must be addressed in order to achieve an optimal integration of AI in education. It is therefore crucial for the Argentine state to promote access to intelligent technology and to foster an appropriate culture of the use of intelligent systems for information management.

REFERENCES

Apolo-Buenaño, D. E., Hermann-Acosta, E. A., García-Herrera, D. G., & Sotaminga-Cinilin, M. J. (2023). Uses of the internet for educational purposes: Perspectives for its strengthening. *Conrado*, 19(90), 233–236.

Ainscow, M. & Miles, S. (2009). Developing inclusive education systems: How we can advance policies? Hosor.

Bajarlía, Á. (2023). Impact of artificial intelligence on leadership. *Perspectivas: Revista Científica de la Universidad de Belgrano*, 6(1), 110–115.

Bolden, R., Petrov, G., & Gosling, J. (2009). Distributed leadership in higher education: Rhetoric and reality. *Educational Management Administration & Leadership*, 37(2), 257–277.

Bolivar, A. (2010). Educational leadership and its role in improvement: a current review of its posibilities and limitations. *Psicoperspectivas*, 9(2), July–December, 9–33.
Bolivar, A. (2014). Educational leadership and teacher professional development: an international review. Chile. RIL Publishers, 61–103.
Camacho, K. (2005). The digital divide. *Words at stake: Multicultural approaches to information societies*, 61–71.
CENIA (2024). *Latin artificial intelligence index*. (2nd ed.).
Cárdenas Tapia, M.J, Callinapa Lupaca, E.A, Canaza Turpo, C.F, Coteviano, A., Cayllahua, J. & Calsin, A. (2022). Educational management: dimensions, factors, and challenges for school transformation. *Revoluciones Magazine*, 4(9), 102–134.
Fadhilah, A. N., & Warnis, S. (2024). Students' perceptions toward the influence of teacher's attitudes on English Learning. *English Learning Achievement,* 164–174.
Fullán, M. (2020). *Leading in a culture of change*. Ediciones Morata.
Flores Vivar, J & García Peñalvo, F. (2023). Reflections on the ethics, potential, and challenges of artificial intelligence in the framework of quality education. *Comunicar*, 74, 37–47. https//doi.org/10.3916/C74-2023-03
Galiani et. al (2008). School decentralization: Helping the good get better, but leaving the poor behind. *Journal of Public Economics*, 92, 2106–2120. https://www.sciencedirect.com/science/article/abs/pii/S0047272708000923
Gvirtz, S., Zacarías, I. & Abregú, V. (2011). *Building a good school: tools for the principal*. Aique Grupo Editor.
Litardo, J. E. T., Arreaga, M. Y. C., Castillo, Y. M. G., & Naranjo, C. E. T. (2024). Artificial intelligence applied to educational management and its impact on the development of teaching skills. *Mapa Magazine*, 8(35).
Loayza Flores, L. J., Marujo Serna, M. P, Primo Mendoza, J. , Alania Coras , E. (2022). Work motivation and teaching performance in Peru. *Propuestas educativas*. 4(2).
Martínez García, I. & Gil Flores (2018). Intercultural competencies in higher education: a key aspect for mobility. *Education in the Knowledge Society*, 19(1).
Northouse P.G. (2021). *Leadership theory and practice*. (9th ed.). SAGE Publications.
Office of the Chief of Cabinet of Ministers, Argentine Republic. (2023). Provision No. 02/23. Recommendations for reliable artificial intelligence. *National Gazette*.
Porres, A. (2018). School leadership in educational transformation. *Clarin*.
Robiolo, G. & Martello, D. (2024). ¿Qué rol juega Argentina en el desarrollo de IA en Latinoamérica? Universidad Austral.
Robinson, V., Hohepa, M. & Lloyd, C. (2009). *School leadership and student outcomes: Identifying what works an why*. The University of Auckland.
Rouhiainen, L. (2018). *Artificial Intelligence*. Alienta Editorial, 20–21.
Sánchez, A. H., & Ainscow, M. (2018). Equidad e Inclusión: Retos y progresos de la escuela del siglo XXI. *Revista Retos XXI*, 2(1), 13–22.
Snyder, H. (2019). Literature review as a research methodology: An overview and guidelines. *Journal of Business Research*, 104(July), 333–339.
Tambingon, H. N., et al., (2024). Principal leadership management. *Return: Study of Management, Economic and Business*, 3(7), 526–537.
Tiramonti, G. (2001). *Modernización educativa de los 90: El fin de la ilusión emancipadora?* Temas.
Lucero Tello, J., Hernandez Davila, C., Gavilanes López, W. (2024). School management and educational quality. *Dialnet*, 9(1), 123–135.

Timperley, H. (2008). Using evidence in the classroom for professional learning. Ontario Education Research Symposium.
Ulloa, M. (2024). Advances in the regulation of artificial intelligence in Latin America: Catastrophic risk observations. University of Cambridge.
UNESCO (2015). *Leadership in education.* UNESCO Publications.
UNESCO (2018). *World education monitoring report.* UNESCO Publications.
UNESCO (2019a). *Education report.* UNESCO Publications.
UNESCO (2021). *Recommendation on the ethics of artificial intelligence.* UNESCO Publications.
UNESCO (2022). *Global education monitoring report 2022.* UNESCO Publications.
UNESCO (2023). *School leadership, evolution of policies and practices and improvement of educational quality.* UNESCO Publications.
Vera, F. (2023). Integración de la inteligencia artificial en la educación superior: Desafíos y oportunidades. *Transformar,* 4(1), 17–34. https://www.revistatransformar.cl/index.php/transformar/article/view/84

9. AI and the ethical dimension of educational leadership

Charles L. Lowery

In this chapter, I explore the ethical dimensions of artificial intelligence (AI) integration in educational leadership, focusing on the importance of balancing authenticity and ethical preparedness with AI prospects: the integration of AI and *authentic* intelligence. I also present the prospect of AI in facilitating the development of ethical decision-making in leaders and introduce foundational concepts for leaders in AI-supported environments.

Increasingly, AI is being assimilated into education and schooling. As we see it used more and more, it presents myriad possibilities for improving educational leadership practice. For example, AI holds the promise of assisting in leader planning and decision-making as well as offering powerful analytic support where large amounts of data are concerned. However, to what degree should school administrators use AI to augment their critical thinking and literacies needed to engage and manage the human aspects of leadership? If school leaders are to *harness AI* (if such a rapidly evolving technology can be harnessed) to augment planning and problem solving, they must also wrestle with the deeper implications. These implications exist within the emotional and social domains of leadership, and educators at all levels must ensure that the moral principles of their work remain at the forefront of what they do.

Therefore, AI presents leadership preparation and practice with certain ethical complexities that demand conscientious consideration. School leaders and other educators are now confronted with a new layer of moral accountability—one that requires them to not only take the lead in using AI for data-driven decision-making, instructional improvements, and community-based problem solving but also to be prepared to act as curators and custodians of rapidly generated texts and information, requiring digital literacy to ensure accuracy, trustworthiness, and, in many cases, equity.

From the position of educational leaders, AI presents opportunities to see things differently and to think about things critically when addressing long-standing dilemmas relating to resource allocation, staff development, stakeholder concerns, and overall implementation of organizational vision. Yet, the benefits of AI must be considered in the context of its limitations—particularly in its capacity (or lack thereof) to distinguish the nuances of ethical and sociocultural contexts. Leaders cannot simply cede their moral responsibilities to AI; conversely, they must find ways to integrate AI-generated insights with their own "authentic intelligence."

In the sections that follow, I outline how leaders can use AI to advance creative thinking, intensify ethical analysis, and explore how AI may help in mitigating crises and dilemmas. I also show that leaders need to remain vigilant about over-reliance on these systems, particularly regarding the phenomenon I term "dilemma latency," in which underlying ethical considerations may remain undiscovered by AI if leaders fail to prompt the tool—or themselves—adequately. Ultimately, this chapter offers a vision for what balanced, ethically prepared AI-enhanced educational leadership might look like, exploring how AI tools can support leaders in making wiser, more deliberate, and inclusive decisions.

BRAINSTORMING AND EXPANDING CRITICAL THOUGHT THROUGH AI

AI can be viewed as a tool for expanding novel, improvisational, and critical thinking by generating ideas outside traditional constraints, promoting innovative reflection, and improving educational leaders' adaptive and contingent thinking abilities. Innovation in educational leadership often stalls when constrained by traditional thinking patterns and "analysis paralysis" (Samimian-Darash & Rabi, 2021). AI may be able to aid school leaders in breaking through *innovation constraints* or "traditional limitations on thinking patterns" by challenging cognitive limitations and fears associated with failure or analysis paralysis. AI can challenge these constraints by generating ideas beyond the scope of human cognitive biases, bridging gaps that commonly limit leaders' willingness to consider creative possibilities. This is particularly useful in contexts where leaders must address complex organizational issues requiring new vantage points.

Therefore, AI's capacity to generate expansive ideas and engage in creative problem-solving complements the leader's moral duty to weigh these ideas within a realistic organizational setting. Leaders must still do the work of evaluating each idea's viability and ethics. Nevertheless, the synergy between AI's generative potential and human critical perspective can be a powerful force for revitalizing the strategic culture of a school or district. Two ways this may be viewed are: 1) AI as a Catalyst for Improvisational Thinking and 2) Tapping into "Blue Sky" Thinking.

AI as a Catalyst for Improvisational Thinking

Generative AI tools (e.g., large language models (LLMs) like ChatGPT) can propose fresh solutions and paths of inquiry, acting as a creative partner that prompts exploration. By proposing unusual or even counterintuitive ideas, AI can help leaders break through "the box" of conventional administrative models. In addition to having the ability to generate "out of the box" solutions and challenging entrenched assumptions, AI may be a tool that leaders can utilize to deepen their capacity for creative, improvisational thought. For example, in a strategic planning session, an AI system could supply a variety of unique staffing solutions, highlighting both logistical challenges and potential ethical pitfalls. Leaders then engage in improvisational thinking to adapt those suggestions to their realities (Beghetto, 2023; Memmert & Tavanapour, 2023).

By integrating AI outputs into reflective protocols or collaborative workshop models, leaders can initiate a process of "idea cross-pollination," where novel suggestions from AI are critiqued, reworked, and contextualized in real time by human stakeholders. This expands the collective imagination of leadership teams, propelling them beyond standard administrative scripts and into generative exploration.

Furthermore, when leaders frame AI-generated suggestions through culturally responsive and equity-focused lenses, improvisational thinking is not simply an abstract exercise; it can be a practical endeavor that assists decision makers in aligning their actions with the visions and missions of their learning organization. Consequently, the creative synergy between human insight and AI-generated pathways can potentially nurture the kind of risk-taking and creative innovation needed for tackling the multifaceted challenges of contemporary schooling.

Tapping into "Blue Sky" Thinking

School leaders may not always consider "far-out" alternatives due to bureaucratic pressure or fear of failure. When AI quickly simulates hypothetical scenarios, those "beyond-the-veil" ideas, what can be thought of as "blue sky" ideas, can be weighed without the immediate financial or political consequences that typically constrain real-world decisions (Pham, 2022). In short, AI can model multiple versions of possible outcomes and "what could be," letting leaders compare projected consequences on a no-stakes basis. Such scenario-based, low-risk exploration fosters the expansion of critical thought in the school administrator as a human agent, enabling educational leaders to deliberate more deeply on feasible action plans.

AI AND PROBLEM-POSING WORK WITH CONFLICTS

What might be AI's role in assisting leaders to ethically analyze complex issues, including crises, dilemmas, and potential controversies? Might we consider ways of using AI to analyze potential ethical conflicts and the importance of leaders maintaining a critical perspective, especially in situations that may involve hidden agendas or biases?

If AI can expand the problem-solving repertoire of school leaders, it can also serve as a valuable sounding board for exploring ethical dilemmas. Educational leaders often navigate tensions where the "right" answer is far from clear. AI can offer a structured approach to analyzing these tensions by identifying underlying variables, stakeholder interests, and potential biases embedded in proposed solutions (Shapiro & Stefkovich, 2016).

Revealing Hidden Agendas and Biases

AI algorithms, especially those trained on large data sets, can detect subtle patterns. For instance, educational leaders might be able to tap into these patterns and discover that specific groups of stakeholders—such as underrepresented parent communities—are consistently omitted from existing decision-making processes. While AI itself might not always catch latent biases (Kumar, 2025), its pattern-recognition capabilities can unearth the historical inequities that leaders might not have recognized on their own. As Arar et al. (2016) emphasize, ethical leadership in education must be acutely attuned to cultural and demographic diversity, and AI can make these dimensions more visible to decision makers.

Problem Posing and Dialogue with AI

Leaders can use AI as a "problem-posing" collaborator to test the moral ramifications of their decisions. By inputting hypothetical conflict scenarios into a generative model, leaders can compare emergent solutions, analyzing how AI frames possible outcomes. This practice sheds light on potential blind spots—areas where the AI solution might inadvertently perpetuate injustice or inequitable resource distributions (Chiu & Chen, 2024). Engaging in dialogue with AI in this way requires that leaders apply a critical lens to AI outputs, ensuring that ethical reasoning supersedes algorithmic convenience.

By drawing upon foundational theories of moral development, leaders can facilitate professional learning sessions or staff dialogues where AI proposals serve as case studies for ethical deliberation. As such, AI would function as a devil's advocate or critical friend providing varying contingencies and hypothetical texts that could help articulate, contest, augment, and refine the leader's assumptions by integrating personal, professional, and collective ethical commitments into "the dialogue."

Beyond merely widening the range of solutions, such critical ethical literacies could deepen a leader's understanding of how policy decisions intersect with the lived realities of stakeholders. Thus, the integration of AI in educational decision-making could possibly be employed to build a capacity for moral discernment, ultimately aligning technology-enhanced solutions with the core values of democratic leadership.

CONDITIONING RESOURCEFULNESS THROUGH SCENARIO-BASED EXERCISES

Segueing from the previous subsection, here I would like to detail how AI can enhance resourcefulness by simulating real-world scenarios that encourage leaders to acknowledge, acquire, allocate, and assess resources innovatively. We can consider how AI exercises might be employed for promoting an asset-oriented mindset, enabling leaders to transform ordinary materials into strategic assets within their educational environments. This prospectively is a means to enhancing human agency and moral autonomy through AI. I argue for the potential of AI to support—not replace—human agency, enhancing leaders' moral autonomy by providing structured ethical insights without undermining independent thinking.

School leaders often confront resource allocation challenges—deciding how to manage limited budgets, staff capabilities, and infrastructure to maximize student success. By simulating scenario-based exercises, AI can cultivate a mindset of resourcefulness. Leaders can systematically examine how to better "acknowledge, acquire, allocate, and assess" existing or new resources (Jonassen, 2010). This presents educational leaders as moral agents who can leverage AI to enhance their ethical decision-making without losing their sense of agency or ethical responsibility.

AI-Enhanced Simulations for Asset-Oriented Thinking

AI can generate multiple variations of a scenario, demonstrating how changes in resource allocation might ripple across a district. For instance, distributing technology resources more equitably among different community schools or redirecting funds to specific after-school programs can be scrutinized in real time (Walter, 2024). Simulation outputs can highlight potential inequities or oversights, encouraging leaders to weigh both immediate outcomes and long-term sustainability (Pham & Sampson, 2022).

Fostering Human Agency and Moral Autonomy

Far from replacing the human aspect of school leadership, AI can serve as a stimulus that sharpens human agency and the leader's moral autonomy. Leaders must remain situated as the moral architects and arbiters of what AI models to reflect on and which suggested actions to adopt. But AI can illuminate resource opportunities or obstacles that might otherwise remain hidden (Cranston & Kusanovich, 2014). In this arrangement, AI brings to the forefront possible pathways, but the educational leader is the one to decide if those pathways align with school values and ethics. This heightened sense of moral autonomy evolves from the leader's capacity to cross-check AI's numerous suggestions and generated recommendations against human considerations such as empathy, equity, and community well-being (Jenlink, 2014; Jenlink & Embry-Jenlink, 2015).

ETHICAL DECISION-MAKING: BALANCING POSITIVE OUTCOMES WITH GROUP IMPACTS

Ethical decision-making often requires reconciling conflicting objectives in which the most favorable outcome for one group might disadvantage another (Thiel et al., 2012). As well, ethical decision-making when facing dilemmas may even be viewed as a no-win situation. In educational leadership, these dilemmas are particularly thorny because choices affect students, teachers, staff, parents, and the broader community.

Leaders need unbiased sounding boards and scenario-sensitive cases to exercise the critical literacies necessary to address these ethical dilemmas. AI-generated replies and case development can assist leaders in strengthening their decision-making through an endless presentation of dialogues and simulations where impacts on various groups are considered. Leaders can then authentically evaluate both positive and negative consequences on stakeholders, ensuring a nuanced understanding of group needs and ethical implications in real-world situations.

AI-Generated Scenarios and Stakeholder Analysis

AI can be seen as an instructive partner in scenario-based decision-making exercises, forecasting potential group-level impacts of a proposed policy or action (Heyman et al., 2024). For example, a leader might query an AI system to project the outcomes of redistributing staff from one department or grade level to another. The AI's analysis could outline benefits to the staffing decisions (such as smaller class sizes or a stronger instructional team) all the while also noting consequences that could prove detrimental (like increased workloads or a diminished sense of morale among a grade level team). Such an assessment provides a more holistic view of stakeholder impacts, which school leaders can then weigh using their own ethical calculus (Hudson, 1997).

Cultivating Nuanced Ethical Literacy

While AI can expand the breadth of leaders' considerations, it is not a substitute for cultivating ethical literacy (Parks-Leduc et al., 2021). Leaders must remain grounded in a moral framework—one informed by democratic values, social justice concerns, and culturally responsive practices (Tenuto & Gardiner, 2018). By integrating AI scenario outputs into their personal and institutional values, leaders refine their capacity to see the full spectrum of group impacts. In this sense, AI functions as a valuable "sparring partner," helping leaders practice moral reasoning in a low-risk environment before making critical real-world decisions.

Building on the imperative to remain grounded in a moral framework, leaders can intentionally cultivate *critical ethical literacies*—glocal literacies for the 21st century (Brooks & Normore, 2010)—by weaving together AI outputs with context-laden judgment. Leaders might feasibly use AI as a sounding board to enhance their socio-historical awareness and approach issues through a critical reflective praxis. This might entail examining AI-recommended courses of action through multiple interpretive lenses (e.g., stakeholder engagement, cultural responsiveness, and equity impact).

DEVELOPING ADAPTIVE THINKING AND CULTURAL SENSITIVITY WITH AI

School leaders often serve in increasingly diverse educational environments where cultural sensitivity and adaptive decision-making are vital. AI can augment leaders' ability to anticipate and manage cultural nuances, provided the tools are used discerningly (Thomson et al., 2007; Samuel et al., 2023). I aver that AI could hypothetically be instrumental in refining leaders' critical thinking and authentic intelligence for culturally sensitive decision-making.

This means considering the problem of whether or not AI can adopt nuanced and socio-culturally appropriate responses. If it can be trained to consider these aspects of sensitivity, then AI can potentially challenge leaders' adaptive decision-making frameworks. This means even engaging school leaders in the consideration of spatio-temporal complexities, encouraging responses that are socially relevant and culturally sensitive. This will include consideration of the educational leader as a critically responsive intellectual and describe how AI can promote a better understanding of past and present contexts to inform ethical decisions.

Culturally Responsive AI?

Emerging research suggests that AI models can be developed to reflect sensitivity to cultural norms and values (Kashyap et al., 2024). However, building culturally responsive AI requires careful training data selection, ethical oversight, and iterative calibration. Hence, leaders must approach AI outputs with skepticism and a willingness to conduct context checks by verifying that recommendations align with local norms, traditions, and social realities (Pham, 2023).

Improving Adaptive Leadership Mindsets

Adaptive leadership calls for a balance between macro-level strategies and micro-level sensitivity (Pherson & Pherson, 2020). AI can push leaders to consider multiple layers of the cultural and temporal context simultaneously. By introducing data about demographic shifts, local historical events, or emerging social concerns into prompts, leaders can ask AI to propose responses that factor in evolving conditions. Through this process, leaders sharpen their contextual intelligence, learning how to pivot effectively in an era characterized by complexity and rapid change (Helbing, 2019).

To further strengthen adaptive leadership mindsets, school leaders can pair AI-driven forecasting with scenario-based simulations that incorporate the dynamic interplay of cultural, social, and economic factors. By thinking critically about multiple "what-if" situations—each iteration reflecting different stakeholder values or shifting contextual conditions—leaders could practice nimbly responding to uncertainty and controversy. This process can be enriched by deliberately incorporating critical literacies, encouraging leaders to question how asymmetrical structures or historical precedents shape the AI's suggestions.

As leaders integrate this adaptive perspective into their strategic routines, they must maintain a space for reflective pauses, stakeholder feedback loops, and continuous learning. This is not a substitute for developing a needed resilience that transcends any given situation and certainly cannot be replaced by a single AI tool. Ultimately, the collaboration between a technologically informed vantage point and a morally responsive approach fosters a type of leadership that can remain flexible in the face of complexity, yet not give up their commitment to the equitable and communal well-being of the school environment.

CAUTIONS ON RELYING SOLELY ON AI: AUTHENTIC INTELLIGENCE AS A MODERATING FACTOR

The potential pitfalls of AI reliance are substantial. Over-reliance can promote complacency or a blind trust in technologically generated insights. Educational leaders must maintain their moral compass, recognizing that AI models, no matter how sophisticated, remain ultimately fallible. In this section, I address the risks of over-reliance on AI, advocating for "authentic intelligence"—human insight that tempers AI-driven responses. There are times, as with all technologies, when we should disconnect from the digital realm and reconnect with ourselves and others. I urge that leaders take heed to ensure a reasonable and critical balance between human judgment and AI input, stressing the importance of maintaining moral responsibility and retaining their personal, ethical intuition in decision-making.

Recognizing Limitations

Generative AI, by its nature, extrapolates from patterns in data—it does not "understand" moral imperatives or local nuances in the way human leaders do (Schiff & Rosenberg-Kima, 2023). For instance, an AI might propose a resource reallocation plan that appears cost-effective but inadvertently perpetuates an existing inequity. Leaders are responsible for auditing outputs against their ethical frameworks and daily lived experiences of their communities (Trevino & Youngblood, 1990).

Prioritizing Human-Centered Leadership

Human-centered leadership underscores the irreplaceable role of empathy, compassion, and personal moral reflection. Authentic intelligence, in this sense, consists of an awareness of local realities, personal experiences, and the capacity for emotional resonance that computers cannot replicate (Jenlink, 2014). Hence, even as AI offers valuable assistance, educational leaders must integrate personal interactions and peer collaboration, recognizing ethical reflection cannot be outsourced to machines (Marbun, 2023).

THE CHALLENGE OF ETHICAL DILEMMA LATENCY IN AI INTEGRATION

Towards a theory of AI Integration for School Leaders, I introduce the concept of what I call "Dilemma Latency," where ethical issues may be latent, unnoticed, or inactive but still influential in decision-making. As noted above, AI is not known for its ability to read nuance. However, if leaders use their own critical inquiry skills, they may be able to innovate and improvisationally create prompts and situations for AI to "get at" these hidden problems. AI can both reveal and obscure these latent factors, and I propose strategies for leaders to stay vigilant to underlying ethical issues that may not immediately surface and use that to their advantage when using AI in their practice.

What Is Dilemma Latency?

One significant risk in AI-mediated decision-making is that key ethical considerations can remain unrecognized or "latent." AI tools tend to respond only to properly-written prompts and the data they have been trained on. Unanticipated dilemmas then can remain dormant if leaders do not explicitly prompt AI to uncover them. Therefore, "dilemma latency" is when ethical or moral conflicts within a given scenario may not surface without intentional inquiry. If certain cultural or contextual intricacies are not specifically included, AI might fail to highlight critical moral issues (Shapiro & Stefkovich, 2016). For example, a query about mitigating a political conflict in a school district might ignore nuanced social tensions or norms that only appear salient when framed in the correct way. To avoid this dilemma latency, leaders need to know how to "ask the right questions" (Pham, 2023).

The problem of dilemma latency emphasizes the importance for leaders to not lose their personal curiosity and reflective judgment. All leaders, particularly school leaders, need to be prepared for and always mindful of less obvious ethical factors embedded in AI-generated recommendations. By systematically probing for oversights—such as unexplored intersectionalities or marginalized perspectives—leaders can preemptively surface emergent moral complexities that AI models might not automatically detect. This process is especially crucial in contexts where deep-seated cultural tensions, historical inequities, or subtle biases may linger beneath the surface.

Leaders who develop robust "prompt engineering" skills can strengthen their ability to generate AI outputs that delve into these less visible dimensions, essentially customizing the AI's analytical lens to reveal hidden ethical terrain. Dilemma latency thus becomes both a cautionary reminder and an opportunity. Leaders must remain cautious against defaulting to AI's first or most convenient answer while also offering a pathway for a more robust, more inclusive inquiry that must remain situated within the school's overall culture and community.

Prompt Engineering as Ethical Inquiry

Leaders can mitigate dilemma latency by devising well-constructed prompts that systematically probe for potential issues. Questions such as, "Which groups might be negatively impacted by this decision?" or "What biases could be embedded in these data?" serve as powerful catalysts. Prompt engineering, in this sense, becomes a tool for ethical inquiry (Walter, 2024). Leaders become, in effect, "scenario designers," controlling how and where the AI directs its analysis and ensuring that latent dilemmas do not remain concealed.

TOWARDS A THEORY OF ETHICALLY AI-ENHANCED EDUCATIONAL LEADERSHIP

In sum, AI integration in educational leadership can significantly expand the boundaries of problem-solving, critical thinking, and ethical decision-making. From brainstorming sessions that prompt innovative solutions to scenario-based exercises that hone resourcefulness, AI offers a trove of potential benefits for school leaders. At the same time, reliance on AI must be tempered by leaders' authentic intelligence—an ethical mindset that values equity, cultural responsiveness, and moral integrity.

Such synergy requires a continued reexamination of what it means to lead ethically in an ever-evolving digital landscape. In terms of AI's potential impact on education, political literacy, information literacy, and pedagogic literacy must always be coupled with moral literacy, spiritual literacy, and temporal literacy (Brooks & Normore, 2010). By weaving AI's analytic power into a leadership approach rooted in empathy, justice, and cultural awareness, school leaders can harness technology not merely to expedite tasks, but to enrich the quality and integrity of their decision-making. In this iterative process, leaders should continually interrogate both AI outputs and their own assumptions—remaining attentive to the potential for bias or oversights within algorithmic models, while affirming their responsibility to uphold democratic principles. This cautious, ethically grounded engagement ensures that AI serves to enhance human vision rather than a replacement for it, helping leaders remain steadfast in their commitment to equitable resource distribution, stakeholder collaboration, and holistic student development.

Educational leaders who adopt these technologies judiciously stand to gain enhanced clarity in ethical dilemmas and greater creativity in organizational problem-solving. Yet, it cannot be stressed enough, the real risk lies in ignoring the possibility of dilemma latency and conferring too much authority on AI. Ultimately, the most responsible path forward is one in which school leaders engage with AI tools in a dialectical manner, inviting new insights while consistently viewing its application through an ethical lens. By balancing AI-informed analysis with their own moral and social sensibilities, we might realize a future in which AI emerges as an invaluable tool for educational leaders as creators of equitable, innovative, democratic, and ethically grounded learning environments for all.

REFERENCES

Arar, K., Haj, I., Abramovitz, R., & Oplatka, I. (2016). Ethical leadership in education and its relation to ethical decision-making: The case of Arab school leaders in Israel. *Journal of Educational Administration, 54*(6), 647–660.

Beghetto, R. A. (2023). A new horizon for possibility thinking: A conceptual case study of Human × AI collaboration. *Possibility Studies & Society, 1*(3), 324–341.

Brooks, J. S., & Normore, A. H. (2010). Educational leadership and globalization: Literacy for a glocal perspective. *Educational Policy, 24*(1), 52–82.

Chiu, Y. H., & Chen, C. C. (2024). Elevating and sharpening convergent thinking: The Potential of generative AI for creative professionals. Available at SSRN 4911494 https://papers.ssrn.com/sol3/papers.cfm?abstract_id=4911494

Cranston, J., & Kusanovich, K. (2014). More drama in school leadership: Developing creative and ethical capacities in the next generation of school leaders. *Canadian Journal of Educational Administration and Policy, 151*(1), 1–33.

Helbing, D. (2019). Societal, economic, ethical and legal challenges of the digital revolution: From big data to deep learning, artificial intelligence, and manipulative technologies. In D. Helbing (Ed.), *Towards digital enlightenment: Essays on the dark and light sides of the digital revolution* (pp. 47–72). Springer International.

Heyman, J. L., Rick, S. R., Giacomelli, G., Wen, H., Laubacher, R., Taubenslag, N., ... & Malone, T. (2024, June). Supermind ideator: How scaffolding human-AI collaboration can increase creativity. *Proceedings of the ACM Collective Intelligence Conference* (pp. 18–28).

Hudson, J. (1997). Ethical leadership: The soul of policy making. *Journal of School Leadership, 7*(5), 506–520.

Jenlink, P. M. (Ed.). (2014). *Educational leadership and moral literacy: The dispositional aims of moral leaders.* Rowman & Littlefield.

Jenlink, P. M., & Embry-Jenlink, K. (2015). Ethical leadership and moral literacy: Incorporating ethical dilemmas in a case-based pedagogy. *Educational Leadership Review, 16*(2), 55–85.

Jonassen, D. H. (2010). *Learning to solve problems: A handbook for designing problem-solving learning environments.* Routledge.

Kashyap, R., Samuel, Y., Friedman, L. W., & Samuel, J. (2024). Artificial intelligence education & governance-human enhancive, culturally sensitive and personally adaptive HAI. *Frontiers in Artificial Intelligence, 7,* 1443386.

Kumar, S. (2025). Ethical Leadership in the Age of AI. In L. Guar (Ed.), *Responsible implementations of generative AI for multidisciplinary use* (pp. 265–290). IGI Global.

Marbun, T. O. (2023). The implementation of artificial intelligence, ChatGPT, And critical thinking method for academic endeavors at Theological Higher Education. *Journal Didaskalia, 6*(2), 84–100.

Memmert, L., & Tavanapour, N. (2023). *Towards human-AI-collaboration in brainstorming: Empirical insights into the perception of working with a generative AI.* Thirty-first European Conference on Information Systems (ECIS 2023), Kristiansand, Norway.

Parks-Leduc, L., Mulligan, L., & Rutherford, M. A. (2021). Can ethics be taught? Examining the impact of distributed ethical training and individual characteristics on ethical decision-making. *Academy of Management Learning & Education, 20*(1), 30–49.

Pham, S. (2022). Multi-dimensional thinking literacy through learning to code: An urgent request for current school leaders. In E. Langran (Ed.), *Proceedings of Society for Information Technology & Teacher Education International Conference* (pp. 1069–1074). Association for the Advancement of Computing in Education (AACE).

Pham, S. T., & Sampson, P. M. (2022). The development of artificial intelligence in education: A review in context. *Journal of Computer Assisted Learning, 38*(5), 1408–1421.

Pham, S. T. (2023). Exploring the Lived Experience of Educators and Business Executives in the Phenomenon of Artificial Intelligence in Education. In J. D. DeHart (Ed.), *Phenomenological Studies in Education* (pp. 182–206). IGI Global.

Pherson, K. H., & Pherson, R. H. (2020). *Critical thinking for strategic intelligence.* CQ Press.

Samimian-Darash, L., & Rabi, M. (2021). Governing uncertainty, producing subjectivity: From Mode I to Mode II scenarios. *Subjectivity, 14*, 1–18.

Samuel, Y., Brennan-Tonetta, M., Samuel, J., Kashyap, R., Kumar, V., Krishna Kaashyap, S., ... & Jain, P. (2023). Cultivation of human centered artificial intelligence: Culturally adaptive thinking in education (CATE) for AI. *Frontiers in Artificial Intelligence, 6*, 1198180.

Shapiro, J. P., & Stefkovich, J. A. (2016). *Ethical leadership and decision making in education: Applying theoretical perspectives to complex dilemmas.* Routledge.

Schiff, D. S., & Rosenberg-Kima, R. B. (2023). AI in education: landscape, vision and critical ethical challenges in the 21st century. In S. Lindgren (Ed.), *Handbook of critical studies of artificial intelligence* (pp. 804–814). Edward Elgar.

Tenuto, P. L., & Gardiner, M. E. (2018). Interactive dimensions for leadership: An integrative literature review and model to promote ethical leadership praxis in a global society. *International Journal of Leadership in Education, 21*(5), 593–607.

Thiel, C. E., Bagdasarov, Z., Harkrider, L., Johnson, J. F., & Mumford, M. D. (2012). Leader ethical decision-making in organizations: Strategies for sensemaking. *Journal of Business Ethics, 107*, 49–64.

Thomson, M. H., Adams, B. D., Taylor, T. E., Sartori, J. A., Authority, D. T. S., & Thompson, M. (2007). The impact of culture on moral and ethical decision-making: An integrative literature review. *Report to Department of National Defence (DRDC No. CR-2007-168).*

Trevino, L. K., & Youngblood, S. A. (1990). Bad apples in bad barrels: A causal analysis of ethical decision-making behavior. *Journal of Applied Psychology, 75*(4), 378.

Walter, Y. (2024). Embracing the future of Artificial Intelligence in the classroom: The relevance of AI literacy, prompt engineering, and critical thinking in modern education. *International Journal of Educational Technology in Higher Education, 21*(1), 15.

PART III

AI for inclusion and equity in curriculum and instruction

10. Trust in artificial intelligence

Challenges of educational equity and ethics in students' practices in German higher education

Therese Rosemann, Marie Rathmann, Jan Schiller, and Sabine Schmidt-Lauff

---

The integration of artificial intelligence in education (AIED) has generated considerable optimism about enhancing educational opportunities, including the support of individualized learning processes (Holmes & Porayska-Pomsta, 2023). While technological sufficiency and feasibility are crucial aspects to consider (Gardner et al., 2021), substantial ethical concerns arise, particularly regarding the types of algorithmic bias in education that have garnered scholarly attention (Fox, 2022; Henking, 2024; Holstein & Doroudi, 2022; Ifenthaler, 2023). Artificial intelligence (AI) applications can create enabling conditions for diverse learning interactions, yet they can also contribute to increased disparities (Reinhardt & Sinn, 2024). The institutional implementation of AIED systems is complemented by students' growing independence in utilizing AI applications based on large language models (LLMs) (Buck & Limburg, 2023; Eager & Brunton, 2023; Renz & Galla, 2024; von Garrel et al., 2023), which gives rise to a distinct set of ethical implications (e.g. between "deontological and consequentialist ethics" cf. Schönmann & Uhl, 2023) through increasingly complex human-machine interactions (Beckers & Teubner, 2024). Despite the widespread prevalence of human-machine interactions in both everyday life and academic settings, as well as the relatively low barrier to accessing digital hardware and software, a digital divide persists. This raises important questions about how human-machine interactions are utilized, or not utilized, in daily life and education, and the ethical challenges they may present. Specifically, to what extent do users and non-users of AI applications differ in terms of their usage behavior, trust in AI, and self-assessment of AI-related knowledge? Moreover, what ethical implications arise from these differences for AI-related practices in higher education?

To address the research questions posed, we first provide the context surrounding AI in education and the digital divide as a framework for examining AI use or non-use in educational settings. Subsequently, we introduce our three central constructs (usage behavior, trust in AI, self-assessment of AI-related knowledge), thereby providing the theoretical foundation for the following statistical analysis. These analyses were conducted as part of the *DigiTaKS** project, which is briefly described and its methodology outlined. The empirical results are subsequently reported in three steps: Initially, the surveyed student population is described in terms of AI users and non-users, then further statistical analysis of differences we performed along the three constructs are shown. Ultimately, a discussion of the results with their implications for the ethical use of AI in higher education and a conclusion will ensue. The article not only demonstrates the usage practices of AI applications in academic settings, but also examines the impact of three core constructs – trust, use, and knowledge – on the adoption and utilization of these technologies. Theoretically and empirically grounded results emerge, enabling conclusions to be drawn about the potential for ethical challenges to arise in the use of AI in higher education, which may exacerbate digital divides. The findings offer an understanding of inequality and social involvement, materializing as a digital divide rather than a structural segregation through physical access to technology and infrastructure. Furthermore, this study sheds light on strategies that universities can employ to mitigate such disparities and ensure educational equity, particularly in the context of ongoing transformations in the field of AIED.

ARTIFICIAL INTELLIGENCE AND DIGITAL DIVIDE IN HIGHER EDUCATION: AN ETHICAL PERSPECTIVE ON THE PHENOMENON

AI is generally understood as not only comprehending intelligent entities but also *building* them: "machines that can compute how to act effectively and safely in a wide variety of novel situations." (Russell & Norvig, 2020, p. 19) This paper specifically examines generative AI, which is understood as generation of synthetic artifacts by using big data and algorithms with the aim of analyzing training examples, identifying and learning their patterns and distributions, and creating matching reproductions. While generative AI can be understood as an umbrella term for AI technologies, LLMs constitute a special type of generative AI. LLMs have "emerged as cutting-edge artificial intelligence systems that can process and generate text with coherent communication and generalize to multiple tasks" (Naveed et al., 2023, p. 2). These models encompass text-generating models, such as ChatGPT or Copilot, as well as visual models, like BingAI or MidJourney. In this context, we adopt UNESCO's

"Recommendation on the Ethics of Artificial Intelligence" (UNESCO, 2022) to define AI as a holistic, integrative, and model-based processing technology:

> AI systems are information-processing technologies that integrate models and algorithms that produce a capacity to learn and to perform cognitive tasks leading to outcomes such as prediction and decision-making in material and virtual environments. AI systems are designed to operate with varying degrees of autonomy by means of knowledge modelling and representation and by exploiting data and calculating correlations. (p. 3)

Processes and methods, which include AI systems, are, among others, machine learning (e.g., deep learning and reinforcement learning) as well as machine reasoning (e.g., search, knowledge representation, planning, etc.). In the following, we will consider such *technical methods* of machine learning to the extent that they enable AI to generate human-like output. Ansari et al. (2024) describe this as follows: "It performs a range of tasks including recording and understanding human input and generating human-like textual responses; it can translate language, complete text, and answer questions" (p. 11283). This output is made possible by algorithms and vast datasets on which the AI has been trained. Esposito (2017) notes that the algorithms "make selections and choices based on criteria that are not random, but that the user does not know and need to know" (p. 260). As a result, questions surrounding big data and AI as a black box come to the forefront, rendering it unclear for most users how algorithms generate a specific output. Nevertheless, they affect both knowledge, access, and practices of users: "The algorithmic effect thus arises from distinctions that flow both unseen and unreflected into the manner of situated knowledge production and the mediation of possibilities for action and agency" (Heinlein, 2024, pp. 419–420, own translation). Considering the *machine reasoning* aspect, specific interactions between AI systems and humans, as well as the resulting dialogue and use of such AI applications, become crucial. The AI system is then viewed as a machine to access (world) knowledge based on interactive practices and dialogue between humans and AI. In and through these interactions, conflicts with content and technology arise – whether it's around deciding to use or not use AI, prompting (how do I formulate my question?), and related reflection processes (can I work further with the output of AI, or must I prompt again? What else is there to know about my content?).

Consequently, AI systems gain significance in educational contexts when they facilitate engagement with both external realities and self-reflection, a process grounded in the humanistic concept of *Bildung* (e.g., Wollersheim, 2023). In this framework, education is understood not merely as the optimization of learning outcomes, but as the cultivation of human independence and self-determination through active engagement with the world. This perspective emphasizes the development of critical thinking and personal agency, rather than the optimized absorption of knowledge. To elucidate theoretical perspectives on inequality regarding the use of AI in studies or higher education, we employ the theoretical framework of the *Digital Divide* as proposed by van Dijk (2020). He defines the digital divide as "the gap between people who do and do not have access to forms of information and communication technology" (van Dijk, 2017, p. 1). Using this framework, it must be highlighted that it does not imply "absolute inequalities between those who are included and those who are excluded, . . . inequalities are more relative in kind" (ibid.). In order to address the digital divide perspective, van Dijk proposes three perspectives:

(a) *innovation* as the acceptance and development of new technology by individuals and societies;
(b) *(in)equality* when people have more opportunities to adopt and use new technology than others; and
(c) *participation* where respect is given to people who are more or less included in or excluded from society (van Dijk, 2020, p. 6).

From van Dijk's point of view, regarding the digital divide, "today, it is impossible to pursue higher education without sufficient digital skills" (van Dijk, 2020, p. 77). Recently, the constant evolution of digital competences has been particularly evident with the emergence of generative AI-based technologies, adding prompt engineering (Eager & Brunton, 2023) to the digital competence spectrum.

Yet, generative AI applications have shifted the foundations of van Dijk's model: While many important AI applications are openly available and free to use on widespread consumer devices like computers and smartphones (open access, physical access) and operate with simple text or voice input (technical competences), motivation and especially competent usage increasingly come into focus regarding a divide in practices. Against this background, the analytical perspective shifts from questions of access to questions of readiness, attitudes, and reflective use. To address this aspect, we adopt the concept of *operational readiness* from the "model for the effective and sustainable implementation of AI in higher education" by Stützer et al. (2023).[1] Operational readiness is defined as the "subjective willingness and capability of stakeholders (students and teaching staff) to engage with digital, intelligent technologies and systems" (ibid., p. 61, own translation). The concept emphasizes the importance of technology acceptance (as an attitude towards AI as a technology, the perceived use and benefits of this technology and the associated use of the technology), trust, as well as social influences alongside usage and competences.

The factors outlined above significantly influence trust in digital infrastructures, which in turn affects the adoption and use of AI applications (Stützer et al., 2023; see also Scheuer, 2020). In conclusion, ethical concerns regarding educational equity and participation are increasingly interconnected with the acceptance and trust in AI-enhanced education (AIED), alongside issues of usage, access, and digital competence. This raises critical questions as: Which dimensions – such as socio-demographic factors, access, acceptance, and digital competencies – affect trust in and the willingness to adopt AI? How can AI usage in academic contexts be differentiated, for example, between receptive and productive uses? What new forms of inequality will emerge as part of a complex, relational digital divide? In response, this study seeks to explore the role of AI-usage, trust in AI and self-assessment of AI-related knowledge in the case of a university in Germany and formulates the research questions: To what extent do users and non-users of AI applications differ in terms of their usage behavior, their trust in AI, and their self-assessment of AI-related knowledge – and what first ethical implications result from this for AI-related practices in higher education? Specifically, it examines the various roles and processes impacted by AI applications from a subjective-individual perspective, including their influence on learning content, scientific methodologies (development), and applications (de Witt et al., 2020). Questions concerning trust in AI, conceptualized as the "AI trust gap" (Chakravorti, 2024) are explored, providing insights into individual perspectives while also offering implications and recommendations for policymakers and higher education institutions. The "AI trust gap" is defined as "the sum of the persistent risks (both real and perceived) associated with AI; depending on the application, some risks are more critical" (ibid.) This gap is bridged when individuals choose to entrust AI with tasks that they would otherwise delegate to qualified professionals, for example. Trust becomes essential not only in terms of placing confidence in the machine but also in our ability to critically evaluate its trustworthiness. This underscores the need for diverse competencies to assess whether AI can be reliably used. For instance, having sufficient contextual information and knowledge about the subject of inquiry is crucial for accurately evaluating AI-generated outputs and determining their reliability for future use. Consequently, the significance of critical trust is growing. Finally, AI and trust are linked to various ethical challenges, as outlined by Chakravorti (2024): disinformation, safety and security, the black box problem, ethical concerns, bias, hallucinations in LLMs, etc.

Moreover, the paper provides an impetus for exploring issues of equality and inequality in the usage and access to AI in terms of a digital divide from van Dijk (2020). According to the OECD, equity in education is defined as ensuring "fair access" to education regardless of social and economic background, thereby enabling and empowering students "to reach their full potential" (OECD, 2024, p. 6). Based on this, we outline initial options for the possible integration of AI applications at universities or at institutions of higher education in order to bridge a digital divide. Thus, we address the inherent ethical dimensions of AI from an educational theoretical perspective, focusing on fairness, equal opportunities, access, and equity at both the individual and educational-institutional levels.

THREE CENTRAL CONSTRUCTS: USAGE, TRUST, AND KNOWLEDGE OF AI APPLICATIONS

In this section, we operationalize three central constructs that are essential to our empirical analysis and serve to contextualize the results of our study (quantitative questionnaire; n = 60) with bachelor students at a German university from different studying fields in the Faculty of Humanity and Social Sciences.

Usage of AI Applications in Studies

When examining the usage of AI applications in education, media practices related to interacting with these technologies are of particular interest. These practices vary based on the context (daily life or studies) and the intended purpose of the interaction. In formal settings within higher education, Tulodziecki (2015) proposes three media usage types, that we transfer to AI applications:

(a) *productive use*, such as generating images or learning materials;
(b) *receptive use*, like automatic translation into a language or literature search functions; and
(c) *interactive use*, for example, interacting with a chatbot as a personal tutor.

The integration of AI applications in education enables new learning processes through formal teaching-learning settings in higher education. For instance, Bhullar et al. (2024) exemplifies this by stating that ChatGPT stands out as a promising tool for open education, enhancing the independence and autonomy of autodidactic learners through personalized support.

AI applications, such as ChatGPT, are transforming practices of knowledge acquisition and transmission. A common criticism of AI systems in education is that "they encourage unethical behavior in learners, for example by facilitating plagiarism or the falsification of intellectual property" (Schönmann & Uhl, 2023, p. 442), just because it is easy to access and the students may not have the reflexive competences. Another – more pedagogical – criticism of the use of AI points to a potential "dumbing down" of learners (ibid., p. 443). The superior problem-solving abilities of AI could lead to students "intellectually withering" (ibid.), losing fundamental academic competences such as scholarly writing, and generally becoming less cognitively engaged (academic debates and discourses). Consequently, new formations and transformations of learning environments are emerging (Ricken et al., 2023, pp. 313–314), raising critical questions regarding access to education and academic equity. The proliferation of AI applications, along with the knowledge of their functionalities and the reflexive, transformative competencies required for their effective use, thus becomes key factors influencing educational (in)equity.

Trust in AI Applications Respectively: Human–Machine Interaction

Whenever AI is prioritized in interactive practices between humans and AI systems – including the user interface and the AI-generated output – human-machine interaction becomes paramount. In conjunction with this, questions surrounding trust in these systems become particularly relevant, encompassing both trust in the functions of the AI and willingness to use it (Liggieri & Müller, 2019, p. 328). Trust becomes central in contexts of uncertainty or lack of knowledge, referring – from a sociological perspective – to the constructed relationship between at least two actors: the trusting individual (in this case: the human), who must place faith and is vulnerable to potential harm due to uncertainty, and the trusted entity (the AI application), which is entrusted with that trust (faith) but possesses the potential power to cause harm to the trust giver (Schäfer et al., 2024).

When we conceptualize AI use as human-machine interaction, the propensity of AI applications to exhibit unexpected behavior or engage in undesirable activities (often described as the "black box" phenomenon) necessitates a delicate balance between anticipated actions of trust, approximation, and recognition. Users (humans) interact with AI systems in a context where their lack of knowledge about the AI often drives the interaction, leading to a situation in which safety and knowledge would ideally replace the dynamic of trust. Reinhardt and Sinn (2024) illustrate this as follows: "I must only trust where I do not know if what I trust will actually materialize" (pp. 229–230). Despite their ability to accurately and reliably solve certain problems – and, to some extent, exhibit intelligent behavior at a human level – such AI systems lack knowledge about how the world operates. Compared to human interaction, AI applications therefore lack common sense, which in turn presents new challenges with regard to trust in interaction (Schönmann & Uhl, 2023, p. 434). This is particularly important in the context of education, for instance when it comes to novel forms of knowledge acquisition and dissemination, providing information for informed decision-making, making personalized learning content available, etc. (ibid., pp. 435–436).

Self-Assessment of AI User Competences Regarding Knowledge, (Learning) Experiences, and Human–Machine Interaction

Knowledge is not only a fundamental prerequisite for trust and the use of AI, but it is also directly linked to digital competencies. The interaction with and use of AI systems translates into action, which results in the accumulation of experiential knowledge related to these interactions. Experience, in turn, forms the foundation for further knowledge development. From an educational theoretical perspective, Tulodziecki (2023) emphasizes: "Experience involves processing one's own activities or observations or mediated information and media messages cognitively, resulting in the formation of knowledge that is available for future perception, thinking, or behavior, or action" (Tulodziecki, 2023, p. 90, own translation).

Thus, the usage of AI and experiences derived from knowledge are closely interconnected. Knowledge influences both the current and future perceptions and usage of AI – hence, shaping the subjective perception of the technology, operational readiness, and usage practices. As a result, questions regarding individuals' self-assessments of their AI-related knowledge and usage are a focal point of interest. When such self-images (perceptions) are empirically assessed, it not only allows for an exploration of trust in one's own abilities and knowledge, but also provides insights into the motivation and reasons behind the use or *non*-use of AI. With easiest access to AI applications given, the person's attitude and motivation, perspective, and self-formation become increasingly important. By drawing further conclusions, we can shed light on consequentialist ethical implications where "the moral assessment of AI in education depends on its consequences for the individual" (Schönmann & Uhl, 2023, p. 442) that are less related to institutional inclusion and exclusion rather than aspects of individual participation.

DigiTaKS* – DIGITAL KEY COMPETENCES FOR STUDIES AND WORK: A RESEARCH PROJECT[2]

In our interdisciplinary research and development project *DigiTaKS** (*Digital Key Competences for Studies and Work – Model for the Transformative Digital Competence Development of Students*), we focus on fostering transformative digital competencies among non-technology bachelor students at a German university, preparing them for both academic and professional success (Schmidt-Lauff et al., 2022). The project aims to empower participants to actively engage in comprehensive transformative processes, equipping them with the digital competence and future-oriented mindset needed for their studies, daily lives, and professional endeavors – ultimately enabling them to become *digital change agents*. To stimulate these competences, three student cohorts (2021–2023) from the Faculty of Humanities and Social Sciences at Helmut-Schmidt-University/University of the Federal Armed Forces Hamburg (HSU) were provided with laptops and a pre-configured software suite, instruments for competency diagnosis and development, as well as barrier-free, collaborative teaching-learning resources. The project is employing a multimethod longitudinal design to investigate the acquisition and development of transformative digital competences, and their iterative developments.

To this end, the *DigiTaKS** research and development project has empirically supported a model for the transformative development of digital skills among students. This model includes a hardware and software package, accompanied by research on everyday and usage practices, tools for skills diagnosis and development (https://www.hsu-hh.de/wb/digitaks/comdigis), synchronous-hybrid teaching/learning formats and spaces, and barrier-free, participatory learning resources for universities (more information and the resulting Open Educational Resources (OER) are adaptively available for further use can be found: https://www.hsu-hh.de/wb/digitaks).

Survey Methodology

Within the multimethodological approach,[3] a *quantitative survey* was conducted to collect (relatively) time-stable characteristics, such as sociodemographic and educational data across the three student cohorts. A total of 240 quantitative surveys were available, which were distributed over the three cohorts as follows: (1) student cohort 2021: 95 questionnaires/completed responses (total number of students: 199), (2) student cohort 2022: 81 questionnaires/completed responses (total number of students: 166), and (3) student cohort 2023 with 64 questionnaires/completed responses (total number of students: 184). Additionally, self-assessments of digital competences and practices with digital media, as well as learning and self-organization strategies, were requested. The goal was to derive insights into the everyday digital practices that guide the acquisition of transformative digital competences. With the free release of LLMs, such as ChatGPT from OpenAI or other text and speech models from fall 2022, this phenomenon was added as an additional part to the quantitative survey (in the student cohort 2023). Consequently, students from the fields of humanities and social sciences, like education and pedagogy, psychology, and history were invited to participate.

The survey questionnaire was digitally dispatched (to n = 184) at the beginning of the first study trimester in October 2023; the data collection period spanned from November 27th to December 14th, 2023. Regarding the questions related to AI, the answers from a total of 60 students (valid cases) are available. This represents a response rate of 32.61% with respect to the overall student population.

A Quantitative Questionnaire with Bachelor Students from Non-Technical Degree Study Programs relating to the Use of AI Applications

Based on several critical questions we identified regarding the relationship between ethical and equity questions and AI in *Artificial Intelligence and Digital Divide in Higher Education: An Ethical Perspective on the Phenomenon*, we systematized dimensions that can affect trust in and the willingness to adopt AI. By integrating aspects of van Dijk's (2020) model of the digital divide and the operational readiness model of Stützer et al. (2023) in *Three Central Constructs*: *Usage*, *Trust*, and *Knowledge of AI Application*, we perceived the divide in digital participation based on motivation and digital competences as crucial for our research question, leading to three sub-areas of interest: student use of AI applications, trust in AI applications and human-machine interaction, and self-assessment of AI user competences. These categorical areas constitute the epistemological focus of our study, which is methodologically operationalized for statistical analysis as follows:

(1) *(Non-)Usage of AI applications in studies*: To gain an initial understanding of the *intensity* (frequency and extent) of AI application usage in everyday contexts, students were asked at the outset whether they had used or were currently using AI applications specifically (dichotomous variable). This question allowed us to differentiate between *users* and *non-users*. The questions were drawn from a brief online study on the usage and attitudes toward AI, specifically ChatGPT, among the general population[4] at the University of Duisburg-Essen, Germany (Kollmann & Civey, 2023). Additionally, we explored the specific *reasons for using AI* tools, which included text generation (e.g., ChatGPT, BingAI), translation (e.g., DeepL), image generation and editing (e.g., Midjourney, DALL-E), as well as tasks such as question comprehension (explorative understanding), text summarization, and information retrieval. These questions are derived and modified from a quantitative survey conducted by von Garrel et al. (2023) on the use of ChatGPT and other AI tools in higher education among students.

(2) *Trust in AI applications respectively – human-machine interaction*: Trust towards AI applications was surveyed using subjective self-assessment on a Likert scale ("not at all" to "very much"). The construct was operationalized using two items that were developed and tested based on the

theoretical background: Firstly, students were asked to assess the *extent to which they trust the accuracy of answers* generated by AI applications. This item aims to assess the personal readiness (subjective) and implicit belief (individual) about the potential quality and reliability of the content of the information produced by AI. Additionally, students were asked to assess their *possibilities of communication* with AI applications: The focus here is on the differentiation between users and non-users about their subjective assessment of the "general possibilities of people to communicate with AI" (as operational readiness), as well as the accuracy of generated answers. The objective was, inter alia, to derive initial conclusions regarding operational readiness and a bit more future-oriented potentials (e.g., less skeptical, more positive) human-machine interaction. The reliability analysis using the Spearman-Brown coefficient indicates a consistent scale (0.79). Both questions also originate from the survey conducted by Kollmann and Civey (2023).

(3) *Self-assessment of AI user competences regarding knowledge*: As knowledge is a key factor influencing trust in AI (Schönmann & Uhl, 2023), the students' knowledge about the possible applications of AI was also requested using a 5-point Likert scale ("do not agree at all" to "fully agree"). This construct was based on the DigComp2.2 (Vuorikari et al., 2022), the Digital Competence framework for citizens from the European Union. The items were slightly modified and integrated into the questionnaire. The reliability analysis indicates a Cronbach's alpha of 0.867.

EMPIRICAL INSIGHTS: USE AND NON-USE OF AI IN STUDIES ALONG TRUST AND KNOWLEGDE

This section presents the results of the survey analysis in relation to the three previously mentioned categories. The aim is to provide a descriptive and – by suggested interpretations and relationships – a deeper understanding of the interplay between students' (1) *use and non-use of generative AI*, (2) *trust in AI applications respectively: human-machine interaction*, and (3) *self-assessment of their AI user competences regarding knowledge*. The objective is to empirically answer the research question of which dimensions can have an impact on the use of AI in studies. For this purpose, the study population is initially described, whereby a distinction is made between users and non-users (Sample Description: Users and Non-Users of AI Applications). Based on this first descriptive analysis, a more detailed statistical examination is then conducted across our three categories use, trust, and user competencies (Deepening Analyses of Students' Use Practices along Usage, Trust, and Knowledge). Subsequently, to identify statistical differences and significance between the two groups (user and non-user), a comparative analysis is performed (A Difference Analysis between AI Users and Non-Users in Terms of Trust in AI applications and Knowledge). Accordingly, as a result of our empirical insights, ethical dimensions of equity in relation to usage, trust, and knowledge are explored, offering insights into the dynamics of AI adoption and non-adoption through the lens of trust in AI.

Sample Description: Users and Non-Users of AI Applications

Of 60 students who participated in the survey, the majority (73%) use AI applications. This suggests the existence of a specific group that has not used such applications or has consciously decided not to use them, which could imply a digital divide. One possible reason is that access to AI applications may be limited, although many are available as open access – so it can also be more of a motivational access than a physical one. Additionally, socio-demographic and societal structural characteristics can influence the intensity of AI use. In terms of gender, we can see slightly fewer female students use AI applications (women: 67%; men: 78%) (see Table 10.1). Parallel to a study by von Garrell et al. (2023) with 6,300 Bachelor's and Master's students from a German university, it can be consistently found that women use AI applications less frequently than men (von Garrel et al., 2023, p. 4). This also indicates a gender-specific difference in AI.

Regarding the *field of study*, it was observed that students from our *DigiTaKS** project majoring in education and pedagogy (79%) as well as history (80%) use AI applications more frequently than psychology students (46%). It can be cautiously assumed that the research methodology and learning settings in formal higher education institutions resp. different fields of study[5] may affect the use of AI applications among students. *Attending a laptop class[6] during school time* as an educational experience and characteristic appears to have less impact on the usage of AI. Out of five students who attended such a class, only three (60%) used AI applications. In contrast, out of the 55 students who did not attend a laptop class, 41 students (75%) still use AI.

Drawing from the study and work-related experiences, it is evident that these can have a modest influence on the use or non-use of AI applications. Specifically, 14 out of 20 students with study experience and 14 out of 18 students with work experience reported using AI applications. Notwithstanding this, there are also many students who utilize AI despite lacking experience. In contrast to the study by von Garrel et al. (2023), which found that experiences can impact AI use, our sample suggests that experience may have a special effect on AI utilization. For instance, master's students tend to use AI more frequently than bachelor's students. The temporal progression of master's students' studies may contribute to their enhanced familiarity and expertise with academic tasks, as well as their broader thematic and methodological

Table 10.1 Sample description regarding AI use

Item	Value/Expression	Users	Non-Users	Total
AI usage	-	44 (73%)	16 (27%)	60
Gender	Female	16 (67%)	8 (33%)	24
Gender	Male	28 (78%)	8 (22%)	36
Study/program	Education and pedagogy	27 (79%)	7 (21%)	34
Program	Psychology	5 (46%)	6 (55%)	11
Program	History	12 (80%)	3 (20%)	15
Laptop class	Yes	3 (60%)	2 (40%)	5
Laptop class	No	41 (74%)	14 (26%)	55
Prior study experience	Yes	14 (70%)	6 (30%)	20
Prior study experience	No	30 (75%)	10 (25%)	40
Prior vocational education and training experience	Yes	14 (78%)	4 (22%)	18
Prior vocational education and training	No	30 (71%)	12 (29%)	42
Migration background*	Yes	11 (73%)	1 (7%)	15
Migration background*	No	33 (69%)	15 (31%)	48
Engagement in volunteering or clubs	Yes	14 (70%)	6 (30%)	20
Engagement in volunteering or clubs	No	30 (75%)	10 (25%)	40

Note: * applies if student or at least one parent was born in a different country.

knowledge (ibid.). Consequently, they may be more competent in the application of AI based on this knowledge. Hence, experience may influence AI usage, but further factors should also be considered. These might include other experiential contexts, such as engagement in volunteer or club activities. Among the surveyed students, 70% of those who engaged in such activities reported using AI applications. Furthermore, the provision of digital media in terms of devices does not appear to have an impact on AI usage. In the survey conducted within the *DigiTaKS** project, students were asked about their ownership and use of ten different types of digital devices. The statistically average number of devices owned by AI users is 4.09, whereas those who do not use AI reported a slightly lower average value of 3.81 devices (see Table 10.1).

Deepening Analyses of Students' Use Practices along Usage, Trust, and Knowledge

Following the description of the surveyed student population within the *DigiTaKS** project and their AI use and non-use, we turn to the AI-based usage practices of students along our three key constructs. The results will not only provide further insights into the research question but also enable a deeper examination of statistical differences.

Usage of AI applications in studies

Among the 44 students who *rely on AI applications*, these are primarily *used for academic tasks* (96%) rather than *private contexts* (77%). Notably, formal learning tasks seem to initiate AI usage, operational readiness, and provide diverse opportunities for learning. The majority of students report using AI applications for *initial information research and thematic overview* (82%), as well as *clarifying understanding questions and discipline-specific concepts* (75%). *Text summarization* is the next most frequently used feature (73%), much less *text translation* (46%). Thus, it appears that *receptive use cases* in a formal study context are primary motivations for students for the usage of AI applications. Receptive use cases can facilitate the expansion of knowledge regarding AI applications in formal learning settings and thus can contribute to the development and acquisition of AI competences. Subsequent *productive use cases* involve academic tasks, with about half of students using AI for *academic task completion* (50%). A much smaller part uses AI applications for *image generation and editing* (11%), while nearly two-thirds use AI for *text generation* (66%).

However, the current study population exhibits relatively rare instances of *interactive use cases*: *formulation help, spelling, and grammar checks* are used by approximately 43%, whereas *organization and planning* of appointments and deadlines are even less frequent (11%). Additionally, advice and support from AI for *decision-making* is utilized by only about one in five students (21%). Based on this analysis, one can infer that students tend to have greater confidence in the reliability and confidentiality of human interactions compared to AI systems. This becomes clear when dealing with sensitive information or personal affairs that necessitate guidance or management within a private setting. This outcome suggests that human interaction plays a vital role in this context, since humans, as Schönmann & Uhl (2023) demonstrate, have expertise in "understanding of how the world functions" and are endowed with common sense, in contrast to a machine (p. 434).

Regarding human-machine interaction, it is noteworthy that AI or machines are predominantly utilized for receptive activities, such as receiving and recording factual knowledge. In contrast, productive interactions with the AI are relatively less frequent, involving the creation of new content or knowledge jointly with the machine. However, when considering more creative or collaborative forms of interaction with the machine, students appear to be more hesitant. This skepticism is evident in their reluctance to engage in interactive use of the machine, which represents one of the rarest reasons for its use among students. Furthermore, students seem to be particularly skeptical about collaborating with the machine, involving a form of dialogical interaction or relational engagement.

Trust in AI applications respectively: human-machine interaction

Regarding trust in AI applications, descriptive results indicate that students generally tend to have a moderate trust in these applications. However, high standard deviations suggest a considerable heterogeneity and situation-specific requirements among students regarding their level of trust in and access to AI (see Table 10.2).

The students exhibit moderate *confidence in the accuracy of the answers generated by AI* (M = 5.05; SD = 2.19). The standard deviation and range of values indicate a diverse assessment, suggesting that trust in the accuracy differs significantly within the group. This moderate confidence may be due to the lack of knowledge about the underlying data, algorithm, and related decision-making processes of AI (black box) among students. Consequently, students need to grant a certain level of trustworthiness to AI applications to trust the accuracy of generated answers. In contrast, the possibility of communicating

Table 10.2 Trust in and access to AI applications

Item	Min	Max	Mean	Standard Deviation
How much do you trust the accuracy of answers generated by AI applications?	1	10	5.05	2.19
How do you generally assess the possibilities for people to communicate with AI applications?	1	10	7.41	2.67

Note: 10-point Likert scale: 1 = not at all; 10 = very much.

with an AI application is generally well evaluated by students – despite high variance – (M = 7.41; SD = 2.67).

This suggests that students have an *optimistic attitude towards the technology and its potential usage* as well as regarding *operational readiness.* Human-machine interaction appears to be positively evaluated by many students. In relation to the accuracy of AI answers, it becomes apparent that students are more skeptical about the output than the general possibility of communicating with AI. This implies that trust in a technology is strongly connected to personal attitudes and dispositions (subjective experience) and can also be linked to technical understanding (knowledge). Trust in the context of AI thus becomes a construct comprising of knowledge and attitude, and influences the operational readiness.

Self-assessment of AI user competences regarding knowledge about AI

The assessment of *knowledge* about the controversial use of AI in relation to ones own performance shows that students are sensitive to the perception of potential risks in their own work (M = 4.42; SD = 0.97). It can therefore be concluded that students evaluate knowledge about the use of AI in a critical and reflective manner. Further, the students rate their own competences of *knowledge* regarding the transformational nature of AI applications high, with a simultaneous understanding that development and impact trends are uncertain (M = 4.31; SD = 1.07). This assessment is more about the status quo of AI but can have an influence on operational readiness. However, most students are also well aware of the practical areas of application of generative AI applications (M = 4.15; SD = 1.14). Interestingly, students rate their *ability to identify relevant areas of application* higher than their *ability to create digital content themselves* (M = 3.64, SD = 1.34) or to *interact with an AI application in a targeted manner* ("prompting"; M = 3.63; SD = 1.02). Similarly, the self-assessment of AI user competences in terms of formulating questions competently (M = 3.63; SD = 1.02) as well as generating content, using this content for their own work, and critically using AI (M = 3.64; SD = 1.34) is less high. A knowledge of broad usage strategies and targeted use of AI and corresponding practical knowledge to generate suitable output thus becomes methodological knowledge that enables an interactive and productive use of AI applications. If this knowledge is considered methodological, it becomes clear that there is still room for improvement in prompting as a prerequisite for competent use. This could be due to a lack of learning experiences for competent use, for example, in formal settings – where they use AI applications the most. Regarding *recognizing possible risks* that could lead to the reproduction of social inequality, such as stereotypes (M = 3.81; SD = 1.22), and the misuse of personal data under data protection law (M = 3.98; SD = 1.21), the students rate themselves mediocre compared to other self-assessments.

This empirical finding shows that students consider themselves less competent regarding knowledge about the datasets underlying AI (black box), which demand ethical considerations about its consequences for AI use. If there is limited understanding regarding the fact that AI applications perpetuate stereotypes and thereby contribute constitutionally to the reproduction of discriminatory inequality, including racist forms, for example, when referencing white scientists or Eurocentric worldviews, this has inevitable implications for ethical considerations in competent handling. This suggests that there is a need

Table 10.3 Self-assessment of AI user competences regarding knowledge about AI

Item	Min	Max	Mean	Standard Deviation
I know how to formulate questions to achieve the required result when dealing with AI (e.g. ChatGPT, BingAI, Alexa, Google Assistant).	1	5	3.63	1.01
I am aware that the data on which the AI depends contains biases, such as stereotypes, and that these can be reinforced by the use of AI (e.g. male bus driver, female shop assistant).	1	5	3.81	1.22
I can recognize signs of wheather I am communicating with a human or an AI-based conversational agent (e.g. speed of response behavior).	1	5	3.41	1.25
I know that AI systems can be used to automatically create digital content.	1	5	4.15	1.14
I know how to create digital content processed by AI and use it for my own work and that this use of AI is controversial.	1	5	3.64	1.34
I am aware that the use of AI is controversial, because the own performance can become unclear (e.g. plagiarism).	1	5	4.42	0.97
I am aware that personal data that I share with an AI could be misused by third parties (e.g. cyber criminnals.	1	5	3.98	1.21
I know how and when I can use AI to solve problems, and I am aware that the automatically generated answerts can be vulnerable to errors.	1	5	4.08	1.15
I am aware that AI is a constantly evolving field whose development and effects are still very unclear.	1	5	4.31	1.07

Note: 5-point Likert scale: 1 = I do not agree at all; 5 = I fully agree.

to further promote the ethical competent usage of data fed to and generated by AI systems, for example in formal educational contexts, to avoid the reproduction of social inequality, to reduce the loss of trust in AI data, and to foster critical reflection on trusting AI with (personal) data.

A Difference Analysis between AI Users and Non-Users in Terms of Trust in AI Applications and Knowledge

Following the prerequisite checks, difference analysis was conducted using an independent samples t-test to compare the groups of users and non-users of AI applications in terms of trust and their own knowledge of various possible uses. This aims to obtain indications on the interactions between corresponding characteristics. In a further step, the effect size was calculated using Cohen's d (Cohen, 1988). The Levene Test revealed that the variances of the two groups were significantly different ($F = 8.457$, $p = 0.005$). Therefore, the t-test in terms of AI knowledge was conducted under the assumption of unequal variances. The results show a significant difference between the means of the two groups ($t(17{,}657) = -2.254$, $p = 0.037$). This indicates that non-users rate their own knowledge of possible uses of AI applications significantly lower ($M = 3.43$; $S = 1.1$) than users ($M = 4.1$; $SD = 0.54$). The effect size, measured with Cohen's d, indicates a small effect in this context ($d = -0.358$). In addition, the group comparisons indicate that the users of AI applications ($M = 5.62$; $SD = 1.96$) trust the accuracy of the results generated by AI applications significantly more than the non-users ($M = 3.50$; $SD = 1.96$). The effect size according to Cohen's d is $d = -0.4$, which also indicates a small effect. A similar result can be seen in the assessment of the given opportunities for people to communicate with AI applications. Here too, users ($M = 8.26$; $SD = 2.01$) rate these opportunities significantly more favorably than non-users ($M = 4.93$; $SD = 2.96$). The effect size, measured with Cohen's d, is $d = -0.551$, which indicates a medium effect. This finding provides initial indicators that active use of AI applications is associated with better knowledge of their possible uses and subsequently higher trust in their results. However, these findings have an impact on *operational readiness* dealing with AI. Thus, AI users exhibit significantly higher trust in AI than non-users. It can be assumed that repeated use culminates in usage, which influences actions leading to an accumulation of experience and subsequent knowledge. Knowledge and usage experiences thus become significant for the use or non-use of AI (see Table 10.4). In a study on the annual status report of the Digital Society in Germany (Initiative D21, 2024), similar findings emerge: Firstly, it is evident that individuals who have acquired new experiences and knowledge with digital technologies and competencies possess significantly better digital literacy than those without such experiences (p. 28). Secondly, within the context of professional activity, it can be inferred that persons who had the opportunity to accumulate positive experiences with ChatGPT in a work setting are likely to hold more favorable attitudes towards AI developments (p. 43).

The statistical parameters were used to gain detailed insights into the differences between the two groups. These indicate some differences between users and non-users of AI in the productive use of AI applications. Users (M = 4.00, SD = 2.69) rate their knowledge of creating digital content and utilizing

Table 10.4 Mean and standard deviation values between AI users and non-users

Item	Users (mean)	Users (standard deviation)	Non-Users (mean)	Non-Users (standard deviation)
Trust: How much do you trust the accuracy of answers generated by AI applications?*	5.61	1.9	3.5	2.2
Trust: How do you generally assess the possibilities for people to communicate with AI applications?*	8.25	1.9	4.93	1.9
Knowledge about possible applications: I know how to formulate questions to achieve the required result when dealing with AI (e.g. ChatGPT, BingAI, Alexa, Google Assistant).	3.91	0.8	2.88	1.2
Knowledge about possible applications: I am aware that the data on which the AI depends contains biases, such as stereotypes, and that these can be reinforced by the use of AI (e.g. male bus driver, female shop assistant).**	3.93	1	3.5	1.7
Knowledge about possible applications: I can recognize signs of whether I am communicating with a human or an AI-based conversational agent (e.g. speed of response behavior).**	3.6	1.1	2.88	1.5

Item	Users (mean)	Users (standard deviation)	Non-Users (mean)	Non-Users (standard deviation)
Knowledge about possible applications: I know that AI systems can be used to automatically create digital content.**	4.4	0.7	3.5	1.7
Knowledge about possible applications: I know how to create digital content processed by AI and use it for my own work and that this use of AI is controversial.**	4	1.1	2.69	1.5
Knowledge about possible applications: I am aware that the use of AI is controversial, because the own performance can become unclear (e.g. plagiarism).**	4.47	0.7	4.31	1.4
Knowledge about possible applications: I am aware that personal data that I share with an AI could be misused by third parties (e.g. cyber criminals).**	4.05	1.1	3.81	1.5
Knowledge about possible applications: I know how and when I can use AI to solve problems, and I am aware that the automatically generated answers can be vulnerable to errors.**	4.3	0.7	3.5	1.8
Knowledge about possible applications: I am aware that AI is a constantly evolving field whose development and effects are still very unclear.**	4.47	0.8	3.88	1.5
Sum Score	4.1	0.5	3.43	1.1

Note: *10-point Likert scale: 1 = not at all; 10 = very much.
**5-point Likert scale: 1 = I do not agree at all; 5 = I fully agree.

it for their own work significantly higher than non-users (M = 2.69, SD = 1.5). Simultaneously, users also report being more competent in recognizing the controversies surrounding AI usage. Non-users, on the other hand, rate their knowledge of productive use and critical reflection lower (M = 2.69, SD = 1.5). A similar difference in self-assessment is observed regarding the knowledge of formulating questions to generate the desired outcome when using AI. Users (M = 4.00, SD = 1.1) rate themselves higher than non-users (M = 2.69, SD = 1.5). Furthermore, a differentiated assessment is evident regarding the knowledge that AI can be used to automatically create digital content. While users tend to rate their competence of knowledge in this area higher (M = 4.40, SD = 1.1), non-users rate themselves lower (M = 2.69, SD = 1.5). This suggests that operational readiness is not only influenced by trust in AI but also by productive usage of AI. Moreover, a relatively small difference between the two user groups is observed regarding the phenomena related to sensitivity towards potential plagiarism. Both user groups report being aware of the controversies surrounding AI usage due to unclear ownership (users: M = 4.47, SD = 0.7 / non-users: M = 4.31, SD = 1.4). Additionally, both groups rate their awareness of stereotypes being reproduced through the datasets used in AI similarly (users: M = 3.93, SD = 1.1 / non-users: M = 3.50, SD = 1.7). The findings suggest that a lack of transparency regarding data-driven functions and algorithms can impact both operational readiness and trust. Failing to recognize the controversies surrounding AI usage is associated with lower self-assessed competence in both user groups.

As expected, the results of the group comparisons regarding AI usage and knowledge about its application areas show corresponding trends. This means that non-users have fewer knowledge resources and trust related to AI use than users. On our questionnaire data, we can show that there is a multifaceted relationship between trust and AI use or non-use across three dimensions – usage, trust, and knowledge. The interaction of these dimensions can have a significant impact on the operational readiness of AI use.

However, it should be noted that the results of the difference analyses do not allow for conclusions regarding causality and should only be interpreted as a cautious first exploration. The results provide insights into inequality and social participation, manifesting as a digital divide rather than a structural separation through physical access to technologies and infrastructure. Instead, the digital divide manifests as a social, not individual phenomenon, characterized by disparities in competency to utilize these technologies effectively, acquire knowledge regarding their functionality and operation, and establish trustworthiness towards AI systems.

DISCUSSION

Both the descriptive analyses and the difference analyses suggest that it is not solely infrastructure-related access to AI applications that determines students' operational readiness and usage, but rather a complex interplay between trust, knowledge, and usage. Our results show that user experiences with AI are primarily gained in study-related contexts (formal contexts), where receptive uses of AI applications are most prevalent. In contrast, more advanced, dialogical, or co-constructive forms of use appear to be less prevalent. At the same time, most students assess their competencies in employing AI in productive and interactive ways as high.

Regarding our three central constructs and the difference analysis, several equity and ethical challenges can be addressed by our research. We observed that the students surveyed *were more skeptical about the output than the general possibility of communicating with AI.* This highlights the important relationship between our constructs of use and trust in practice: Because AI is easy to access and students may lack the reflexive competences, trust on the level of human-machine interaction is needed, as AI use has the potential power to cause harm to the student trust giver (Schäfer et al., 2024). As study-related contexts are important instances for AI experiences of students, higher education institutions like universities now have the opportunity to utilize AI to open up new chances for the education system with new formations and transformations of learning environments (Ricken et al., 2023, pp. 313–314), for example, open education, autonomy of autodidactic learning, and motivation. Yet simultaneously, they must address the requirements of ensuring educational equity and social participation to prevent a renewed digital divide. By promoting competent handling of AI and making transparent the underlying data sets and algorithms of AI systems on a meta-level as well, transparency can be created, and trust in human-machine interaction can increase. This could foster the operational readiness of AI not only regarding students' technology acceptance through trust but through competent assessment of benefits, limitations, and risks. Ideally, safety and knowledge would replace the dynamic of trust over time. Transparency at the institutional level on the permitted ways to use AI for students is equally important, as it gives institutional contextualization to the trust in AI. Otherwise, we might face a new digital divide for the worse between those able to assess the risks and benefits of AI use, participate in new learning environments that utilize AI, recognize AI systems and output generated by them, and those who are not. This poses the harm of fostering educational inequities through digital technology and decreases overall operational readiness to use AI in higher education.

To further analyze their access to AI, it would be sensible to consider students not only as actors within higher education but also as experts in their everyday study lives. Conducting expert interviews with them could provide deeper insights into their experiences, behavior, and perceptions of AI. Additionally, incorporating other status groups of institutions of higher education into the analysis, such as teachers or supervisors, and examining institutional regulations and documents related to the operational readiness of AI could offer a more comprehensive understanding of the interplay between trust, knowledge, and usage, resp. insights into AIED.

CONCLUSION

Our research in the project *DigiTaKS** highlights the importance of considering the complex relationships between trust, knowledge, and usage in the context of operational readiness for AI. By doing so, higher education institutions can promote the development of AI operational readiness and resilience among students. The findings of this study suggest that it is not solely infrastructure-related access to AI applications that determines students' operational readiness but rather a complex interplay between trust, knowledge, and usage. Implications for teaching and learning in higher education are multifaceted. On the one hand, the use of AI can open new opportunities for the education system (e.g., open education, autonomy of autodidactic learning, motivation). On the other hand, it is essential to address the requirements of ensuring educational equity and social participation to prevent a digital divide. By promoting competent handling of AI, knowledge and experience regarding human-machine interaction can be fostered. This requires a nuanced understanding of the interplay between trust, knowledge, and usage and highlights the importance of considering students' experiences and perceptions of AI in study-related contexts. By enabling interactions with external realities and prompting reflective examinations, educators can actualize an educational philosophy that is grounded in humanistic values like the concept of "*Bildung*."

NOTES

1. Stützer et al. (2023) orient themselves on evidence-based technology acceptance models such as the *Technology Acceptance Model* (TAM), the third generation of which (TAM3) provides a very good overview of indicators and attitudes (including *prospective*, *psychological*, and *emotional readiness*) to use technology.
2. This chapter was developed as part of the project "Digital Key Competencies for Studies and Careers – Model for the Transformative Digital Competence Development of Students (*DigiTaKS**)" (2021–2024). The project is funded by the

Center for Digitalization and Technology Research of the Bundeswehr (dtec.bw) and supported by the European Union under the "NextGenerationEU" initiative.

3. As an *initial needs and requirements analysis* (Rathmann et al., 2022), various stakeholder groups at HSU were surveyed regarding the (post-)pandemic starting conditions for digital learning (focus group discussion: 6 master's students in GeiSo; secondary data analysis of EvaSyS across all faculties: n = 4,782 evaluation forms FT20-WT21; 11 expert interviews [6 instructors from GeiSo; 5 military superiors from all StudB]; survey: n = 45 instructors from GeiSo). Following this, *longitudinal, multimethod usage studies* were conducted to analyze the acquisition and application of transformative digital competencies by students (cf. Schmidt-Lauff, i.p.), including: *(a) a quantitative baseline survey* (first-year students n = 176; online questionnaire via SoSciSurvey) on media usage patterns, self-assessed digital competencies, and learning and self-organization (with additional data for cohort 2023 in Q4/2023). Two *additional (3) quantitative non-usage studies* (2021 cohort [n = 29], 2022 cohort [n = 9]) to explore reasons for non-participation in the basic program (rejection of devices, the study concept, etc.). These also provided interesting comparative aspects for interviews and could be used in the longer term in the context of divergent attitudes towards digital technology usage. Additionally, *(b) episodic interviews* (n = 31) were conducted to gain in-depth insights into specific digital everyday and study practices, complemented by *(c) a learning and usage diary study* (n = 58) in digital format over two 10-day collection periods (Feb 23/Jun 23; an additional round for cohort 2023 in Q4/2023) focusing on study-related, leisure, and learning-relevant (digital/analog/mixed) everyday practices of students (e.g., analyzing critical and positive challenges from the students' perspective). In *(d) ethnographic studies*, seven students from the 2021 cohort have been ethnographically followed since mid-2022 in their (study) everyday life. The aim was to examine practices of media appropriation as well as learning and work organization among students. Based on these research findings, a learning unit on digital self- and work-organization has been integrated as an Open Educational Resource OER (available for download in German): https://www.hsu-hh.de/wb/digitaks/comdigis) into the self-learning tool ComDigiS* (SCORM module 4; cf. Schmidt-Lauff i.p.).
4. Four target groups were surveyed: >5,000 German citizens, >1,500 ChatGPT users, >1,000 employed individuals, and >500 employed individuals who had already used ChatGPT.
5. Furthermore, it is not possible to compare a technology-intensive field with a non-technology-intensive field within this sample, which would allow for insights into the relationship between study-related technological understanding and use, as demonstrated by von Garrel et al. (2023). In their study, they show that students from technology-oriented fields, such as natural sciences or mathematics, use AI applications more frequently during their studies (pp. 21–23).

6. In these laptop-based learning environments, students engage with digital tools, including laptops, with a deliberate focus on developing skills and competences through hands-on practice and collaborative activities.

REFERENCES

Ansari, A. N., Ahmad, S., & Bhutta, S. M. (2024). Mapping the global evidence around the use of ChatGPT in higher education: A systematic scoping review. *Education and Information Technologies, 29*(9), 11281–11321. https://doi.org/10.1007/s10639-023-12223-4

Beckers, A., & Teubner, G. (2024). Die digitale Verantwortungslücke: Vorschläge zur Haftung für algorithmisches Fehlverhalten. In M. Heinlein & N. Huchler (Eds.), *Künstliche Intelligenz, Mensch und Gesellschaft* (pp. 153–177). Springer Fachmedien Wiesbaden. https://doi.org/10.1007/978-3-658-43521-9_7

Bhullar, P. S., Joshi, M., & Chugh, R. (2024). ChatGPT in higher education – A synthesis of the literature and a future research agenda. *Education and Information Technologies.* https://doi.org/10.1007/s10639-024-12723-x

Buck, I., & Limburg, A. (2023). *Hochschulbildung vor dem Hintergrund von Natural Language Processing (KI-Schreibtools).* https://doi.org/10.3278/HSL2306W

Chakravorti, B. (2024). AI's trust problem: Twelve persistent risks of AI that are driving skepticism. *Harvard Business Review.* https://hbr.org/2024/05/ais-trust-problem

Cohen, J. (1988). *Statistical Power Analysis for the Behavioral Sciences* (2nd ed). Taylor and Francis.

de Witt, C., Rampelt, F., & Pinkwart, N. (2020). *Whitepaper "Künstliche Intelligenz in der Hochschulbildung."* https://doi.org/10.5281/ZENODO.4063722

Eager, B., & Brunton, R. (2023). Prompting Higher Education Towards AI-Augmented Teaching and Learning Practice. *Journal of University Teaching and Learning Practice, 20*(5). https://doi.org/10.53761/1.20.5.02

Esposito, E. (2017). Artificial Communication? The Production of Contingency by Algorithms. *Zeitschrift Für Soziologie, 46*(4), 249–265. https://doi.org/10.1515/zfsoz-2017-1014

Fox, A. (2022). Educational research and AIED. Identifying ethical challenges. In W. Holmes & K. Porayska-Pomsta, *The Ethics of Artificial Intelligence in Education* (1st ed., pp. 47–73). Routledge. https://doi.org/10.4324/9780429329067-4

Gardner, J., O'Leary, M., & Yuan, L. (2021). Artificial intelligence in educational assessment: 'Breakthrough? Or buncombe and ballyhoo?' *Journal of Computer Assisted Learning, 37*(5), 1207–1216. https://doi.org/10.1111/jcal.12577

Heinlein, M. (2024). Künstliche Intelligenz als kontingenzerzeugende Technik: Eine praxistheoretische Perspektive. In M. Heinlein & N. Huchler (Eds.), *Künstliche Intelligenz, Mensch und Gesellschaft: Soziale Dynamiken und gesellschaftliche Folgen einer technologischen Innovation* (pp. 391–430). Springer Fachmedien Wiesbaden. https://doi.org/10.1007/978-3-658-43521-9

Henking, T. (2024). Moral Decision-Making via AI – deep ethics? About shifting or losing responsibility. In M. Reder & C. Koska (Eds.), *Künstliche Intelligenz und ethische Verantwortung* (1st ed., pp. 49–62). transcript Verlag. https://doi.org/10.14361/9783839469057

Holmes, W., & Porayska-Pomsta, K. (Eds.). (2023). *The ethics of artificial intelligence in education: Practices, challenges, and debates.* Routledge.

Holstein, K., & Doroudi, S. (2022). Equity and Artificial Intelligence in education. In W. Holmes & K. Porayska-Pomsta, *The Ethics of Artificial Intelligence in Education* (1st ed., pp. 151–173). Routledge. https://doi.org/10.4324/9780429329067-9
Ifenthaler, D. (2023). Ethische Perspektiven auf künstliche Intelligenz im Kontext der Hochschule. In T. Schmohl, A. Watanabe, & K. Schelling (Eds.), *Künstliche Intelligenz in der Hochschulbildung: Chancen und Grenzen des KI-gestützten Lernens und Lehrens* (1st ed., Vol. 4, pp. 71–86). transcript Verlag. https://doi.org/10.14361/9783839457696
Initiative D21. (2024). D21-Digital-Index 2023/24. Jährliches Lagebild zur Digitalen Gesellschaft (1. Auflage). Initiative D21. https://initiatived21.de/uploads/03_Studien-Publikationen/D21-Digital-Index/2023-24/d21digitalindex_2023-2024.pdf
Kollmann, T., & Civey. (2023). *Kurzstudie Uni Duisburg-Essen & Civey.* https://app.civey.com/dashboards/kurzstudie-uni-duisburg-essen-civey-14024
Liggieri, K., & Müller, O. (Eds.). (2019). *Mensch-Maschine-Interaktion: Handbuch zu Geschichte – Kultur – Ethik.* J.B. Metzler Verlag. https://doi.org/10.1007/978-3-476-05604-7
Naveed, H., Khan, A. U., Qiu, S., Saqib, M., Anwar, S., Usman, M., Akhtar, N., Barnes, N., & Mian, A. (2023). *A Comprehensive Overview of Large Language Models* (Version 10). https://doi.org/10.48550/ARXIV.2307.06435
OECD. (2024). *Education at a glance 2024: OECD indicators.* OECD Publishing. https://doi.org/10.1787/c00cad36-en
Rathmann, M., Rosemann, T., Schiller, J., Schmidt-Lauff, S., & Schwarz, J. (2022). Digitalität als Herausforderung und Chance. Eine multiperspektivische Analyse zu Bedarfslagen. openHSU. https://doi.org/10.24405/14354
Reinhardt, K., & Sinn, J. (2024). Einleitung: Neue Vertrauensfragen? Digitalisierung und Künstliche Intelligenz. *Zeitschrift Für Praktische Philosophie, 11*(1). https://doi.org/10.22613/zfpp/11.1.13
Renz, A., & Galla, N. (2024). KI in der Bildung. Viel mehr als eine Utopie – Dystopie – Dualismus? In S. Hartong & A. Renz (Eds.), *Digitale Lerntechnologien. Von der Mystifizierung zur reflektierten Gestaltung von EdTech* (1. Auflage, pp. 131–159). Transcript.
Ricken, N., Reh, S., & Scholz, J. (2023). Transformationen des Bildungswissens – eine wissenstheoretische und -geschichtliche Per-spektive auf digitale Wissenskulturen. In S. Aßmann & N. Ricken (Eds.), *Bildung und Digitalität: Analysen – Diskurse – Perspektiven* (pp. 313–347). Springer Fachmedien Wiesbaden. https://doi.org/10.1007/978-3-658-30766-0
Russell, S., & Norvig, P. (2020). *Artificial intelligence: A modern approach* (4th ed.). Pearson.
Schäfer, A., Esterbauer, R., & Kubicek, B. (2024). Trusting robots: A relational trust definition based on human intentionality. *Humanities and Social Sciences Communications, 11*(1), 1412. https://doi.org/10.1057/s41599-024-03897-3
Scheuer, D. (2020). *Akzeptanz von Künstlicher Intelligenz: Grundlagen intelligenter KI-Assistenten und deren vertrauensvolle Nutzung.* Springer Fachmedien Wiesbaden. https://doi.org/10.1007/978-3-658-29526-4
Schmidt-Lauff, S. (2025). (Transformative) Digitale Kompetenzen – Entwicklungen für Hochschule, Studium und Gesellschaft. WBV Publikation.
Schmidt-Lauff, S., Schwarz, J., Rosemann, T., Rathmann, M., & Schiller, J. (2022). DigiTaKS*-Digitale Schlüsselkompetenzen für Studium und Beruf. In D. Schulz, A. Fay, W. Matiaske, & M. Schulz (Eds.), *Dtec.bw-Beiträge der Helmut-Schmidt-Universität / Universität der Bundeswehr Hamburg. Forschungsaktivitäten im*

Zentrum für Digitalisierungs- und Technologieforschung der Bundeswehr dtec. bw (Vol. 1). Helmut-Schmidt-Universität Hamburg. https://openhsu.ub.hsu-hh.de/handle/10.24405/14573

Schönmann, M., & Uhl, M. (2023). Eine ethische Perspektive auf KI in der Bildung. In C. De Witt, C. Gloerfeld, & S. E. Wrede (Eds.), Künstliche Intelligenz in der Bildung (pp. 433–453). Springer Fachmedien Wiesbaden. https://doi.org/10.1007/978-3-658-40079-8_21

Stützer, C. M., Gaaw, S., Herbst, S., & Pengel, N. (2023). Ménage à trois. Zur Beziehung von künstlicher Intelligenz, Hochschulbildung und Digitalität. In T. Schmohl, A. Watanabe, & K. Schelling (Eds.), *Künstliche Intelligenz in der Hochschulbildung: Chancen und Grenzen des KI-gestützten Lernens und Lehrens* (1st ed., Vol. 4, pp. 51–70). transcript Verlag. https://doi.org/10.14361/9783839457696

Tulodziecki, G. (2015). Dimensionen von Medienbildung: Ein konzeptioneller Rahmen für medienpädagogisches Handeln. *MedienPädagogik: Zeitschrift Für Theorie Und Praxis Der Medienbildung*, 31–49. https://doi.org/10.21240/mpaed/00/2015.06.05.X

Tulodziecki, G. (2023). *Individuelles Handeln und Gemeinwohl: Eine interdisziplinäre Handlungstheorie im Kontext von Freiheit, Verantwortung und künstlicher Intelligenz* (1. Auflage). Transcript Verlag.

UNESCO (Ed.). (2022). *Recommendation on the Ethics of Artificial Intelligence.* https://unesdoc.unesco.org/ark:/48223/pf0000381137

van Dijk, J. A. G. M. (2017). Digital Divide: Impact of Access. In P. Rössler, C. A. Hoffner, & L. Zoonen (Eds.), *The International Encyclopedia of Media Effects* (1st ed., pp. 1–11). Wiley. https://doi.org/10.1002/9781118783764.wbieme0043

van Dijk, J. A. G. M. (2020). *The digital divide.* Polity.

von Garrel, J., Mayer, J., & Mühlfeld, M. (2023). *Künstliche Intelligenz im Studium Eine quantitative Befragung von Studierenden zur Nutzung von ChatGPT & Co.* https://doi.org/10.48444/H_DOCS-PUB-395

Vuorikari, R., Kluzer, S., & Punie, Y. (2022). *DigComp 2.2, The Digital Competence framework for citizens: With new examples of knowledge, skills and attitudes.* Publications Office of the European Union. https://data.europa.eu/doi/10.2760/115376

Wollersheim, H.-W. (2023). Bildung durch Künstliche Intelligenz ermöglichen. Ein Beitrag aus bildungstheoretischer Perspektive. In C. De Witt, C. Gloerfeld, & S. E. Wrede (Eds.), Künstliche Intelligenz in der Bildung (pp. 3–29). Springer VS. https://doi.org/10.1007/978-3-658-40079-8_1

11. Digitalization and artificial intelligence for enhancing inclusive and equitable education in Finland

Sari Havu-Nuutinen and Sini Kontkanen

THE FINNISH EDUCATION SYSTEM

Key Political, Social, and Economic Drivers of Education

The Finnish education system is renowned for its high quality, equity, and efficiency (Chung, 2019). Educational policy is consistent and committed to a knowledge-based society and enhanced local authority (Sahlberg et al., 2021). Finland's high-quality education relies on broad national guidance and stricter local administration. The Basic Education Act (628/1998) sets the principles and norms of basic education, which are implemented by national authorities. The Finnish education system has a two-tier administrative structure: the Ministry of Education and Culture, which is the highest authority over education, and the Finnish National Agency for Education (EDUFI), which operates under the Ministry but is relatively autonomous within its own working area. The EDUFI operates educational programs from early childhood education and care to upper secondary education, in addition to adult education. Higher education is regulated by the Ministry of Education and Culture.

Finnish education has several key drivers. First, pre-primary through higher education is free, including meals, transportation, and all learning supplies, including digital devices. Second, all people have the right to education in accordance with their abilities and special needs. Compulsory education begins the year a child turns six and ends the year they turn eighteen. This means that after basic education, young people have the right to continue their studies either at a general high school or a vocational school without tuition (Act on Compulsory Education, 1214/2020).

Free education increases equity, which is a significant driver for Finnish success in international evaluations as well. There is a strong focus on ensuring equal opportunities for all students, regardless of their background. For

Finland, this degree of equity in educational achievement is a result of its explicit vision for equity in education, which was established in the early 1970s with the equity-based school reform movement. In particular, early childhood education and basic education have been organized so that students enter public schools near where they live. Private education options are limited, so there are not many opportunities for "school shopping." Schools demonstrate little between-school variation, and very high academic and social inclusion (see Thrupp et al., 2023).

Educational policy also highlights lifelong learning. Early childhood education and care are prioritized to ensure a strong foundation. Every child, regardless of background or ability, gets an equal start, and cooperation with parents is imperative (Harju-Luukkainen et al., 2022). After the nine-year basic education, free education at a high school or vocational school is provided to ensure knowledgeable and skilled Finnish workers. Throughout an adult's work life, educational opportunities are provided and supported by the government. Open universities and community colleges provide access to a wide range of courses for developing academic and practical skills, including digital skills. In addition, in vocational training, adults can gain new qualifications or enhance existing skills. Additionally, many employers support ongoing professional development by offering courses and training, often during work time (see Ministry of Education and Culture, Finnish National Agency for Education, 2022).

One key driver of the Finnish education system is the high number of competent teachers. Teachers are respected professionals with advanced education and significant autonomy in their decision-making. Thus, there are numerous applicants for teacher education, and placement is competitive. Finnish teacher education is implemented at universities following a nationally shared framework. Universities' curricula vary, but they all follow the same national guidelines and legislation for university teacher education (Mikkilä-Erdmann et al., 2019). In the university training schools, student teachers practice teaching, applying their theoretical knowledge and skills in actual school environments. This combination of theory and practice in a context designed to foster the development of student teachers is a key element of Finnish educational consistency (Mononen et al., 2023). A large review of the Finnish education system (Ustun & Eryilmaz, 2018) highlights that there is a system of interrelated factors to explain Finland's efficiency and consistency in education. The quality of teachers and teacher education seems to be one of the prominent factors because only the selected students are educated in teacher education.

The final key driver of the Finnish education system is trust. Teachers have high freedom to implement their pedagogy and there are no inspections of Finnish schools. The education system and Finnish society rely on the proficiency of the teachers. (Ustun & Eryilmaz, 2018.) The Finnish Education Evaluation Centre conducts nationwide evaluations of education; however, the main purpose of these evaluations is to provide educational stakeholders with appropriate feedback, and they do not include teacher inspections (www.karvi.fi).

School Policy and National Core Curriculum for Basic Education

Until the 1970s, the Finnish school system could be described as segregated, consisting of six years of elementary school followed by two options for secondary school: vocational and academic (Hausstätter & Jahnukainen, 2014). However, in the 1970s, the school system underwent a fundamental reform due to growing social awareness regarding social participation. It became apparent in several scientific studies that students' choice between vocational and academic careers was largely determined by socioeconomic factors and generational traditions. These findings were the main reason for Finland's fundamental school reform, and in 1972, the nine-year comprehensive school system was successively introduced in Finland (Hausstätter & Jahnukainen, 2014). At the same time, a new system of internal differentiation was introduced, which enabled individual schools to freely dispose of a specially allocated hourly allowance and use it, for example, for remedial measures. Thus, individual schools were given a high degree of pedagogical autonomy, creating a culture of trust in teachers' work (see also Sahlberg et al., 2021).

Comprehensive schooling follows the decentralized school policy. This means that local municipalities have significant autonomy in planning, implementing, and running schools. The public school system is funded by the government, but municipalities are responsible for schools' day-to-day operations, including the use of financial resources, staffing, and curriculum planning and implementation. Schools, municipalities, and other stakeholders often collaborate to ensure that education policies are effectively implemented and adapted to local needs.

Local, school-based curricula follow the national core curriculum for basic education (Finnish National Agency for Education, 2014), which sets a national framework for general aims and standards of basic education, as well as general aims for each school subject (Lavonen, 2020). Education is similarly guided in early childhood education and high school. Finland's educational policies expect teachers to organize support for their students in collaboration with other teachers and professionals at school. In general, Finnish teachers' pedagogical position is autonomous, giving them the freedom to resolve pedagogical issues and determine practices themselves.

The latest curriculum reform in 2014 started after public discussion about the need for general work and life skills and how this should be considered more broadly in schools. Researchers and policymakers debated what kind of school was necessary to ensure future competence for students. This discussion led to reforms in the national curriculum to reflect the requirements of the twenty-first century (Vahtivuori-Hänninen et al., 2014). While designing the curriculum, work-related transversal competences were also considered beside the subjects. Transversal competences were grouped under the following competence areas: taking care of oneself; managing daily life; multiliteracy, information, and communication technology (ICT) competence; working life competence; entrepreneurship; participation and involvement in building a sustainable future; thinking and learning to learn; and cultural competence, interaction, and expression.

The defined transversal competences confirm that these skills are systematically considered in all subjects. For example, the use of digital technology in education is not optional. ICT competence should be developed in all subjects, and technology should be used as an integrated tool for learning. The current national core curriculum for basic education emphasizes that future jobs will require broad competences and skills that are developed through school subjects. Developing competences and skills is influenced by the individual's values and attitudes and by their own goals and ambitions (Finnish National Agency for Education, 2014).

National assessment criteria have been reviewed in the national core curriculum for basic education with two core aims. The first is to focus on formative assessment and support self-assessment skills. The second focus is on summative assessment by indicating how well students achieve in learning. There are no national tests for students, and the nature of the evaluation of learning outcomes at schools is defined as encouraging and supportive. Assessment and evaluation are based on local schools' evaluation culture, which needs to be transparent and used similarly across schools (Finnish National Agency for Education, 2014).

INCLUSION AND EQUITY IN FINNISH EDUCATION

Inclusion and equity are fundamental principles that are strongly ingrained in the Finnish education system. Finland's approach to education prioritizes providing equal opportunities for all students regardless of their background, socioeconomic status, abilities, or geographic location (Thrupp et al., 2023). In this sub-chapter, we present how key drivers of Finnish education and other principles support the development of inclusion and equity: equal access to schools, free education for all, special education integration, quality teacher education, and a strong focus on parental involvement.

School for all has been the reality in Finland for several decades, and its basic structure is undisputed by public educational policy. The special educational support system was gradually integrated into the mainstream school system in the 1970s, with special needs education increasingly being provided in different organizational forms under the umbrella of comprehensive schooling. The next phase of the reform led to inclusive education, and this discussion has been active for more than a decade. School-based reforms have supported organizing all education types in mainstream schools (Pulkkinen & Jahnukainen, 2015).

In Finland, inclusive education is most often understood as a pragmatic approach to offering the best possible support for those who need it, particularly students defined as having special educational needs (Malinen et al., 2012). All this support is provided in comprehensive schools. In some schools, the students are integrated into mainstream classrooms, while others establish special education classes. When inclusion has been successful, this approach has increased feelings of equity and belonging, though there have been experiences of segregation and feelings of distance (Niemi & Mietola, 2023). However, inclusive education has encouraged teachers to utilize and develop pedagogical approaches and devices that support students with different skills and abilities. For example, with the wide use of digital devices, modern teaching approaches and new learning environments have become available for all learners. This integrated support system is considered by many Finnish special educators to be one of the reasons for the success of the Finnish school system (Hausstätter & Takala, 2011; Bernelius & Kosunen, 2023).

The success and equity of the Finnish school system is monitored and audited by the independent evaluation center KARVI (www.karvi.fi). KARVI evaluates all education from early childhood through higher education. One of the key aims of this center is to evaluate the equality and equity of education in Finland. According to its latest report (Ukkola & Väätäinen, 2021), comprehensive schools meet the targets, and the majority of students have similar opportunities for education despite their language, living situation, or economic background. Individual variation in learning outcomes is significant, however, and comprehensive schools are not able to compensate for the differences resulting from family backgrounds because of lack of resources. In addition, the differences between residential areas comparing the cities and rural areas are growing, and these gaps are reflected after basic education in higher education and worklife (Ukkola & Väätäinen, 2021).

DIGITALIZATION IN FINNISH EDUCATION

Digitalization describes the spread of digital information technology into everyday functions and environments, such as schools, workplaces, and community services. It has the potential to offer a wide range of opportunities, but it can also be a major challenge, for example, in terms of equality. Digitalization is linked to many of the major challenges of our time, such as marginalization and school well-being. Digital transformation is a broader concept that refers to a comprehensive change in how organizations and institutions act, driven by the integration of digital technologies. Finland follows the goals of the European Union's (EU) 2030 digital policy program and encompasses national goals and themes in Finland's digital compass, which outlines the nation's vision and targets for digital transformation up to 2030 (Finnish Government, 2022). Finland's digital compass has four main topics: skills, secure and sustainable digital infrastructures, the digital transformation of businesses, and the digitalization of public services. In Finland, the significance of digital transformation has been increasingly recognized, prompting substantial investments in digital infrastructure for education in recent years. This includes enhancements in high-speed internet connectivity, cloud computing, and online learning platforms (Leino et al., 2023). Such investments have facilitated the integration of digital learning tools and platforms within basic education, thereby ensuring that students have access to high-quality education irrespective of their geographical location, including those residing in the rural regions of northern and eastern Finland (Tanhua-Piiroinen et al., 2020). This has been confirmed by various project funding and initiatives from the EDUFI and the Ministry of Education and Culture, which have continued to enable the development of digital learning and teaching in different educational contexts and levels, as well as support teachers' digital pedagogical skills (Näykki & Häkkinen, 2023).

Digitalization in Finnish education refers to the integration of technology into teaching and learning processes across all levels of education, from early childhood to higher education. It consists of integrating digital applications, learning tools, and environments into classes and administrative tasks (Finnish National Agency for Education, 2014). Characteristic of Finland is an emphasis in curricula on examining digital competence from social perspectives, as well as critical and ethical approaches (Godhe, 2019). Competence in digital technologies is one of the transversal competences in the Finnish national core curriculum for early childhood education and care, and basic education. Competence in digital technologies is therefore seen as an important civic skill, both in itself and as a part of multiliteracy (another transversal competence area in the national core curriculum for basic education). It is both an objective and a tool for learning. In basic education, all students should have opportunities to develop their digital skills. Digital technologies should be systematically used in basic education at all grade levels, in different disciplines, in multidisciplinary learning modules, and in other schoolwork. Competence in digital technologies is built around four core learning areas: practical skills and personal production, responsible and safe use of digital technologies, information management, and inquiry-based and creative work, interaction, and networks (Finnish National Agency for Education, 2014, 2018). In addition to these transversal skills, coding, programming, and computational thinking are added under the objectives of mathematics and craft education. This is a new subject area that was brought into the latest core curriculum of basic education (Erstad et al., 2021).

Even though the current revised curriculum in Finland strongly emphasizes digital competence, curriculum texts leave much room for discretion in practical implementation. For instance, a review study examining the curriculum of Finnish early childhood education and care found that although it is considered to comprehensively develop children's digital competence, the curriculum text does not sufficiently describe concrete methods and means for this development (Kontkanen et al., 2023). Only some schools have created their own local plans for developing pupils' competences in digital technologies in different grade levels to make learning in this area a logical continuum in basic education. This places students from other schools in an unequal position. Therefore, to open and concretize competences in digital technologies in the national core curriculum, the EDUFI and the National Audiovisual Institution published a new literacies development program. It describes over 300 learning goals for using digital technologies and programming for early childhood education and care, preschool, and grades one through nine. These goals are built around four core learning areas of competence in digital technologies in the curriculum. The program emphasizes the importance of self-expression and engagement, the cultivation of active and responsible participation, and the enhancement of diverse critical thinking abilities—all of which are crucial in a society that is becoming progressively more digitalized (Finnish National Agency for Education, 2022).

In Finland, there is good infrastructure and equipment in education compared to many other countries. Almost all Finnish basic education schools have good-quality network connections, and most teachers have personal digital devices provided by the school (Tanhua-Piiroinen et al., 2020; Fagerlund et al., 2024). Most schools are equipped with simulation and modeling software, drawing or graphic software, programmable robots, and 3D printers. However, sensors for data collection and analysis, adaptive learning systems, and virtual reality devices are uncommon. There are approximately two to four students per ICT device (including desktop computers, laptops, and tablets). While in Finland the foundation of schooling is equality, education providers mainly offer the supplies, materials, and devices necessary for studying. This is one reason why Finnish students do not bring their own devices to school (Fagerlund et al., 2024), but there is also intense discussion about the relevance of the use of students' own mobile devices at school. Starting from the beginning of the 2025 school year, the Basic Education Act has been amended so that a pupil may use a mobile phone or other mobile devices during school hours only for educational purposes defined by the teacher, or if the pupil has a medical reason to use such devices (Ministry of Education and Culture, 2024).

In a large international study of students' computer and information literacy ICILS (European Commission: Directorate-General for Education, Youth, Sport and Culture, 2024), Finnish eighth-grade students ranked among the top performers by country in an assessment of multiliteracy and computational thinking skills. Girls achieved significantly better scores than boys in multiliteracy. Compared to a previous study by ICILS in 2018, the proportion of weak performers in Finland increased by one percent. In computational thinking, the number of both weak and strong performers increased. These differences were explained by students' socioeconomic backgrounds (Fagerlund et al., 2024).

Finnish educators and institutions possess significant independence in delivering instruction in alignment with the national curriculum's guidelines. Consequently, the implementation of digital technologies differs widely across Finnish schools and among individual teachers. According to Halinen et al. (2024), on average, teachers in Finland very rarely assign students the role of active participants as users of digital technology. Digital technology requiring basic skills was utilized in teaching only about once a month. Advanced skills requiring digital technology were hardly used at all. This is supported by the finding of the ICILS study (European Commission: Directorate-General for Education, Youth, Sport and Culture, 2024), in which the use of ICT devices in various subjects in Finnish schools was found to be below the international average (Fagerlund et al., 2024). According to students, different areas of digital learning are practiced at schools, but only occasionally and often only in optional subjects (Oinas & Hotulainen, 2024). Students receiving support for learning and schooling, those with foreign backgrounds, and those performing less well reported using digital technology at school more often than other students (Nazeri & Vainikainen, 2024; Hienonen et al., 2024). The ICILS study (European Commission, 2024) also indicates that Finnish youth have mostly learned ICT skills outside school. For example, skills concerning data protection and security were rarely learned in school.

The transition of educational materials to online platforms facilitates individualized and differentiated instruction as the internet offers a plethora of tasks for students at various levels (Kiili & Laurinen, 2019). Computers can provide new learning opportunities for students with learning difficulties. Digital tools also support continuous learning, enabling both formal and informal education regardless of time and place. However, for young individuals with specific language impairments, the accessibility of digital services may pose challenges if accessibility is not considered in the design. Important factors for accessibility include a clear site structure, readability, and reliability (Autere et al., 2019). Linguistic challenges and learning difficulties can weaken digital skills, potentially leading to inequality and the assimilation of incorrect information online (Kaarakainen & Saikkonen, 2022).

THE ROLE OF DIGITALIZATION IN TEACHER EDUCATION

The digitalization of education culminates with teachers and the pedagogical solutions they implement. Therefore, it is important to examine the skills and attitudes of pre-service and in-service teachers related to digitalization and how these are supported by the Finnish education system. It is widely accepted that institutions responsible for initial teacher education are crucial for equipping pre-service teachers to effectively utilize digital technologies in their future careers (Häkkinen et al., 2017). Because of the decentralized teacher education system and the autonomy of teacher education institutions, there are no common procedures in Finland for how and what should be taught about digitalization. According to Tondeur et al.'s (2012) review of strategies for preparing pre-service teachers' digital competence, it is important to support teachers' competence by modeling technology use, providing opportunities to design technology use, and scaffolding teachers in authentic technology experiences. In a recent study of Finnish teacher educators, it was found that teachers' attitudes toward digitalization were mainly positive, but there was large variation in their self-reported skills. Teacher educators see modeling technology use and offering authentic experiences with technology as easy, whereas instructional design, reflection, collaborative use of technology, and giving feedback are seen as difficult (Kukkonen et al., 2025). According to several studies, Finnish pre-service teachers' confidence in their skills and attitudes regarding the integration of technology in teaching and learning varies significantly (Lehtinen et al., 2024; Mertala, 2019; Valtonen et al., 2017; Valtonen et al., 2021).

The adoption of digital technologies varies significantly between individual teachers. The differences in teachers' utilization of educational technology in Finland are mainly explained by individual factors, such as age and digital skills, rather than school or municipal factors (Kaarakainen & Saikkonen, 2022). According to Halinen et al. (2024), one factor that particularly predicts technology use is teachers' confidence in their own digital skills. Therefore, it is important to develop ways to improve these skills.

In recent years, Finland has invested significantly to improve teacher education nationally. The Ministry of Education and Culture initiated the Finnish Teacher Education Forum in 2016 to prepare a national teacher education strategy. The forum identified key competences and actions for improving teacher education and financed several projects for which digitalization was a leading theme (Lavonen et al., 2021). At the same time, the Ministry of Education and Culture and the EDUFI supported pre- and in-service teachers' digital competence by developing various networks for digital learning and modes of in-service training. For example, in new forms of in-service training, teacher specialization programs related to teaching and learning in digital environments have been effective for developing teachers' evidence-based use of technology (Kontkanen et al., 2024). Even though there are multiple ways for in-service teachers to improve their digital competence, participation in continuing education varies widely between teachers. The COVID-19 pandemic reduced the amount of teacher participation, for example, in courses about certain applications and programs or the educational use of digital technologies for students with special needs and support (Leino et al., 2023).

ARTIFICIAL INTELLIGENCE FOR ENHANCING INCLUSIVE AND EQUITABLE EDUCATION IN FINLAND

Artificial intelligence (AI) refers to the simulation of human intelligence processes, such as learning, reasoning, and self-correction, by machines, particularly computer systems. AI encompasses a wide range of technologies and methodologies, including machine learning, deep learning, natural language processing, robotics, and computer vision (Baker & Smith, 2019). Particularly, generative AI (GAI), a subfield of AI that produces novel and unique outputs such as images, music, and text, has sparked discussion in recent years within the educational sphere regarding various ethical, privacy, and authorship issues. In the discourse surrounding GAI within the educational sector, the emphasis is largely on the potential misuse of such technology by students, often overshadowing the possible benefits that GAI tools might offer (Pack & Maloney, 2023). There are several challenges associated with the safety, bias, and misinformation of GAI systems, including ensuring fair access, protecting student privacy, and addressing misinformation generated by AI (Han & Cai, 2023). However, GAI tools hold the promise of improving accessibility for a diverse range of students, opening new avenues for creative expression, and supporting the development of immersive and interactive learning environments (Baidoo-Anu & Ansah, 2023; Chheang et al., 2024; Kadaruddin, 2023). In the educational context, it is important to proactively engage students in understanding and managing their interactions with GAI by exploring how GAI can enhance their thinking and creativity (Kasneci et al., 2023). It is essential to nurture the upcoming generation with a critical perspective and the ability to effectively use these innovative tools for their creative pursuits and to critically evaluate the work of others (Han & Cai, 2023). As AI-driven tools like GPT-4 become more widespread in education, it will become increasingly vital to educate students about digital literacy, critical thinking, and the ethical considerations of employing AI across various scenarios.

In Finland, AI is an emerging topic within educational institutions, including teacher training programs. There is a noticeable deficiency in curriculum resources that are tailored to these topics, as well as a lack of educational technology and methodologies that facilitate teachers in integrating AI into their instructional practices (Kahila et al., 2024). Enhanced awareness of how algorithms and AI function lays the groundwork for active engagement and equips individuals with tools to comprehend the surrounding world (Gran et al., 2021; Vartiainen et al., 2020). Recently, AI and machine learning have been incorporated into the computational thinking segment of curriculum texts in Finland (Tedre et al., 2021). Research on the application of AI in the Finnish educational context is still at an initial phase. However, Finland is actively investing in research and development projects to explore ways to leverage AI's potential for educational purposes. For instance, the Strategic Research Council, an independent body within the Research Council of Finland (www.aka.fi), is financing the Generation-AI research project, which aims to establish a foundation for the technology education of the "AI generation." This project focuses on educating individuals about the principles of AI, its potential advantages, and its dynamic effects, while also addressing its limitations and risks. It underscores the importance of understanding how AI systems might contribute to conflict, discrimination, insecurity, and the erosion of trust (Kahila et al., 2024).

The AI act of the EU (European Commission, 2024) is the first comprehensive regulatory framework in the world for the use and development of AI. The goal of the AI act is to promote responsible use of AI in the EU and to protect citizens' health, safety, and fundamental rights. Based on the AI act, the Finnish government has prepared supplementary national legislation to be applied even by education and training providers for early childhood education and care. The EDUFI published recommendations and legislation regarding the use of AI in early childhood education, basic education, liberal adult education, and secondary education in 2025 (Finnish National Agency for Education, 2025). This support material, titled "Artificial Intelligence in Education—Legislation and Recommendations," aims to assist organizers of early childhood education and educational institutions in integrating AI as part of the educational process. During the preparatory phase, the support material was open to commentary by professionals in the field of education. The published material includes a list of obligations for both education providers and teaching and guidance staff based on the legislation. Additionally, there are recommendations for both education providers and teaching and guidance staff and background material about topics such as the use of AI in teaching, the assessment and recognition of skills, AI literacy, and ethical and sustainable development issues associated with the use of AI. The support material leans strongly on the AI act of the EU and underlines the responsibilities of education providers (educational institutions and municipalities) to ensure the proper use of AI in education.

Despite its potential, AI entails many challenges and risks when used in education, especially from an ethical perspective. Privacy and data protection issues, lack of transparency, accountability and decision-making issues, as well as bias and discrimination challenge the use of AI in learning (Nguyen et al., 2023). The AI act of the EU and the support material from the EDUFI (Finnish National Agency for Education, 2025) provide guidelines for the ethical use of AI for both education providers and teaching and guidance staff in Finland. For example, education providers are obligated to offer devices and AI services, and teaching staff cannot oblige learners to register or create IDs for other systems or applications. It is recommended that teaching staff only use AI services accepted by education providers and ensure data protection according to the education providers' guidelines. The need to follow curriculum guidelines for different levels of education is emphasized, and AI's use always must be pedagogically justified, followed by aims and content of the curriculum. Additionally, the use of AI by education providers should be open and transparent, and staff and learners should be informed when AI is used in education and assessment. In the support material (Finnish National Agency for Education, 2025), possible biases and misconceptions in AI are recommended for consideration and discussion with learners.

Although these recommendations and laws on the use of AI in education exist, practice and understanding of the ethical use of AI are still in the early stages and arouse uncertainty and fears. For example, the AI act of the EU has led to a total ban on the use of AI in education in some Finnish municipalities. Therefore, there is a need for education around these topics for both teachers and education providers. This is also a strong message from the EDUFI (Finnish National Agency of Education, 2025): "all the users of AI [must] have sufficient understanding and ability to interpret and critically evaluate the outputs by AI." It is recommended that education providers ensure sufficient education for the ethical use of AI for both staff and learners. However, the overall national picture of Finnish teachers' AI skills and training needs is not clear. Relevant studies are currently being launched, and teacher education on this topic should be a significant target for the coming years.

IMPLEMENTATION AND OUTCOMES OF DIGITALIZATION AND AI IN K–12 EDUCATION

Digitalization, particularly the rapid development of AI tools, is challenging teachers to improve their classroom practices. In this chapter, we present research-based experiences with using digital devices and AI in school learning. Examples include how third- and fourth-grade students have used VR glasses for water purification learning, how mobile learning has been used for science education and assessment, and how GAI can support creative writing skills in second graders. In addition, the critical, ethical, and equity perspectives when using digital devices and AI with young students are explored.

Case 1: Digital Devices and AI in Developing the Science Capital of Third- and Fourth-Grade Students

This case was implemented in a Finnish elementary school with 108 third- and fourth-grade students (ages nine to eleven) in rural eastern Finland. The teaching period was carried out within the regular curriculum, meeting its aims and content. Consent was given by the school and parents for research purposes. The teaching period was planned by a teacher and a group of researchers in educational science. The core aim of the lesson was to support the students' science capital, their literacy skills in science, and their intentions and attitudes towards science and provide pedagogical tools to examine water and nutrition from different viewpoints. The teaching period was part of a larger project studying Finnish science capital from different perspectives (the FINSCI research project). The teaching period aimed to foster students' knowledge, skills, and attitudes related to doing science and help them see science careers as a possibility. Besides science competence, the teaching periods aimed to provide inclusive and sustainable tools for science using digital technologies (Fischer et al., 2024).

A total of 15 45-minute lessons were carried out: two introductory lessons, eight lessons on water content, four lessons on nutrition content, and one concluding lesson. To examine water and nutrition, the students had several opportunities to increase their knowledge and skills by using AI-based digital tools, such as Google Earth, VR glasses, and Google Classroom. Some had good experiences, while others faced challenges.

In the pilot phase of the teaching period, the students collected their initial thoughts and field notes in a Google Classroom environment. However, the digital environment took too much time to use, and the teacher decided to change from a digital platform to paper worksheets for field notes. In the first phase of each topic, the students watched topical orientation videos created for the project. The videos activated the students' thoughts and inspired them to investigate the selected topics. They also provided multichannel opportunities to orient to the topic. Google Earth was used to explore water-related attractions in Finland. This provided easy access to locate the selected places on the map and see the three-dimensional photos related to the locations. Water samples, which students collected from nearby lakes, were analyzed afterwards with Easi-scope digital microscopes (see Figure 11.1). The digital microscopes provided additional information to consider the litter, color, and structure of

Source: Finsci-intervention documentation.

Figure 11.1 *Analyzing water samples with digital microscopes*

the water and stimulated discussions about water purity. The devices also provided easy and equitable access to microscopy without any specific spaces or expensive devices. In addition, this supported individual learning skills and student engagement.

This pedagogical approach to science capital suggests visiting places where science is involved and where people work with science. In this project, the students were invited to visit water purification centers, but there was no access in the local area. Thus, VR glasses were used, and students had virtual experiences with the water purification processes. Again, this approach provided equal opportunities for students to learn and have experiences without physically visiting locations. Students who were not eager to use VR glasses engaged in similar tours with their tablets.

Additionally, to communicate with workers at water purification centers, the students contacted experts via Microsoft Teams meetings and interviewed them online. The interviews were recorded and summarized by the students using their tablets to create short presentations. Tablets and laptops were systematically and continually used for the reporting, ensuring equal and responsible participation in the lessons.

Case 2: Digital Devices and GAI in Supporting Creative Writing with Second-Grade Students

The second case is a description of two lessons that were part of a single school year experiment in which a class of second-grade students (ages eight to nine, n = 23) used digital devices and applications to support their creative writing. The teaching experiment was carried out within the regular curriculum, and consents were given by the school and parents. The experiment took place at a university training school with a one-to-one policy for technological devices. All students have personal tablets, and they begin learning to use them in first grade. In the case lessons, students were asked to create a fictional forest animal character using different applications. The teacher created a wall in the Padlet application (https://padlet.com/) on which students posted their forest animal pictures. Students created characters with the GAI tool integrated into Padlet. The AI service provider in Padlet does not train with users' data. Students did not log into the Padlet wall; the teacher did this to create the learning environment. Students practiced prompting, and they were advised to prompt the GAI in English as follows: "name of the animal," "location/place of the animal," "adjective describing the animal." After the GAI created a list of optional pictures, the student chose one and added it to the Padlet wall (see example in Figure 11.2). In this phase, the teacher and students discussed pictures added to the wall, whether they were proper according to the assignment, and possible biases/misinformation present in them.

After choosing their pictures, students saved them to their tablets. Then they logged into the Thinglink application (https://www.thinglink.com/). In Thinglink, students used their GAI-generated animal pictures as a base (wallpaper) and added "hotspots" of images, sound, and text describing their chosen animals. At the end of the lesson, students were asked to present their animals to others and make self-assessments of their digital learning on the Padlet wall

Source: Padlet.

Figure 11.2 *Example of a student's prompt and chosen picture in Padlet*

created by the teacher. Students assessed their learning according to the lesson goals by choosing one of three statements: "I need practice," "I am familiar with this, and I can do it," or "I can help others with this topic." With most of the learning goals, the majority of the students assessed that they could help others with the topic or that they could do it themselves. Only the learning goal of logging into Thinglink was seen as more challenging, with over 25% of students saying they needed practice with this (see Table 11.1).

Based on the experiences with this case, it is vital to select applications carefully to ensure that privacy and other critical aspects are appropriately considered with young students. Including children in digital culture is a significant step toward equality and accessibility as children should have the opportunity to participate in this essential part of modern life. It was noted that young students were capable of handling complex processes during the lessons, and their abilities were often underestimated. In this case, AI tools supported and inspired young students' creative writing skills and, according to the teacher, motivated them. For this reason, experiments and research are needed to create new effective models and practices. In this way, we can ensure that digital environments are safe, educational, and inspiring for all children.

Table 11.1 Students' self-assessments of their digital learning during the case lessons

Learning goal of digital learning	I need practice	I am familiar with this, and I can do it	I can help others with this topic
To practice picture saving to iPad (n = 19)	5.3%	36.8%	57.9%
To practice integrating different functions, such as images, sound, and text, into the picture (n = 19)	15.8%	36.8%	47.4%
To practice creating a picture using a prompt (n = 18)	0%	27.8%	72.2%
To practice evaluating if the created information is reliable (n = 16)	18.8%	0%	81.3%
To practice logging into Thinglink (n = 19)	26.3%	47.4%	26.3%

CONCLUSION AND FUTURE STEPS

In Finland, ICT is taught in all subjects, and its contents and objectives have been defined as part of teaching as a broad-based knowledge entity. In addition, education providers can locally emphasize some of the contents of this wide-ranging competence, add topics in addition to the national curriculum, and use optional lessons for teaching, for example, programming, according to class divisions.

ICT competence includes skills belonging to everyone, such as multiliteracy, information management, creative work, and networking, but that have not been developed as estimated. There are multiple educational programs to support digital learning and competence in schools, but teachers and the learning culture are still struggling to create effective learning outcomes. According to several researchers (Brinck et al., 2023), students should familiarize themselves with different ICT skills and AI (Niemi et al., 2023) at an early age. This helps develop skills in problem-solving, creativity, and collaboration and increases interest in science, technology, engineering, and mathematics careers. In addition, strengthening digital competence promotes educational equality among students. At the same time, there is active discussion related to students' learning difficulties, psychological challenges, and holistic well-being. Many of these issues have been caused by the huge increase in the use of digital devices and therefore Finnish Government has given restrictions for use of personal devices in schools. However, there is a need to create a school culture where technology can be used in versatile and appropriate ways to promote equality and agency of students to participate in digital society.

Finnish students have easy access to digital devices at early ages, and they use a variety of tools at home with their parents, in school, and with their peers. Digital games and social communication arenas, as well as AI-supported applications, increase equality and create similar opportunities to participate and engage. At the same time, they present certain challenges in school contexts. The use of digital devices requires skills that students are still learning and are unable to monitor or control. This may lead to overemphasizing the role of digital devices in everyday use and social relations. Some studies (Tammisalo et al., 2020) have pointed to behavioral problems, sleep challenges, problems in social relations, and even burnout symptoms. These reactions are evident at all levels of education, and they need to be monitored and controlled to use digital environments appropriately.

The number of AI applications is dramatically increasing, and children in multiple age groups may access them easily. In Finnish society, digital learning is systematically applied in various educational phases because of its significant relevance to successful learning. Digital and AI learning increase students' problem-solving skills and creativity, but at the same time, they cause concerns regarding data protection and skill confidence.

Many teachers appreciate that digital learning material is easily available and that it is of high quality. This is ensured because schools use learning environments for large program agencies, which are well planned and designed for school use. However, the environments contain separate applications that leak information, causing problems from a data protection perspective.

Fortunately for schools, there are great materials available in Finland, for example in digital libraries, a joint search service for archives, libraries, and museums. However, the research indicates high variation in teachers' digital competences. This trend might increase along with the use of AI in school contexts. Currently, the development of competence is very much dependent on teachers' own interest and willingness to participate in service training, which is not mandatory. However, we also have good experiences of school-based professional development programs, which have produced promising results (Kontkanen et al., 2024; Oikarinen et. al., 2026).

Even though the digital competences of teachers have been emphasized in teacher education for several years, and there have been various projects, training, and pre- and in-service education opportunities, there is a need to effectively continue teacher education. Particularly, the role of AI and GAI needs additional consideration with a focus on ethical issues. Teachers need to become aware of the role of technology and AI in school and how it provides opportunities for equal learning and individuals' rights to control their learning. At the same time, the multiple uses of technology might cause ethical concerns related to autonomy, respect for rights, trust, and democracy. These issues are rarely discussed and require research and development in education.

REFERENCES

Act on Compulsory Education 2014/2020: https://www.finlex.fi/fi/lainsaadanto/saadoskokoelma/2020/1214

Autere, N., Talvinen, A., Hankala, M., & Pöysä-Tarhonen, J. (2019). Esteettömyys digitaalisissa ympäristöissä kielellisten erityisvaikeuksien näkökulmasta. *Oppimisen ja oppimisvaikeuksien erityislehti: NMI-bulletin, 29*(2).

Baidoo-Anu, D., & Ansah, L. O. (2023). Education in the era of generative artificial intelligence (AI): Understanding the potential benefits of ChatGPT in promoting teaching and learning. *Journal of AI, 7*(1), 52–62. https://doi.org/10.61969/jai.1337500

Baker, T., & Smith, L. (2019). *Educ-AI-tion rebooted? Exploring the future of artificial intelligence in schools and colleges.* https://www.nesta.org.uk/report/education-rebooted/

Bernelius, V., & Kosunen, S. (2023). "Three bedrooms and a nice school"—Residential choices, school choices and vicious circles of segregation in the education landscape of Finnish cities. In M. Thrupp, P. Seppänen, J. Kauko, & S. Kosunen (Eds.),

Finland's famous education system: Unvarnished insights into Finnish schooling (pp. 175–192). Springer. https://doi.org/10.1007/978-981-19-8241-5

Brinck, J., Leinonen, T., Lipponen, L., & Kallio-Tavin, M. (2023). Open design pedagogy: Revealing openness in early childhood education with digital technology. *International Journal of Education Through Art*, *19*(2), 223–240. https://doi.org/10.1386/eta_00128_1

Chheang, V., Sharmin, S., Márquez-Hernández, R., Patel, M., Rajasekaran, D., Caulfield, G., Kiafar, B., Li, J. Kullu, P., & Barmaki, R. (2024). Towards anatomy education with generative AI-based virtual assistants in immersive virtual reality environments. In *2024 IEEE International Conference on Artificial Intelligence and eXtended and Virtual Reality (AIxVR)* (pp. 21–30). https://doi.org/10.48550/arXiv.2306.17278

Chung, J. (2019). *PISA and global education policy: Understanding Finland's success and influence.* Brill Sense.

Erstad, O., Kjällander, S., & Järvelä, S. (2021). Facing the challenges of "digital competence". A Nordic agenda for curriculum development for the 21st century. *Nordic Journal of Digital Literacy*, *16*(2), 77–87. https://www.scup.com/doi/full/10.18261/issn.1891-943x-2021-02-04

European Commission. (2024). *The EU AI Act.* https://artificialintelligenceact.eu/ai-act-explorer/

European Commission: Directorate-General for Education, Youth, Sport and Culture. (2024). *International Computer and Information Literacy Study (ICILS) in Europe, 2023 – Main findings and educational policy implications.* Publications Office of the European Union. https://data.europa.eu/doi/10.2766/5221263

Fagerlund, J., Leino, K., Niilo-Rämä, M., Puhakka, E., & Markkanen, I. (2024). *Kohti digiosaamisen strategista kehittämistä. Kansainvälisen monilukutaidon ja ohjelmoinnillisen ajattelun tutkimus (ICILS 2023).* Koulutuksen tutkimuslaitos. Jyväskylä.

Finnish Government. (2022). *Government report on the digital compass sets the course for Finland's digital transformation.* https://valtioneuvosto.fi/en/-/10623/government-report-on-the-digital-compass-sets-the-course-for-finland-s-digital-transformation

Finnish National Agency for Education. (2014). *National core curriculum for basic education.* Helsinki.

Finnish National Agency for Education. (2018). *National core curriculum for early childhood education and care.* Finnish National Agency for Education.

Finnish National Agency for Education. (2022). *Uudet lukutaidot – kehittämisohjelmasta tukea tieto- javiestintäteknologian opetukseen.* [The new literacy skills – development program provides support for teaching information and communication technology]. https://www.oph.fi/fi/kehittaminen/uudet-lukutaidot-kehittamisohjelmasta-tukea-tieto-ja-viestintateknologian-opetukseen

Finnish National Agency for Education. (2025). *Tekoäly varhaiskasvatuksessa ja koulutuksessa—lainsäädäntö ja suositukset.* [Artificial intelligence in early childhood education and training—legislation and recommendations]. https://www.oph.fi/fi/tekoalysuositukset

Fischer, A., Havu-Nuutinen, S., Kontkanen, S., & Suortti, E. (2024). Investigating sustainability education in the science capital teaching approach: Competence development and pillar considerations. *Interdisciplinary Journal of Environmental and Science Education*, *20*(4), e2418. https://doi.org/10.29333/ijese/15038

Godhe, A.-L. (2019). Digital literacies or digital competence: Conceptualizations in Nordic curricula. *Media and Communication*, *7*(2), 25–35. https://doi.org/10.17645/mac.v7i2.1888

Gran, A. E., Booth, P., & Bucher, T. (2021). To be or not to be algorithm aware: A question of a new digital divide? *Information, Communication & Society*, *24*(12), 1779–1796. https://doi.org/10.1080/1369118X.2020.1736124

Häkkinen, P., Järvelä, S., Mäkitalo-Siegl, K., Ahonen, A., Näykki, P., & Valtonen, T. (2017). Preparing teacher students for twenty-first century learning practices (PREP 21): A framework for enhancing collaborative problem-solving and strategic learning skills. *Teachers and Teaching: Theory and Practice*, *23*(1), 25–41. https://doi.org/10.1080/13540602.2016.1203772

Halinen, J., Schöning, O., & Nazeri, F. (2024). Opettajat koulujen digitalisaation käytännön toteuttajina. In S. Oinas & M-P. Vainikainen (Eds.), *Digitalisaatio oppimisen ja oppimistulosten selittäjänä.* Suomen kasvatustieteellinen seura. Kasvatusalan tutkimuksia 86, 63–92.

Han, A., & Cai, Z. (2023). Design implications of generative AI systems for visual storytelling for young learners. In *Proceedings of the 22nd Annual ACM Interaction Design and Children Conference* (pp. 470–474).

Harju-Luukkainen, H., Kangas, J., & Garvis, S. (2022). *Finnish early childhood education and care: A multi theoretical perspective on research and practice.* Springer. https://doi.org/10.1007/978-3-030-95512-0

Hausstätter, R. S., & Jahnukainen, M. (2014). From integration to inclusion and the role of special education. In F. Kiuppis & R. S. Haustätter (Eds.), *Inclusive education twenty years after Salamanca* (Vol. 19, pp. 119–132). Disability studies in education. Peter Lang.

Hausstätter, R. S., & Takala, M. (2011). Can special education make a difference? Exploring the differences of special educational systems between Finland and Norway in relation to the PISA results. *Scandinavian Journal of Disability Research*, *13*(4), 271–281. https://doi.org/10.1080/15017419.2010.507372

Hienonen, N., Lintuvuori, M., & Vainikainen, M-P. (2024). Tehostettua ja erityistä tukea saaneet oppilaat valtakunnallisessa DigiVOO-aineistossa—Digitaalisen teknologian käytön yhteys äidinkielen ja matematiikan tehtävistä suoriutumiseen. In S. Oinas & M-P. Vainikainen (Eds.), *Digitalisaatio oppimisen ja oppimistulosten selittäjänä.* Suomen kasvatustieteellinen seura. Kasvatusalan tutkimuksia 86, 167–194.

Kaarakainen, M. T., & Saikkonen, L. (2022). Remark on digital accessibility: Educational disparities define digital inclusion from adolescence onwards. *Universal Access in the Information Society*, 22, 1279–1292. https://doi.org/10.1007/s10209-022-00908-5

Kadaruddin, K. (2023). Empowering education through generative AI: Innovative instructional strategies for tomorrow's learners. *International Journal of Business, Law, and Education*, *4*(2), 618–625. https://doi.org/10.56442/ijble.v4i2.215

Kahila, J., Vartiainen, H., Tedre, M., Arkko, E., Lin, A., Pope, N., Jormanainen, I., & Valtonen, T. (2024). Pedagogical framework for cultivating children's data agency and creative abilities in the age of AI. *Informatics in Education*, *23*(2), 323–360. https://doi.org/10.15388/infedu.2024.15

Kasneci, E., Seßler, K., Küchemann, S., Bannert, M., Dementieva, D., Fischer, F., Gasser, U., Groh, G. Günnemann, S., Eyke Hüllermeier, E., Krusche, S., Kutyniok, G., Michaeli, T., Nerdel, C., Pfeffer, J., Poquet, O., Sailer, M., Schmidt, A., Seidel, T., Stadler, M., Weller, J., Kuhn, J., & Kasneci, G. (2023). ChatGPT for good? On opportunities and challenges of large language models for education. *Learning and Individual Differences, 103*. https://doi.org/10.1016/j.lindif.2023.102274

Kiili, C., & Laurinen, L. (2019). Näkökulmia tutkivan nettilukemisen opettamiseen. *Oppimisen ja oppimisvaikeuksien erityislehti: NMI-bulletin, 29*(2).

Kontkanen, S., Piispa-Hakala, S., Pöntinen, S., & Valtonen, T. (2024). Effects of professional development programme for teaching and learning in digital environments from the perspective of teachers: Case study from Finland. In *Global perspectives on teaching with technology* (pp. 214–230). Routledge.

Kontkanen, S., Pöntinen, S., Kewalramani, S., Veresov, N., & Havu-Nuutinen, S. (2023). Children's digital competence in early childhood education: A comparative analysis of curricula. *Eurasia Journal of Mathematics, Science and Technology Education, 19*(1), em2215. https://doi.org/10.29333/ejmste/12798

Kukkonen, J., Kontkanen, S., Kontturi, H., Nenonen, S., Parpala, M., Tahvanainen, V., & Valtonen, T. (2025). Examining teacher trainer roles in developing preservice teachers' digital competence. *European Journal of Teacher Education*, e-print, 1–24. https://doi.org/10.1080/02619768.2025.2505021

Lavonen, J. (2020). Curriculum and teacher education reforms in Finland that support the development of competences for the twenty-first century. In F. M. Reimers (Ed.), *Audacious education purposes: How governments transform the goals of education systems* (pp. 65–80). Springer. https://doi.org/10.1007/978-3-030-41882-3_3

Lavonen, J., Mahlamaki-Kultanen, S., Vahtivuori-Hanninen, S., & Mikkola, A. (2021). Implementation of a national teacher education strategy in Finland through pilot projects. *Australian Journal of Teacher Education (Online), 46*(10), 21–42. https://search.informit.org/doi/10.3316

Lehtinen, A., Kostiainen, E., Martin, A., & Näykki, P. (2024). Pre-service teachers co-constructing narratives about the future of education. *European Journal of Teacher Education*, 1–23. https://doi-org.ezproxy.uef.fi:2443/10.1080/02619768.2024.2393329

Leino, K., Puhakka, E., & Niilo-Rämä, M. (2023). *Tieto—ja viestintäteknologia koulujen arjessa. ICILS Opettajapaneeli 2020—tutkimuksen tuloksia.* Finnish Institute for Educational Research, University of Jyväskylä. http://urn.fi/URN:ISBN:978-951-39-8913-2

Malinen, O.-P., Väisänen, P., & Savolainen, H. (2012). Teacher education in Finland: A review of a national effort for preparing teachers for the future. *The Curriculum Journal, 23*(4), 567–584. https://doi.org/10.1080/09585176.2012.731011

Mertala, P. (2019). Digital technologies in early childhood education—A frame analysis of preservice teachers' perceptions. *Early Child Development and Care, 189*(8), 1228–1241. https://doi-org.ezproxy.uef.fi:2443/10.1080/03004430.2017.1372756

Mikkilä-Erdmann, M., Warinowski, A., & Iiskala, T. (2019). Teacher education in Finland and future directions. *Oxford research encyclopedia of education.* https://oxfordre.com/education/view/10.1093/acrefore/9780190264093.001.0001/acrefore-9780190264093-e-286

Ministry of Education and Culture (2024). Restrictions to be placed on the use of phones and mobile devices in schools. https://valtioneuvosto.fi/en/-/1410845/restrictions-to-be-placed-on-the-use-of-phones-and-mobile-devices-in-schools

Ministry of Education and Culture, Finnish National Agency for Education (2022). Finnish education in a nutshell. https://www.oph.fi/en/statistics-and-publications/publications/finnish-education-nutshell

Mononen, M., Havu-Nuutinen, S., & Haring, M. (2023). Student teachers' experiences in teaching practice using team teaching in flexible learning space. *Teaching and Teacher Education, 125*, 1–11. https://doi.org/10.1016/j.tate.2023.104069

Näykki, P., & Häkkinen, P. (2023). Trends and issues of digital learning in Finland. *Trends and Issues of Promoting Digital Learning in High-Digital-Competitiveness Countries: Country Reports and International Comparison*. Technological and Vocational Education Research Center (TVERC), National Taiwan Normal University.

Nazeri, F., & Vainikainen, M-P. (2024). Suomen kielen taito ulkomaalaistaustaisten oppilaiden koulumenestyksen esteenä?—Valtaväestön ha ulkomaalaistaustaisten oppilaiden matematiikan osaamiserot ja niiden selittäjät. In S. Oinas & M-P. Vainikainen (Eds.), *Digitalisaatio oppimisen ja oppimistulosten selittäjänä*. Suomen kasvatustieteellinen seura. Kasvatusalan tutkimuksia 86, 115–132.

Nguyen, A., Ngo, H. N., Hong, Y., Dang, B., & Thi Nguyen, B-P. (2023). Ethical principles for artificial intelligence in education. *Education and Information Technologies, 28*, 4221–4241. https://doi-org.ezproxy.uef.fi:2443/10.1007/s10639-022-11316-w

Niemi, A.-M., & Mietola, R. (2023). Exclusively included? Finland's inclusion success story and hidden dual system of mainstream and special needs education. In M. Thrupp, P. Seppänen, J. Kauko, & S. Kosunen (Eds.), *Finland's famous education system: Unvarnished insights into Finnish schooling* (pp. 417–434). Springer. https://doi.org/10.1007/978-981-19-8241-5_26

Niemi, H., Pea, R. D., & Lu, Yu. (Eds.). (2023). *AI in learning: Designing the future*. Springer Nature. https://doi.org/10.1007/978-3-031-09687-7

Oikarinen, M., Havu-Nuutinen, S., Pöntinen, S., & Oikarinen, J. K. (2026). The school community in developing teachers' digital competence. *Professional Development in Education*, 1–21. https://doi.org/10.1080/19415257.2026.2625129

Oinas, S., & Hotulainen, R. (2024). Havaintoja ja yläkoululaisten ajatuksia digitalisaatiosta oppitunneilla. In S. Oinas & M-P. Vainikainen (Eds.), *Digitalisaatio oppimisen ja oppimistulosten selittäjänä*. Suomen kasvatustieteellinen seura. Kasvatusalan tutkimuksia 86, 427–452.

Pack, A., & Maloney, J. (2023). Potential affordances of generative AI in language education: Demonstrations and an evaluative framework. *Teaching English with Technology, 23*(2), 4–24. https://doi.org/10.56297/BUKA4060/VRRO1747

Pulkkinen, J., & Jahnukainen, M. (2015). Finnish reform of the funding and provision of special education: The views of principals and municipal education administrators. *Educational Review, 68*(2), 171–188. https://doi-org.ezproxy.uef.fi:2443/10.1080/00131911.2015.1060586

Sahlberg, P., Gardner, H., & Robinson, K. (2021). *Finnish lessons 3.0: What can the world learn from educational change in Finland?* (3rd ed.). Teachers College Press.

Tammisalo, K., Rotkirch, A., Alanko, L., Danielsbacka, M., Honkanen, J., Hämäläinen, M., & Prusskij, C. (2020). *Digitaalinen hyvinvointi perheissä: Suomi hyvin käytetyn ajan mallimaaksi* (Valtioneuvoston selvitys- ja tutkimustoiminnan julkaisusarja 2020:43). Valtioneuvoston kanslia.

Tanhua-Piiroinen, E., Kaarakainen, S. S., Kaarakainen, M. T., & Viteli, J. (2020). *Digiajan peruskoulu II*. Opetus- ja kulttuuriministeriö. https://julkaisut.valtioneuvosto.fi/handle/10024/162236

Tedre, M., Vartiainen, H., Kahila, J., Toivonen, T., Jormanainen, I., & Valtonen, T. (2021). Machine learning introduces new perspectives to data agency in K–12 computing education. *2020 IEEE Frontiers in Education Conference (FIE)* (pp. 1–8). IEEE.

The Basic Education Act 628/1998. (1998). Ministry of Education and Culture. https://www.finlex.fi/en/laki/kaannokset/1998/en19980628.pdf.

Thrupp, M., Seppänen, P., Kauko, J., & Kosunen, S. (Eds.). (2023). *Finland's famous education system: Unvarnished insights into Finnish schooling*. Springer. https://doi.org/10.1007/978-981-19-8241-5.

Tondeur, J., Van Braak, J., Sang, G., Voogt, J., Fisser, P., & Ottenbreit-Leftwich, A. (2012). Preparing pre service teachers to integrate technology in education: A synthesis of qualitative evidence. *Computers & Education*, *59*(1), 134–144. https://doi.org/10.1016/j.compedu.2011.10.009

Ukkola, A., & Väätäinen, H. (2021). *Equality and participation in education—An overview of national evaluations* (Summaries 18:2021). Finnish Education Evaluation Centre.

Ustun, U., & Eryilmaz, A. (2018). Analysis of Finnish education system to question the reasons behind Finnish success in PISA. *Studies in Educational Research and Development*, *2*(2), 93–114.

Vahtivuori-Hänninen, S. H., Halinen, I., Niemi, H., Lavonen, J. M. J., Lipponen, L., & Multisilta, J. (2014). A new Finnish national core curriculum for basic education and technology as an integrated tool for learning. In H. Niemi, J. Multisilta, L. Lipponen, & M. Vivitsou (Eds.), *Finnish innovations & technologies in schools: A guide towards new ecosystems of learning* (pp. 33–44). Sense Publishers.

Valtonen, T., Hoang, N., Sointu, E., Näykki, P., Virtanen, A., Pöysä-Tarhonen, J., Häkkinen, P.,Järvelä, S., Mäkitalo, K., & Kukkonen, J. (2021). How pre-service teachers perceive their 21st-century skills and dispositions: A longitudinal perspective. *Computers in Human Behavior*, *116*, 106643. https://doi.org/10.1016/j.chb.2020.106643

Valtonen, T., Sointu, E. T., Kukkonen, J., Häkkinen, P., Järvelä, S., Ahonen, A., Näykki, P., Pöysä-Tarhonen, J., & Mäkitalo-Siegl, K. (2017). Insights into Finnish first-year pre-service teachers' twenty-first century skills. *Education and Information Technologies*, *22*(5), 2055–2069. https://doi.org/10.1007/s10639-016-9529-2

Vartiainen, H., Tedre, M., & Valtonen, T. (2020). Learning machine learning with very young children: Who is teaching whom? *International Journal of Child–Computer Interaction*, *25*, 100182. https://doi.org/10.1016/j.ijcci.2020.100182

12. Educational integration of artificial intelligence

Like it or not AI is changing the way we teach and learn

María Dolores Lasso and Camila Carpio Frixone

Artificial intelligence (AI) has revolutionized our reality in recent years in all fields, and education is no exception (Milberg, 2024). The world is constantly changing, and to better respond to the new realities, it is crucial to ensure a flexible curriculum design to adopt new needs, integrate trends, and facilitate continuous improvement in educational settings (Lasso, 2024). Whether we like it or not, AI has already invaded academic environments: its adoption and presence in the classrooms is no longer a choice; it is already part of most students' access to information and is constantly used as a tool for learning. Therefore, we need to find ways to formally integrate it and teach it, not as a trend but as the acceptance of a new reality (Pearson, 2023). As an educator in the 1990s, I witnessed the impact of search engines in every aspect of access to content, lesson design, and didactic resources, among others. A paradigm shift took place for educators when long hours in libraries and bookstores consulting about topics to gain understanding as we prepared our classes was no longer a need. Today, educators are facing a new paradigm shift through all the applications that AI has to offer to synthesize information, create reports, contrast contents, and so many other current student competencies that technology can do for them. As technology continues to evolve, education continues to be a human act; therefore, as educators, we must conceive AI as a powerful learning tool but understand that human interaction, personal considerations, contextual-based needs, and emotions are still the heart of the educational practice. In the past, people had extended periods to adapt to changes, to adopt and accept technologies; today, the massification of technology access makes the transition time almost nonexistent, particularly for those individuals that are used to adopting technologies as part of their cultural and generational context. In education, adopting change is particularly challenging for educators, while adopting new technologies is particularly easy for students, creating an immediate gap that forces teachers to embrace technologies faster than ever before. As part of confronting any challenge (in this case, the adoption of AI in educational settings), the first step is an honest acknowledgment of its existence, a clear assessment of our current situation, and finding viable ways to confront this challenge in the best possible manner.

Most teachers have a difficult time understanding the uses, effects, and potential of AI in educational settings. The acknowledgment and understanding of the evolving process of access to content is essential for teachers to be able to reflect on AI and identify ways for initial adoption. AI has the potential to tailor teaching and learning processes to individual needs. However, it is crucial to approach it critically and reflectively, ensuring that it complements rather than replaces the relational and human-centered aspects of education. For this reason, professional development for educators is essential. Rather than passively adopting AI-driven solutions, educators should actively engage in their analysis and interpretation. This enables them to enhance their skills, drive innovation in educational practices, and foster greater inclusion (Zurru, 2024). The effective integration of new practices often happens in stages; the adoption of AI is no exception. The most common concerns about the use of AI in the classroom are often associated with teachers' lack of control and insufficient familiarity with AI. Schools and educational institutions should plan for an AI integration process that explicitly confronts teachers' concerns as they become familiar with the myriads of ways in which AI can be used as part of their students' learning process. Teachers consistently express their ethical concerns around the following issues concerning the integration of AI: students will not develop the analytical perspective to contrast different sources of information if all the content is provided by one source, in some cases an unreliable reference; students will not learn to organize their ideas and knowledge; and how will teachers be able to tell when the written work was crafted by the students or created by AI. To address these valid ethical concerns, the starting point is addressing the limitations of AI and valuing the student role as a key element of the learning process: teachers should make sure that students double-check the information provided by AI and cite sources; student work should explicitly integrate AI as a source for consultation and guidelines, but teachers should expect students' work to focus on contextual application of concepts, creative, and practical solutions to specific problems; and, particularly, have them engage in meaningful and critical dialogues that promote reasoning and argument development. Once again, learning should be assessed based on the process that takes place for understanding to occur and not based on the final product that might not be able to showcase the student's progress and individual learning and performance. It is also essential to recognize that the goal is not only to certify students' knowledge but also to encourage their awareness of their own learning process and support the development of their autonomy. A student can be considered autonomous when they understand the purpose of what they need to learn, make decisions about how to approach their learning, and reflect on their progress and journey (Anijovich & Cappelletti, 2017).

As we embark on a reality in which AI is part of our daily lives, students must develop their ability to make informed decisions, assess content bias, question the source's reliability, and understand that AI uses information from databases that might not be representative of their work. Exploring AI for different learning purposes, playing with AI during class time, exercising with prompt construction, and testing the reliability of AI should be part of all educational experiences.

Using AI to support teacher administrative tasks could be helpful for data analysis and to create personalized assessment cues. AI is not here to replace teachers; it is the teachers' responsibility to review their students' work, to ensure the fairness of the assessment process, and to consider individual traits that can easily be missed by a novice AI user. Educational decisions can never be taken solely based on AI outputs; the analysis and considerations that involve human-made decisions are still direly needed and will continue to be in the future.

To assess the myriad of ways in which teachers and students are already using AI and to determine possible ways to integrate AI in a higher education setting, Universidad San Francisco de Quito (USFQ), a private university in Quito, Ecuador is set to lead and learn. As an institution, it was important to acknowledge that AI had arrived to change the way we learn and teach immediately; the mere access of the public to AI showed that there was no time to embark on philosophical debates or strategic data analysis to determine a path of action. The institution had acknowledged there was an immediate challenge to address. While conducting a general assessment of how to embrace AI into the organization, it was clear that many members of the academic community were already using and integrating AI into their classes. The next step to confront the challenge was to have a strategy to facilitate the familiarization of our faculty members and staff with AI.

The adoption of AI has several challenges, particularly external pressures for its adoption in education that are becoming more evident as time passes. Educational policies and regulations are showcasing the presence of AI as an expectation in educational systems, accreditation processes, and rankings. In 2027, the Ecuadorian Higher Education system will undertake a national accreditation process; the assessment model has recently been published. In contrast to the last accreditation process five years ago, the model mentions the integration of AI in different indicators throughout the national assessment model (CACES, 2023).

This chapter will review four ways AI integration has been encouraged at USFQ since 2022: identifying AI champions across the different academic fields, making AI integration visible to the institutional academic community, fostering the integration and application of AI inside and also outside the classroom for management and decision-making purposes, and exposing the community to several opportunities for approximation and adoption of AI in daily academic life.

CONTEXTUAL OVERVIEW

Higher Education in Ecuador

Ecuador's higher education system has evolved significantly over the past decades. After the Higher Education Law of 2010 (LOES), important reforms were introduced to ensure quality and accountability in universities and polytechnic schools. Today, the system includes public universities, private universities, polytechnic schools, and technical institutes, each with specific roles defined by law. The Council for the Evaluation, Accreditation and Quality Assurance of Higher Education (known in Spanish as CACES) oversees accreditation processes and enforces national quality standards.

In the last decade, the country has made efforts to promote digital transformation in education. While there is no national policy that fully regulates the use of AI in higher education yet, there is a growing interest in integrating digital technologies into teaching, learning, and management. This has been accelerated by the COVID-19 pandemic, which highlighted challenges related to internet access and digital literacy, especially in rural areas.

Universidad San Francisco de Quito (USFQ)

The Universidad San Francisco de Quito (USFQ), founded in 1988, is a private liberal arts university based in Quito, Ecuador. USFQ has gained national and international recognition for its academic quality, innovation, and autonomy. The university's academic structure includes eleven colleges covering diverse fields such as Liberal Arts, Sciences, Engineering, Medicine, and Business.

Administratively, USFQ operates under a model that promotes academic freedom, student-centered learning, and constant innovation. In recent years, the university has embraced digitalization as part of its strategic development. Initiatives include the implementation of digital platforms for learning management, online resources for research, and most recently, the integration of AI tools and training for faculty and students.

The institution has recognized the urgency of adapting to AI-driven transformations in education. Therefore, USFQ is proactively developing guidelines and fostering a community of practice that promotes responsible, ethical, and contextually relevant uses of AI in both academic and administrative processes.

IDENTIFYING MOTIVATED EDUCATORS IN AI INTEGRATION

Research consistently shows how teacher attitude and pedagogy are essential in the learning process (Hattie, 2009). It is essential to highlight that when implementing AI in the educational field, the role of the teacher is fundamental and influenced by their skills, digital literacy, the support they receive, and the resources they have access to. In a rapidly transforming educational environment, teachers must stay caught up. Although generational gaps may make it harder for some educators to incorporate new technologies, many have demonstrated that it is possible organically and effectively. Roger's diffusion of innovation theory outlines that people rarely adopt a new idea on a whim. Instead, they typically go through five stages: (1) *knowledge*: becoming aware of the existence of a new idea; (2) *persuasion*: developing a positive attitude toward the idea; (3) *decision*: making a choice to adopt the innovation; (4) *implementation*: applying the idea in practice; and (5) *confirmation*: gathering additional information to either reinforce continued adoption or decide to discontinue its use (Rogers, 1995, p. 326).

Nonetheless, educators are often pressured to integrate technology into their classrooms due to external demands rather than doing so naturally and in alignment with their pedagogical methods. This can lead to superficial or ineffective adoption of digital and technological tools when often teaching resources are scarce. The effectiveness of educational policies often depends more on the strategic allocation and utilization of resources rather than on the sheer number of resources invested (Hanushek, 2020, pp. 161–170). In this section, we describe how teachers have managed to integrate technology, particularly AI, in their teaching, which can play a crucial role in motivating and guiding their colleagues.

Often educational institutions organize professional development opportunities as a way to deal with teacher needs or institutional goals. When USFQ decided to promote the integration of AI in the classes, the first step was fostering a culture of collaboration among educators, where those who have successfully adopted AI share their experiences and teach others. This strategy was particularly powerful to motivate teachers, and presenters were trusted members of the community willing to share their experiences, mishaps, and tips. This initial stage resulted in inviting more teachers to overcome the fear of change, considering that implementing AI in classrooms through concrete, realistic practices can enrich their individual pedagogy. Ultimately, the use of any technological tool, particularly AI, generally aims to optimize teaching tasks and enhance students' learning experiences, which should be the common goal of all educators. As a way to boost interest in AI, it is essential to identify which teachers are organically integrating AI into their classrooms; in our experience, there were many more than expected, and their experiences ranged from creating learning resources to designing higher-order learning tasks.

AI Integration Strategy 1

It is time for institutions to find AI champions of their own. It can easily happen through an internal contest or a simple survey to start the process of spreading staff experiences and knowledge throughout the educational community.

Communicating and rewarding success cases visibly

Several authors have studied the different processes that accompany the adoption of new technologies in educational settings (Granić, 2022; Oyetade et al., 2020; Wilson et al., 2002). Barriers such as fear of change, lack of training, or resistance to traditional methodologies are common when fostering the integration of new technologies in the classroom (Ali et al., 2023; Ertmer & Ottenbreit-Leftwich, 2010). In this context, this section of the chapter describes the second strategy to promote AI integration by making it visible and doable within the community.

On one hand, sharing concrete examples of trustworthy educators who have successfully implemented AI in the same educational context is a powerful tool for inspiring others and showing realistic applications and expectations. These real-life contextualized cases are presented publicly and their message is accessible to the whole community as a way to allow other educators to see how AI can enhance learning and create an environment of trust, collaboration, and curiosity. Testimonials from colleagues who have achieved positive results by integrating AI show that innovation is attainable and practical.

On the other hand, public recognition of educators who innovate strengthens their motivation and creates a healthy environment of continuous improvement among academic staff. Visibly recognizing those who try new approaches and tools and adapt their lessons to their students' needs and demands becomes a clear message: innovation is possible and valued in our educational community. These acknowledgments, ranging from newsletters, formal awards, and opportunities for teachers to showcase their experiences, act as tangible catalysts for other educators to ignite their curiosity and willingness to step up and begin to experiment with AI integration in their classrooms.

Additionally, understanding the variety of AI educational tools available is essential for institutions aiming to implement AI effectively. Many schools and universities adopt AI tools based on their specific needs and objectives. There are AI tools designed for content personalization based on individual learning needs. Personalized content can be created; the tool provides students with learning experiences based on their skills and progress, and it automatically adapts, providing practice and challenges using previous interactions as the input. There are tutoring AI tools that create individual lesson plans that adjust based on responses and student feedback. AI has also played a key role in gamifying learning environments to ensure students' engagement while they monitor their performance. Furthermore, AI is increasingly used in educational management, making tasks such as creating student schedules and classroom assignments more efficient. In higher education, AI is commonly used as a tool for data management, content analysis, synthesis, research, creating multiple-choice exams based on class content, personalized virtual learning certifications, and language learning, among other applications. By making these AI implementations visible and recognizing educators who successfully integrate them, institutions can foster a culture of trust and curiosity, encouraging more teachers to explore and embrace AI-driven innovations.

AI Integration Strategy 2

Finding ways to acknowledge and motivate educators who dare to try, enrich, and innovate their students' learning experiences by adopting new technologies, such as integrating AI in the classroom, is a crucial strategy for advancing an institution´s approach to technology in education. Thus, promoting, making visible, and rewarding AI integration in the classroom encourages educators to innovate and creates an educational culture where change is seen as an opportunity to offer students the best learning experiences.

AI beyond the classroom

Integrating technologies, in this case particularly AI in educational settings, should not be limited to classroom use. Innovation and willingness to improve should be considered an essential and organic part of the organizational culture. Innovation is widely recognized as a critical driver of an organization's long-term success. Research highlights that fostering and strengthening a culture that promotes innovation within the organization is essential to achieving it (Bendak et al., 2020). AI is already being used in several managerial tasks as a critical tool for optimizing all academic and administrative processes. Identifying opportunities for implementation beyond classes is crucial for creating an organizational culture centered around AI, ensuring that teachers, students, and administrative staff find the best and most efficient ways to solve problems and learn about different phenomena.

In the following section, we describe how AI was also integrated into different academic management systems and data analysis, finding ways to automate and improve administrative tasks such as scheduling, enrollment management, and academic performance tracking. These tools increase operational efficiency and allow leaders and teachers to dedicate more time to quality assurance and pedagogical activities, facilitating more personalized teaching tailored to individual student needs.

For administrative staff, AI systems can optimize decision-making through predictive analysis, identifying trends that anticipate future needs or improve organizational processes.

This integration must be accompanied by adequate training for teachers and administrative staff to utilize the available tools fully. This way, the efficient use of AI is encouraged, and an organizational culture is created where all educational stakeholders, from students to administrative staff, are aligned with leveraging this technology.

AI Integration Strategy 3

Creating an environment where AI is an integral part of educational processes promotes greater openness to innovation and continuous evolution in teaching, learning, and managing educational institutions. This allows AI to shift from being seen as a future technology to becoming a fundamental pillar of the current academic ecosystem.

Provide the community with learning opportunities

Integrating AI in education is transforming how we teach and learn. However, for this transformation to be effective and beneficial, it is crucial to support the educational community through specific training that addresses the various facets of this technology. This training should equip teachers, students, and administrative staff with the skills to use AI optimally and consciously.

A vital aspect of this training is the introduction and practical use of AI tools. This includes everything from adaptive learning platforms to virtual tutoring systems and educational data analysis software. By familiarizing academic community members with these tools, they are empowered to use them in the classroom and identify opportunities in administrative management and learning assessment.

In addition to the tools, it is crucial that the training also focuses on the benefits that AI can bring to education. For example, AI can personalize learning, identify each student's needs, automate repetitive tasks, and improve decision-making by analyzing large volumes of data. Teachers and administrative staff can better leverage AI to improve educational quality and operational efficiency by understanding these benefits.

However, it is equally important to recognize AI's limitations. Training should include a frank discussion of areas where AI cannot replace human judgment, such as empathy, critical thinking, and creativity. Additionally, it is necessary to understand the potential risks of over-relying on technology, such as the dehumanization of the educational process or biases present in algorithms.

Finally, ethics in AI integration in the educational environment should be a central component of the training. Decisions about using AI should consider student privacy, equitable access to technology, and the social impacts of its implementation. Teachers and administrators must be equipped to make informed decisions that respect students' rights and promote responsible use of AI.

AI Integration Strategy 4

AI training in the educational field is vital for the community to adopt this technology in an informed and effective manner. Providing knowledge about tools, benefits, limitations, and ethical considerations strengthens their ability to integrate AI responsibly and efficiently, contributing to a more innovative, inclusive, and future-ready educational system.

The role of AI in promoting inclusion in education

Inclusion in education is essential to ensuring that all students, regardless of their background or abilities, have equal opportunities to learn and succeed. However, traditional teaching methods may not always address the diverse needs of students. AI has emerged as a transformative tool that can help bridge these gaps, making education more accessible and personalized. By leveraging AI technologies, educational institutions can create a more inclusive learning environment that benefits all students from early childhood to higher education.

In this context, AI plays a crucial role in designing learning environments that consider diverse abilities, backgrounds, and learning preferences. Technologies powered by AI such as virtual reality, augmented reality, and assistive tools can support students with disabilities by offering alternative ways to engage and participate in the learning process. Additionally, AI enables educators to personalize instructional materials, adapt learning settings, and provide tailored support, fostering inclusive classrooms that meet the unique needs of every learner (Pawar & Khose, 2024).

A major way AI fosters inclusion is by improving accessibility. AI-powered tools such as speech-to-text applications, real-time transcription services, and screen readers enable students with disabilities to engage more effectively with learning materials. Furthermore, AI-powered language translation tools help non-native speakers better understand course content, creating a more inclusive classroom experience. Beyond accessibility, AI also enhances student support through chatbots and virtual assistants, which provide continuous academic assistance by answering questions and offering study resources. By making educational support available at all times, AI helps reduce the challenges students face, particularly those who require additional guidance throughout their learning journey.

Ultimately, AI has the potential to make education more inclusive through improved accessibility, personalized learning experiences, and enhanced student support. By integrating AI thoughtfully, education can become not only more inclusive but also more engaging and effective for all students. As AI continues to evolve, it is crucial for educators and institutions to embrace its benefits while ensuring its ethical and responsible implementation to maximize its positive impact on education.

ECUADORIAN LANDSCAPE

For Ecuador's 2026 National Accreditation process, universities are expected to integrate AI into their institutions. However, there are currently no regulations or guidelines to guide the use and application of AI in higher education, so the involved parties are presently "playing by ear."

Currently, the integration of AI in Ecuadorian higher education faces significant challenges, such as a lack of faculty readiness, professional development opportunities focused on AI, and socio-economic disparities affecting access to AI tools and resources; thus, strategic efforts from both government and institutions can lead to successful adoption that benefits both students and educators.

The Ecuadorian education environment faces many challenges, among the most relevant being students' and teachers' low performance in reading and mathematics, lack of resources and trained teachers to accommodate students with learning needs in the public and private school systems, and limited access to the internet in rural areas or urban underprivileged areas. AI tools can become very useful in efforts to shorten the educational gaps within Ecuadorian society. Self-paced personalized education could be a viable solution to overcome the educational delay that most students are showing and could become a valuable tool for students with learning needs who need personalized pacing and attention. Access to the internet and technology is currently a need, and it is no longer a utility service. Public policy and national efforts should focus on providing access to the internet and monitoring learning using AI as a way to identify needs and implement context-based solutions.

Universities and other higher education institutions should lead their efforts to integrate AI in the educational fields to find context-based practices that will benefit the academic field, but mostly the future generations.

In conclusion, the integration of AI in higher education, as analyzed in the case of Universidad San Francisco de Quito, represents a pivotal opportunity to transform both teaching and educational management. However, its success depends on various factors, including teachers' willingness, digital skills training, and access to adequate resources. Making visible and rewarding successful initiatives by professors who have effectively implemented AI inspires other educators to innovate and fosters a culture of continuous improvement within institutions. AI should not be limited to the classroom but should be leveraged to optimize administrative and academic processes, creating a more efficient, inclusive, and future-adapted educational environment. Finally, the implementation of AI in higher education in Ecuador, while promising, faces significant challenges. Overcoming these challenges will depend on a collaborative approach involving teachers and administrators, promoting a culture open to change and technological innovation.

REFERENCES

Ali, Z., Younis, S., Ahmad, N., Saba, F., & Ullah, N. (2023). Teachers' perspective of technology integration effects on students learning at university level. *Gradiva, 62*(5), 29–38.

Anijovich, R., & Cappelletti, G. (2017). Más allá de las pruebas: la retroalimentación. In *La evaluación como oportunidad* (pp. 85–100). Paidós.

Bendak, S., Shikhli, A. M., Abdel-Razek, R. H., & Ardito, L. (2020). How changing organizational culture can enhance innovation: Development of the innovative culture enhancement framework. *Cogent Business & Management, 7*(1). https://doi.org/10.1080/23311975.2020.1712125

CACES. (2023). Modelo de evaluación externa con fines de acreditación para el aseguramiento de la calidad de las UEP. Consejo de Aseguramiento de la Calidad de la Educación Superior. https://www.caces.gob.ec/wp-content/uploads/2023/12/Modelo-de-Evaluacio%CC%81n-Externa-UEP-2023-1.pdf

Ertmer, P., & Ottenbreit-Leftwich, A. T. (2010). Teacher technology change: How knowledge, confidence, beliefs and culture intersect. *Journal of Research on Technology in Education, 42*, 255–284. http://dx.doi.org/10.1080/15391523.2010.10782551

Granić, A. (2022). Educational technology adoption: A systematic review. *Educ Inf Technol* 27, 9725–9744. https://doi.org/10.1007/s10639-022-10951-7

Hanushek, E. A. (2020). Education production functions. In S. Bradley & C. Green (Eds.), *The Economics of Education* (2nd ed., pp. 161–170). Academic Press. https://www.sciencedirect.com/book/edited-volume/9780128153918/the-economics-of-education

Hattie, J. (2009). *Visible Learning: A synthesis of over 800 meta-analyses relating to achievement.* Routledge, New York, United States.

Lasso, M. D. (2024). Flexible curriculum design models to embrace innovation. [presentation]. QS Higher Ed Summit: Americas 2024, Mexico City, Mexico.

Milberg, T. (2024, April 28). *The future of learning: how AI is revolutionizing education 4.0.* World Economic Forum. https://www.weforum.org/stories/2024/04/future-learning-ai-revolutionizing-education-4-0/

Oyetade, K. E., Zuva, T., & Harmse, A. (2020). Technology adoption in education: A systematic literature review. *Advances in Science, Technology and Engineering Systems Journal*, *5*(6), 108–112. https://doi.org/10.25046/aj050611

Pawar, G., & Khose, J. (2024) Exploring the role of artificial intelligence in enhancing equity and inclusion in education. *International Journal of Innovative Science and Research Technology*, *9*(4). https://doi.org/10.38124/ijisrt/IJISRT24APR1939

Pearson T. (2023). AI – like it or not, it is here to stay. *ADCES in Practice*, *11*(5), 6–7. https://doi.org/10.1177/2633559X231191659

Rogers, E. M. (1995). Lessons for guidelines from the diffusion of innovations. *The Joint Commission Journal on Quality Improvement*, *21*(7), 324–328. https://doi.org/10.1016/s1070-3241(16)30155-9

Wilson, B., Sherry, L., Dobrovolny, J., Batty, M., & Ryder, M. (2002). Adoption factors and processes. In H. H. Adelsberger, B. Collis, & J. M. Pawlowski (Eds.), *Handbook on Information Technologies for Education and Training* (pp. 293–307). Berlin: Heidelberg. https://doi.org/10.1007/978-3-662-07682-8_18

Zurru, A. L. (2024). Reverting to the Oracle. Anthropological, ethical, and pedagogical questions about artificial intelligence. *Journal of Inclusive Methodology and Technology in Learning and Teaching*, *4*(1). https://doi.org/10.32043/jimtlt.v4i1.158

13. Mitigating teacher burnout and facilitating career pathways

Claire Ramsey

INTRODUCTION

Teacher burnout and career pathway challenges represent two critical issues in the education sector, particularly within the United States of America (USA). Burnout, characterized by emotional exhaustion, depersonalization, and a reduced sense of personal accomplishment, significantly impacts educators' ability to deliver effective instruction (Maslach & Leiter, 2016). This leads to severe consequences for the holistic health of educators in terms of personal well-being and instructional quality. In turn, this negatively impacts student learning, contributes to higher turnover rates, and impedes overall school effectiveness (Maslach & Leiter, 2016; Skaalvik & Skaalvik, 2017). Compounding this problem is the issue of career pathway instability, where teachers exit the profession prematurely or shift to alternative roles, further straining educational systems and disproportionately impacting under-resourced schools and marginalized student populations (Ingersoll, 2001). Career pathway changes, whether voluntary or forced due to burnout, disrupt educational stability and contribute to inequities, particularly for students in under-resourced schools (Skaalvik & Skaalvik, 2017). These challenges affect not only teachers but also the broader educational ecosystem, including students and administrative systems, leading to reduced academic success and increased costs for recruitment and training (Ingersoll, 2001; Barnes & Crowe, 2007).

Teacher burnout has been studied in a variety of ways. For example, Mota et al. (2021) evaluated teacher burnout via the Maslach Burnout Inventory (MBI), a self-report tool used to measure burnout through three key dimensions: emotional exhaustion (e.g., feelings of being emotionally overextended by work), depersonalization (e.g., emotional detachment or indifference toward others in the work environment), and personal accomplishment (e.g., sense of competence and success at work). It is available in different versions tailored to general use, teachers, and health professionals (Mota et al., 2021).

By measuring these three components, Mota et al. (2021) found that the analysis of factors linked to burnout indicates that personal and organizational variables are the most commonly examined in research on teacher burnout, making them key contributors to understanding the elevated levels across various burnout dimensions. Alternatively, Lindqvist et al. (2021) examined how Swedish student teachers discussed burnout during focus group conversations, using a constructivist grounded theory approach to analyze how burnout was framed and negotiated. Rather than measuring symptoms, the study explored how burnout was socially constructed through language, revealing that student teachers viewed it as an expected risk tied to workload and emotional demands. Participants often minimized their concerns with humor or disclaimers, reflecting tensions between vulnerability and professional resilience (Lindqvist et al., 2021). Unlike quantitative studies that use tools like the MBI, this research highlighted burnout as a culturally shaped experience, underscoring the need for teacher preparation programs to address both structural challenges and identity formation.

The demands placed on teachers to plan, implement, and assess curricula, while simultaneously addressing diverse student needs, create a landscape rife with stressors. This is especially true in an environment where differentiated instruction, standardized testing, and the integration of technology are integral components of educational delivery (Fischl, 2024). The holistic health of teachers, which includes their physical, emotional, mental, and social well-being, is crucial to their ability to perform effectively in the classroom (Fairbanks, 2023). For instance, when burnout occurs, teachers face emotional exhaustion, depersonalization, and a diminished sense of personal accomplishment (Maslach & Leiter, 2016). These symptoms not only diminish the capacity of educators to engage with their students but also lead to higher absenteeism, reduced job performance, and increased turnover (Skaalvik & Skaalvik, 2017). This, in turn, compromises the quality of education that students receive, particularly in under-resourced schools where the teacher-student relationship is critical for curriculum development and student success.

Amid these challenges, Artificial Intelligence (AI) offers promising solutions by alleviating workload burdens, enhancing professional growth opportunities, and creating adaptive career pathways for educators. This chapter seeks to understand AI's transformative potential in education. By leveraging tools such as AI-powered grading systems, virtual assistants, and predictive analytics, educators can reduce stress, find tailored career guidance, and improve their overall job satisfaction (Fischl, 2024; Klein, 2020; Price, 2024; Samuels-White, 2024; Teachflow, 2023a). This chapter explores how AI applications can address these critical issues, guided by two research questions: (a) How can AI, particularly machine learning programs like ChatGPT, help prevent teacher burnout? and (b) How can AI address educator career exits and facilitate career pathway changes? The discussion integrates findings from peer-reviewed studies and case analyses, contextualized within an inclusion and equity framework focused on intentional AI integration.

This chapter focuses on the context of holistic health in K–12 education in the USA, then discusses the connection between teacher burnout and curriculum and instruction for K–12 teachers before providing insight on opportunities surrounding educator career exit and educator career pathway swerve. Throughout, the author uses "educator" and "teacher" interchangeably. Additionally, the USA provides a unique backdrop for education and encourages more academic contributions surrounding the uses of AI and machine learning internationally, as there are many opportunities to understand the holistic health of K–12 education, globally.

BACKGROUND AND LITERATURE REVIEW

Teacher Burnout: Prevalence and Impact

Burnout among educators is a multifaceted problem deeply rooted in systemic issues such as inadequate resources, excessive administrative demands, and increasing classroom challenges. Lindqvist et al. (2021) identify relational dynamics between teachers, students, and administrators as significant contributors to burnout, highlighting the need for systemic interventions. Mota et al. (2021) emphasize that burnout disproportionately affects educators in under-resourced schools, exacerbating educational inequities and negatively impacting student achievement. Additionally, teachers experiencing burnout are more likely to disengage from their instructional responsibilities, leading to diminished learning outcomes and weakened student-teacher relationships (Skaalvik & Skaalvik, 2017).

Burnout undermines the holistic approach that curriculum and instruction require. Educators are expected to foster student growth by tailoring instruction to meet diverse needs. However, when teachers are burnt out, their ability to deliver personalized and effective instruction is significantly impaired. The integration of AI tools to reduce teacher workload, streamline administrative tasks, and provide personalized professional development emerges as a vital strategy for protecting the holistic health of K–12 educators (Fairbanks, 2023; Fischl, 2024; Takyar, n.d.; Teachflow, 2023b). By automating routine tasks such as grading and lesson planning, AI enables teachers to redirect their energy toward more personal well-being and meaningful instructional activities. AI-driven platforms such as Eduaide and Gradescope can reduce the cognitive load on teachers, offering them a reprieve from the exhaustive administrative work that often leads to burnout (Klein, 2020; Piech et al., 2015; Price, 2024). These tools allow teachers to focus on core teaching responsibilities, thereby enhancing their professional satisfaction and overall health. Since the prevalence and impact of teacher burnout create unique career pathway challenges that are felt across the entire system, AI may provide valuable insights to address educator career exits and facilitate alternative career pathway changes.

Career Pathway Challenges

With high attrition rates posing significant challenges for educational systems, career pathway instability is another pressing concern. Educator career exit, or attrition, is influenced by several factors, including high stress levels, inadequate support, lack of professional growth opportunities, and work-life balance issues (Ingersoll, 2001). Ingersoll (2001) notes that teacher turnover incurs substantial financial costs for recruitment and training, while also disrupting continuity in student learning. Additionally, Barnes et al. (2007) conducted a pilot study examining the financial impact of teacher turnover in five USA school districts. They found that turnover costs ranged from $4,000 to nearly $18,000 per teacher depending on location and experience level, with urban districts bearing the highest costs. These expenses included recruitment, hiring, training, and lost productivity. The study emphasized that reducing teacher attrition could result in substantial savings and improved educational continuity, especially in high-needs districts. These findings underscore the importance of addressing the root causes of attrition, such as burnout and limited access to professional growth, which Madigan and Kim (2021) identify as key drivers of career instability in the teaching profession. Specifically, Madigan and Kim (2021) link burnout to career instability, demonstrating that teachers who lack access to professional growth opportunities are more likely to leave the profession. These trends disproportionately affect schools in marginalized communities, where turnover rates are higher, further deepening systemic inequities (Barnes & Crowe, 2007).

Since burnout and educator attrition are established issues in education, advancements in AI and machine learning may be providing viable solutions and alternatives; however, these benefits are not distributed equitably. A persistent and widening digital divide complicates the picture. While some well-resourced schools have adopted AI tools to support instruction, assessment, and educator career development, others—particularly in low-income or rural areas—struggle with limited access to basic digital infrastructure (Alpha School, 2025; Reynolds, 2020; Vesna et al., 2025; Warschauer & Matuchniak, 2010). Moreover, differing institutional policies on AI reflect broader inequities in educational governance. Some districts are embracing AI integration, training teachers and students to use it responsibly and creatively. Others, citing concerns about academic dishonesty, algorithmic bias, and data privacy, have issued sweeping bans on its use (Selwyn, 2024; Zawacki-Richter et al.,

2019). This inconsistency in AI policy exacerbates disparities in teacher support, student preparedness, and institutional innovation.

Even when AI tools are technically available, affordability, digital literacy, and implementation support present further challenges. Teachers in under-resourced schools may lack the training, time, or broadband access needed to effectively incorporate AI into their workflow (Beaunoyer et al., 2020). Without equitable infrastructure, the potential of AI to improve teacher retention and enhance career pathways may remain unrealized for those who need it most. Thus, while AI presents promising solutions, educational leaders and policymakers must prioritize strategies that bridge the digital divide. This includes not only expanding access to high-speed internet and devices but also investing in culturally responsive professional development and inclusive policy frameworks to ensure that technological advancements reinforce, rather than undermine, equity in education.

AI AS A POTENTIAL SOLUTION

Emerging research highlights the potential of AI to address these challenges. Duan and Zhao (2024) demonstrate that AI-powered tools, such as virtual assistants and automated grading systems, reduce workload burdens and enhance teacher autonomy. Chamorro-Premuzic et al. (2017) emphasize the role of AI in facilitating personalized professional development, enabling educators to explore new career opportunities while remaining engaged in their current roles. These findings suggest that AI can play a transformative role in creating more equitable and sustainable educational systems.

AI and machine learning platforms offer several tools and applications to help mitigate teacher burnout by reducing workload, providing personalized professional development, and offering emotional support (Fischl, 2024; Fairbanks, 2023; Teachflow, 2023b). In their study, *AI to the Rescue: Exploring the Potential of ChatGPT as a Teacher Ally for Workload Relief and Burnout Prevention*, Hashem et al. (2024) seek to understand teacher burnout in the United Arab Emirates by critically evaluating the machine learning platform itself. Their findings confirmed a strong link between high workload and increased teacher stress, while also offering promising evidence that generative AI tools like ChatGPT can serve as effective teaching assistants to reduce workload and help prevent burnout. Furthermore, Furze (2024) argues that while generative AI holds promise for reducing teacher workload, its true potential lies not in automating lesson planning but in assisting with administrative tasks, strategic planning, and data analysis, thereby allowing educators to focus more on meaningful teaching activities. For instance, Marzuki et al. (2023) interviewed Indonesian teachers who were already using AI in their higher education English as a Foreign Language curriculum, noting that English as a Foreign Language (EFL) teachers use a variety of AI writing tools—such as Quillbot, Jenni, ChatGPT, WordTune, Copy.ai, Paperpal, and Essay Writer—to support student writing. These tools were reported to improve the clarity and logical structure of students' work and contribute to a more effective learning environment. However, teachers also raised concerns that overreliance on these tools might hinder students' development of critical thinking and problem-solving abilities. Overall, the findings suggest that when used thoughtfully, AI writing tools can enhance the quality of EFL student writing (Marzuki et al., 2023). Studies like these suggest that AI and machine learning may have promising applications in the K–12 classroom, particularly in enhancing teaching and learning processes.

AI-powered tools can support teachers by improving professional development for online teaching and reducing digital burnout. Additionally, AI writing tools help students enhance the clarity, organization, and overall quality of their writing, especially in EFL contexts (Marzuki et al., 2023). However, it remains essential to balance AI use with strategies that encourage students' independent critical thinking and problem-solving skills to prevent overreliance (Marzuki et al., 2023). Still, AI has potential in creating more adaptive, supportive, and effective learning environments in K–12 education, while also calling for thoughtful integration to maximize benefits without compromising students' intellectual growth (Marzuki et al., 2023). Another example of a case study on high school educators in China, Duan and Zhao (2024) found that teachers who used AI-powered applications reported increased autonomy across various aspects of their work, including instructional practices, curriculum implementation, school decision-making, and overall professional agency. Further, Duan and Zhao (2024) reported that AI-powered tools were effective in enhancing professional development for online teaching, showing how these tools can adapt training practices for digital education. Additionally, their study demonstrates that AI applications can help reduce digital burnout among teachers, supporting broader discussions on technology's role in managing stress (Duan & Zhao, 2024). This research provides empirical evidence of AI's practical benefits in supporting teachers' well-being in a tech-centered educational landscape.

In many cases, research appears to demonstrate the effectiveness of AI in reducing teacher burnout. For instance, Fitzpatrick et al. (2017) found that teachers using the Woebot chatbot reported significantly lower levels of stress and burnout (Fischl, 2024). Additionally, case studies have shown that AI-powered tools significantly reduce the administrative burden on teachers, allowing them to focus on core teaching activities and thereby improving overall job satisfaction and well-being (Duan & Zhao, 2024; Marzuki et al., 2023; Teachflow, 2023b). With that said, in Al-Zahrani's (2024) *Unveiling the Shadows: Beyond the Hype of AI in Education*, Al-Zahrani critically examines the often-overlooked challenges associated with integrating AI into educational settings. Through a comprehensive literature review and a survey conducted with 260 participants from a Saudi Arabian university, the study identifies key concerns including data privacy, algorithmic bias, transparency, ethical issues, and the potential erosion of human connections in learning environments. The findings suggest that while AI holds transformative potential, its uncritical adoption may lead to unintended negative consequences. The study advocates for holistic policymaking that addresses these concerns to ensure responsible and ethical AI integration in education. While AI tools show promise in alleviating teacher burnout and enhancing professional satisfaction, these benefits must be weighed against ethical, practical, and relational concerns—underscoring the need for a structured framework to guide responsible implementation.

CONCEPTUAL FRAMEWORK: COMPREHENSIVE AI ASSESSMENT FRAMEWORK

This chapter draws upon the Comprehensive AI Assessment Framework (CAIAF) developed by Kilinç (2024), which refines and extends the earlier Artificial Intelligence Assessment Scale (AIAS) presented by Perkins et al. (2024). The CAIAF is a five-level classification system designed to evaluate AI integration in education, particularly in assessment, instructional delivery, and administrative support. These levels offer a continuum from traditional, non-AI instructional approaches to full AI integration, each with increasing degrees of technological complexity, ethical consideration, and human–AI interaction.

- *Level 1—No AI (Human-Only)*: Instructional and evaluative processes are entirely human-driven, prioritizing conventional pedagogical strategies and direct student-teacher engagement.
- *Level 2—AI-Assisted Idea Generation*: AI supports brainstorming or organizational tasks but does not generate final products or learning artifacts.
- *Level 3—AI-Assisted Refinement*: AI is used to edit and improve student work or teaching materials, maintaining the original human-generated content.
- *Level 4—AI Task Completion with Human Oversight*: AI completes parts of educational tasks (e.g., grading or drafting resources), which are then reviewed and validated by educators.
- *Level 5—Full AI Integration*: AI is embedded across the instructional process, including personalized learning, assessment design, feedback, and continuous improvement loops.

Beyond simply categorizing AI use, the CAIAF incorporates five ethical dimensions to ensure responsible, equitable AI integration:

- *Transparency*: Students and educators must disclose AI use, enabling clear identification of AI's role in academic outputs.
- *Equity and Inclusivity*: All learners, regardless of socioeconomic status, must have access to AI technologies and support systems to ensure fair participation.
- *Pedagogical Alignment*: AI applications should align with learning goals, encouraging student creativity and deep learning rather than superficial automation.
- *Accountability*: AI integration should not erode academic integrity; students and educators remain responsible for the authenticity of the work.
- *Privacy and Data Protection*: AI systems must comply with data protection laws, safeguarding sensitive student information throughout the learning process (Kilinç, 2024).

Kilinç (2024) argues that these enhancements are essential given the rising influence of generative AI in education. The framework is both a pedagogical and ethical tool—emphasizing thoughtful AI adoption that improves learning without compromising human-centered education. It aligns closely with this chapter's focus on competence, fairness, and excellence, offering a practical and principled roadmap for using AI to mitigate burnout and enhance career development while maintaining educational integrity and inclusivity.

METHODOLOGY

In this chapter, the author synthesizes findings from peer-reviewed studies, case analyses, journal articles, and policy reports to produce a literature-based analysis of the impact of AI on teacher burnout and career pathway evolution. Data selection was guided by relevance to the research questions and alignment with CAIAF (Kilinç, 2024). While the founding framework for CAIAF, AI Assessment Scale (AIAS) (Perkins et al., 2024) offered a progression-based view of AI integration, CAIAF expands on this foundation by incorporating ethical dimensions—such as transparency, pedagogical alignment, and equity—that are essential in evaluating AI's systemic impact. This broader framework allows for a more nuanced analysis, recognizing that AI's influence extends beyond reducing teacher workload to shaping student learning environments, guiding data governance, and advancing systemic equity. Whether applied to grading, career development, or emotional support, each AI use case is examined in light of CAIAF's ethical criteria to assess both its functionality and its implications for inclusive educational practice.

DISCUSSION

The guiding questions for this chapter are: (a) *How can AI—particularly tools like ChatGPT—help prevent teacher burnout?* and (b) *How can AI address educator attrition and support evolving career pathways?* Literature reviewed through the lens of the CAIAF reveals that AI interventions can revitalize the educator workforce through support in areas such as automated grading and feedback, streamlined lesson planning, and enhanced emotional well-being and professional development. Grounded in CAIAF, this chapter evaluates these interventions not only by their efficiency but also by their adherence to ethical principles: transparency, equity, pedagogical alignment, accountability, and privacy (Kılınç, 2024). Within the parameters of these ethical principles, the content of this chapter also identifies connections within the literature to Perkins et al. (2024) AIAS: (1) No AI; (2) AI-Assisted Idea Generation and Structuring; (3) AI-Assisted Editing; (4) AI Task Completion, Human Evaluation; (5) Full AI. As demonstrated in subsequent sections, predictive analytics for teacher retention, AI-powered career development platforms, and digital tools that foster skill-building and mentorship represent promising solutions when aligned with these criteria. In this way, CAIAF dually serves as a classification system for AI use in education and also a guiding ethical lens, linking educator support, equity in student learning, and institutional accountability.

Teacher Burnout and AI Interventions

As the demands of the teaching profession grow more complex and emotionally taxing, AI presents innovative solutions to support educators. This section examines how thoughtfully-implemented AI tools can lighten administrative loads, streamline instructional tasks, and offer mental health support. While promising in their ability to improve work-life balance and foster professional growth, these interventions must be deployed thoughtfully to avoid reinforcing inequities or undermining pedagogical trust.

Automated grading and feedback

AI, and more specifically machine learning programs like ChatGPT, can significantly reduce teacher burnout by automating time-consuming tasks and providing personalized support. AI-powered tools such as Gradescope and Turnitin automate grading processes, reducing the time and effort teachers spend on routine assessments (Turnitin, n.d.). Gradescope, for example, uses machine learning to evaluate multiple-choice exams and written assignments, providing immediate feedback to students and freeing up teachers' time for instructional planning and student engagement (Klein, 2020; Piech et al., 2015). For example, Piech et al. (2013) developed probabilistic models to correct for grader biases and reliabilities in MOOC (Massive Open Online Courses) (p. 1): peer assessments that significantly enhance grading accuracy and provide insights into student engagement and performance. These applications correspond to Level 4 of the AIAS, where AI assumes responsibility for operational tasks under human oversight (Perkins et al., 2024). Studies have shown that AI's ability to streamline these tasks can significantly reduce the workload on teachers, ultimately lowering stress levels (Teachflow, 2023a). However, growing literature warns of potential algorithmic biases embedded in automated grading and AI-based writing assessment tools. Notably, researchers have identified that AI detectors and grading algorithms may disproportionately flag or score lower the work of non-native English speakers (Liang et al., 2023; Smith, 2025). For instance, Liang et al. (2023) and Jiang et al. (2024) found that GPT detectors and automated assessment tools were significantly more likely to misclassify essays written by multilingual writers as AI-generated or less coherent, even when the content was original and thoughtful. In kind, Smith (2025) discusses findings from a study by The Learning Agency, which evaluated ChatGPT's essay scoring ability using the ASAP 2.0 benchmark dataset. The study revealed that while ChatGPT's scoring closely mirrored human grading overall, it failed to recognize exceptional writing and replicated existing human biases, particularly toward Black students. These biases, if unaddressed, risk reinforcing linguistic discrimination and further marginalizing students from diverse backgrounds.

Similarly, Baker and Hawn (2022) provide a comprehensive review of algorithmic bias in educational AI systems, noting that models trained on predominantly native English data may inadvertently penalize valid linguistic patterns common among English language learners. The Markup's investigation into AI cheating detectors revealed real-world consequences of such biases, where international students were falsely accused of academic dishonesty due to flawed detection logic (The Markup, 2023). A growing body of research also highlights the potential for AI systems to improve equity in assessment when designed thoughtfully (Wargo & Anderson, 2024). Some AI tools have incorporated adaptive language models and culturally responsive training data to mitigate linguistic bias (Khare et al., 2024). Furthermore, Jiang et al. (2024) suggest that with human-in-the-loop oversight and targeted calibration, detection and grading tools can achieve more accurate and equitable outcomes. Given these findings, it is imperative that educational leaders and developers approach the integration of AI grading systems with a commitment to fairness and transparency. Shute and Rahimi (2017) note that well-designed computer-based assessment for learning systems that deliver manageable, elaborated feedback effectively enhance student learning across various subjects. Clear guidance on best practices, including teacher review of flagged responses, continuous monitoring for demographic disparities, and the inclusion of diverse and representative linguistic datasets in training models, is essential to ensure that AI enhances rather than hinders equitable instruction.

Lesson planning and curriculum design

AI assists in lesson planning and curriculum design by providing personalized content recommendations based on student needs and learning styles, reducing the time teachers spend on preparing differentiated instruction (Brusilovsky & Millán, 2007; Fischl, 2024). Additionally, AI platforms can assist in lesson planning by analyzing student performance data to recommend tailored instructional materials. For example, the AI platform Eduaide allows teachers to create tailored lesson plans, incorporating insights from student data to better address diverse learning needs, thus enhancing both efficiency and effectiveness in instructional delivery (Fischl, 2024). However, limitations such as algorithmic bias underscore the need for teacher oversight to ensure the inclusivity and relevance of AI-generated recommendations. This aligns with Level 3 of the AIAS (Perkins et al., 2024), where AI enhances the refinement of instructional materials. However, teachers must evaluate AI-generated recommendations to ensure inclusivity and relevance, addressing limitations like cultural bias in algorithmic outputs. AI's potential to streamline administrative duties, such as grading, lesson planning, and communication, ensures that educators spend more time on meaningful teaching tasks and less on routine administrative work. This balance is essential for preventing burnout, which is often exacerbated by overwhelming workloads and limited support (Maslach & Leiter, 2016; Skaalvik & Skaalvik, 2017). AI tools create opportunities for teachers to regain control over their time, leading to improved job satisfaction and well-being.

While AI tools like Eduaide offer promising avenues for personalized lesson planning and curriculum design, it's essential to approach their integration with caution. Yan et al. (2023) highlight several ethical challenges after conducting "a systematic scoping review of 118 peer-reviewed papers published since 2017 to pinpoint the current state of research on using LLMs to automate and support educational tasks" (p. 1). Yan et al. (2023) underscore the importance of maintaining human oversight in educational processes, which is supported across much of the literature (Jiang et al., 2024; Kılınç, 2024; Trucano, 2023). For instance, the potential for algorithmic bias necessitates that educators critically evaluate AI-generated content to ensure it meets the diverse needs of all students. Moreover, the lack of transparency in some AI systems can make it difficult for teachers to understand the rationale behind certain recommendations, potentially leading to mistrust or misuse. Privacy concerns also arise when student data is used to inform AI-driven decisions, emphasizing the need for strict data governance policies. Therefore, while AI can enhance efficiency in lesson planning, educators must remain vigilant, ensuring these tools are used ethically and effectively to support inclusive and equitable learning environments.

Emotional support and professional development

Madigan and Kim's (2021) meta-analysis reveals that teacher burnout—particularly emotional exhaustion—is a stronger predictor of intentions to leave the profession than low job satisfaction, with the impact of burnout intensifying over time. AI-driven chatbots like Woebot provide emotional support by offering conversational therapy and stress management resources. Fitzpatrick et al. (2017) found that teachers using Woebot reported reduced stress and improved well-being, demonstrating the potential of AI to address mental health challenges. Additionally, platforms like Coursera and edX offer personalized professional development opportunities, enabling educators to acquire new skills and advance their careers while remaining in their current roles (Fairbanks, 2023). The integration of AI in professional development also provides real-time feedback and personalized learning pathways, which are essential for continuous growth and adaptation in teaching practices (Teachflow, 2023b). These applications reflect Level 5 of the AIAS, emphasizing full AI integration to address both personal and professional needs (Perkins et al., 2024).

AI's role in career development also extends to proactive planning and long-term goal alignment. As Sahota (2024) highlights, AI-powered tools are increasingly capable of analyzing an individual's skills, experiences, and aspirations to generate tailored upskilling and transition pathways. When used effectively, these technologies can democratize access to career guidance, especially in schools where counseling and mentorship are limited (Sahota, 2024). Moreover, AI-powered platforms can offer personalized learning paths and real-time skill assessments, enabling students and educators alike to identify strengths, address learning gaps, and align with career goals more effectively (Takyar, n.d.).

However, the integration of digital technologies into teaching environments is not without challenges. Gupta and Irwin (2016) found that in-class use of social media platforms like Facebook significantly distracted students from primary learning tasks, negatively affecting academic performance—particularly when engagement occurred during instruction. This finding underscores the need for boundaries and intentional design when integrating AI and digital tools into educators' routines. While AI holds immense promise for alleviating emotional exhaustion and enhancing professional development, unstructured or poorly aligned technological adoption can introduce new forms of cognitive load and distraction. Therefore, school leaders must implement digital literacy programs and provide guidance on effective AI tool usage to ensure that the intended benefits (e.g., reduced burnout, enhanced performance, and personalized growth) are realized without unintended disruptions.

Career Pathway Challenges and AI Solutions

Educator turnover remains a pressing challenge across K–12 systems, often stemming from unmanageable workloads, limited advancement options, and insufficient institutional support. Emerging AI technologies, when designed and implemented with care, can mitigate these challenges by providing actionable insights, flexible learning pathways, and meaningful mentorship. Drawing on CAIAF, this section examines how AI can support educator retention and reinvention by enabling proactive retention strategies, facilitating personalized growth, and ensuring equitable access to career advancement opportunities within this shifting professional landscape.

Predictive analytics for retention

Predictive analytics can be used to identify teachers at risk of burnout or attrition by analyzing data related to workload, stress levels, and job satisfaction. Sparks (2011) highlights how predictive models guide administrators in improving teacher retention rates and fostering systemic equity. This enables schools to offer targeted support and resources before teachers reach the point of leaving the profession (Klein, 2020; Sparks, 2011). Early intervention through AI-driven predictive analytics is critical for maintaining a fair and equitable educational environment, as it ensures that teachers in challenging circumstances receive the support they need. This approach fosters excellence by addressing issues before they become crises, enabling educators to continue contributing their expertise in the classroom. As part of Level 4 in the AIAS, these tools support decision-making by integrating human oversight with AI-driven insights (Perkins et al., 2024).

Leveraging AI as a retention tool offers a strategic opportunity to prevent the exit of highly effective educators, which can serve as a powerful incentive for educational leaders and policymakers. By using AI-driven solutions to address key factors contributing to teacher attrition, institutions can better support teachers in their roles, reduce workload pressures, and ultimately foster a more inclusive and equitable educational environment. AI's potential to improve teacher retention aligns with a framework centered on competence, fairness, and excellence, ensuring that all educators have the opportunity to thrive in their careers, regardless of their location or the resources available to them.

When effective educators leave the profession, the students most negatively affected are those from marginalized backgrounds, further widening the achievement gap (Chandra, 2024; Fairbanks, 2023). AI offers powerful tools to retain these educators by enhancing career development, improving work-life balance, and enabling early interventions, thus promoting long-term retention (Teachflow, 2023a). For educational leaders and policymakers, investing in AI-driven solutions is not only a means of retaining talented teachers but also a commitment to creating an equitable, inclusive, and high-performing educational environment where all students and educators can feel invested.

Personalized career development

AI platforms such as LinkedIn Learning and Pymetrics offer personalized learning pathways, enabling teachers to advance in their careers, explore new roles within the education sector, and increase their social capital (Bankins et al., 2024). These tools help educators develop professionally while keeping them engaged in their current roles, thereby increasing job satisfaction and retention rates (Fischl, 2024; Madigan & Kim, 2021; Slagg, 2023). Particularly in under-resourced schools, personalized AI platforms can enhance teachers' sense of competence by offering tailored growth opportunities (Chamorro-Premuzic et al., 2017). These interventions align with Level 5 of the AIAS, where adaptive technologies are fully integrated to support long-term career development (Perkins et al., 2024).

For additional upskilling and networking opportunities, platforms like Coursera enable educators to earn new credentials or explore alternative pathways, while networking tools like MentorCloud connect teachers with mentors for collaboration and professional growth—an especially meaningful resource for educators from underrepresented groups (Bankins et al., 2024; OECD, 2020). These examples span Levels 4 and 5 of the AIAS by combining task automation with comprehensive, personalized support (Perkins et al., 2024). When implemented equitably, such tools may help strengthen the teaching workforce and improve student outcomes by fostering teacher competence, confidence, and career satisfaction.

However, the benefits of AI-driven career tools are not universally accessible. Al-Zahrani (2024) cautions that the automation of mentorship and career planning risks undermining key human dynamics such as trust, nuanced guidance, and interpersonal collaboration. Similarly, Beaunoyer et al. (2020) emphasize that persistent digital inequalities—including disparities in infrastructure, technological skill, and meaningful use—pose serious challenges for equitable adoption. These concerns suggest that institutional support and inclusive design are critical to ensuring that personalized AI tools truly benefit all educators. Sahota (2024) adds that even with advanced AI, the success of upskilling technologies depends on users' digital fluency and consistent access—two factors not guaranteed across all educational contexts. As educators experience the evolving landscape of AI-supported professional growth, it is equally important to consider how these developments translate into student learning and long-term academic outcomes.

IMPLICATIONS FOR STUDENTS' ACADEMIC SUCCESS

Thoughtful and sustainable integration of AI into educational systems can enhance instructional quality, support equity, promote stable learning environments, and yield long-term systemic benefits. When used to alleviate teacher burnout and reduce administrative workload—such as through automated grading and AI-assisted lesson planning—these tools enable educators to devote more time to meaningful, student-centered instruction. This increased instructional capacity is closely linked to improved student learning outcomes, particularly in under-resourced schools where student-teacher ratios are less favorable (Fischl, 2024; Piech et al., 2015).

Beyond improving efficiency, AI systems that adapt to students' individual needs help narrow achievement gaps by supporting teachers in differentiating instruction and delivering timely, targeted interventions. Adaptive learning platforms, for example, use real-time data to adjust content based on performance, ensuring students receive appropriate levels of challenge and support (Kılınç, 2024). However, equitable access to such tools remains a critical challenge. Beaunoyer et al. (2020) found that the COVID-19 pandemic laid bare longstanding digital inequalities—especially in terms of access, digital literacy, and meaningful use—disproportionately affecting marginalized students and educators. These disparities risk compounding existing inequities if left unaddressed by institutional policies and targeted supports. Moreover, Al-Zahrani (2024) warns that overreliance on AI can erode the human relationships foundational to effective learning. His findings highlight the risk of diminishing teacher-student interaction in overly automated classrooms. These factors are key for trust, motivation, and educational equity. This concern aligns with decades of research underscoring the importance of interpersonal connection in fostering both academic and social-emotional growth (Ingersoll, 2001; Sparks, 2011). Thus, technology-enhanced classrooms must intentionally preserve space for human interaction. Retaining experienced educators through AI-enabled career development and predictive analytics further supports classroom continuity and relational stability.

To ensure these tools are implemented ethically and equitably, CAIAF provides a critical reminder for structure. CAIAF not only categorizes the degree of AI integration in educational environments but also evaluates it through five ethical pillars: transparency, equity and inclusivity, pedagogical alignment, accountability, and data protection (Kılınç, 2024). For example, transparency protocols require students to disclose their use of AI tools, preserving academic integrity and trust in the learning process. Equity-focused policies are needed to ensure that all students—regardless of socioeconomic status—can access and benefit from AI-enhanced instruction. CAIAF also promotes pedagogical alignment by encouraging the use of adaptive systems that foster creativity, critical thinking, and personalized learning pathways. These technologies can support student agency and close opportunity gaps by aligning instructional delivery with diverse learner profiles (OECD, 2020; Kılınç, 2024). Finally, its emphasis on data privacy and accountability addresses growing concerns about surveillance and the ethical use of student data in digital education platforms (Beaunoyer et al., 2020). In sum, AI has the potential to support more inclusive, effective, and responsive learning environments—but only when its integration is guided by a clear ethical framework like CAIAF. With deliberate attention to both instructional design and structural equity, AI can help create educational ecosystems that cultivate educator support and all students are positioned to thrive academically, emotionally, and socially.

CONCLUSION

AI has the potential to revolutionize education by addressing critical challenges such as teacher burnout, career exit, and career pathway changes. By leveraging AI tools and applications, educators can enhance their professional development, improve work-life balance, and explore new career opportunities (Fairbanks, 2023; Fischl, 2024; Teachflow, 2023a). To fully realize these benefits, it is essential for educational institutions to integrate AI tools into their support systems, ensuring that educators have equitable access to these resources. Certainly, there are valid concerns that should be addressed when using AI and machine learning platforms; however, there is also opportunity (Tlili et al., 2023). By embedding AI into educational systems with a focus on inclusion and equity, institutions can enhance teacher well-being, improve retention rates, and create adaptive career pathways. Sustained collaboration among educators, technologists, and policymakers will be critical to refining AI applications and addressing potential challenges, ensuring their transformative potential in fostering a more equitable and effective educational system.

Educational leaders must prioritize the integration of AI tools to empower teachers, particularly in under-resourced schools. Adopting AI solutions that streamline administrative tasks and reduce workloads may create systemically sustainable foundations that encourage teachers to focus more on student engagement and instructional innovation while simultaneously providing equitable access to AI-driven professional development and targeted support systems. These systems and continuous training programs equip educators to effectively use AI tools, fostering a culture of technology integration, professional growth, and authentic, responsible modeling for students.

Policy recommendations should align with the tenets of the CAIAF and AIAS frameworks, where appropriate, for intentional inclusion and equity integration that emphasizes competence, fairness, and excellence (Kılınç, 2024; Perkins et al., 2024). By advocating for funding initiatives that prioritize inclusive AI applications, policy recommendations can be seen as strategic pathways aligned with these values instead of prescriptive actions, ensuring that all educators and students benefit from these advancements. For instance, policymakers and educational leaders might focus on fostering the development of AI platforms that prioritize the well-being and professional growth of educators, making these technological advancements accessible to all teachers, regardless of their background or location. To promote competence, educational leaders must view AI not merely as a technological solution but as a tool for empowering educators to excel in their roles. This means creating robust professional development systems that include AI-driven personalized learning opportunities. AI should be integrated in ways that support teachers' unique instructional needs and help them build expertise, ensuring that competence is fostered across all levels of the teaching workforce, particularly in under-resourced schools where teachers often lack access to such resources. Furthermore, as AI technologies evolve, sustained research and collaboration among educators, technologists, policymakers, and mental health professionals will be crucial to refining these tools and maximizing their positive impact on the education sector (Fischl, 2024; Samuels-White, 2024; Teachflow, 2023b).

AI tools should be implemented with a focus on equitable access. Leaders must ensure that all educators, regardless of their background or the resources of their institutions, can benefit from AI tools. Policymakers should advocate for initiatives that prioritize the development of AI platforms tailored to diverse educational environments, especially those serving marginalized communities. This approach ensures fairness by creating an even playing field where all teachers, not just those in well-resourced schools, have access to the technology needed to reduce workloads and improve student outcomes. Furthermore, fostering excellence requires a shift in how we approach the implementation of AI technologies. Excellence in education is not just about improving efficiency but about creating systems that allow educators to focus on high-impact instructional strategies. Educational leaders must prioritize AI solutions that free teachers from administrative burdens and allow them to concentrate on student-centered learning and innovation in pedagogy. By doing so, institutions can promote excellence across the board, from classroom engagement to professional growth. Additionally, successful integration of AI must involve sustained research and collaboration among multi-sector stakeholders, including educators, technologists, policymakers, and mental health professionals. Collaboration ensures that the development and application of AI technologies are responsive to the actual needs of educators and students.

For instance, predictive analytics should be informed by not only technical experts but also mental health professionals, ensuring early interventions are both data-driven and humane, ultimately supporting educators' well-being and longevity in their careers.

In conclusion, AI holds transformative potential for addressing teacher burnout, preventing educator career exits, and enabling career pathway changes. Educational leaders, in collaboration with policymakers, must champion AI as a strategic tool for fostering competence, fairness, and excellence in the teaching profession. By embedding AI into educational support systems with a focus on inclusion and equity, institutions can enhance teacher well-being, improve retention rates, and create adaptable career development models. As AI continues to evolve, its successful integration will depend on ongoing research, multi-sector collaboration, and a deep commitment to addressing both the opportunities and challenges inherent in AI-driven education.

REFERENCES

Al-Zahrani, A. M. (2024). Unveiling the shadows: Beyond the hype of AI in education. *Smart Learning Environments, 11*(1), Article 18. https://pmc.ncbi.nlm.nih.gov/articles/PMC11087970

Alpha School. (2025, May 15). *AI Powered Private School.* Alpha School. https://alpha.school/#:~:text=AI%20Powered%20Private%20School,do%20and%20develop%20life%20skills

Baker, R. S., & Hawn, A. (2022). Algorithmic bias in education. *International Journal of Artificial Intelligence in Education, 32*, 1052–1092. https://doi.org/10.1007/s40593-021-00285-9

Bankins, S., Jooss, S., Restubog, S., Marrone, M., Ocampo, A., & Shoss, M. (2024). Navigating career stages in the age of artificial intelligence: A systematic interdisciplinary review and agenda for future research. *Journal of Vocational Behavior, 153*, Article 104011. https://doi.org/10.1016/j.jvb.2024.104011

Barnes, P. D. & Crowe, E. (2007). The cost of teacher turnover in five school districts: A pilot study. *The National Commission on Teaching and America's Future.* https://www.policyarchive.org/handle/10207/96339

Beaunoyer, E., Dupéré, S., & Guitton, M. J. (2020). COVID-19 and digital inequalities: Reciprocal impacts and mitigation strategies. *Computers in Human Behavior, 111*, 106424. https://doi.org/10.1016/j.chb.2020.106424

Brusilovsky, P., & Millán, E. (2007). User models for adaptive hypermedia and adaptive educational systems. In P. Brusilovsky, A. Kobsa, & W. Nejdl (Eds.), *The adaptive web: Methods and strategies of web personalization* (pp. 3–53). Springer. https://doi.org/10.1007/978-3-540-72079-9_1

Chamorro-Premuzic, T., Akhtar, R., Winsborough, D., & Sherman, R. A. (2017). The datafication of talent: How technology is advancing the science of human potential at work. *Current Opinion in Behavioral Sciences, 18*, 13–16. https://doi.org/10.1016/j.cobeha.2017.04.007

Chandra, V. (2024, April 19). 22: Predictive analytics in education: Anticipate student needs and proactive interventions. *LinkedIn.* https://www.linkedin.com/pulse/22-predictive-analytics-education-anticipate-student-needs-chandra-nxdsc/

Duan, H., & Zhao, W. (2024). The effects of educational artificial intelligence-powered applications on teachers' perceived autonomy, professional development for online teaching, and digital burnout. *International Review of Research in Open and Distributed Learning*, *25*(3), 57–76. https://doi.org/10.19173/irrodl.v25i3.7659

Fairbanks, C. C. (2023). How AI could prevent teacher burnout. *Sutherland Institute.* https://sutherlandinstitute.org/how-ai-could-prevent-teacher-burnout/

Fischl, B. (2024). Reducing workload with Eduaide AI, an educator's assistant – AI-enhanced instructional design. In P. MacDowell, D. Desjardins, B. Drought, B. Fischl, S. Frampton, M. Giannios, H. Jodrey, K. Korchinski, S. Moser, K. Moskalyk, J. Neibrandt, P. Neufeld, A. Peters, T. Otegbade, A. Schindelka, D. Tide, L. Tilford, K. Tooke, & M. Washlowsky (Eds.), *AI-Enhanced Instructional Design.* University of Saskatchewan. https://www.saskoer.ca/etad873aienhancedinstructionaldesign

Fitzpatrick, K. K., Darcy, A., & Vierhile, M. (2017). Delivering cognitive behavior therapy to young adults with symptoms of depression and anxiety using a fully automated conversational agent (Woebot): A randomized controlled trial. *JMIR Mental Health*, *4*(2), e7785. https://doi.org/10.2196/mental.7785

Furze, L. (2024, March 21). Artificial intelligence and teacher workload: Can AI actually save educators time? *Leon Furze.* https://leonfurze.com/2024/03/21/artificial-intelligence-and-teacher-workload-can-ai-actually-save-educators-time/comment-page-1/

Gupta, N., & Irwin, J. D. (2016). In-class distractions: The role of Facebook and the primary learning task. *Computers in Human Behavior*, *55*, 1165–1178. http://dx.doi.org/10.1016/j.chb.2014.10.022

Hashem, R., Ali, N., El Zein, F., Fidalgo, F., & Abu Khurma, O. (2024). AI to the rescue: Exploring the potential of ChatGPT as a teacher ally for workload relief and burnout prevention. *Research and Practice in Technology Enhanced Learning*, *19*(23), 1–26. https://doi.org/10.58459/rptel.2024.19023

Ingersoll, R. M. (2001). Teacher turnover and teacher shortages: An organizational analysis. *American Educational Research Journal*, *38*(3), 499–534. https://doi.org/10.3102/00028312038003499

Jiang, Y., Hao, J., Fauss, M., & Li, C. (2024). Detecting ChatGPT-generated essays in a large-scale writing assessment: Is there a bias against non-native English speakers? *Computers & Education*, *217.* https://doi.org/10.1016/j.compedu.2024.105070

Kilinç, S. (2024). Comprehensive AI assessment framework: Enhancing educational evaluation with ethical AI integration. *Journal of Educational Technology & Online Learning*, *7*(4), 521–540. http://doi.org/10.31681/jetol.1492695

Khare, S. K., Blanes-Vidal, V., Nadimi, E. S., Acharya, U. R. (2024). Emotion recognition and artificial intelligence: A systematic review (2014–2023) and research recommendations. *Information Fusion*, *102*, 156–183. https://doi.org/10.1016/j.inffus.2023.102019

Klein, A. (2020, January 8). Artificial intelligence could free up 13 hours a week for teachers, report finds. *Education Week.* https://www.edweek.org/technology/artificial-intelligence-could-free-up-13-hours-a-week-for-teachers-report-finds/2020/01

Liang, W., Yuksekgonul, M., Mao, Y., Wu, E., & Zou, J. (2023). GPT detectors are biased against non-native English writers. *Patterns*, *4*(7), 100798. https://doi.org/10.1016/j.patter.2023.100798

Lindqvist, H., Weurlander, M., Wernerson, A., & Thornberg, R. (2021). Talk of teacher burnout among student teachers. *Scandinavian Journal of Educational Research*, *65*(7), 1266–1278. https://doi.org/10.1080/00313831.2020.1816576

Madigan, D. J., & Kim, L. E. (2021). Towards an understanding of teacher attrition: A meta-analysis of burnout, job satisfaction, and teachers' intentions to quit. *Teaching and Teacher Education, 105*, 103425. https://doi.org/10.1016/j.tate.2021.103425

Marzuki, W., Widiati, U., Rusdin, D., Indrawati, D., & Indrawati, I. (2023). The impact of AI writing tools on the content and organization of students' writing: EFL teachers' perspective. *Cogent Education, 10*(2), Article 2236469. https://doi.org/10.1080/2331186X.2023.2236469

Maslach, C., & Leiter, M. P. (2016). Understanding the burnout experience: Recent research and its implications for psychiatry. *World Psychiatry, 15*(2), 103–111. https://doi.org/10.1002/wps.20311

Mota, A. I., Lopes, J., & Oliveira, C. (2021). Burnout in Portuguese teachers: A systematic review. *European Journal of Educational Research, 10*(2), 693–703. https://doi.org/10.12973/eu-jer.10.2.693

Perkins, M., Furze, L., Roe, J., & MacVaugh, J. (2024). The artificial intelligence assessment scale (AIAS): A framework for ethical integration of generative AI in educational assessment. *Journal of University Teaching and Learning Practice, 21*(6). https://doi.org/10.53761/q3azde36

Piech, C., Huang, J., Chen, Z., Do, C. B., Ng, A., & Koller, D. (2013). Tuned models of peer assessment in MOOCs. In *Proceedings of the 6th International Conference on Educational Data Mining* (pp. 153–160). https://web.stanford.edu/~cpiech/bio/papers/tuningPeerGrading.pdf

Piech, C., Huang, J., Chen, Z., Do, C., Ng, A., & Koller, D. (2015). Tuned models of peer assessment in MOOCs. *International Journal of Artificial Intelligence in Education, 25*(2), 130–145. https://doi.org/10.1007/s40593-014-0029-5

Price, M. (2024, October 2). *How AI is changing the role of teachers in Education.* Forbes. https://www.forbes.com/councils/forbestechcouncil/2024/10/02/how-ai-is-changing-the-role-of-teachers-in-education/

Organisation for Economic Co-operation and Development (OECD). (2020). *A framework to guide an education response to the COVID-19 pandemic of 2020.* OECD Publishing. https://doi.org/10.1787/6ae21003-en

Sahota, N. (2024, July 25). AI energizes your career path & charts your professional growth plan. *Forbes.* https://www.forbes.com/sites/neilsahota/2024/07/25/ai-energizes-your-career-path--charts-your-professional-growth-plan/?ss=ai

Samuels-White, S. (2024). Beyond burnout: AI as an academic ally in the "publish or perish" culture. *Faculty Focus.* https://www.facultyfocus.com/articles/teaching-with-technology-articles/beyond-burnout-ai-as-an-academic-ally-in-the-publish-or-perish-culture/

Selwyn, N. (2024). On the limits of artificial intelligence (AI) in Education. *Nordisk tidsskrift for pedagogikk og kritikk: Special Issue on Artificial Intelligence in Education, 10*, 3–14. http://doi.org/10.23865/ntpk.v10.6062

Shute, V. J., & Rahimi, S. (2017). Review of computer-based assessment for learning in elementary and secondary education. *Journal of Computer Assisted Learning, 33*(1), 1–19. https://doi.org/10.1111/jcal.12172

Skaalvik, E. M., & Skaalvik, S. (2017). Teacher stress and teacher self-efficacy: Relations and consequences. In T. McIntyre, S. McIntyre, & D. Francis (Eds.), *Educator stress: Aligning perspectives on health, safety and well-being* (pp. 101–125). Springer. https://doi.org/10.1007/978-3-319-53053-6_5

Slagg, A. (2023, November 14). AI for teachers: Defeating burnout and boosting productivity. *EdTech Magazine.* https://edtechmagazine.com/k12/article/2023/11/ai-for-teachers-defeating-burnout-boosting-productivity-perfcon

Smith, K. (2025, May 6). *AI shows racial bias when grading essays — and can't tell good writing from bad.* The 74. https://www.the74million.org/article/ai-shows-racial-bias-when-grading-essays-and-cant-tell-good-writing-from-bad/

Sparks, S. D. (2011, June 30). Schools find uses for predictive data techniques. *Education Week.* https://www.edweek.org/teaching-learning/schools-find-uses-for-predictive-data-techniques/2011/06

Takyar, A. (n.d.). AI in education: Use cases, benefits, solution and implementation. *LeewayHertz.* https://www.leewayhertz.com/ai-use-cases-in-education/

Teachflow. (2023a). The impact of AI on teacher workload and mental health: A white paper. *Teachflow Research Briefs.* https://www.teachflow.ai/research/teacher-wellbeing-ai

Teachflow. (2023b). The impact of AI on teacher well-being and burnout. *Teachflow.ai.* https://teachflow.ai/the-impact-of-ai-on-teacher-well-being-and-burnout/

The Markup. (2023, August 14). AI detection tools falsely accuse international students of cheating. *The Markup.* https://themarkup.org/machine-learning/2023/08/14/ai-detection-tools-falsely-accuse-international-students-of-cheating

Tlili, A., Shehata, B., Adarkwah, M. A., Bozkurt, A., Hickey, D. T., Huang, R., & Agyemang, B. (2023). What if the devil is my guardian angel: ChatGPT as a case study of using chatbots in education. *Smart Learning Environments, 10*(1), Article 15. https://doi.org/10.1186/s40561-023-00237-x

Trucano, M. (2023, July 10). AI and the next digital divide in education. *Brookings Institution.* https://www.brookings.edu/articles/ai-and-the-next-digital-divide-in-education

Turnitin. (n.d.). *Turnitin originality and feedback studio.* https://www.turnitin.com/

Reynolds, Rebecca. (2020). [Review of the book *The Digital Divide*, by J. Dijk]. *Journal of the Association for Information Science and Technology, Name of Journal, 72*(1), 136–138. https://10.1002/asi.24355

Vesna, L., Sawale, P. S., Kaul, P., Pal, S., Murthy, B. S. R. (2025). Digital Divide in AI-Powered Education: Challenges and Solutions for Equitable Learning. *Journal of Information Systems Engineering and Management, 10*(21s), 300–308. https://doi.org/10.52783/jisem.v10i21s.3327

Warschauer, M., & Matuchniak, T. (2010). New technology and digital worlds: Analyzing evidence of equity in access, use, and outcomes. *Review of Research in Education, 34*(1), 179–225. https://doi.org/10.3102/0091732X09349791

Wargo, K., & Anderson, B. (2024, December 5). Striking a balance: Navigating the ethical dilemmas of AI in higher education. *EDUCAUSE Review.* https://er.educause.edu/articles/2024/12/striking-a-balance-navigating-the-ethical-dilemmas-of-ai-in-higher-education

Yan, L., Sha, L., Zhao, L., Li, Y., Martinez-Maldonado, R., Chen, G., Jin, X. L. Y., & Gašević, D. (2023). Practical and ethical challenges of large language models in education: A systematic scoping review. *British Journal of Educational Technology, 55*(1), 90–112. https://doi.org/10.1111/bjet.13370

Zawacki-Richter, O., Marín, V. I., Bond, M., & Gouverneur, F. (2019). Systematic review of research on artificial intelligence applications in higher education: Where are the educators? *International Journal of Educational Technology in Higher Education, 16*(1), Article 39. https://doi.org/10.1186/s41239-019-0171-0

14. Reclaiming AI equity in special education

Justice in a post-federal era

Jimmy R. Caldwell

INTRODUCTION

Artificial Intelligence (AI) is rapidly transforming education, offering both opportunities and potential harms for students historically marginalized by traditional schooling structures. In special education, AI's emergence has sparked optimism for personalized learning, assistive technologies, and data-informed decision-making. Proponents argue that AI tools can reduce barriers, adapt to student needs in real time, and support inclusive instructional design (Hopcan et al., 2022; Ahmad et al., 2025). Yet these claims require critical scrutiny. Without ethical oversight or cultural responsiveness, AI systems risk reproducing the same racialized and ableist hierarchies that have long excluded students with disabilities—particularly those who are Black, multilingual, or situated at other points of systemic marginalization (Harkins-Brown et al., 2025; Kong & Yang, 2024).

AI is not a neutral tool. It is a sociotechnical system shaped by policy, power, and capital—forces that have historically sustained educational inequities. In special education, its integration must be reclaimed from logics of surveillance, automation, and efficiency, and reoriented toward collective visions of equity, justice, and inclusion. This moment demands both visionary and vigilant approaches: ones that recognize AI's liberatory potential while confronting its role in reinscribing oppression.

This chapter's analysis is grounded in two critical frameworks: Universal Design for Learning (UDL) and Disability Critical Race Theory (DisCrit). UDL offers a lens to assess whether AI tools reflect principles of access, flexibility, and learner agency. DisCrit, drawing from the foundational work of Annamma et al. (2013), examines how algorithmic systems may recode longstanding exclusions—embedding racialized disability classifications, deficit logics, and exclusionary practices into new technological infrastructures. Together, these frameworks underscore that inclusive AI must be rooted in both pedagogical intentionality and a structural critique of how race and disability are constructed in education (Alkan & Yildiz, 2024; Harkins-Brown et al., 2025).

The chapter pursues four aims: (1) to examine the current landscape of AI in special education, including its applications and promises; (2) to surface equity concerns related to algorithmic bias, digital surveillance, and access disparities; (3) to analyze the ethical and legal dimensions of AI integration through policy critique; and (4) to offer practice-based recommendations for educators, developers, and policymakers committed to inclusive design. This inquiry draws from systematic literature review and policy document analysis, with an emphasis on equity-centered critique. Sources include peer-reviewed research, global and U.S. policy frameworks (e.g., the Individuals with Disabilities Education Act (IDEA), Section 504, EU AI Act), and case examples from special education contexts.

Ultimately, the future of AI in special education must be intentionally shaped. When developed with and for students with disabilities, AI can serve as a tool for accessibility, autonomy, and justice. Without that intentionality, however, it may simply digitize and accelerate long-standing inequities.

From Assistive Tech to Algorithmic Harm: Trends in AI and Special Education

AI in education has evolved from rule-based systems and programmed instruction to advanced machine learning, natural language processing, and adaptive analytics. In special education, this technological shift mirrors a broader trend: moving from isolated assistive technologies toward AI-powered tools embedded throughout instruction, assessment, and service delivery (Ahmad et al., 2025). What began as hardware-driven solutions (speech devices, screen readers, communication boards) has expanded into predictive analytics, virtual agents, and real-time personalization. However, AI adoption in education has outpaced critical examination of its equity implications.

A bibliometric analysis by Chen et al. (2020), reviewing over 45 studies across two decades, confirms AI in education has grown exponentially in both scope and scholarly interest. However, this growth has disproportionately focused on general education applications, with fewer studies addressing disability, access, or culturally responsive design. In special education, where technological interventions have long been shaped by deficit logics, this silence is telling. AI systems continue to encode ableist assumptions about behavior, cognition, and "normal" progress. Global rhetoric about AI inclusion often masks technocratic logic that prioritizes efficiency over justice (Ahmad et al., 2025).

Current trends include the use of AI to support Individualized Education Programs (IEPs), monitor student behavior, enhance communication for non-verbal learners, and assist in the diagnostic classification of disabilities. While such tools may offer efficiency and responsiveness, they can also deepen educational surveillance. Hopcan et al. (2022) highlight how AI tools are most often deployed in contexts like autism support or emotional-behavioral intervention, areas historically associated with over-surveillance and subjective judgment. Without safeguards, these systems risk reifying exclusion under the guise of objectivity. These concerns echo the principles of Disability Critical Race Theory (DisCrit), which interrogates how systems reproduce racialized and ableist exclusions through seemingly neutral mechanisms.

AI technologies in education rarely include the voices of students with disabilities, their families, or communities. Alkan and Yildiz (2024) critique current models for lacking participatory design, noting that students with disabilities are often positioned as data points rather than collaborators. This exclusion replicates historical dynamics in special education, where decisions have traditionally been made for students rather than with them. The absence of culturally and linguistically diverse perspectives in algorithmic training data further compounds these risks. As AI shapes the future of educational service delivery, the central question is not just what AI can do—but for whom, by whom, and to what end? In special education, AI's trajectory must move beyond narrow definitions of success and toward inclusive, justice-centered approaches. Without active resistance to digitized forms of exclusion, AI will not disrupt inequity; it will deepen it.

Core AI Applications in Special Education

Building on AI's evolution in education, this section examines six core AI applications in special education through DisCrit and UDL frameworks, analyzing how each technology may either enhance or hinder inclusive education. AI now permeates technologies supporting students with disabilities across instructional, communicative, behavioral, and administrative domains. While framed as innovations, these tools are neither neutral nor universally accessible. Their design, implementation, and outcomes reflect embedded assumptions about ability, normalcy, and educational value.

Adaptive learning systems

AI-powered adaptive platforms, such as DreamBox Learning and Lexia Core5, adjust content difficulty, pacing, and feedback in real time. Marketed as personalized supports for IEP goals, these systems often rely on static definitions of ability and rarely incorporate disability-specific insights (Hopcan et al., 2022). When efficiency is prioritized over learner agency, such tools reinforce normative standards and contradict UDL principles that call for multiple means of engagement and expression.

AI-powered assistive technologies

Speech-to-text converters (like Dragon NaturallySpeaking), text-to-speech readers, predictive text software, and real-time captioning represent widely used AI applications in special education (Ahmad et al., 2025). These technologies serve as essential supports for students with sensory, mobility, or communication-related disabilities. Goldman et al. (2025) highlight AI writing tools that help students plan, organize, and revise writing using self-regulated strategies, aligning with UDL's multiple means of action and expression. However, accessibility remains uneven, contingent on school funding and infrastructure. Their development has centered on dominant language users, marginalizing multilingual students, those with dialectal variations, or users of alternative communicative modalities (Alkan & Yildiz, 2024), which is a concern highlighted by DisCrit's emphasis on intersectional exclusion.

Natural language processing (NLP)

NLP enables AI to interpret, generate, and respond to human language. In special education contexts, tools like Google's Live Transcribe or Microsoft's Immersive Reader support non-verbal communication, automate documentation, and provide real-time feedback. However, these tools inadequately accommodate speech variations and accents, resulting in miscommunication or exclusion that disproportionately affects students at racial, linguistic, and disability intersections.

Computer vision tools

Emerging AI systems incorporate computer vision to interpret gestures, facial expressions, or visual cues, supporting students who use sign language or facial expression-based communication. However, equity concerns are urgent. Facial recognition software used for engagement tracking or behavioral analysis encodes racial and gender bias, particularly problematic in special education classrooms where surveillance has long been a concern (Hopcan et al., 2022). Through a DisCrit lens, these technologies risk digitizing racialized surveillance practices under the guise of objective monitoring.

Automated assessment and progress monitoring

AI applications analyze student performance data, identify patterns, and flag areas needing intervention. While potentially streamlining IEP monitoring, they introduce datafication risks. When AI-driven assessments like DIBELS

8th Edition or AIMSweb Plus are treated as objective indicators, they override teacher judgment and ignore contextual factors such as trauma, language variation, or cultural norms. Through both UDL and DisCrit frameworks, we must question whether these systems accommodate genuine learning variability or merely reinforce standardized expectations.

AI in educational decision-making

The most ethically fraught application is using AI to inform high-stakes special education decisions: eligibility classification, intervention planning, and placement recommendations. Waterfield et al. (2024) explore how SPED-specific AI platforms aid these decisions but operate as "black box" systems with limited transparency. Without critical oversight, these tools risk reinforcing racialized disability labels, silencing families, and narrowing educational possibilities, thus directly contradicting the participatory decision-making mandated by IDEA.

Collectively, these applications reveal both potential and peril. While they may increase efficiency and expand access, they risk digitizing existing inequities unless designed with students with disabilities and their intersectional identities at the center. The next section examines specific equity challenges these technologies present and explores possibilities for more inclusive AI development.

Digitizing Disparities: Algorithmic Bias and the Politics of Labeling in SPED

AI is often framed as neutral or liberatory in educational reform. Yet when AI systems develop and deploy without critical understanding of power, equity, and systemic exclusion, they reproduce and amplify the inequities they claim to address (Caldwell, 2023). In special education, these concerns are urgent, material, and deeply consequential for students with disabilities who also navigate racial, linguistic, and socioeconomic marginalization.

Algorithmic bias represents a pressing equity concern, arising when training data reflects dominant norms and inadequately represents disabled, racialized, or linguistically diverse learners (Zhou et al., 2022). Biased datasets embed discriminatory patterns into prediction systems, disproportionately flagging non-white students or those with disabilities as "at risk" or "non-compliant." These biases aren't incidental; they're historical and systemic, shaped by long-standing practices of racialized surveillance and deficit-based special education placement.

Critiques of predictive labeling center on the politics of who gets flagged, categorized, or denied support. Pham et al. (2024) examine how AI-driven predictive analytics in education disproportionately classify Black, Latinx, and other racial minorities as less likely to succeed academically, with Wisconsin's early warning system generating 42% higher false alarm rates for Black students than White students. This pattern extends globally, as the UN Special Rapporteur on racism reports that such tools systematically steer marginalized students away from opportunities that would maximize their potential (Ashwini, 2024). Rather than representing technological failures, these disparities reflect how AI systems replicate historical biases embedded in educational data—the tools aren't broken; they're operating as designed within systems that normalize educational stratification.

This critique is central to Disability Critical Race Theory (DisCrit), which asserts that race and ability are co-constructed categories maintaining educational stratification (Annamma et al., 2013). Within AI contexts, DisCrit examines how "objective" technologies encode subjective values about who is teachable, disruptive, or worthy of resources. Labeling systems powered by AI don't escape these logics; they digitize them. Machine learning-driven labeling tools replicate traditional classification exclusions, particularly when developers lack engagement with equity frameworks that consider multiple identities.

From a Universal Design for Learning perspective, algorithmic bias fundamentally contradicts core UDL principles. When AI systems misclassify students based on racial, cultural, or linguistic differences, they undermine multiple means of engagement by privileging normative expressions of learning. Similarly, predictive models that pathologize diverse communicative styles (e.g., African American Vernacular English) violate UDL's commitment to multiple means of expression, effectively narrowing rather than expanding pathways to educational participation (Intachomphoo & Gundersen, 2020). Because of this, natural language processing systems introduce another layer of harm when linguistic benchmarks draw from normative English. Hofmann et al. (2024) demonstrate these tools frequently misinterpret multilingual students' speech patterns, leading to misclassification or behavior flagging. These risks compound in school districts with fewer resources or culturally responsive training opportunities, making algorithmic injustice both technical and geographic.

AI's equity failures are not isolated glitches; they reflect deeper patterns in educational technology and data governance. Research demonstrates that language models exhibit systematic implicit bias against people with disabilities, consistently scoring disability-related language more negatively than standard text across multiple model architectures (Venkit et al., 2022). Instead of disrupting structural inequities, these tools often reproduce them through unexamined assumptions and poorly curated data. Institutional governance plays a significant role in this dynamic. AI policy frameworks often privilege standardization and datafication over inclusion and justice (Williamson & Piattoeva, 2019). When systems are guided by metrics of efficiency rather than principles of human dignity, students with disabilities are reduced to data points flagged, categorized, and managed, rather than supported as full participants in learning. These challenges demand not only technical solutions but a reimagining of AI development grounded in disability justice. The sections that follow examine the ethical and policy dimensions of this work and consider how AI can be reclaimed as a tool for equity rather than exclusion.

Surveillance, Consent, and Algorithmic Harm: Ethics in Special Education AI

AI in education raises profound ethical questions, particularly in special education, where technologies influence how students are assessed, taught, tracked, and defined. These systems demand scrutiny through the lenses of consent, transparency, autonomy, and harm prevention. In environments where students are already over-surveilled and over-classified, ethical concerns take on heightened urgency.

One major issue is the erosion of informed consent. AI tools are frequently embedded in instructional platforms and assessments without meaningful disclosure to families or students. Hakimi et al. (2021) note that schools often lack clear policies for how AI handles student data, raising serious concerns about transparency and governance. This issue is particularly troubling for students with disabilities, where ethical obligations around informed consent and participation are often poorly addressed in AI-driven systems. Schiff (2021) and Mintz et al. (2023) warn that AI systems in schools are often developed and deployed without democratic oversight, bypassing student and family input in ways that deepen existing inequities.

Data privacy and surveillance also raise serious concerns. AI systems continuously collect behavioral, biometric, and linguistic data, often retained long-term. For students with disabilities, this creates a permanent digital record of deviation from normative benchmarks, increasing exposure to institutional scrutiny. When data is shared across platforms or vendors without oversight, student privacy protections can be bypassed entirely. In already racialized and ableist school environments, surveillance becomes digitized and even more difficult to detect.

Ethical design must also align with the values of inclusion and dignity. Ethical concerns cannot be resolved through compliance checklists alone. Too often, AI tools are built around normative assumptions about intelligence, behavior, and communication. Instead, ethical design must be rooted in relationships with the communities it serves. Alkan (2024) maintains that when early intervention tools treat disability as a problem to be fixed, they violate student rights and marginalize neurodiverse ways of learning.

Accountability remains a final, unresolved ethical challenge. Who is responsible when AI systems misclassify students, restrict services, or cause exclusion? Legal frameworks such as IDEA and Section 504 offer procedural safeguards, but few of these laws anticipate the complexities of algorithmic decision-making. Hanna et al. (2025) emphasize that in the absence of clear accountability structures, ethical harms become systemic and normalized.

Taken together, these concerns illustrate that AI ethics in special education is not merely about minimizing harm—it is about designing systems grounded in justice. As the next sections explore legal and policy dimensions, the challenge is to ensure that ethical design is not optional but foundational to how AI is used in schools.

COMPLIANCE OR COMPLICITY? POLICY MISALIGNMENT IN SPED AI

AI is increasingly positioned as a tool to modernize and support inclusive education. Yet its rapid adoption has outpaced the evolution of legal frameworks, especially those governing special education. As AI becomes embedded in classrooms, assessments, and administrative workflows, it collides with policies never intended to regulate algorithmic decision-making. This section assesses how current AI tools align, or fail to align, with special education law, surfacing critical gaps that demand urgent policy intervention.

At the federal level, IDEA and Section 504 of the Rehabilitation Act guarantee students with disabilities the right to a Free Appropriate Public Education (FAPE), individualized supports, and protection from discrimination. Yet, as Swiecki and Staples (2023) caution, AI-driven tools often rely on standardized algorithms that may conflict with IDEA's mandate for flexibility and personalization. These systems can reinforce rigid classifications, overlook contextual and cultural factors, and introduce bias—raising serious concerns about their alignment with both the intent and implementation of special education law.

Similarly, the Americans with Disabilities Act (ADA) requires nondiscrimination and equal access across educational environments. Yet AI tools often fail to comply with accessibility standards, such as not accommodating screen readers or nonverbal communication devices. Zhuang and Goggin (2024) point out that most edtech developers operate from normative assumptions, excluding disabled stakeholders from the design process. As a result, AI systems often reproduce exclusion under the guise of inclusion.

UDL offers a compelling pedagogical alternative. It promotes multiple means of engagement, representation, and expression—principles that align with AI's potential. While tools like Immersive Reader reflect UDL values, most implementations are shallow. Ainscow and Messiou (2018) warn that layering technology onto inequitable systems widens gaps without systemic reform. Kasneci et al. (2023) similarly critique the illusion of personalization in AI, noting that most tools rely on narrow datasets and rigid models that erase learner variability. Song (2022) underscores how these technologies often reflect commercial priorities rather than pedagogical ones, reinforcing exclusion through assumptions of neutrality and objectivity.

These misalignments create compliance challenges. When AI-generated recommendations shape IEP decisions or behavior tracking without transparency, they infringe upon families' legal right to informed participation. Although the U.S. Department of Education (2023) has warned that AI tools must not violate civil rights protections, its guidance remains nonbinding and lacks enforcement mechanisms. Existing disability laws anticipate human discretion, not opaque, automated processes.

Globally, the United Nations Convention on the Rights of Persons with Disabilities (CRPD) enshrines the right to equitable, inclusive education. Yet most AI education tools are developed without meaningful consultation with disabled communities or alignment with disability rights principles (UNESCO, 2021). Similarly, (UNESCO, 2024) found that large language models often reflect and amplify structural bias, with disabled, gender-marginalized, and racialized users disproportionately harmed. This growing gap between global ideals and local practice underscores the need to embed disability justice and community accountability into the governance of AI systems.

Current special education policies presume human-led decision-making, team-based planning, and contextual assessments. In contrast, AI systems automate, predict, and standardize, often beyond the bounds of legal safeguards. Closing this gap will require more than minor policy updates. It demands reimagining how education, disability, and technology intersect, and crafting new laws that address algorithmic systems, mandate inclusive design, and give students, families, and educators tools to challenge unjust outcomes.

Opaque by Design? Legal Ambiguities and Ethical Tensions

While IDEA, ADA, and Section 504 offer foundational protections for students with disabilities, these laws were created for human decision-making, not for algorithmic judgment. As AI becomes more deeply embedded in special education, new legal and ethical tensions emerge. These uncertainties expose students to harm while limiting families' and educators' capacity for recourse.

A core challenge is accountability. When an AI system misclassifies a student, denies necessary services, or recommends an inappropriate placement, it is often unclear who bears responsibility. Current education laws like IDEA establish clear accountability frameworks with identifiable human decision-makers, such as IEP teams composed of parents, teachers, and specialists who develop individualized education programs and can be held responsible for educational decisions (Dragoo, 2024). However, the U.S. Department of Education (2023) recognizes that AI introduces new complexities to these established frameworks, noting that AI systems can "automate decisions about instruction and other educational processes" and create risks of "algorithmic discrimination" that may result in "systematic unfairness in the learning opportunities or resources recommended to some populations of students." This shift from human decision-making to automated processes introduces what the Department calls "infrastructural and invisible" uses of AI that create "concerns about transparency and trust." The technical opacity inherent in AI systems obscures the clear lines of accountability that laws like IDEA assume, leaving families with potentially fewer avenues for redress when algorithmic decisions affect their children's legal entitlements and educational trajectories. Without mechanisms for explainability and auditability, neither families nor educators can effectively challenge or correct harmful automated decisions in the way that traditional special education law envisions.

Emerging research has demonstrated educators' growing concern about this opacity. Song (2022) critiques how algorithmic decision-making in education often functions as a "black box"—systems whose internal logic is hidden from users—preventing educators and families from understanding or contesting AI-generated outputs. This lack of transparency consolidates power in the hands of developers and administrators, disempowering those most affected by these systems. In special education, where decisions about eligibility and support services carry legal and ethical weight, such opacity undermines trust and reinforces hierarchies that marginalize the lived knowledge of educators, students, and families.

These problems are compounded by gaps in procedural safeguards. IDEA gives families the right to participate in educational planning and challenge school decisions. But when AI tools influence decisions behind the scenes, by pre-filling IEPs, flagging "noncompliance," or ranking eligibility, those rights can be eroded without notice (Yuan & Hart Barnett, 2024). Currently, AI implementation has outpaced policy, leaving families vulnerable to decisions that feel authoritative yet lack legal legitimacy. Data privacy further complicates matters. The Family Educational Rights and Privacy Act (FERPA) governs access to and protection of student data, but it was not designed for systems that aggregate behavioral and biometric information across platforms. Poth (2024) suggests that third-party AI vendors often operate in ways that circumvent FERPA, creating loopholes in consent and data control. Moreover, laws like COPPA (Children's Online Privacy Protection Act), while designed to protect student data, offer little clarity when AI tools fail to disclose how information is collected, stored, or monetized. For students with disabilities, this lack of transparency constitutes both a legal and ethical breach.

The international landscape offers little additional clarity. The CRPD mandates inclusive education free from discrimination and undue restriction. Yet UNESCO (2023) finds that AI tools used globally rarely offer opt-outs, informed consent, or community governance. Zhuang and Goggin (2024) describe this dynamic as "algorithmic disenfranchisement," where students with disabilities are subjected to high-stakes systems that ignore their rights and erase their agency. Collectively, these legal ambiguities represent a structural governance failure. As AI reshapes how education decisions are made, existing laws are increasingly out of step with the systems they are supposed to regulate. Without explicit legal frameworks for algorithmic accountability, students with disabilities remain vulnerable to harm, and families are left without meaningful recourse. The next section explores how these gaps can be addressed through proactive policy reforms and practice-based approaches that embed equity, transparency, and disability justice at every level of AI governance.

FROM PARTICIPATION TO POWER: INCLUSIVE AI DESIGN IN SPED

Calls for "inclusive AI" are increasingly common in educational discourse, yet the term is often used without clarity or substance. Too often, inclusion is reduced to accessibility features or adaptive content. In special education, where technologies have historically reflected deficit-based assumptions, inclusive design must move beyond compliance. It must begin with the recognition that systems are never neutral—that AI, like education, encodes values, power, and exclusion.

Inclusive design in special education AI requires more than technical accessibility; it demands a fundamental rethinking of how systems are conceived, developed, and implemented. The question is not whether students with disabilities can be accommodated, but whether systems are designed *with* their identities, needs, and lived realities at the center. Kasneci et al. (2023) argue that AI systems often emphasize personalization rhetorically while failing to operationalize it meaningfully. True inclusion also requires confronting racialized and ableist assumptions embedded in AI design. Inclusive AI must reject frameworks that equate "normal" with whiteness, standard English, or neurotypical behavior. Instead, it must support students at the intersection of race, language, and disability. This vision aligns with the concept of liberatory AI design—a process that not only accommodates difference but reconfigures systems to redistribute power and expand educational justice.

Participatory design is central to this shift. Alkan and Yildiz (2024) critique how most AI tools are developed without the involvement of students with disabilities, leading to systems that reflect external assumptions rather than lived experience. AI must be co-created with students, families, educators, and advocates through processes that compensate participants, value diverse communication, and embed feedback loops throughout design cycles.

Significant structural barriers stand in the way. Under-resourced districts often adopt standardized, off-the-shelf solutions that prioritize efficiency over equity. Budget constraints limit time and capacity for meaningful collaboration. And few development teams integrate both AI expertise and disability studies. These challenges are not merely technical; they are institutional. Addressing them requires systemic investment, policy reform, and a shift in design ethics. Inclusive design is not a checklist. It is a political commitment to justice, rooted in community expertise and accountable to those most impacted.

Designing With, Not For: Community-Led AI in SPED

Inclusive design cannot be achieved without the active leadership of the communities most affected. Yet in the field of AI and special education, co-design remains underdeveloped, frequently tokenized, or treated as optional. When students with disabilities, their families, educators, and cultural communities are excluded from design processes, the resulting tools reflect institutional priorities, not lived expertise. Co-design must be understood not as consultation, but as an ethical commitment to shared authorship and power redistribution.

Authentic participation directly responds to the algorithmic bias concerns raised in previous sections. When diverse stakeholders help shape training data and feature selection, they can identify discriminatory patterns before they are encoded. Co-design also helps address the legal and ethical accountability gaps explored earlier by embedding transparency and collective responsibility into AI development. However, systemic barriers persist. Commercial developers and school districts operate under time constraints, rigid procurement processes, and accountability systems that reward scale over equity. These pressures marginalize those with the least institutional power, particularly students and families who are Black, disabled, multilingual, or economically disenfranchised. The exclusion of disabled voices is not incidental; it is structurally embedded. Remedying this exclusion requires redistributing resources, decision-making power, and design ownership, not merely adding advisory panels.

Still, viable strategies exist. Schools can create AI review committees that include students and families, offering compensation and structured input opportunities. Districts can revise procurement policies to require documentation of community collaboration. Developers can implement participatory practices like "design sprints" or "accessibility jams" that center disabled users in early prototyping. Even modest pilot projects can demonstrate the value of co-ownership before scaling up.

Global examples of community-led AI design demonstrate that authentic participation can fundamentally reshape both technological outcomes and power dynamics in special education. When students with disabilities and their families co-author AI interfaces and define ethical boundaries, as demonstrated in Ahmad et al.'s (2025) cross-national case studies, the resulting systems reflect lived experiences rather than institutional assumptions. Similarly, Parveen et al.'s (2025) documentation of AI projects in India shows how grounding development in local pedagogies and disability justice frameworks creates more responsive and culturally relevant tools. These initiatives succeeded not because of advanced technology, but because they were built on sustained, culturally responsive partnerships that positioned disabled communities as experts in their own needs.

While these international examples demonstrate the transformative potential of community-led design, U.S. implementation faces distinct challenges rooted in compliance-driven educational systems and fragmented governance structures. The Center for Innovation, Design, and Digital Learning (CIDDL, 2024) promotes frameworks like SETT (Student, Environment, Tasks, Tools) to center students in team-based decision-making, yet these efforts often remain constrained by existing power hierarchies. Waterfield et al.'s (2024) analysis of co-design implementation in AI-based IEP platforms reveals this tension: while meaningful participation increased user trust and system adoption rates, persistent structural limitations emerged including transparency gaps, fragmented feedback systems, and difficulties incorporating community insights into technical logic. These findings reaffirm that co-design must be ongoing, embedded in governance structures, and reflexively updated—not a one-time checkbox exercise—echoing the accountability mechanisms discussed in earlier sections on bias mitigation and algorithmic transparency.

REWRITING THE RULES: LEGISLATIVE GAPS IN AI AND SPECIAL EDUCATION

The increasing use of AI in special education requires coordinated legislative and regulatory responses to ensure equity, transparency, and accountability. While federal laws such as IDEA and Section 504 mandate service access for students with disabilities, they do not explicitly regulate algorithmic tools. This omission creates serious oversight gaps in how AI impacts student placement, accommodations, and disciplinary decisions (Washington Office of Superintendent of Public Instruction, Washington OSPI, 2024; U.S. Department of Education, 2023).

At the state level, policy remains fragmented. States like California and Washington have developed guidelines for AI in K–12 education, while most others offer no direction. This results in disparate implementation, with students in unregulated states more vulnerable to algorithmic misclassification, surveillance, and privacy violations (Oregon Department of Education, 2023). These disparities are particularly pronounced in under-resourced districts. Limited capacity intersects with absent state guidance, leaving administrators to make high-stakes AI procurement and implementation decisions with minimal training or oversight.

To address these gaps, lawmakers must require bias audits for all AI tools used in special education, including IEP generators, progress monitoring systems, and predictive behavioral interventions (Waterfield et al., 2024). These audits should measure disparate impacts across race, language, disability category, and socioeconomic background. IDEA and Section 504 should expand to account for algorithmic decision-making and mandate that human educators retain final authority in high-stakes decisions. Data privacy laws such as FERPA and COPPA also need modernization. Current provisions inadequately prevent vendors from using student data to train commercial algorithms or sharing sensitive disability data beyond educational contexts (Washington OSPI, 2024).

Critically, legislation must prevent using AI as justification for teacher displacement. While AI can support documentation and offer learning insights, it must never replace the relational, contextual, and sensitive decision-making of educators, families, and service providers. Without enforceable regulation and transparency mechanisms, AI risks becoming a cost-saving tool that compromises equity rather than promoting it (Carey et al., 2022).

Justice Demands Data: Reimagining Research for Inclusive AI

While policy reform is vital, research must play an equally transformative role in evaluating, regulating, and reimagining AI in special education. Policy can constrain harm, but research drives the knowledge systems that shape innovation, accountability, and design. To date, empirical studies remain limited, and much of the existing research relies on short-term metrics or assumes that AI's technical precision inherently yields educational improvement, a dangerous assumption for marginalized learners (CRPE, 2023).

Future research must examine the long-term, cumulative impacts of AI in disability classification, IEP planning, and service eligibility. Early findings suggest AI-powered referral systems may replicate, and even amplify, racial disproportionality in special education placement (Filgueiras, 2023). Comparative research is needed to assess how AI-mediated decisions differ from traditional models, particularly when considering race, language, and disability as intersecting factors.

Multilingual and neurodivergent learners are especially vulnerable to misrepresentation in AI systems. Tools trained on English-dominant, neurotypical data often misinterpret speech patterns, literacy expression, and behavior (Oh-Young & Karlin, 2024). These misinterpretations are frequently framed as deficits, leading to inaccurate assessment and inappropriate intervention.

Beyond technical performance, research must also explore participatory governance models where students, families, educators, and disability advocates co-design and co-regulate AI tools and policies (Washington OSPI, 2024). DisCrit-informed methodologies are essential for examining how algorithmic systems reproduce historical logics of racism, ableism, and linguistic bias—moving beyond narrow conceptions of "bias" to address systemic injustice (Filgueiras, 2023). These critical frameworks become even more urgent as federal oversight structures erode.

As the U.S. Department of Education faces institutional dismantling, the research landscape must shift. Leadership, funding, and accountability will increasingly fall to state agencies, universities, and community-based institutions. Projects grounded in UDL, disability justice, and culturally sustaining pedagogy must receive priority support to counterbalance corporate influence. In this moment, research is not neutral; it is a form of advocacy, resistance, and infrastructural repair. Without it, ethical AI in special education will remain a rhetorical ideal rather than a lived reality.

Justice Without the Department: Reclaiming AI Equity in a Post-Federal Era

To avoid reproducing past harms through new technological infrastructures, AI governance in special education must be led by inclusive coalitions—not driven by fragmented policy or private-sector priorities. Yet Donald Trump's March 2025 executive order dismantling the U.S. Department of Education marks a seismic shift in educational governance. With responsibilities for civil rights enforcement and special education oversight reassigned to agencies like the Department of Health and Human Services (Jimenez, 2025), key accountability mechanisms are collapsing. As federal infrastructure erodes, the risk of algorithmic harm accelerates.

Hundreds of federal education staff, including civil rights investigators, disability researchers, and accessibility specialists, have already faced layoffs. Core offices such as the Office of Special Education Programs (OSEP) and the Office for Civil Rights (OCR) face defunding, restructuring, or relocation to agencies lacking historical expertise in education equity. These entities have functioned as the institutional foundation for monitoring IDEA compliance, investigating systemic discrimination, and providing technical guidance to states and districts. Their dismantling removes both the capacity and mandate to ensure algorithmic accountability in special education. In this context, coalitions must become the new infrastructure for justice, rooting themselves not in symbolic inclusion but in real power at the levels where AI is deployed: states, districts, schools, and classrooms.

STATE-LEVEL ACTION

States must adopt robust, equity-driven AI policies, establishing ethics boards, mandating algorithmic bias audits, and requiring procurement input from students with disabilities, educators, and disability advocates (Parveen et al., 2025). Without this, AI adoption will prioritize efficiency over justice.

District and Local Governance

Superintendents and school boards must embed AI ethics reviews and equity audits into school improvement frameworks (Christian, 2024). Incident-reporting mechanisms for students, families, and staff should be built into every district's AI deployment strategy.

School Leaders and Principals

Principals must lead cultural shifts around AI use, supporting professional learning communities, modeling equity-minded engagement, and balancing innovation with caution (Sajjad et al., 2025; Eltantawy & Alsudairy, 2024).

Teachers and Classrooms

Educators must become critical filters of AI, developing skills in AI literacy, bias recognition, and systems-level resistance (Searson et al., 2024). Solidarity networks can sustain ethical teaching under political pressure.

Reframing the Moment

Inclusive governance isn't the product of better tools; it is a collective political commitment. Without organized, disability-led, and justice-driven coalitions across all educational ecosystem levels, AI will reflect the ideological drift now underway, where efficiency replaces equity and automation supplants human responsibility. But with sustained action from state policymakers, district leaders, educators, families, and advocates, AI can still be reclaimed as a tool for inclusion and possibility.

CONCLUSION: RECLAIMING AI FOR JUSTICE IN SPECIAL EDUCATION

AI in special education is not a neutral innovation; it is a defining inflection point in the intersection of technology, power, and education. AI's capacity to support students with disabilities depends less on technical sophistication than on the values embedded in its design, deployment, and governance. Without an explicit commitment to equity, AI will not disrupt systemic injustice; it will accelerate and automate it (Filgueiras, 2023; Oh-Young & Karlin, 2024).

This chapter outlines strategies for shifting that trajectory through a justice-centered AI framework that emphasizes bias audits, algorithmic transparency, cultural responsiveness, and community accountability. Professional learning must reject corporate techno-solutionism and instead embrace critically engaged, culturally sustaining pedagogies (Sajjad et al., 2025). At the policy level, urgent reforms are required—including the modernization of FERPA and IDEA, the institutionalization of bias audits, and ethical procurement policies (Waterfield et al., 2024; Washington OSPI, 2024). Equally vital is a robust research agenda rooted in Disability Critical Race Theory (DisCrit), which interrogates how algorithmic decision-making reproduces historical inequities in new digital forms (Annamma et al., 2013; Filgueiras, 2023).

DisCrit reminds us that we cannot evaluate AI's outcomes in isolation from the power structures that shape them. Technologies are never neutral; they reflect decisions about which minds are valued, which bodies are welcomed, and which futures are deemed worth investing in. Inclusive design, if understood only as technical compliance, risks flattening the radical possibilities of disability justice. In education, AI is already influencing who is labeled, who is included, and who is excluded. The redistribution of decision-making authority to those with lived experience at the margins is not just a design choice; it is a political imperative.

This urgency is amplified by the dismantling of federal education infrastructure. The rollback of the U.S. Department of Education and its civil rights and special education offices signals systemic retreat (Jimenez, 2025). As national protections erode, ethical implementation of AI increasingly falls to under-resourced local actors, who often lack the tools, training, or support to challenge harmful systems. This decentralization amounts to a redistribution of ethical burden.

In this uncertain landscape, reclaiming AI as a tool of liberation begins by centering students with disabilities, especially those living at the intersections of race, language, gender, and economic injustice. Anything less is not innovation; it is complicity. Technological reform without structural transformation will only reinforce what has always been unequal.

Justice, not efficiency, must drive the future of AI in special education. Transparency must take precedence over expediency. Collective accountability must replace algorithmic convenience. That future will not be delivered by compliance alone. It will be claimed through coalition, imagination, and the radical belief that every learner deserves more than access.

They deserve freedom.

REFERENCES

Ahmad, W., Raj, R., & Shokeen, R. (2025). Reshaping special education: Strategic use of artificial intelligence. In W. B. Mallik & R. Sengupta (Eds.), *Artificial Intelligence and Inclusive Education* (pp. 1–22). IGI Global. https://doi.org/10.4018/979-8-3693-5538-1.ch001

Ahmad, W., Shokeen, R., & Raj, R. (2025). Artificial intelligence: Solutions in special education. In W. B. Mallik & R. Sengupta (Eds.), *Artificial Intelligence and Inclusive Education* (pp. 459–472). IGI Global. https://doi.org/10.4018/979-8-3693-5538-1.ch017

Ainscow, M., & Messiou, K. (2018). Engaging with the views of students to promote inclusion in education. *Journal of Educational Change*, *19*(1), 1–17. https://doi.org/10.1007/s10833-017-9312-1

Alkan, A. (2024). The role of artificial intelligence in the education of students with special needs. *International Journal of Technology in Education and Science*, *8*(4), 542–557. https://doi.org/10.46328/ijtes.569

Alkan, A., & Yildiz, E. P. (2024). Artificial intelligence and education: A metaphorical analysis on the perceptions of students with special abilities. *International Journal of Research in Education and Science*, *10*(4), 761–775. https://doi.org/10.46328/ijres.3520

Annamma, S. A., Connor, D. J., & Ferri, B. A. (2013). Dis/ability critical race studies (DisCrit): Theorizing at the intersections of race and dis/ability. *Race Ethnicity and Education*, *16*(1), 1–31. https://doi.org/10.1080/13613324.2012.730511

Ashwini, K. P. (2024). Contemporary forms of racism, racial discrimination, xenophobia and related intolerance: Report of the Special Rapporteur on contemporary forms of racism, racial discrimination, xenophobia and related intolerance (A/HRC/56/68). United Nations Human Rights Council.

Carey, J., D'Aoust, C., Vaughan, M., & Johnston, T. (2022). Equity-oriented implementation of assistive technologies in under-resourced schools. *Journal of Special Education Technology*, *37*(4), 289–302. https://doi.org/10.1177/01626434211056658

Caldwell, J. (2023). All education is political: Critical race theory, white power, and the killing of Black academic freedom. *Journal of Academic Freedom*, *14*. https://www.aaup.org/JAF14

Center on Reinventing Public Education. (2023). *AI is already disrupting education, but only 13 states are offering guidance for schools*. https://crpe.org/ai-is-already-disrupting-education/

Chen, X., Xie, H., Zou, D., & Hwang, G.-J. (2020). Application and theory gaps during the rise of artificial intelligence in education. *Computers and Education: Artificial Intelligence*, *1*, 100002. https://doi.org/10.1016/j.caeai.2020.100002

Christian, J. (2024). Predictive algorithms in K–12 behavior systems: Transparency, legality, and bias. *Education Policy Analysis Archives, 32*(1), 22–39.

CIDDL. (2024). *Inclusive intelligence: Harnessing AI to support all learners.* Center for Innovation in Disability and Design in Learning. https://ciddl.org/wp-content/uploads/2024/01/InclusiveIntelligence_a11y_navadded.pdf

Dragoo, K. E. (2024). *The Individuals with Disabilities Education Act (IDEA), Part B: Key statutory and regulatory provisions* (CRS Report No. R41833). Congressional Research Service. https://www.congress.gov/crs-product/R41833

Eltantawy, M. M., & Alsudairy, N. A. (2024). Special education teachers' perceptions of using artificial intelligence in educating students with disabilities. *Journal of Intellectual Disability – Diagnosis and Treatment, 12*(2), 92–102. https://doi.org/10.6000/2292-2598.2024.12.02.5

Filgueiras, T. (2023). Algorithmic classification and racial disproportionality in special education. *Disability Studies Quarterly, 43*(2). https://dsq-sds.org/index.php/dsq/article/view/8625

Goldman, S. R., Smith, S. J., & Carreon, A. (2025). Artificial intelligence to support writing outcomes for students with disabilities. *Journal of Special Education Technology, 0*(0), 1–9. https://doi.org/10.1177/01626434251326328

Hakimi, L., Eynon, R., & Murphy, V. A. (2021). The ethics of using digital trace data in education: A thematic review of the research landscape. *Review of Educational Research, 91*(5), 671–717. https://doi.org/10.3102/00346543211020116

Hanna, M. G., Pantanowitz, L., Jackson, B., Palmer, O., Visweswarane, S., Pantanowitz, J., Deebajah, M., & Rashidi, H. H. (2025). Ethical and bias considerations in artificial intelligence/machine learning. *Modern Pathology, 38*, Article 100686. https://doi.org/10.1016/j.modpat.2024.100686

Harkins-Brown, A. R., Carling, L. Z., & Peloff, D. C. (2025). Artificial intelligence in special education. *Encyclopedia, 5*, Article 11. https://doi.org/10.3390/encyclopedia5010011

Hofmann, V., Kalluri, P. R., Jurafsky, D., & King, S. (2024). AI generates covertly racist decisions about people based on their dialect. *Nature, 633*(8033), 147–154. https://doi.org/10.1038/s41586-024-07856-5

Hopcan, S., Polat, E., Ozturk, M. E., & Ozturk, L. (2022). Artificial intelligence in special education: A systematic review. *Interactive Learning Environments.* Advance online publication. https://doi.org/10.1080/10494820.2022.2067186

Intachomphoo, C., & Gundersen, O. E. (2020). Artificial intelligence and race: A systematic review. *Legal Information Management, 20*(3), 74–84. https://doi.org/10.1017/S1472669620000183

Jimenez, C. (2025, March 21). Will Education Department closure harm students with disabilities? *USA Today.* https://www.usatoday.com/story/news/education/2025/03/21/education-department-closing-disability-rights/70211235007/

Kasneci, E., Sessler, K., Küchemann, S., Bannert, M., Dementieva, D., Fischer, F., & Kasneci, G. (2023). ChatGPT for good? On opportunities and challenges of large language models for education. *Learning and Individual Differences, 103*, 102274. https://doi.org/10.1016/j.lindif.2023.102274

Kong, S.-C., & Yang, Y. (2024). A human-centered learning and teaching framework using generative artificial intelligence for self-regulated learning development through domain knowledge learning in K–12 settings. *IEEE Transactions on Learning Technologies, 17*, 1562–1575. https://doi.org/10.1109/TLT.2024.3392830

Mintz, J., Holmes, W., Liu, L., & Perez-Ortiz, M. (2023). Artificial intelligence and K–12 education: Possibilities, pedagogies and risks. *Computers in the Schools, 40*(4), 325–333. https://doi.org/10.1080/07380569.2023.2279870

Oh-Young, C., & Karlin, M. (2024). Artificial intelligence... in the early childhood special education classroom!!? *Teaching Exceptional Children, 57*(5), 348–356. https://doi.org/10.1177/00400599241231237

Oregon Department of Education. (2023). *Guidelines for AI use in K–12 education: Supporting equity and transparency.* https://www.oregon.gov/ode

Parveen, A., Zimik, P., Bashir, F., Ganie, A. N., & Jan, S. (2025). AI and special education: Inclusive practice and support. In *Teaching in the Artificial Intelligence Era: Empowering Educators for the Future* (Chapter 8) (pp. 72–85). IIP Series.

Pham, H., Kohli, T., Llano, E. O., Nokuri, I., & Weinstock, A. (2024, June 29). How will AI impact racial disparities in education? *Stanford Center for Racial Justice.* https://law.stanford.edu/2024/06/29/how-will-ai-impact-racial-disparities-in-education/

Poth, R. D. (2024). AI and the law: What educators need to know. *Edutopia.* https://www.edutopia.org/article/laws-ai-education/

Sajjad, M., Batool, Z., & Amjad, R. (2025). Building educator capacity for ethical AI use in inclusive classrooms. *International Journal of Inclusive Education.* Advance online publication. https://doi.org/10.1080/13603116.2025.2301186

Schiff, D. (2021). Education for uncertain futures: Designing socially just AI policy with and for young people. *Learning, Media and Technology, 46*(3), 264–277. https://doi.org/10.1080/17439884.2021.1876089

Searson, M., Langran, E., & Trumble, K. (2024). Preparing teachers for AI: Literacy, ethics, and advocacy. *Journal of Technology and Teacher Education, 32*(1), 1–17.

Song, K. (2022). Critical perspectives on the algorithmic turn in education. *Educational Philosophy and Theory, 54*(14), 2310–2321. https://doi.org/10.1080/00131857.2022.2046174

Swiecki, Z., & Staples, S. (2023). Leveraging artificial intelligence to support students with disabilities: Promise and peril. *Intervention in School and Clinic, 59*(1), 3–11. https://doi.org/10.1177/10534512231186914

Trump, D. J. (2025, March 20). *Improving education outcomes by empowering parents, states, and communities* [Executive order]. The White House. https://www.whitehouse.gov/briefing-room/presidential-actions/2025/03/20/improving-education-outcomes/

UNESCO, IRACAI. (2021). *AI and education: Guidance for policy-makers.* United Nations Educational, Scientific and Cultural Organization. https://unesdoc.unesco.org/ark:/48223/pf0000376709

UNESCO, IRCAI (2024). *Challenging systematic prejudices: an investigation into gender bias in large language models.* https://ircai.org/project/challenging-systematic-prejudices/

U.S. Department of Education. (2023). *Artificial intelligence and the future of teaching and learning: Insights and recommendations.* Office of Educational Technology. https://www.ed.gov/sites/ed/files/documents/ai-report/ai-report.pdf

Venkit, P. N., Srinath, M., & Wilson, S. (2022). A study of implicit language model bias against people with disabilities. In *Proceedings of the 29th International Conference on Computational Linguistics* (pp. 523–532). International Committee on Computational Linguistics.

Washington Office of Superintendent of Public Instruction. (2024). *Responsible AI in education: Equity guidelines for Washington public schools.* https://www.k12.wa.us/policy-funding/technology/responsible-ai-guidelines

Waterfield, B., Watson, J., & Day, M. (2024). Auditing AI in education: Legal requirements and ethical frameworks. *Harvard Journal of Law & Technology, 37*(1), 92–117.

Williamson, B., & Piattoeva, N. (2019). Objectivity as standardization in data-scientific education policy, technology and governance. *Learning, Media & Technology.* https://doi.org/10.1080/17439884.2018.1556215

Yuan, C., & Hart Barnett, J. E. (2024). Developing quality IEP goals in the age of artificial intelligence. *Teaching Exceptional Children.* https://doi.org/10.1177/00400599241239311

Zhou, N., Zhang, Z., Nair, V. N., Singhal, H., & Chen, J. (2022). Bias, fairness and accountability with artificial intelligence and machine learning algorithms. *International Statistical Review, 90*(3), 468–480. https://doi.org/10.1111/insr.12492

Zhuang, K. V., & Goggin, G. (2024). New possibilities or problems for disability and inclusion? The case of AI and ADMs across work. *Telematics and Informatics, 92*, Article 102156. https://doi.org/10.1016/j.tele.2024.102156

Index